PAPERS IN ECONOMIC PREHISTORY

PAPERS IN ECONOMIC PREHISTORY

BRITISH ACADEMY MAJOR RESEARCH PROJECT

The Early History of Agriculture

Management Committee:
    Professor J. G. D. Clark, Sc.D., F.B.A.
    Professor Sir Joseph Hutchinson, C.M.G., Sc.D., F.R.S.
    Dr G. H. S. Bushnell, Ph.D., F.S.A.
    Dr R. G. West, Ph.D., F.R.S.
    E. S. Higgs, M.A., B.Comm. (Director)

Assistant Director, Wenner-Gren Fellow:
    M. R. Jarman, B.A.

British Academy Fellow:
    S. Payne, B.A.

Documentary Secretary:
    H. N. Jarman, B.A.

Associates:
    C. Vita-Finzi, Ph.D., University College, London
    J. Renfrew, Ph.D., University of Sheffield
    D. Webley, B.Sc., D.I.C., M.A., Agricultural Development and
        Advisory Service, Cardiff

Research Associates:
    A. J. Legge, B.A., Churchill College
    R. W. Dennell, B.A., Pembroke College
    D. A. Sturdy, B.A., Trinity College
    P. F. Wilkinson, B.A., Gonville and Caius College (Musk-ox Project,
        College, Alaska)

Collaborators:
    D. H. French, Ph.D., Director of the British Institute of Archaeology
        at Ankara
    G. C. Hillman, B.Sc., University of Reading
    J. A. Charles, B.Sc., M.A., A.R.S.M., C.Eng., I.A.M.M., F.I.M.,
        Department of Metallurgy, Cambridge University
    R. J. Payne, B.A., Girton College

The help of the following bodies and institutions is also acknowledged:
The Institute of Animal Physiology, Babraham; The Plant Breeding
Institute, Cambridge; The National Institute of Agricultural Botany,
Cambridge; and The Department of Quaternary Research, Cambridge
University

PAPERS IN ECONOMIC PREHISTORY

Studies by Members and Associates of the
British Academy Major Research Project in the
Early History of Agriculture

edited by

E. S. HIGGS

Faculty of Archaeology and Anthropology, University of Cambridge

CAMBRIDGE

AT THE UNIVERSITY PRESS 1972

Published by the Syndics of the Cambridge University Press
Bentley House, 200 Euston Road, London NW1 2DB
American Branch: 32 East 57th Street, New York, N.Y. 10022

© Cambridge University Press 1972

Library of Congress Catalogue Card Number: 78-180019

ISBN: 0 521 08452 0

Printed in Great Britain by W. Heffer & Sons Ltd., Cambridge.

CONTENTS

Foreword by Grahame Clark   page vii

Section I   Theory   1

1. E. S. Higgs and M. R. Jarman: The origins of animal and plant husbandry   3

2. H. N. Jarman: The origins of wheat and barley cultivation   15

3. E. S. Higgs and C. Vita-Finzi: Prehistoric economies: a territorial approach   27

Section II   Methods and techniques   37

1. H. N. Jarman, A. J. Legge and J. A. Charles: Retrieval of plant remains from archaeological sites by froth flotation   39

2. S. Payne: Partial recovery and sample bias: the results of some sieving experiments   49

3. S. Payne: On the interpretation of bone samples from archaeological sites   65

4. M. R. Jarman and P. F. Wilkinson: Criteria of animal domestication   83

5. A. J. Legge: Cave climates   97

Section III   Field and case studies   105

1. P. F. Wilkinson: Current experimental domestication and its relevance to prehistory   107

2. A. J. Legge: Prehistoric exploitation of the gazelle in Palestine   119

3. M. R. Jarman: European deer economies and the advent of the Neolithic   125

4. R. W. Dennell: The interpretation of plant remains: Bulgaria   149

5. D. A. Sturdy: The exploitation patterns of a modern reindeer economy in west Greenland   161

6. D. Webley: Soils and site location in prehistoric Palestine   169

7. D. H. French, G. C. Hillman, S. Payne and R. J. Payne: Excavations at Can Hasan III 1969-1970   181

8. S. Payne: Can Hasan III, the Anatolian aceramic, and the Greek Neolithic   191

Conclusion: The biology of domestication by Sir Joseph Hutchinson   195

Bibliography   199

Name index   213

General index   216

FOREWORD

The present volume is only one of many outcomes of a plea made by Lord Robbins in his presidential address to the British Academy for 1965.[1] Lord Robbins suggested that the time was ripe for the Academy to consider initiating and carrying through major research projects on its own account. He did not envisage any diversion of resources from the support of individual or corporate scholarly enterprise. His hope was rather that additional subventions might be obtained to further long-term research on topics of major interest, sponsored directly by the Academy. To this end he invited the various sections to submit proposals for submissions to the Council. One of the first to be approved by the Council of the British Academy was a proposal by Section X (Archaeology) to undertake research on the early history of agriculture.

A point worth emphasizing is that the topic was chosen in full realization that success would depend on securing and maintaining close and intimate cooperation between the human and natural sciences. Indeed, one might go further and say that an attractive feature of this proposal was that it involved dialogue between natural scientists and humanistic scholars. When in due course the Academy appointed a standing Committee on the Early History of Agriculture, it included two distinguished Fellows of the Royal Society, Sir Joseph Hutchinson, Draper's Professor of Agriculture, and Dr Harry Godwin, Professor of Botany and Director of the Sub-department of Quaternary Research at Cambridge, alongside four of its own fellows, Professors Martyn Jope, Grahame Clark, Stuart Piggott and Christopher Hawkes, holders of chairs of Archaeology respectively at the Universities of Belfast, Cambridge, Edinburgh and Oxford. When this Committee met on 23 April 1966, at Peterhouse, Cambridge, it began by appointing Sir Joseph Hutchinson as chairman and affirming its primary task as the promotion of research into the early history of agriculture. As a first step it was decided to set up a project in the Department of Archaeology and Anthropology at Cambridge under the direction of Mr E. S. Higgs.

The Committee was anxious to initiate research without delay and Cambridge offered obvious advantages. For one thing interdisciplinary team-work of the kind needed for investigating the manner in which early man utilized natural resources to subserve social ends was well established there. The concept of quaternary research already had a long history at Cambridge. The Sub-department of Quaternary Research established in the Botany School in 1948 with the aid of the Nuffield Foundation rested to a significant degree[2] on the basis of experience between 1932-40 of the work of the Fenland Research Committee, which under the chairmanship of Sir Albert Seward, F.R.S.,[3] had systematically deployed archaeological, palaeobotanical and geological techniques to investigate the Postglacial settlement of the Fenland; and it is an interesting indication of the durability of interdisciplinary research that no less than four of the six original members of the Academy Committee[4] were former members of the Fenland Research Committee founded thirty-five years previously. The scope of the Sub-department as this developed under the direction first of Dr (later Professor Sir) Harry Godwin, F.R.S., and later of Dr Richard West, F.R.S., was greatly expanded both in range of reference and in technical facilities – the addition of a radio-carbon laboratory was of particular importance as Godwin illustrated so well in respect of prehistoric England at the recent joint symposium of the Royal Society and the British Academy;[5] but well-tried procedures of special relevance to the study of early agriculture and land-clearance, including pollen-analysis and the identification of macroscopic plant remains, continued to play central roles in the day-to-day work of the Sub-department.

Another reason why Cambridge was considered to be a suitable centre was its importance as a focus of agricultural research. The location of the National Institute of Agricultural Botany in the city, of the Plant Breeding Institute at Trumpington and of the Institute of Animal Physiology at Babraham meant that expert and friendly advisers as well as reference collections were available close at hand. Even more important from a university point of view was the personal interest and involvement of Sir Joseph Hutchinson, head of the Department of Agriculture, an interest stemming in part from insights gained during his service in tropical countries into the workings of agricultural societies at a relatively simple level of technology and in part from his professional concern as a geneticist with the history of the crop plants themselves, an interest displayed among other ways in the organizing of the Cambridge Symposium of 1962.[6]

If Cambridge was a likely centre on general grounds, there were particular reasons for locating the project in the Department of Archaeology and Anthropology. Despite inadequate premises and serious understaffing at both graduate and assistant level, the department had two priceless advantages: an increasing flow of able students and a strand of teaching particularly relevant to the aims and objects of the project. Since the war Cambridge had taken a lead in developing interest in economic prehistory, that is fundamentally in the manner in which prehistoric man utilized natural resources to maintain life in society. This interest was not merely theoretical.[7] It was also practical in the sense that it determined objectives and the means for attaining them. The series of excavations at Star Carr (1949-51) translated theory into fact and this translation was achieved by the labours of twenty-five students from the department.[8] This was an aspect of the Cambridge teaching to which Eric Higgs responded most warmly when he came as a mature graduate student in 1954 to read for the Diploma in Prehistoric Archaeology. He obtained his Diploma and has stayed on ever since. By the time we were ready for the project Higgs had been holding a research post in the department for a decade. During this time he had made fundamental contributions to our thinking, in particular by focusing attention on the biological data from a.chaeological sites and by developing, in conjunction with Dr Claudio Vita-Finzi, a concern for the territorial basis of prehistoric economies. His presence was another strong argument for locating the project in the department.

Since Sir Mortimer Wheeler has already described the steps by which the project was set up at Cambridge in his book *The British Academy 1949-1968*,[9] it is only necessary to state that no time was lost in following up recommendations of the Academy's Committee. As soon as the university gave its consent a Management Committee was appointed by the Faculty Board of Archaeology and Anthropology to mobilize financial resources and supervise such matters as the recruitment of research staff. A prompt and generous grant from the Academy, supplemented by substantial help from the Wenner-Gren Foundation of New York, made it possible for the project to start operations with a minimum staff at the beginning of the academic year 1967-8.

From the outset the view was taken that the opportunities presented by a major research project would be wasted if work was limited by existing concepts and procedures. There was an obligation to test new ways of thought and devise new techniques. On the other hand archaeological excavation was an ongoing activity and, since the project could only under exceptional conditions initiate excavations on its own account, it was necessary to take advantage of opportunities that might never recur. It required no prodigies of thought to appreciate that no useful samples could be obtained by sitting at home and waiting in the old style for excavators to produce whatever animal bones or plant remains they or their helpers happened to notice and collect. This means that there has been a marked seasonal rhythm in the work of the project team. During the summer small groups have gone off to conduct investigations on the sites of major excavations. Up to date these have lain in southern and south-eastern Europe and in south-western Asia. In most instances opportunities have been provided by British institutes or schools of archaeology, including those at Ankara, Athens, Baghdad and Rome, but important sites have been opened up by the Israeli authorities and, thanks to liaison with the British Academy, by the Bulgarian Academy of Sciences. Much time during the winter and spring has been spent dealing with the samples collected during the summer and preparing reports for publication. On the other hand this is the time of the year when opportunity is greatest for discussion and the formulation of ideas. The chapters which form this present book were written in between rounds of field activities and the busy work of routine work on the primary data.

The present volume is no more than a beginning. Fundamental research into a topic as complex as early agriculture is a slow matter. Members of the project and their associates have published many interim reports on materials from particular excavations and a number of brief papers exploring ideas. What is aimed at here is, first, to open up the field by questioning some well-established dogmas and suggesting new ways of approach; second, to consider means of obtaining samples adequate to support critical conclusions; and, thirdly, to illustrate by examples what is being done in particular regions.

Under the first head there is a marked reaction against the long-standing preoccupation with developmental stages. The progress of excavation has thrown increasing doubt on the validity of the concept of the Neolithic Revolution as this is featured in the conventional wisdom. Braidwood's work in south-west Asia and MacNeish's in Mesoamerica have shown that in each of these areas the process of taming and exploiting animals and plants has been gradual and long-drawn-out. Even more to the point, the application of modern research techniques to territories outside the immediate range of the earliest literate civilizations suggests that the relationships established between men and the animals and plants on which they live are far too complex to be explained in terms of an elementary dichotomy. Interest has therefore shifted from developmental to functional and specifically ecological concerns, a shift which in due course may be expected paradoxically to lead to more soundly-based explanations of large-scale economic change. Another reaction is away from fixations on individual sites of the kind encouraged by the allocation of funds almost exclusively for particular excavations. As Higgs and Vita-Finzi emphasize, it is essential to consider the biological data from archaeological sites in relation to the territories exploited by their inhabitants. It is only when excavated material is considered in relation to the resources of the territory utilized, the nature of the technology and the size of the community, that a meaningful picture is likely to emerge of the manner in which economic needs were met.

The fact remains that definitive evidence about the pattern of utilization of resources, including the question of seasonality, can only be obtained from archaeological sites; and if it is to provide a basis for rigorous analysis this needs to be secured under closely controlled conditions. To be sure of the archaeological context of biological samples it has been necessary for teams from the project, not only to work on archaeological sites and understand their complexities, but personally to obtain the samples needed. It is not merely a question of establishing the precise cultural and chronological context of samples, but also of determining how the organic materials in question became incorporated in the deposits in which they are found and what they mean in terms of the life of the people who discarded them. The other crucial point about samples is that they should be adequate in content: that is that they should be well enough preserved to permit accurate determination and abundant enough to provide a basis for valid statistical analysis. Since the validity and meaning of samples is basic to the whole enterprise, this was one of the first topics to be tackled by the project. As Payne's article in Section II of this volume shows, research into problems of data-retrieval and sampling has involved a good deal of experimentation on archaeological sites as well as work on the development of apparatus. The most striking piece of hardware is that devised to facilitate the extraction of plant materials from archaeological deposits by means of froth-flotation described by Jarman, Legge and Charles. By making it possible to process rapidly deposits which in the past would have been regarded as sterile or at best as sources for occasional finds, this apparatus has revolutionized the prospects of gaining an insight into the plants utilized by man as far back as the Palaeolithic.

Analysis of the samples obtained by such methods opens up a new field for discussion. Much has been said and rightly said of the need to study the utilization of natural resources in the context of the natural sciences. The converse also needs emphasis, namely that archaeologists are not as such concerned with the environment, but rather with the use made of it by early man. No information can be obtained without asking questions and the people best qualified to ask the questions are those who most need the answers. The appendices to too many archaeological papers record reports by specialists, which, though often compiled at great cost, tell us distressingly little of what we need to know. In part this is due to the nature of the samples. As a rule these are not only inadequate in themselves, but the

expert has frequently no first-hand idea of their context. Even more important he often has no real conception of what is required of him and solves his problem by listing identifications and offering such comments as he has time for or feels inclined to make. If interdisciplinary research is to be effective it implies a large degree of autonomy. The help which archaeologists and natural scientists can give each other depends to a significant degree on respecting their independence. This applies even when, as in the case of the Fenland Research Committee, the problem was the elementary one of establishing the environmental context of successive phases of occupation in a defined territory. In the case of economic prehistory the questions are more complicated and they need to be framed, at least in the first instance, by archaeologists. It is not infrequently lamented that experts are hard to find. Two things might be said. For one thing archaeologists ought to be more sparing of experts' time by undertaking routine identifications for themselves, a problem which should largely solve itself as more archaeologists appreciate that biological clues are every bit as important as artifactual ones — or to be more accurate, if they accepted the fact that assemblages of biological materials from archaeological sites are in a real sense artifacts themselves. An essential part of the instruction now being given to many students of archaeology[10] includes not only the ability to identify, but the rarer one of knowing at what point to turn for expert advice. This brings me to my second point. When the expert is approached he is entitled to expect intelligent questions.

Geographically the project has initially been concentrated for the most part on the territories in south-west Asia and south-east Europe where agriculture first became effective in the sense of supporting the earliest historic civilizations of the Old World. Much of the time and effort of those concerned has been expended on collecting and analysing assemblages of animal bones from such key Early Neolithic sites as Knossos and Nea Nikomedeia, the reports on which are now complete. Most of the contributions to Section III of the present volume are concerned with the same area of concentration, including studies based on work carried out in Palestine, Anatolia, Greece, Bulgaria and Italy. Given the concern with living systems that goes with the functional approach, however, it should be no surprise that the project should have reached out to territories remote from the early centres of Old World civilization. Wilkinson's experience with Professor Teal's crash-programme on the domestication of the musk-ox in Alaska, and Sturdy's first-hand observations on the management of reindeer in west Greenland have each in their way yielded insights of value for interpreting data from the remote past. They remind us that prehistory is or should be as world

FOREWORD

wide in its reference as natural science. This is well exemplified in the history of the Academy's project. The problems under study are of world-wide interest and continuing relevance. It is small wonder that they should have called forth cooperation on an international scale.

Grahame Clark

[1] *Proceedings of the British Academy,* 51 (1965), 43.

[2] The point is well made by Sir Harry Godwin in the preface to his *The History of the British Flora,* 7 (Cambridge, 1956).

[3] See C. W. Phillips 'The Fenland Research Committee, its past achievements and future prospects', in *Aspects of Archaeology in Britain and Beyond*, ed. W. F. Grimes (London, 1951), 258-73.

[4] Of the other two, Sir Joseph Hutchinson was working as a geneticist overseas and Martyn Jope was still engaged as a natural scientist on medical research.

[5] T. E. Allibone (ed.), *The Impact of the Natural Sciences on Archaeology* (London, 1970), 69-71, fig. 8.

[6] Sir Joseph Hutchinson (ed.), *Essays on crop plant evolution* (Cambridge, 1965).

[7] For an explicit statement, see the present author's Albert Reckitt Archaeological Lecture for 1953, 'The Economic Approach to Prehistory', *Proceedings of the British Academy,* 39, 215-38. The same approach was implicit in a series of papers published in preparation for *Prehistoric Europe: the economic basis* (London, 1952).

[8] A reprint of the definitive account *Excavations at Star Carr, Yorkshire* is now available from the Cambridge University Press and a reconsideration by the present author entitled *Star Carr, a case study in bioarchaeology* (1971) has been published by Addison-Wesley as an item in their modular program in Archaeology and Anthropology.

[9] Pp. 93-8 (Oxford University Press, 1970).

[10] Instruction on these lines has for some years been on offer in the Department of Archaeology and Anthropology at Cambridge and in the Department of Environmental Archaeology at the Institute of Archaeology in London. A new series, *Studies in Archaeological Sciences*, planned by the Seminar Press with Professor G. W. Dimbleby as consulting editor should prove useful in promoting greater self-reliance and understanding on the part of archaeologists.

EDITORIAL NOTE

Internal cross-references are in the form, 'Payne (II. 2)', denoting that his is the second paper in Section II.

SECTION I
THEORY

1. THE ORIGINS OF ANIMAL AND PLANT HUSBANDRY

E. S. HIGGS AND M. R. JARMAN

For a quarter of a century much archaeological activity has centred on the Near East as the 'hearth area of domestication' and the cradle of civilization. Clear evidence for the early occurrence here of certain phenomena — large towns, writing, metallurgy — has encouraged the search for other and earlier origins and to a considerable extent this has been justified. As an outcome, the long-standing belief that the inventions associated with 'food production' and the consequent economic revolution probably took place for the first time in this area, received a considerable measure of support.

The pioneer work of Braidwood & Howe (1960) set out to document and explain the transition from 'half a million years of savagery' through the stage of the 'effective village-farming community' to urban civilization. They took it as a reasonable hypothesis that the 'hilly flanks of the Fertile Crescent' presented a natural nuclear area within which the origins of the transition might be sought. Since then the area of interest has widened to include Anatolia (Çambel & Braidwood, 1970), but the Near East remains the focus of attention. Zoological and botanical considerations have tended to support this interpretation of the archaeological data so that together they form a formidable obstacle to the consideration of alternative hypotheses and new data tend to be considered only in the light of the existing framework. The development of our knowledge of early agriculture in the Americas has however raised a number of questions which require an answer, which is all the more necessary in view of the fact that vast new areas of the world are opening up for the study of prehistoric agriculture, areas which in this respect have hitherto remained largely unexplored. We need therefore to remember that up to now only certain restricted regions in the Americas and the Near East have been adequately investigated from this point of view, and it is imperative to ask if our current opinions and interpretations have been biased by discoveries in these very restricted areas. Are the factors which we have become accustomed to consider as critically important of more than local significance, and are the areas which we have for so long considered the crucial centres upon which subsequent developments depended, part of a much wider phenomenon in time and space? Indeed it seems unlikely that when the history of agriculture in India and the Far East and Africa has been better

explored there will not be some sharp redress to our current views. It may be thought that no new early civilizations are now likely to be discovered, and if this is so any further developments of our knowledge will be of secondary importance compared with that which we now have, but on the other hand there cannot be sound understanding of the causes of successful developments if cultural and economic cul-de-sacs remain little understood.

In the opinion of the authors there is a need for a reconsideration of the situation as a whole, the basic data available, and possible alternative hypotheses which can be derived from it. As a preface to attempting such a task it is worthwhile to summarize the accepted interpretations of animal and plant evidence for early domestication in the Near East. Next we will consider the criteria and beliefs which shaped the interpretations, and we will continue by discussing some factors and hypotheses which appear to us to have been given little or no attention hitherto. The animals we will discuss in the first instance are the sheep, goat, cattle, pig, and dog; the plants, wheat and barley. These will serve our purpose of providing a means of examining the existing data and exploring alternative ways of approaching it.

The sheep. Perkins' (1964) report of domestic sheep at Zawi Chemi Shanidar is the earliest record which is generally accepted, with a ^{14}C data of about 9000 B.C. The criterion used was the high percentage of immature animals in the sample and a sharp change in the economy relative to the neighbouring Shanidar Cave, where the earlier levels contained a goat-dominated fauna, sheep being uncommon. The evidence relates to economic change and is not based on zoological criteria. By about 7000 B.C. domestic sheep are present at Ali Kosh in Iran (Hole, Flannery & Neely, 1969) on the fragile basis of the presence of a hornless individual, and at Çayönü in Turkey (Reed, 1969). By 6000 B.C. they are widespread in Greece, present at Argissa-Magula, Nea Nikomedeia, and Knossos (Boessneck, 1962; Higgs, 1962a; Jarman & Jarman, 1968). Sheep appear to have been rare in the Pleistocene and common in the Holocene. Payne (1968) has pointed out the dubious nature of so many of the identifications of Pleistocene sheep, and has suggested that the appearance of *Ovis* in the sense of a

3

breeding population isolated from *Capra* may be a very recent occurrence.

The goat. Domesticated goats are claimed first at Ali Kosh (7500-6750 B.C.) on the basis of a mortality pattern which differs from a 'natural' one, and on the ecological position of the site; they also appear at Beidha, *c.* 7000 B.C. (Perkins, 1966), where there was a high proportion of immature individuals. At Ali Kosh a morphological criterion by which domestic goats are often distinguished, the medial flattening of the horn cores, does not occur until a later date. Before 6000 B.C. domestic goats appear in Greece at Argissa, Nea Nikomedeia, and Knossos.

Cattle. All the earliest dates for domestic cattle, on the criterion of their small size, now occur in Greece, first at Argissa (6500 B.C.), and then at Nea Nikomedeia (6200 B.C.) and Knossos (6100 B.C.). Perkins (1969) has identified small cattle by 5800 B.C. at Çatal Hüyük, but his arguments for domestication in earlier levels on the basis of anatomical representation are inconclusive in the absence of fuller discussion of this and other evidence. The dates proposed for domestic cattle in the hinterland of the Fertile Crescent area are uniformly later in date (5500 B.C. or later, as at Ali Kosh).

The pig. The pig is claimed to be domestic at Çayönü about 7000 B.C. (Reed, 1969), and at some time after 6500 B.C. it appears at Jarmo (Reed, 1961). By then, or soon after, domestic pigs occur in the earliest Greek Neolithic, at Argissa, Nea Nikomedeia, and Knossos. As with cattle the evidence for domestication is their small size relative to the wild pigs of the area.

The dog. The earliest ^{14}C date reported for domestic dogs comes from Idaho, in North America (Lawrence, 1967). The Jaguar Cave finds, *c.* 8400 B.C., support the identification of a probable domestic dog in an early Postglacial context (Galbreath, 1938). Star Carr, *c.* 7500 B.C., remains the next oldest ^{14}C dated find (Degerbøl, 1961). The criteria used to identify domestication are changes in morphology and size relative to the supposed wild ancestor, the wolf. Two other finds seem likely to pre-date the earliest Near Eastern dogs of which accounts have been published, but we have as yet only their geological context from which to infer their early date. Specimens indistinguishable from recent dogs of the area come from several Late Pleistocene cave deposits in Japan, in one case associated with and distinguishable from those of the local wolf (Shikama & Okafuji, 1958). Pidoplichko (1969) reports Late Pleistocene dog from Mezin, in the Ukraine, with mammoth, reindeer, horse, and musk-ox and Musil (1970) another in the Magdalenian of the Kniegrotte Cave in Germany. The earliest dog reported from the Near East is from Çayönü (Lawrence, 1967) at 7000 B.C.

Wheat. Early domestic wheats are reported from a wide area of the Near East; several sites with dates around 7000 B.C. contain domestic einkorn, or emmer, or both: the lowest levels of Ali Kosh (Helbaek, 1969), the lower levels at Hacılar (Helbaek, 1970). By about 6000 B.C. these forms are very widespread, and the genetically more complex hexaploid wheats are found, as at Tell Ramad (van Zeist & Bottema, 1966), Knossos (Evans, 1964), and a few hundred years later, at Çatal Hüyük (Helbaek, 1964) and Tell es-Sawwan (Renfrew, 1969). The identification of these as domestic rather than wild samples relies almost exclusively upon morphological criteria; in particular, grain shape and the brittleness of the rachis.

Barley. In some ways the barley situation parallels that outlined for wheat. Two-row domesticated barleys are reported from a number of early (*c.* 7000 B.C.) sources, including Ali Kosh and Jericho. At Beidha, Helbaek reports the presence of a barley which, although by definition morphologically wild, was probably cultivated. Many sites provide comparable evidence by about 6000 B.C., including the early Greek Neolithic sites. The six-row barleys, which are usually held to be a product of human selection upon the two-row form, seem on the whole to have a slightly later distribution; they occur early at one site (Haçilar, 7000 B.C.), but other records are all later than this. The criteria for distinguishing the wild from the domestic forms are again primarily morphological considerations of grain shape, and the nature of the rachis and the structures which enclose the grain, the palea and lemma.

This data of itself presents certain problems if the customary hypothesis of an invention of the techniques of domestication by Mesolithic (Neolithic, 'Pre-pottery-Neolithic', or proto-Neolithic) peoples in the Fertile Crescent, is to be maintained. The domestication of the dog appears to have been accomplished or in progress by the Late Glacial/Early Postglacial period in many areas of the Northern Hemisphere from North America to Japan. Our present data suggest that the Near East was late in this development. Further, small forms of pigs and cattle, which thus accord to current criteria as 'domesticated', certainly occur in Greece and Turkey as early as or earlier than anywhere else.

It seems desirable then to consider the criteria which determine whether the bones from archaeological sites represent wild or domesticated animals.

THE ZOOLOGICAL AND BOTANICAL APPROACH

Detailed consideration has been given elsewhere in this volume to the criteria employed to separate wild and domestic animals (Jarman & Wilkinson, II. 4) and plants

(Jarman, I. 2). It is thus unnecessary to treat this subject in detail here.

It is common today to speak of animals and plants as either wild or domestic. Clearly some animals and plants are in a close relationship with man, and these are called domesticated; with others, the relationship is distant, or indeed imperceptible in some cases except to the biologist, and these are called wild. For considerations of the modern situation this is generally adequate at a superficial level. Most, though not all, modern animals and plants fall neatly enough into one category or the other. Difficulties arise, however, as soon as we attempt to define the categories precisely; to perceive not only the existence of the categories but also the factors producing them or to project the present situation into the past in order to assess the manner and situation in which the categories began to emerge. It is thus to some extent unfortunate that the zoologist and botanist have retained classification terms which work well in most general discussions of modern situations, but which are not really adequate to deal with the complex situation which their studies have revealed. Relationships between man and other organisms are varied, and the 'wild' class of plants and animals merges by a series of imperceptible stages into the 'domestic' class. It is clear that here the ecologists are ahead of us in the consideration of biological relationships, and their studies of symbiosis, mutualism, commensalism, and of a wide variety of predator-prey and other relationships, have a direct bearing on considerations of man-animal and man-plant relationships.

In order to study effectively the animals and plants concerned, the zoologist must try to draw firm dividing lines to distinguish classes which are helpful in the consideration of his data and problems. For this reason it is necessary, so that they may be satisfactorily studied, especially in the case of past situations, that the domestic class should be distinguishable in some physical characteristic from the wild class.

SELECTION

All organisms are thought to owe their nature and form in some degree to 'natural selection', the various pressures imposed upon them from the external environment as a whole. The hypothesis has been put forward that human selection upon domestic species, even in the early stages of the domestication process, will have been sufficiently different from natural selection in its impact for changes to have taken place which can be used to distinguish domestic from wild species. Many, like Zeuner (1963a), have compiled lists of changes which are thought to have arisen from such selection, which can be classified as either unconscious or conscious selection.

Unconscious selection is considered to have played an especially important role in the early stages of the history of domestication. Man is believed to have isolated small numbers of individuals from the natural wild breeding populations. At this stage two factors are thought to be of significance. In the first place, the operation of selective pressures consequent upon human influence but not consciously willed by man: in this category come the size decrease in pigs and cattle, and the appearance of tough rachis cereals (thought to result from unconsciously exerted selection during harvesting). Secondly it is believed that the very act of isolating segments of the wild population and causing restricted breeding to take place will necessarily cause changes, especially in the case of small groups where 'genetic drift' is thought to operate.

Conscious selection is thought to come at a fairly late stage in the history of domestication, and this term is reserved for the intentional application of controlled breeding with specific objectives in mind. For animals, this is usually inferred from the existence of different breeds of a species within a single area, but some authors (Bökönyi, 1969a) consider the appearance of castrated animals as a first step in the process. In some species evidence of intentional selection has been traced back to prehistoric, or at least protohistoric, times, as with the predynastic dogs in Egypt, which included a greyhound breed, and the sheep breeds of the Uruk period in Mesopotamia. Similar criteria are applied to intentional selection in plants, but the evidence is more scanty and the question has received little systematic attention from the point of view of prehistoric studies. Conscious selection for certain characters can occur early in the history of plant husbandry; for instance Mangelsdorf (1965) notes evidence for wide-spread intentional selection on maize, which had produced a large number of varieties, apparently by Pre-Columbian times.

Isolation is thought to have played an important part in domestication, especially in the early stages. The hypothesis is that man will have captured and tamed a few, probably young, individuals of the wild species, and that these will have been maintained as an isolated breeding group having little or no further contact with the local wild population. For this reason it is believed that the anatomical changes by which domesticates are identified will have arisen within a short space of time after the initiation of the new relationship.

Thus while it is generally agreed that the very first generations of domestic forms may not have changed sufficiently to be recognized as such by the methods available at present, nevertheless it is felt that isolation and changed selective pressures together induced perceptible changes so quickly that as far as the beginning of domestication is concerned any time lag can be ignored. If this approach is to be of value in indicating the time of an original domestication it is essential that any time lag should be insignificant on an archaeological time scale.

There are two basic tenets involved in this hypothesis which require consideration; each has been discussed in more detail elsewhere in this volume (Jarman & Wilkinson, II. 4. pp. 86, 87ff.; Jarman, I. 2). The first is that changes produced by human interference can be distinguished from the products of non-human selective forces. For example, size decrease is widely employed as a criterion of domestication of pigs and cattle; yet the Late Glacial and Postglacial periods are marked by dramatic size changes in many wild animals such as the Cave Hyena (*Crocuta crocuta*). Similarly this can also be said of certain samples of pig bones in the Crimea. Though small, they are considered to be of wild rather than of domesticated animals apparently because their chronological and cultural context is thought to be incompatible with domestic status (Tringham, 1969). The same limitations apply to many morphological features. Tooth crowding is considered by many to be a good criterion of domestication in the dog. But it has been pointed out that this condition certainly occurs in the wolf, and that we have no knowledge of how frequently it occurs (Clutton-Brock, 1963). Similar doubt has been thrown recently upon other criteria held to distinguish dogs and wolves (Herre & Roehrs, 1971). As far as plants are concerned, a comparable situation exists. Certain features, such as possession of tough rachises, seem in general well correlated with human influence (although we should note that even this may not be an inviolable rule, Jarman, I. 2. p. 19); other features seem more ambiguous.

The second tenet we must consider is that early domestication was accomplished by the isolation of small numbers of animals from the parent wild population, with subsequent maintenance of a sexual-genetic barrier between the wild and domestic populations; and that this was a major factor in the initiation of the physical changes which occurred. There is some doubt however whether or not isolation of itself does give rise to change. Certainly many isolated populations such as those on islands (Foster, 1964) do undergo changes relative to their parent populations. However, it is questionable whether or not it is isolation rather than a change in selective pressures, which causes the observed changes to take place. Ehrlich & Raven (1969) have argued strongly that gene flow between populations is in general at a much lower level than has been assumed previously, and that it plays little part in maintaining morphological similarity within species; by their hypothesis selection pressure plays a dominant role in controlling variability and similarity.

Most zoological work on this question has been concerned with total isolation in situations where the sea or other geographical barriers result in an absolute minimum, or indeed a total absence, of gene flow between the isolate and the parent population. The archaeological situation is, however, likely to have been such that total isolation will rarely have taken place. The difficulties of keeping wild and domestic stock apart are well known today, even with the aid of modern facilities, and when the wild populations are in a minority. Even in cases like that of the recently domesticated elk, where the new domesticates show no apparent desire to return to wild, there is a likelihood of mixture and inter-breeding; in this case the wild elk are apparently attracted to and join the domesticates (Knorre, 1961). In the past, with wild individuals greatly outnumbering the domestic, and with less technological sophistication, the task of maintaining total isolation is likely to have been an impossible one; partial isolation is probably the best that was achieved in most prehistoric situations.

The same conclusion seems reasonable of the early stages of plant husbandry. As long as agriculture was being carried out within the habitats of wild cereals a certain degree of cross-fertilization, and probably actual mixture of forms, would be inevitable. The prevalence of primitive forms occurring as 'weeds of cultivation' in many prehistoric grain samples suggests that this situation may indeed have been maintained long after the development of agriculture outside the area of early Postglacial cereal distribution. Doggett (1970) has discussed this in some detail with relation to sorghum. Even today, the virtual impossibility of keeping fields clear of hedgerow grasses indicates the likelihood of a high degree of physical and genetic contamination of crops when cereals themselves form a part of the local vegetation.

There is also strong anthropological evidence suggesting that total isolation may have been a comparatively rare occurrence. Quite apart from the many instances when inter-breeding is deplored and discouraged but cannot be entirely avoided, as in Tungus reindeer (Shirokogoroff, 1935) and Russian horses (Gmelin, 1768-9, quoted in Zeuner, 1963a), numerous cases are recorded where inter-breeding between wild and domestic animals is a matter of indifference to man, or indeed has been actively encouraged as an important part of the animal husbandry process. Thus the inter-breeding of the domestic Chukchi reindeer with the local wild population is thought to be beneficial by the herders (Leeds, 1965); the Naga go to great lengths to encourage crossing between the wild form of *Bibos*, the banteng, and the domestic Gayal, supplying salt-licks in order to attract the wild bulls (Zeuner, 1963a); in parts of New Guinea all domestic female pigs are served by captured wild (or, strictly speaking, feral) boars. Males born to domestic sows are castrated (Bulmer, 1968). Similar examples can be quoted for dogs, asses (Groves, Ziccardi & Toschi, 1966), and sheep (Carruthers, 1949). The Chukchi reindeer and New Guinea pigs are examples where barriers to gene flow between wild and domestic populations are virtually absent. Here there is a conflict between anthropological evidence and zoological hypothesis.

Even if we assume *a priori* that isolation took place and that changes in animals and plants took place as a result, Ehrlich & Raven's (1969) work suggests that as long as the selective pressures remained similar, changes could be very slow or of an infinitesimal nature.

Therefore we are presented with unknown vistas of time during which man could have been husbanding morphologically unchanged, and thus by zoological and botanical definition 'wild', plants and animals. The flourishing fields of many European botanical institutes show that there is no difficulty in cultivating as a successful crop for many generations cereals which are, morphologically speaking, wild. The many examples of present-day situations in which little or no barrier exists to free genetic exchange between wild and domestic populations indicate that the appearance of morphological differences may have been delayed indefinitely, particularly where selective pressures in the two populations remained similar. It seems almost a commonsense proposition that under the conditions in which primitive agriculture must have arisen, isolation and the consequences of isolation are hardly likely to have occurred except on rare occasions.

The accepted interpretations of the present record also include instances in which, it is claimed, pastoralism and cultivation of plants has taken place in the absence of morphological change. At Zawi Chemi Shanidar, morphologically unchanged sheep have been identified as domestic on the basis of an economic change relative to the neighbouring Shanidar Cave, and because of the high percentage of immature specimens (Perkins, 1964). The same author (1969) has inferred from details of anatomical representation that cattle from the lower levels at Çatal Hüyük were domestic, in spite of the absence of morphological differences from local wild specimens. Helbaek's (1966) 'cultivated wild barley' from Beidha falls into a comparable position as far as plants are concerned; it is not considered by Helbaek to be domestic, botanically speaking, as it is morphologically similar to the wild form, but its large size leads him to infer that it was husbanded by man. Faced with a similar situation in the evolution of maize, Mangelsdorf, MacNeish & Galinat (1964) adopt a rather simpler position. Their 'early cultivated' maize is distinguished from the wild form only by size, but they infer a change in the man-plant relationship at this point, with the practice of simple husbandry measures, and thus take this as a clear classificatory dividing line. Such instances are usually considered to be representative of a brief period of time when the human economic relationship had altered, but morpho-

logical change had not started. As we have indicated above, this is not necessarily so. The change in human economic behaviour could have occurred at any time previously, and need not necessarily have been associated with morphological change within a short period of time, or indeed at all. The presence of such changes can be taken to indicate that some form of agriculture existed at that time and that a farming economy was in operation; their absence cannot be taken to indicate that 'farming' was not present and the economy was one of hunter-gatherers.

POPULATION STRUCTURE

Recently a further attempt to distinguish between pastoral and hunting economies has been made by comparing the age and sex composition of prehistoric animal bone collections with the estimated 'natural' pattern, by which is meant the pattern in situations unaffected by human selective influence (Ducos, 1968, 1969; Bökönyi, 1969*a*). This approach has been considered in more detail elsewhere (Jarman & Wilkinson, II. 4). The basic hypothesis is that pre-agricultural man will have exploited resources in a 'natural', i.e. random, fashion, and that the increased control over his resources given by domestication allows planned cropping, which will be seen in the form of exploitation patterns which deviate from the natural random one. The information yielded by such studies is clearly of great importance for the study of prehistoric economies, but further consideration is required before the way in which the results have been interpreted can be accepted. Studies of predator-prey relationships between animals show the frequent occurrence of selective predation; selection of species, sex group, and age group are all recorded for a number of predators. Indeed, far from a random exploitation pattern being typical of all 'natural' relationships, it appears on available evidence to be a rarity. Comparable evidence is available for hunting economies, although studies of this are commonly not sufficiently detailed for our purposes.

SPECIALIZED ECONOMIES

Specialization has sometimes been regarded as a possible step towards domestication, particularly in connection with the Late Glacial reindeer economies of western Europe. A prolonged high degree of economic dependence on a single species does suggest the possibility of a close man-animal or man-plant relationship favouring the survival of both parties to the relationship. Legge (III. 2) and Jarman (III. 3) have discussed some aspects of this kind of relationship of man with gazelle and with deer.

Consideration of these examples leads to the realization that up till now economic studies of early domestication have been confined to a very small range of species, primarily those which are the staple food resources of civilized societies today. Many other plants and animals have, however, clearly been of great importance in the past, and it does not seem unlikely that some of these may have been in a close relationship with man, similar or indeed in some cases identical to relationships within the range of those we now regard as characteristic of domestication.

We know that certain individuals of the modern *Elephas maximus* are in a close relationship with man, and we call them domesticated in spite of the fact that no physical differences are perceptible between the wild and domestic individuals. As Zeuner noted, all the current methods of capturing elephants for domestication are 'well within the capabilities of primitive man, and even of Palaeolithic man'. It does not seem at all unlikely that species of elephant other than *E. maximus* were to some degree husbanded in the past. Recent suggestions by Dart (1967) and Eaton (1969) indicate possible examples of other such relationships. We do know that the onager was used extensively in Mesopotamia as a draught animal and, although still extant, was superseded by the horse and fell out of use. Columella relates that the onager was crossed with female asses to obtain an improved animal, an excellent example of conscious selective breeding. In addition a wide variety of species was kept in recorded herds in Egypt in Old Kingdom times. Legge's work (III. 2) allows the suggestion to be made that the gazelle in Egypt was not used as an experiment in domestication, but had long been domesticated in the Near East (Zeuner, 1963a; Vita-Finzi & Higgs, 1970).

We have therefore to conclude that zoological and botanical techniques cannot as a rule tell us at the present time whether or not the occupants of a site were farmers or hunter-gatherers. They can help to tell us that farming was practised but not that it was not practised. Rather than 'agriculture', in our view it would be preferable in future to refer to animal and plant 'husbandry' which stresses the important human element in man-animal and man-plant relationships and which would indicate in a single category pastoralists, herders, herd followers and the like, *where some form of intentional conservation was practised*. The precise method of killing or cropping would then be of lesser importance in our considerations. The term domestication we would prefer to confine to later agricultural practices where *intentional selective purposeful breeding can be demonstrated*.

If, however, we continue to attempt to distinguish between hunter-gatherers and farmers we have to take into account other than botanical and zoological considerations.

SETTLEMENT PATTERNS

The mode of settlement is considered by many an important feature distinguishing hunter-gatherers from communities with animal and plant husbandry. Hobler & Hester (1969) indeed make evidence of permanent settlement their basic criterion for classifying sites as Neolithic or non-Neolithic. Similarly, Braidwood & Howe (1960) considered the appearance of 'the effective village-farming community' to be intimately bound up with early domestication. The situation is more complex than this, however. An increasing number of villages have been reported from the Near East (e.g. Mallaha, Mureybit, Suberde) at which it is claimed that subsistence is based entirely on hunting and gathering. The Pleistocene sites of the Ukraine show that substantial structures are by no means restricted to the Postglacial. On the other hand it is quite obvious that permanent villages are by no means a prerequisite of the development of close man-animal and man-plant relationships. As discussed below, the Mesoamerican evidence illustrates this point clearly, and the many modern examples of mobile pastoralism should also warn us of the dangers of this hypothesis. Nor is there any guarantee that 'villages' will necessarily be permanently, rather than seasonally occupied. The latter situation is a commonplace in many modern pastoralist societies. Furthermore, it is not logical to maintain both that the hunter-gatherer existence was a random, 'catch-as-catch-can' affair, and that hunter-gatherers occupied settled villages otherwise indistinguishable from those of early agriculturalists.

An alternative interpretation would be that permanent settlement, or the regular seasonal occupation of substantial structures, depend on particular economic circumstances. Permanent houses represent a considerable investment, a capital outlay in terms of time, effort, and resources. In order for this to be worthwhile a dependable long-term incentive must be present within the exploitation territory of the site (Higgs & Vita-Finzi, I. 3). Obviously in exceptional circumstances this can occur in hunter-gatherer economies; certain Indians of the north-west coast of North America offer a well-known ethnographic example of such a case. However, the relatively sudden appearance of large numbers of villages in the Near East is evidently connected with the large-scale cultivation of cereals, and it seems most likely that the so-called hunters' villages at Mallaha, Mureybit and Suberde may represent sites at which close man-plant relationships had arisen without concomitant changes in plant or animal morphology.

In Mexico, villages appear at a time when maize is increasing in economic importance, appearing more prominently in the diet than previously, and developing more advanced forms. In the Far East, the appearance of villages seems to be closely involved with rice cultivation, as at Non Nok Tha and Ban Kao in Thailand (Gorman, 1971), and with *Setaria*, as at Pan-p'o in China (Ho, 1969). The effective village stage arose not from the invention of particular agricultural techniques which had probably long been known, but from the chance selection of particular plant and animal species with exceptional potentials and which were favoured almost on a world-wide scale by Postglacial climatic change.

ARTEFACTS

It might be thought that hunter-gatherer tool-kits would be sufficiently distinct from those of agriculturalists and pastoralists to provide a clear dividing line of some use to archaeologists. We know little about the precise function of Stone Age tools. Certainly there are some, like the shouldered points of some Palaeolithic industries, which seem best explained as projectile points. The work of Semenov (1964) has given a rebuff to even this conservative view. Clark (1952) has shown that some microliths were indeed tips, and possibly barbs of arrows in the Mesolithic of north-west Europe, but microliths are common in some industries in Australia, where, however, it is believed that the bow was absent. Not only are many industries which (by archaeological hypothesis) relate to hunter-gatherer economies without unequivocal hunting equipment, but on the other hand the industries which are most prominent in possession of such items are frequently chronologically late and apparently connected with farming economies. Unmistakable arrow heads are one of the commonest flint types in many western European sites dating from the Late Neolithic to Early Bronze Age times. Other artefacts usually associated with hunting, such as barbed bone points and harpoons, and spear throwers, are very restricted chronologically and geographically, and in the case of spear throwers, are few in number (Garrod, 1955). Other common Palaeolithic tools, such as burins and scrapers also occur in Neolithic and even Bronze Age contexts.

'Neolithic tools' present a similarly uncertain picture. Grindstones and mortars are known from many Palaeolithic sites; sickle flints occur in Natufian sites where there is no evidence for cultivation of cereals, and where indeed it seems that this would have been an unsatisfactory form of economy (Vita-Finzi & Higgs, 1970). Some authorities believe that sickles were multi-purpose tools and were used for the cutting of reeds and grasses. Sickle flints have been reported recently from pre-Holocene contexts in Sudan (Wendorf, 1968). The digging stick, a common tool in many primitive African agricultural societies, is also an important tool for hunter-gatherers like the Hadza (Woodburn, 1968).

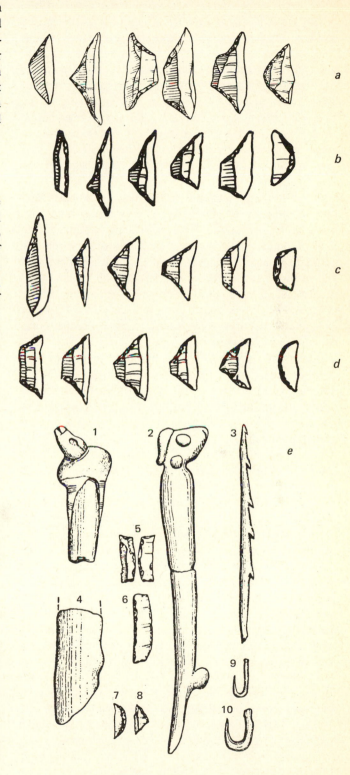

Fig. 1.   Mesolithic/Neolithic artefacts: *a* Star Carr, England; *b* La Cocina, Spain; *c* Palegawra, Iraq; *d* Jarmo, Iraq; *e* Natufian, Palestine (after Clark & Piggott (1965), 152).

As Clark has pointed out many times (1962, 1967, 1970a) there is a large measure of continuity between the tool-kits and technology of the two groups and this is nowhere more strongly marked than in the area of south-west Asia conventionally held to be the earliest home of Old World agriculture. Whether one looks to the so-called 'Pre-pottery Neolithic' farmers in the Levant or in the Zagros extending from Anatolia to Iran, the basic lithic industry and much of the equipment made from antler or bone is typologically 'Mesolithic', in the former case Natufian, in the latter Palegawran. This is so whether one looks to microliths with steep retouch (objects which must have served many purposes other than arrow barbs and tips), to the use of slotted tools or weapons with flint insets, to barbed points of antler or bone to barbless fish-hooks. Similar parallels have been drawn between the nature of personal ornaments, down to quite fine details, or even between ritual practices associated with human skulls. And some of these, most notably the microlithic forms, occur in certain contexts quite far back in the Upper or Advanced Palaeolithic sequence of southern Europe, north Africa, and south-west Asia.

Conversely, there is evident continuity in the opposite direction. Many of the type fossils which help to define the threshold of the Neolithic were in fact developed among communities which would not in conventional terms be so classified. Thus rubbers and grinding-stones, associated with the preparation of plant food occur as far back as the Advanced Palaeolithic in south Russia. Edge-ground stone axes are of great antiquity in regions as far apart as Japan and Australia and even polished ones occur in 'Mesolithic' contexts in Denmark and north-west Russia. Pottery, again, may appear under certain conditions in very early contexts as we are reminded by its occurrence even in Early Jomon deposits in Japan.

It is only where new economies have been introduced rather abruptly from one region to another — a process by no means as common as archaeological textbooks might suggest — that any very marked contrast appears between the equipment of farmers and antecedent populations. The lithic component of the material equipment of many Neolithic groups in Italy is basically Gravettian, carrying on a tradition that goes well back into the Late Glacial. Examination of the inventory of Neolithic settlements in Switzerland, the west Baltic area, or Iberia would tell much the same story. There is evidence of continuity in material equipment quite as much as in modes of subsistence.

THE NEED FOR A WORLD VIEW

It is obvious from what has preceded that the existing archaeological view of the origins of agriculture in the Old World is based on data derived not only from a very small number of species, but also from a very small area of western Asia, with the recent addition of a little of eastern Europe. Little is known of economic development in most of Asia, Africa, or Australasia. Despite the many discoveries concerned with early domestication in the New World little attempt has been made to consider Old World data in the light of this additional information. Indeed, the lack of impact which the models derived from Mesoamerican research have had upon the conventional archaeological view of the origins of domestication is most remarkable. In the New World the early domesticates include some apparently very unlikely plants, such as the avocado, bottle gourd, and various squashes, and not the present-day world staples. Not only does maize appear at a secondary stage in this development of man-plant relationships, but Mangels-dorf et al. (1964) have shown how slow was the development of the importance of maize as a staple domesticate; morphologically wild maize continues to account for fifty percent or more of all maize found in the Tehuacán Valley for some two millennia after the appearance of the 'early cultivated' form, a development which continues with the gradual evolution of new forms through later periods. Callen (1967) has shown that in some areas at least, a form of millet (Setaria geniculata) was grown prior to maize, and that its importance was only superseded when the development of maize had considerably progressed, in the first millennium B.C. This is a good example of a plant which, although it was apparently once an important crop, has been superseded by a more effective economic species, and has consequently dropped out of cultivation.

No parallels are known to the New World situation in the Near East. This may in part be due to the excellence of preservation in Mesoamerica, and the importance of copro-lites as a source of data here, as opposed to the grain caches and scatters of carbonized material on house floors which provide the bulk of information in the Near East. However, it is not improbable that a determined search for early plant and animal domesticates over a wider area of the Old World, including a wider range of species, will indicate a situation here more comparable with that in the New World. There early domestication appears to have arisen in many places over a wide area at least from Peru to Arizona, and not in a small circumscribed area like that around the Fertile Crescent. A recent review of the botanical data (Harris, 1967) has argued strongly for the need to look away from the major modern cultigens 'to some of the minor cultigens before agricultural systems became specialized toward the production of one or more major crops'. The same author has urged a greater interest in areas of the world other than the Near East and Mesoamerica.

Recent work in south-east Asia gives some support to these suggestions. Plant remains from the Spirit Cave in

Thailand have been interpreted as suggesting 'a stage of plant exploitation beyond simple gathering' at an early date, c. 7000 B.C. (Gorman, 1971). The plants concerned include legumes, bottle gourd, and water chestnut. Ho (1969) has argued that a species of millet and certain Chenapodiaceae were extensively grown in the dry loess areas of China from the fifth millennium onwards; and Smalley (1968) has suggested that the Chinese loess lands were colonized by agriculturalists virtually as soon as they were available for cultivation. It is noticeable in both China and Thailand that the modern staple, rice, appears as a late-comer in the plant husbandry of the region. At the other geographical extreme, it has been pointed out (Dimbleby, 1967) that hazel which flourishes ill in shadow may have been husbanded in Mesolithic times in north-west Europe by shade clearance; and the hypothesis of Helbaek (1960a) that *Chenopodium* may have been cultivated in the European Bronze Age again underlines the dangers of confining our interest to modern staples.

Thus from the point of view of the available data and the objectives of future research there is a need for a broadening of outlook. This is perhaps still more urgent from the point of view of the overall hypotheses in the light of which we interpret the data. Former explanations and suggested causes of the rise of agriculture have recently become less convincing. Childe's propinquity theory suggested drastic Postglacial dessication as the major causative factor, but this view has been steadily eroded over the past twenty years by the data and opinions of palynologists, botanists, and zoologists, who have cast doubt on the theory of a sudden dessication, and have queried the accuracy of Childe's model for human behaviour in such conditions, even had they occurred. Hypotheses of a religious motivation for animal domestication have, at best, no factual support at present. Zeuner's (1963a) belief that animal domestication was not economic in its origins but the 'almost inevitable' outcome of social interaction between man and certain other species, has received little attention. It appears to be based on the misconception that taming would necessarily be an uncertain and difficult process at first, and that man first acquired as domesticates those species which thrust themselves upon him as scavengers or crop-robbers, or to which he had attached himself as a 'social parasite'. Only a small number of species in these categories is today domesticated; and there is nothing in Zeuner's arguments to indicate why this should have occurred first at the time when he believed that it did.

The hypothesis that agriculture arose automatically as a result of human culture having attained a certain level (Braidwood & Howe, 1960; Braidwood & Willey, 1962), or of a combination of this and climatic factors (Reed, 1969), looks far less attractive in the light of the New World and other evidence. The artefactual evidence is contradictory; many features thought typical of economies with domestic plants and animals, including villages, grinding equipment, and polished stone, are reported from a variety of other and earlier situations. In many areas there is considerable cultural continuity between sites thought to have domesticated species and those thought to be hunter-gatherer settlements. In addition, cultural and climatic conditions are sufficiently diverse in the different areas to cast doubt upon this hypothesis. Thus village life, thought by many to be the necessary prerequisite or concomitant of domestication in the Near East, comes later than the cultivated plants of the El Riego phase in the Tehuacán Valley and the Infiernillo phase in Tamaulipas. In south-east Asia the earliest close man-plant relationships are claimed not from village sites, but cave sites. Similar objections exist to the vague proposition that we are dealing with part of a process of 'Postglacial readaptation'; the areas concerned are so diverse in every aspect of their climates and external environments that it can hardly be argued that each gave rise to such similar phenomena at nearly identical periods. A step forward here is Binford's hypothesis (1968) that stress situations caused by population pressure may have been a potent goad to economic and technological advance. However, his view that the Holocene is likely to have been the first time that such pressure was applied does not appear to be tenable; there is good reason to believe that both population pressure and productive economies may have been recurrent features throughout prehistory.

Permanently settled villages, and still more so stratified urban societies, depend upon reliable and readily storable surpluses of real (as opposed to symbolic) wealth. On the present evidence it seems that the modern cereal staples, in particular wheat, barley, rice, and maize played a crucial part in the rapid developments of such socio-economic organizations over wide areas of the world, and that this was a Postglacial phenomenon. The great economic impact of man's close exploitive relationships with cereals should not be allowed to convince us that these were the first relationships of their kind, however. Dynastic Egyptian sculptures and reliefs give us a picture of a complex range of close man-animal relationships, many of which were with species which are considered to be wild today, and for which there is no zoological or osteological evidence that they were ever anything but wild. Plants such as *Setaria geniculata* in the New World and *Chenopodium* in the Old World illustrate the same situation. The prehistoric, and in some cases, historic, importance of a wide range of plant species in Europe is well known, and points in the same direction. Indeed, it is becoming clear that many species which were 'domesticated' in the past have ceased to be so as more effective species and relationships have become available, and as economic requirements of the situation have changed. This is a process which continues today, as is exemplified by the rapidly dwindling number of camels and mules, the decline in the world importance of rye and oats, and the need to take positive measures to keep in cultivation such plants of declining economic interest as finger millet and Galla potatoes.

AN ALTERNATIVE HYPOTHESIS

At the present time it is clear that the development of tillage and pastoralism is being studied piecemeal on the basis of a series of different geographical entities; the data is uneven, having been collected in different areas, and derived from a variety of sources by a variety of techniques. Too little consideration has been given to possible underlying causes of economic changes, or to the mechanisms of change themselves (Higgs & Jarman, 1969). Attention is concentrated upon the search for first instances and the historical description of subsequent developments. Where they are discussed at all the origins are usually referred to inventions by 'innovating societies', the inevitable results of cultural development, or unspecified Postglacial adaptations. An overall hypothesis within which individual pieces of information from a wide variety of areas can be integrated is required.

We can see no reason for making the assumption that husbandry is an exclusively Postglacial phenomenon. This view is largely due to the confining of interest to present-day important domesticates. There is no reason to believe that other animals and plants have not been associated with man in close economic relationships in the past, and many of these relationships may well have been within the range of present-day pastoralist and agricultural economies.

The view taken by the authors is that animal and plant domestication were not the result of a series of Postglacial inventions, but were natural developments of processes common in human and non-human exploitation patterns (Higgs & Jarman, 1969). Like Zeuner (1963a) we feel that human domestication is not essentially a different pattern of behaviour from many visible between other species. But while Zeuner viewed the coming of domestication as a relatively sudden occurrence, limited to the last few millennia of human prehistory, and thought of it as originally a non-economic relationship born of the social interactions of different species, we believe that its roots go back much further, and that the relationships were always essentially economic, with great adaptive value. While it may be in some instances convenient to do so, it can also be misleading to talk of the 'origins' of domestication at all, if by this one means a well-defined point at which a totally new type of economic relationship came into being. It is certainly

true that modern conscious selective breeding is drastically increasing the degree to which man changes other organisms, and the speed with which the changes take effect. These are no more than intensifications of processes inherent in the situation, however. Obviously the techniques whereby man has extracted his economic surpluses have changed enormously with time, but the objective has remained the same throughout. By and large it seems permissible to see human economic developments as a general trend to increasing control over resources and a concomitant rise in productivity per unit of land surface. We do not feel that it is necessary or useful to break this development into a hunter-gatherer stage, from the origins of humanity until some point about 10 000 years ago, and an agricultural 'food producer' stage from there on. Man has always had a selective effect upon many of his prey populations, as do many other predators. One of the main points to arise from the studies of early economies is the strong ties linking many animal predator-prey relationships with early human exploitation patterns, and these again with many subsequent 'domestic' relationships, at least in their underlying economic principles, if not in the way in which we now rationalize the different practices. A glance at the relevant literature (e.g. Slobodkin, 1962; Wynne-Edwards, 1962) will show clearly the impact and relevance of terms and ideas arising from human economics in studies of animal relationships. Thus as Carr-Saunders (1922) said of the social system, the 'origins of domestication' lie far back in the realms of the evolution of animal behaviour, and are thus beyond the scope of archaeological study.

To deal with the more specifically archaeological aspect of the problem, we believe that man-animal and man-plant relationships similar to modern domestication will have tended to occur throughout the Pleistocene wherever this was the most profitable economic strategy in the prevailing circumstances. Similarly, eclectic, or 'broad spectrum' hunting and gathering will also have tended to occur where this was a successful economic solution to the problems posed by population pressure upon the available resources. Short-term fluctuation obscures this picture to some degree, but we need not be distracted by this from perceiving the existence of a rationally explicable pattern. In many ways the diversity of economy which existed in the Palaeolithic was comparable with that of today, but with a continuing trend to an increase in high productivity economies under the urgings of sustained population pressure. There is no reason to suppose that there was ever a 'Hunter-Gatherer Age' in the sense of a time when all men were eclectic hunter-gatherers. We think it unlikely that from say Middle Palaeolithic to Postglacial times economies remained static at a hunter-gatherer stage. It seems much more likely that economic practices changed and developed throughout this period. Patterns of exploitation resulting in a husbanding of plant and animal resources (whether by chance or design is immaterial) is too common a feature elsewhere in the animal world for us to believe that man did not evolve similar economic mechanisms, and the evidence suggests positively that he did.

We think, therefore, that the search for origins of agriculture and pastoralism will not continue to be rewarding as it has been in the past. The present hypotheses have taken the data as far as they are able to go, and a new framework is more likely to yield insight. We prefer to study the development of agriculture not essentially as an invention or a series of inventions designed to control man's environment, but as a continuously developing natural process of great selective value, in which adjustments to climatic and other ecological factors are visible up to the present day. A wide variety of man-animal and -plant associations took place from time to time and were repeatedly superseded by more successful associations. We now know only the end-products of continual elimination. Figure 2 shows that, even accepting the traditional static-historical model, domestication can be regarded as a long-term process whose limit at one end is defined by the present day, and at the other only by the earliest date that anyone has yet had the temerity to propose. There seems no reason why certain species may not have been domesticated a number of times as occasion demanded; thus Knorre (1961) has pointed out that the modern Russian domestication of the elk is almost certainly not the first similar economic exploitation of this species. We believe that if a serious attempt is to be made to understand human development more archaeological re-sources might well be devoted to the study of the economic mechanisms involved rather than to a search for first instances and rival 'hearths of domestication'.

Turning to the more parochial problems of Europe, of which we believe the above consideration is an essential preliminary, the weight of the evidence today seems to lead to the following conclusions. Wheat, barley, sheep and goats were probably introduced into Europe from the East although on this point some reservations should still be made (Jarman, I. 2). With other domesticates, in particular the pig, cattle and the dog, the evidence is either equivocal or to the contrary. We think it is unlikely that pastoral and agricultural techniques were introduced into a Europe entirely exploited by hunter-gatherer economies. We think it is unlikely that the exploitation of the resources of Europe was so uniform in Glacial and Postglacial times. There appears to us to be a strong possibility that European reindeer-based economies in the Late Glacial are more likely to have more in common with pastoralism or reindeer herding than with eclectic random hunting. We think that there is some evidence to support this and little to support the opposite view. As for evidence for plant husbandry, the consideration of the data is more or less confined to a search for morphological change. Valuable indicators as such changes are, their absence cannot demonstrate that plant husbandry did not take place, and research in other directions should not be inhibited by the absence of a particular form of evidence. The study of site territories and land utilization in prehistoric times may be expected to give an informative lead in this direction.

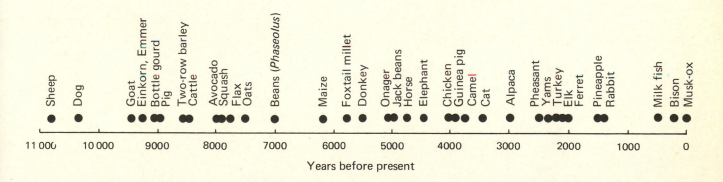

Fig. 2.   Accepted dates for the domestication of some plants and animals, showing the continuing development of the process. (The dates are approximate owing to the lack of resolution in most archaeological data.)

2. THE ORIGINS OF WHEAT AND BARLEY CULTIVATION

H. N. JARMAN

The study of the evolution of crop plants has attracted considerable interest among archaeologists in recent years. Mangelsdorf's detailed study (Mangelsdorf, MacNeish & Galinat, 1964; Mangelsdorf, 1965) of the development of maize on the basis of archaeological remains has been especially influential, and in the Old World the study of the evolution of wheat and barley has come to form an integral part of Near Eastern Neolithic archaeology. Most of our present understanding of crop plant evolution has come to us from the findings of botany, plant genetics, and ecology. It is evident, however, that the specialist contributions which have most impact on the archaeological literature are those which confirm the hypotheses which the prehistorian has arrived at by the consideration of other forms of data. Information and opinions which appear contradictory to those derived from 'cultural' material tend, on the contrary, to reach the archaeologist seldom or not at all. Similarly, the interest in and collection of palaeobotanical data is on the whole focused in those areas which appear crucial in terms of their 'cultural' development. The limitations arising from such an approach are apparent; the hypothesis of agricultural origins in the Near East tends to be self-fulfilling, in the absence of organized efforts to test it in other areas.

At our present state of knowledge one must accept that in the evolutionary studies which are central to our ideas concerning cereal development, patterns of evolution and their causes cannot be perceived with certainty. The data and techniques of the time will tend to support a particular hypothesis or hypotheses, and one may be tempted to overlook the inconsistencies until the development of new techniques makes greater understanding possible. But to lose sight meanwhile of the weaknesses in the preferred hypothesis may close possible avenues of research and produce a stagnation of ideas which new techniques unsupported by new concepts will not overcome. Therefore, this critique of the current view of the domestication of wheat and barley is not intended to point out hitherto unnoticed discrepancies, but to discuss in greater depth some questions which have only been touched upon in the past and to examine their implications for future archaeological research.

Recent discussion on the nature of the domestication relationship (Higgs & Jarman, 1969) has thrown doubt on the value of the words 'wild' and 'domesticated' to describe the full range of man-animal and man-plant relationships which may have existed in the past. In his treatment of the subject, Helbaek (1969, 1970) avoids the problem by defining 'domestication' in terms of the physiology of the plant concerned: 'domestication depends on some physiological inefficacy in a plant of which man takes advantage' (Helbaek, 1970). Although ambiguities may be eliminated in this definition, it focuses attention upon the plant morphology rather than the man-plant relationship with which prehistory is concerned. On the other hand, Helbaek's description of 'cultivated' as 'a complex of measures by which ecology is influenced in order to further the growth and output of one or more plant species', correctly places emphasis on the processes which create the contact between man and plants and defines a category which is useful to the archaeologist. A classification with more universal application could distinguish between husbanded and non-husbanded plant resources. The division would be based on economic criteria rather than botanical criteria and might or might not coincide with traditional botanical groupings. 'Cultivation' fits into this scheme as a husbandry practice; it is, in fact, a rather nebulous collection of husbandry practices variously including ploughing, sowing, weeding, fertilizing, and harvesting. In this paper the term is used to include both sowing and harvesting but not to imply any particular treatment of the crop between sowing and harvesting.

The term 'domestication' is unnecessary in the economic classification, but it is convenient when used in conjunction with the botanical classification. For example, those who are unfamiliar with Latin names for plants will probably find 'domesticated-type' and 'wild-type' einkorn more comprehensible than *Triticum monococcum* and *T. boeoticum*. Therefore it is suggested that these terms be used solely as a readily comprehensible botanical classification, distinguishing between morphologically wild and morphologically domesticated plants. This taxonomy has existed in the past in an undefined and often confusing form. In the literature one finds several meanings attached to the words 'cultivated', 'cultivate', and 'wild'. The adjective 'cultivated' is sometimes used to indicate the state of being under cultivation, but is often used to describe the morphology or genetic constitution of a plant possessing traits considered typical of modern cultivated plants. The verb 'to cultivate', on the other hand, is always used to refer to the activities of man toward the plant. Similarly, 'wild' has been used with both economic and morphological connotations. The complications and ambiguities which arise from the use of a single word in two entirely different ways are well illustrated in Helbaek's (1966) description of the Beidha barley as 'cultivated wild barley'. As he suggests (Helbaek, 1970), the two terms are not incompatible if 'cultivated' is construed in an economic sense, and 'wild' in a morphological sense, but it would help to clarify thinking on this subject if the morphology of a plant were kept terminologically distinct from the man-plant relationship. For this reason the terms 'domesticated-type' and 'wild-type' are used in this paper strictly as descriptions of plant morphology.

BASIC ASSUMPTIONS

The current hypothesis proposes that wheat and barley were both brought into cultivation in south-west Asia, primarily on the hilly flanks of the 'Fertile Crescent' about 10 000 years ago. Evidence to support this view has been obtained from plant remains which resemble modern cultivated forms from sites of this period, such as Ali Kosh, Beidha, Jarmo, and Jericho. An increasing number of early sites with similar remains in Anatolia has led to the suggestion that the area of initial cultivation of these cereals may have extended slightly beyond the boundaries of the 'Fertile Crescent'. Additional evidence has come from studies of the modern distribution of wild wheat and barley (Harlan & Zohary, 1966; Zohary, 1969) and from genome analysis work by plant geneticists (Bell, 1965; Riley, 1965).

The interpretation of this evidence has relied on two basic assumptions: (1) that the conditions under which the cereal grew (that is, whether or not it was assisted by man) can be determined by the morphology of remains of that cereal found on archaeological sites; (2) that the distribution of wild progenitors of wheat and barley has remained largely unchanged during the past 10 000 years, and where it has changed, the original pattern can be detected by a study of the context in which it is growing at the present day. This latter assumption, in fact, contains a further assumption: that close genetic relationship between modern wild and modern cultivated species of cereals implies close evolutionary relationship, and it assumes that the wild progenitor has remained the same since the time the cultivated form became a distinct species. Although many workers are probably aware of the limitations of these assumptions, they are nevertheless almost invariably relied upon in the interpretation of prehistoric plant remains, and in the reconstruction of the early development of agriculture. Yet there exists no thorough discussion of the validity of the assumptions nor of the implications for further research if they were rejected. A closer analysis of them may illuminate their relevance to the study of past human behaviour.

MORPHOLOGY

A close connection between morphology and conditions under which a plant has developed has been assumed by many concerned with identifying and interpreting remains of plants from archaeological sites. It is obvious from a study of the anatomy of modern cereals that differences do exist between those which are cultivated and those which grow under wild, or weedy, conditions. Even considering only the caryopsis, which is often the only portion of the plant preserved in archaeological deposits, seemingly primitive domesticated-type einkorn and emmer, *T. monococcum* and *T. dicoccum*, can be distinguished on morphological grounds from the very similar wild forms *T. boeoticum* and *T. dicoccoides*. It has further been commonly assumed that the morphology of modern cultivated cereals is associated with cultivation in a one-to-one relationship. In other words, every time cultivation occurs so too does modern cultivated morphology and vice versa. Schwanitz (1966), however, does not agree that the appearance of cultivated forms need be coincident with the beginnings of cultivation:

> Do wild species, if they are grown by man, turn directly into cultivated plants? By no means. The plants remain wild plants even when they are grown under the improved conditions of cultivation, showing better development and a higher yield than those plants gathered in the fields and forests. They still have not lost any of the properties that mark them as wild plants and have not yet taken on any characteristics that make them more useful or desirable than wild plants, and so they do not differ in any way from the wild form. They are as useful as gathered plants, but can in no way be considered true cultivated forms, for a genuine cultivated plant always differs from its wild ancestor in certain of its hereditary characters.

Stated more concisely, Schwanitz is saying that at least some plants which are being cultivated are not cultivated plants taxonomically speaking. Here there is a linguistic confusion which has already been discussed; but the linguistic complexities do not solve the problem of how far we can rely upon morphological characteristics of plant remains to indicate whether or not the inhabitants of a particular site were practising agriculture. For this, one must examine each of the traits usually considered to be typical of 'domesticated-type' wheat and barley in order to determine how closely tied they are to the practice of agriculture.

Three criteria have commonly been used to assess the economic status of prehistoric cereal remains. The shape of the grain is frequently used to identify remains at the specific level. It has been assumed that if the identified species is the same as a modern or historically cultivated species that the remains came from domesticated plants, but if the species identified is at present wild, this is usually accepted as sufficient evidence that the prehistoric crop was a wild, gathered one. Two problems arise in the use of this criterion. The first, a technical problem, involves the fact that many species vary only slightly in grain shape and size, and that the distortions resulting from carbonization may be greater than the species' differences, making it very difficult to identify the grain to species level unless other portions of the plant are preserved as well, or preservation is by some means other than carbonization. The second problem is a theoretical one involving the link between morphological characteristics, such as grain shape or glume and rachis form, and conditions of cultivation. No special study has been made of morphological changes which occur in grain shape and glume and rachis form when species such as *T. boeoticum* or *H. spontaneum* are taken from the wild and grown in the cultivated conditions of botanical gardens, especially those of north-western Europe with their different climate and soil. Thus, although it is to be expected that some changes may take place, they have not been so great as to attract the attention of the botanists dealing with them or to warrant the creation of new taxonomic groupings. When cereals began to be cultivated in or near the regions of their wild distribution, one would expect even less morphological change. Much of course depends upon the selection pressures both on the wild and cultivated population, but one cannot postulate an immediate and automatic change in grain shape as an inevitable result of domestication, and how long a time might elapse before such a change would occur is unknown.

The size of prehistoric grain has sometimes been used as a criterion of cultivation, but no consistent discussion of the nature of this relationship is available. Helbaek (1966) interpreted the large size of barley kernels at Beidha as evidence for its cultivation; but in the case of emmer he sees cultivation as resulting in a decrease in the size of the spikelets (Helbaek, 1960b). A recent study of the physiological aspects of wheat evolution (Evans & Dunstone, 1970) shows a consistent increase in grain weight proceeding from wild diploid to cultivated hexaploid forms. As the authors suggest, it is likely that grain size would have been an early criterion for human selection. However, a general trend toward increasing grain size does not necessarily

demonstrate the incidence of cultivation at any particular point on the scale. In particular, the significance of Early Holocene grain size cannot be adequately discussed until something is known of the Late Pleistocene populations which preceded it. It is interesting to note that wild-type einkorn, *T. boeoticum*, grown at the Institute of Plant Breeding at Wageningen was demonstrably larger than that found at the prehistoric site of Mureybit (van Zeist & Casparie, 1968) and might for this reason be regarded as domestic grain if found in an archaeological context. Cereal grain size depends not only upon the economic status of the crop, but on the total ecological circumstances of its growth, and one would expect that the protected environment of crops grown in botanical institutes, as well as the conditions of climate and soil fertility will have some effect on both size and physical characteristics of the populations concerned. The likelihood of Postglacial climatic change or more localized ecological events having important repercussions on plant growth and form should be considered before relating size change to domestication. Some of these variables might be eliminated if size and shape comparisons were made between archaeological samples of different ages, but care must be taken to confine such work to a restricted geographical or ecological zone.

The means of seed dissemination in cereals as expressed by the fragility of the rachis has been one of the morphological traits most frequently used in distinguishing between wild and cultivated forms of wheat and barley found on archaeological sites. In support of the use of this criterion, Zohary (1969) emphasizes the fact that the brittle rachis is part of an integrated mechanism for efficient seed dispersal in a non-agricultural environment. Under conditions of cultivation, where man contributes to the continued propagation of the plant population, the high selective value of this mechanism would presumably be decreased. However, the relaxation of selection pressures on a particular trait is not sufficient in itself to eliminate it from a population. This fact is immediately obvious on the basis of physical evidence alone without the ample evolutionary theory to back it up. Schwanitz (1966) notes some general examples of cultivated plants which have not yet lost their highly efficient mechanisms for dissemination of fruits and seeds: 'Thus, in isolated districts of Spain even today is grown a primitive variety of flax having fruits that burst open when ripe; and every so often we find the black poppy, which scatters its seeds when ripe, like the wild species of poppy.' As to the disappearance of the brittle rachis itself under conditions of cultivation, modern *T. monococcum* and *T. dicoccum* have a rachis only slightly less brittle than their wild counterparts. Percival (1921) describes *T. monococcum* as follows: 'The ears of *T. monococcum* are very brittle, and it is stated that the plant sometimes sows itself among other crops from which it is difficult to extirpate it when once established; it was reported in 1871 as a troublesome weed in cornfields round Montpellier.' The hexaploid wheat *T. spelta*, which has been under cultivation since at least the second millennium B.C., retains a rachis so brittle as to necessitate special treatment in harvesting to avoid shattering and loss of grain (Percival, 1921). Among the durum wheats, too, Percival describes some varieties which disarticulate more or less easily especially near the base of the ear. It is evident then that cultivation and the relaxation of selection for wild-type seed dispersal has not fully eliminated the brittle rachis in many varieties even after several thousands of years of cultivation, although in some cases this may be due to the genetic potential of the crop involved. Indeed, in the case of *spelta* the brittle rachis may have been selected for or be genetically linked with other desirable characteristics, making it unlikely that it will ever disappear from the species (Riley, pers. comm.).

This continued existence of brittle rachis forms into the present day weakens the argument that man's harvesting and/or sowing methods would have necessarily produced unconscious selection for tough rachis plants. *Triticum spelta* is harvested before it is fully ripe; no loss of grain occurs, and therefore, a tough rachis plant has no advantage in this case over the brittle rachis one. Similarly, Harlan (1967) found that only minor losses of grain occurred in harvesting wild wheat when almost fully ripe, even if a sickle were used. He demonstrated the possibility of harvesting brittle rachis plants efficiently by hand, in which case one would expect even less loss of grain. In any case, if cultivation were taking place in an area where wild cereals occurred naturally, those spikelets of brittle rachis ears lost during the harvest would seed themselves and become part of the following year's crop. There is the further problem that since ears of *T. monococcum* and *T. dicoccum* break up during threshing, the refuse deposited after threshing will appear to have come from a brittle-eared cereal. The existence today of tough rachis cereals means that at some time, in some place, it became advantageous either to man, or to the plant, or both, for cereal ears to possess a tougher rachis. That selection for this trait would have gone on rapidly and automatically from the earliest cultivation is by no means certain; although the practice of fallow may have helped to eliminate the brittle rachis, crop rotation on the other hand might have helped to preserve it.

There seems, therefore, to be no commonly recognized morphological characteristic which can be shown either to occur immediately upon full cultivation (sowing and harvesting) or to express itself in all cultivated forms. Why then has morphology come to be almost the sole tool for distinguishing plants grown in wild conditions from those grown under cultivation? It is largely due to the fact that archaeologists have fallen into the habit of passing the responsibility for archaeological as well as botanical interpretation of plant remains to plant specialists. Geneticists and botanists have been primarily interested in the evolution of modern domesticated plants and not in the origins of particular practices of cultivation, although these aspects have been considered in as much as they could be used to explain species differentiation. It is reasonable, and indeed necessary in our present state of knowledge, that the taxonomy of fossil populations should rely upon morphological evidence. From the point of view of palaeobotanical classification, the line dividing an ancestral wild species from its cultivated descendant must be drawn at a point where the morphology of the latter is sufficiently distinct to allow practical separation of the two. But it must always be remembered that this is a line drawn to suit the requirements of botanical taxonomy; it is the most distant point in time to which particular characteristics of modern cultivated plants can be traced. It is not necessarily the line between plant gathering and agriculture. Yet it is this latter distinction, one of human behaviour, which is the primary concern of archaeologists.

As an example of the distinction between the botanical and archaeological interpretations, we can consider the barley remains from Beidha about which Helbaek (1966) writes:

> There is no evidence of articulated internodes such as in domesticated barley so what we are dealing with is, strictly speaking, cultivated wild barley (*Hordeum spontaneum*). After a longer period of cultivation and automatic harvesting selection the crop changes physiologically in that the spike axis becomes tough and the grains can be beaten loose while the internodes remain attached to each other as a unit, the rachis or axis. Only then can barley be described as domesticated.

This is a botanical statement about the changes of morphology of the barley and the possible causes of these changes. Certainly the archaeological implication to be drawn from this evidence is that throughout its existence as a village, the arable economy of Beidha was probably based on the cultivation of barley (whether it was *Hordeum spontaneum* or *H. distichum*), and that the very location of the village would have been influenced by its suitability for cereal cultivation. The fact that the brittle rachis changes to a tough rachis at some point in the archaeological sequence may be interesting from the point of view of illuminating details of agricultural method, although it is by no means certain that it will provide even this information; but these details cannot be considered as central to problems of economy and culture as a whole.

The cereal remains from Mureybit could be reconsidered in the light of the above interpretation of the Beidha barley. Van Zeist and Casparie (1968) have suggested that since wild einkorn does not grow in the vicinity of the site at the present time, and since there is no evidence for climatic change since 8000 B.C., the inhabitants of Mureybit harvested their einkorn in south-eastern Turkey, a distance of 100 to 150 km from the site, and carried the year's supply of grain back to Mureybit with them. However, two other explanations are possible. First, the wild einkorn distribution may have changed, for although the interpretation of the scarce palynological evidence may be correct in proposing similar overall climatic conditions throughout the last 10 000 years, local environmental conditions in the past may have been more suitable to wild einkorn, or the ecological tolerances of wild einkorn may have changed since Mureybit was inhabited. This possibility will be discussed more fully in the section on distribution. The second alternative is that although the morphology of the grain at Mureybit places it securely within the taxonomic groupings of the wild species *Triticum boeoticum* and *Hordeum spontaneum*, there is no reason to suppose that it was not sown and harvested in the vicinity of the site, thus falling into Helbaek's (1966) 'longer period of cultivation' before the crop changes physiologically. The site is located along the Euphrates River which would have provided extra moisture whether or not it was manipulated by man. From an economic point of view the pattern of exploitation suggested by van Zeist and Casparie seems least likely of these three. Flannery (1969) has calculated that about one metric ton of grain would be necessary to feed a family group for one year. In view of the distance involved and the means of transportation then available, the yearly movement of this bulk and weight of food would have been so uneconomic as to make it, while still possible, highly unlikely.

It is not intended, however, totally to divorce the study of man from that of plant morphology, but rather to clarify their relationship to each other. Given a plant with a particular set of characteristics, man will adapt his method of exploitation in such a way as to exploit it efficiently. These methods may have no long term effect upon the plant morphology or physiology. On the other hand they may exert an evolutionary pressure (whether by conscious or unconscious selection) causing considerable changes in the crop and thus producing a feedback which may alter the methods of exploitation. The degree to which each member in the interaction will change in order to produce a successful relationship is neither predetermined nor uniform. Within the single genus *Triticum* both processes are evident to varying degrees. Most of the tetraploid and hexaploid wheats have very tough rachises and naked grain.

They are left in the field until fully ripe with only minor loss of grain during harvesting, and can be threshed with a minimum of time and effort. *Triticum spelta*, on the other hand, possesses a brittle rachis and hulled grain. It must be harvested before it is fully ripe, and the grain is freed from the ears by the use of a special mill (Percival, 1921). In spite of the adjustments made in human behaviour to grow spelt profitably, Percival records it grown as late as 1901 over large areas in Germany and also in Switzerland, Austria, northern Spain, France and Italy. Even today there are 10 000 hectares of spelt in the Belgian Ardennes (Riley, pers. comm.). Percival mentions its special advantages over the more prolific and more easily processed bread wheat in winter hardiness, resistance to smut, bunt, and rust fungi. The way in which spelt is handled does not result in selection for a tough rachis or naked grain; these disadvantages are accommodated by adjustments in human behaviour and technology, and at least up to 1901 the advantages of spelt wheat must have outweighed the disadvantages in some areas, or it certainly would not have continued as a crop for 3000 years.

It should now be possible to draw some conclusions regarding the interpretation of samples of wheat and barley from archaeological sites. From a positive point of view, some characteristics of many, but not all, modern cultivated varieties of wheat and barley may be fairly safely assumed to put the plants in an inferior position if placed in direct competition with the native wild flora. Two of these traits which may be preserved in archaeological material are the tough rachis and loose glumes. Even here, however, there are exceptions to the rule: one form of a wild *Aegilops* species has been recorded as possessing a non-fragile rachis (Sarkar & Stebbins, 1956). This can be taken as a salutary warning of the dangers of simplistic and absolutist hypotheses. One may nevertheless reasonably assume that when cereal remains can be shown to possess a tough rachis or naked grain, they were probably assisted by man in their continued propagation. This is supported by the fact that providing their advantages are recognized and that therefore a positive selection was exercised in their favour, plants with a tough rachis would have enjoyed a privileged position in cultivation relative to those with a brittle rachis. Tough rachis plants can be allowed to ripen longer without increased loss of grain; the riper grain germinates better, has increased productivity, and contributes an increasing proportion to the seed corn. As long as conditions of cultivation and growth continue to favour them, the tough rachis plants will thus tend to spread throughout the crop. However, while husbandry techniques are adapted to brittle rachis plants, the cereal will probably be harvested before the ears are fully ripe, or by a technique which successfully allows for the limitations of the crop. Tough rachis mutants, with their potential for more complete ripening, will have no selective advantage, because the human behaviour patterns have in this instance been successfully adapted to the behaviour of the brittle rachis plant. Under these circumstances the plant morphology might have remained unchanged for an indefinite period, until by chance or design the human economic practices altered to produce an effective evolutionary pressure for toughness. Thus one cannot assume that because cereal remains do not show any morphological differentiation from modern wild cereals that they were not cultivated. There are no characteristics inherent in wild cereals which render them uneconomical to cultivate even with a minimum of technological sophistication, assuming that man is at least flexible enough to live within that rather large geographic and climatic range in which wild wheat and barley will grow (it is possible to grow these species and the wild goat-face grasses out-of-doors in England). Therefore, the lack of any or all characters considered to be typical of modern cultivated cereals cannot be used to demonstrate the absence of agriculture at a particular site.

One might argue that, even assuming the wild cereals to be suitable for cultivation without modification, the probable selection by man of superior individuals for seed grain would quickly produce noticeable physiological changes in the crop. However, historical records do not indicate that this was the case. In discussing the history of agricultural research Salmon & Hanson (1964) state that although much progress was made in improvements in early agriculture 'it was always distressingly slow'. Similarly, Schwanitz (1966) records that apart from choosing the largest grain for seed as was recommended by the Romans, 'efforts to obtain hereditary improvement in cultivated plants were rather slight and hence not very effective. It is understandable that the origin and development of cultivated plants took a long time, under the circumstances, and led only to relatively insignificant improvement in their performance'. This very slow rate of change is no doubt partly due to the limited stock of grain at the disposal of any one group. Most improvements in cultivated crops rely on combining and selecting among naturally occurring variations between individuals and populations. Whereas modern means of communication bring the variations of the plant populations of the world to the plant breeder's doorstep, until recently man was limited to the varieties in his own neighbourhood. To this one must add the fact that the variations which do occur are by no means always an improvement over existing plant types. Even now the majority of scientifically bred varieties, when subjected to field trials, turn out to be no better than varieties already under cultivation (Gill & Vear, 1966). Also, it should be noted that the selection in the field of superior ears to

provide the following year's seed grain does not necessarily ensure a better crop the next year. Variations in individual plants in the field are often due to localized environmental fluctuations, a patch of more fertile soil or a drainage pattern favouring one section of a field, rather than to genetic factors which can be maintained in the progeny. Therefore, one cannot rely on rapid and consistent progress in prehistoric crop improvements.

In addition, it has usually been implicitly assumed that the obvious morphological changes, such as increase in grain size and establishment of tough rachis forms, would be of prime importance to early agriculturalists and would be selected for, whether consciously or unconsciously, rapidly and uniformly. However, other characteristics, not tied to particular morphological features, might equally have been considered of importance by early agriculturalists. For instance, selection may have been for high productivity, uniform germination and ripening, disease resistance, and other physiological properties. The selection actually applied would depend largely upon the economic circumstances involved. A group of people relying upon their cereal crop as a staple food source probably could not afford to select for ease of processing to the detriment of productivity. This factor may explain the persistence of *T. spelta* in the face of the more easily harvested and threshed *T. aestivum*; Percival (1921) quotes Stoll's figures that after the winter of 1900-1, 38 percent of the winter wheat of Germany had to be ploughed up in May, because of frost damage, whereas less than 1 percent of the spelt sown was destroyed.

The difficulties involved in interpreting archaeological samples of grain must now be apparent. It is possible to cultivate the wild forms of wheat and barley while effecting little or no morphological or physiological change in the plants. Changes in selection pressures under cultivation may have affected features not detectable in the material preserved on archaeological sites. It would appear that at the present state of knowledge, one must admit that morphological criteria are of limited use in establishing the practice of agriculture in general. The resulting implications include the possibility that grain from early sites, such as Mureybit, may have been the result of an agricultural economy, and that cereal cultivation in earlier times cannot be ruled out.

GEOGRAPHICAL AND ECOLOGICAL DISTRIBUTION

The currently accepted hypothesis concerning the link between the modern distribution of wild cereals and the origin of cereal cultivation is clearly stated by Helbaek (1959):

The locus for the domestication of a wild plant must necessarily be its area of natural distribution ... [Gives modern distribution]. Thus, we may conclude from present distribution studies that the cradle of Old World plant husbandry stood within the general area of the arc constituted by the western foothills of the Zagros Mountains (Iraq-Iran), the Taurus (southern Turkey), and the Galilean uplands (northern Palestine) ...;

and more recently by Zohary (1970):

A logical and most sound approach to the problem of place of origin would be to find out (on the basis of genetic affinities) which are the wild progenitors of cultivated plants and where they are distributed. If one can plot the distribution of a given progenitor (or more specifically the area where this progenitor occupies primary habitats and is genuinely wild!) one can delimit the area in which domestication could have taken place.

Contrary to the faith placed in morphological studies, however, most authors discussing the use of modern distributions of wild wheat and barley often make the proviso that distributions may not have remained constant throughout the past 10 000 years. However, this possibility is usually subsequently ignored, and conclusions are drawn on the basis that distributions have remained the same. This is surprising in view of the fact that some specific problems arise from such an assumption, and that our knowledge of the distribution of wild wheats and barley outside the Near East is almost non-existent and even within the Near Eastern area seems to be highly inadequate. Renfrew (1969) notes the anomaly between the modern distribution of single- and twin-grained races of wild einkorn and their occurrence on archaeological sites. Although the single-grained variety is now characteristic of the southern Balkans and west Anatolia, it has been found at Ali Kosh and Jarmo, far to the east of its present distribution. A similar problem is raised by the supposed most likely place of origin of hexaploid wheat near the south-west corner of the Caspian Sea (Zohary, 1969) and its earliest recorded occurrences in Stratum X (6100 B.C.) at Knossos on Crete (Evans, 1964) and at Tell Ramad (c. 6200 B.C.) in Syria (van Zeist & Bottema, 1966). The inadequacy of our knowledge of modern distributions is well demonstrated by Zohary (1969, footnote p. 66) who notes some new finds from south-eastern Turkey pertaining to the modern distribution of *T. dicoccoides*. These finds, which materially alter our conception of where emmer might have been taken into cultivation, come from an area which has been relatively intensely explored compared to regions outside the Near East. Another possible flaw in our knowledge of this area is noted in a review of Japanese work on the

genetics of *Triticum* and *Aegilops* (Lilienfield, 1951), which states that the distribution of *Ae. squarrosa*, one of the likely progenitors of hexaploid wheat, 'seems to be out of place' compared to the other *Aegilops* species, and suggests that either the original habitat has changed or that the data on distribution is incorrect. If data from the well explored areas of the Near East are still so patchy that new data continue to subject our conception of cereal domestication to major alterations, one wonders what effect concentrated exploration in central Asia would have upon the current hypothesis. Strong recommendations for exploration in central Asia were made at the First International Barley Genetics Symposium (Åberg, 1963), but up-to-date information from this area is still conspicuously lacking. In view of these problems and gaps in our knowledge the case for the distribution hypothesis and its alternatives needs reconsideration.

Two factors are usually mentioned as possibly having contributed to changes in distribution: climate and man. Butzer (1964) writes: 'If one can assume that the distribution of wild wheat and barley was 12 000 years ago as it is today, it would seem that the cradle of the "western" plant husbandry cultures lies in the winter rainfall zone of the Near East.' He qualifies this statement, however, and concludes that it would be 'unjustified to say that ecologic conditions were truly "modern" prior to ca. 8000 B.C.'. Van Zeist (1969) also warns of the lack of adequate data: 'One tries in such a case to make the utmost of the little information on palaeo-environment so far available; but this easily results in generalizations and far-reaching conclusions which are not justified at the present state of knowledge. . . . I wish to stress that one should not rely too heavily on these reconstructions, since they are based on too scanty evidence.' Using the little evidence available to him from present natural vegetation zones and from pollen cores, van Zeist reconstructs the Late Pleistocene distribution of wild cereals in the Near East as being restricted to small isolated populations. On the basis of pollen cores from Lake Zeribar and Lake Mirabad, both in western Iran, he suggests that the Postglacial vegetation was more open than modern 'natural' vegetation would be; presumably a reflection of drier conditions. However, he qualifies these conclusions, because of the archaeological evidence for cereal agriculture at this time. If the total annual rainfall during that period had been less than modern rainfall irrigation would have been necessary at a time when it is generally believed that it would have been technologically unlikely. His conclusion, therefore, is that the pollen diagrams reflect a longer summer dryness, which would affect neither wild nor cultivated cereals dependent upon autumn, winter, and spring rain. This interpretation of the data is certainly plausible, but the alternative that the inhabitants of Pre-pottery Neolithic sites in the Near East were capable of small-scale irrigation, as can be observed in the Pindus Mountains and in many areas in Iraq today, is equally possible. There are no data conclusively supporting or refuting either argument. New data may suggest an entirely different picture. Braidwood (Çambel & Braidwood, 1970) reports that new pollen samples from the Zagros Mountains suggest greater climatic and vegetational changes in the last 17 000 years than had previously been supposed. It is hoped that archaeologists will heed van Zeist's warnings, and reserve judgement as to the climate and distribution of vegetational zones in the Late Pleistocene and Postglacial time in the Near East until more data are available.

The anthropogenic factor is, if anything, even more difficult to assess than the climatic one. Historical records may give us some clues as to the changes in plant distributions brought about by activities of man, but the effect of the hunter, gatherer, pastoralist, and subsistence farmer in prehistory can only be guessed at. It is fairly obvious that man has served both as a spreading and restricting agent for the distribution of plants. The weedy nature of the wild cereals and goat-face grasses has recently been discussed by Hawkes (1969) and can be attested by anyone who has attempted to grow them. Harlan & Zohary (1966) in their distributional studies distinguish those wild cereals in segetal habitats, which they believe to have spread to these areas as weeds of agriculture, that is, solely by the agency of man. Such instances certainly must be very common, but it should be emphasized that the distinction between alien and native is not always simple or clear-cut. Harlan and Zohary argue that where wild cereals occur today in massive stands in primary sites, they should be considered a natural part of the native flora, that is 'genuinely wild', as opposed to imports in areas where they occur only in highly disturbed habitats. However, Heiser (1965) notes that it is impossible to reconstruct the original distribution of wild sunflowers in North America on the basis of a study of habitats and varieties of modern sunflowers and similar difficulties are evident in cereal distribution. Salisbury (1961), in discussing the problems of determining whether a species is alien to an area, concludes that the pitfalls are so numerous that 'any discussion or statement that a particular species is, or is not, a "native" is rather an idle one and of little if any, real scientific value'. After all, if the question of native versus introduced is viewed in the long term, all life must be considered as intrusive at one time or another. The designation 'natural' or 'native' is only a relative description and must be defined on an absolute time scale before it can become meaningful to a discussion of this sort. Harlan and Zohary apparently conceive of 'native' as pre-agricultural and 'alien' as post-agricultural, but due to the paucity of pollen cores and other palaeobotanical

remains, distinguish native from alien species not on the basis of their history of colonization of an area, but on the basis of modern ecological associations. How long these associations can be projected into the past is of critical importance. One wonders, for instance, whether in the course of man's modification of the vegetation since the time that agriculture appeared in the area, only those plants which could colonize disturbed ground, wild cereals and other weedy plants, survived the introduction of agriculture, while the rest of the native vegetation largely disappeared. And conversely, whether perhaps at some time in the past 10 000 years, if indeed one can limit the timespan to that period, some cereals introduced by man either as crop weeds or as crop plants, may not have become an integral part of the local plant community. Such changes in distribution must be even more likely if cereal cultivation can be shown to have been practised in suitable areas in the Pleistocene.

Such suggestions cannot be 'proved', but they can be shown to provide plausible alternatives to the usual picture of relatively static plant communities. On a broad scale a factor of great importance would be the degree to which the area had been grazed or cultivated in the past. It is evident that in some areas human activity could have affected the local biotope to so great an extent that no floral communities could now exist which would be considered 'natural' by Harlan and Zohary. Some of the best specific instances of a restriction in range of the wild cereals and the associated forest and steppe-forest formations come from Harlan and Zohary themselves. Zohary (1965) states: 'The Old World belt of Mediterranean agriculture (Southwestern Asia and the Mediterranean basin) furnishes one of the most conspicuous examples of widespread destruction of indigenous vegetation cover and its replacement by open, man-made formations.' Again Harlan & Zohary (1966) describe a race of *H. spontaneum* from Afghanistan which 'may have been a natural component of the open grasslands before they were degraded and nearly destroyed by farming and overgrazing'. In the same paper they note that since wild emmer is not weedy, 'its range and abundance may well have become restricted since the land was disturbed by agriculture', and they quote its increased abundance in Israel after the establishment of grazing controls. Although this may be interpreted as evidence that past patterns of grazing and cultivation would have made only temporary inroads on the range of wild cereals, the degree of disruption to plant communities would depend upon the intensity of the disturbing factors and the length of time over which they operated. In the analogous situation of the over-grazed California grasslands, the native bunch grasses have almost entirely disappeared within the last hundred years (Ellison, 1960). It has been suggested (Baker, 1965) that even if the present disturbance were removed, the bunch grass would never re-establish itself, as the seed sources have now disappeared, and the weedy invaders would probably come to form their own closely adapted climax vegetation.

Baker's conclusion leads to a consideration of the second suggestion presented above, that is, that what appear to be truly wild populations may have become established since the introduction of agriculture. It is already widely accepted that the wild cereals have spread into new territory as weeds of agriculture. There is also the possibility that cultivated varieties have become feral, especially if one allows the possibility of a long period of cultivation before the appearance of tough rachis forms of wheat and barley. However, as mentioned above, the rachis of *T. monococcum* and *T. dicoccum* is only slightly less brittle than that of their wild counterparts, and *T. monococcum* has been known to continue propagating even though it is not resown. Indeed, even modern *T. aestivum* will produce a second crop if left unharvested. Gill & Vear (1966) warn: 'In most cereals, breaking-up of the inflorescence to set free the grain takes place readily when the dead-ripe stage is reached, or the straw becomes brittle so that whole ears are lost. Although such shedding is very much less rapid and less complete than in wild forms, it is still necessary to take precautions against it, and to select varieties which do not shed readily when ripe...'. And in its British Cereal Seed Scheme the National Institute of Agricultural Botany requires that no cereal crop be grown on land within the Scheme for two years prior to sowing of approved seed in order to fully eliminate contamination. *T. aestivum* has never been recorded in the wild or as a weed, and it would appear that it does not compete well with the existing vegetation in countries where it has been grown. However, contrary to the general view that no wild hexaploid wheats exist, one form (*T. macha* var. *megrelicum*) which has been discovered in west Georgia (Transcaucasia), possesses a fragile rachis, as in *T. dicoccoides*, and occurs in the wild (Kuckuck, 1970). Whether or not this is a feral variety is not discussed, but one cannot rule out the possibility that other tough rachis hexaploid wheats may escape from cultivation in the future. Baker (1965) reports that very recently the cultivated radish has become a weed in the western United States and Canada. Through introgression with a weedy relative most of the effects of centuries of human selection have been reversed, and the crop plant has acquired all those specializations essential for it to exist without continued propagation by man. Hybridization and subsequent introgression in wild and cultivated cereals is recorded by Zohary (1960, 1969) and under suitable conditions could lead to the formation of a wild population with a genetic constitution differing from either the local wild or cultivated species.

Again, there is no way of proving that any particular population, or vegetational formation, has existed for a specified length of time unless there happen to be historical records documenting the fact. Salisbury (1961) notes non-cereal introductions to Australia and New Zealand where the introduced species have lost their aggressive character and become normal constituents of the vegetation since European colonization. Aliens are obviously not always at a disadvantage in competition with native species. Nor need the period of invasion and adaptation be long compared to the archaeological time scale. Even the development of a full climax vegetation is measured in tens or hundreds of years, rather than the thousands in which archaeologists deal. Certainly if one is to take seriously the suggestion of palynologists that in less than 5000 years man has destroyed the great Postglacial forests of north-west Europe, one must also allow that in 10 000 years or more he has probably had considerable impact on stands of wild cereals.

Involved in the problem of using distribution data on modern wild cereals, is the question of ancestral relationships between the modern wild and cultivated forms. The area of distribution of a wild cereal is only potentially relevant to the origins of cultivation of a species if it is known to be ancestral to that species. The work of plant geneticists has contributed a great deal of information on the subject of relationships between the various cereals (for brief reviews see Bell, 1965, and Riley, 1965). However, the information appearing in the archaeological literature has been limited and in some cases very one-sided. Communication between the two disciplines has usually consisted of an exchange of broad generalizations, resulting in misinterpretations on both sides, often through lack of appreciation of the limitations of the data in the desire for simple positive statements.

The first point to consider is the usual interpretation of data on genome analysis. Genome analysis has been used when it is known that a particular species is a hybrid of two or more other unknown species, in order to discover what the component species are. The technique determines the degree of genetic similarity between the hybrid and suspected parent species as measured by the frequency of chromosome pairing. However, the system of notation of genome types does not take into account minor genetic variation, and therefore, the similarity does not necessarily indicate precise morphological and ecological similarity; nor does the identification of a genome donor necessarily identify an ancestral population. Thus statements found in archaeological discussions asserting that *T. dicoccoides* derived its genome components from einkorn and *Aegilops speltoides* and that subsequently *Ae. squarrosa* combined with a tetraploid wheat to form hexaploid wheat are not strictly correct. The more exact wording of the following statement (Riley, Unrau & Chapman, 1958) includes an important evolutionary aspect which is missing from the usual archaeological view: 'It might be speculated, therefore, that originally a form very like *Ae. speltoides* crossed naturally with a diploid wheat growing in the same area. . . . The original tetraploid would in fact, be very similar to the artificial amphiploid *T. monococcum* × *Ae. speltoides* investigated in this study.' Similarly, although the goat-face grass *Ae. squarrosa* has been identified as one of the genome donors to hexaploid wheat, the original hybridization took place so long ago (more than 8000 years ago) that *Ae. squarrosa* itself may have altered either morphologically or ecologically or both to a significant degree since then without exceeding the limits of sensitivity of genome analysis. The possibility of a change in the ecological tolerances of *Ae. squarrosa* could also be inferred from Lilienfield's (1951) suggestion noted above, that the original habitat of this species may have changed. There are no data available at present which would allow confirmation of this possibility; but it indicates the logical inconsistency of the argument that since *Ae. squarrosa* contributed the D genome to hexaploid wheat, hexaploid wheat must have first appeared within the present distribution of *Ae. squarrosa*.

There are some specific questions which plant geneticists themselves are still in disagreement about, but which archaeologists seem only slightly aware of. It is usually assumed in archaeological discussions that tetraploid wheat arose in the wild, being represented today by *T. dicoccoides* and was subsequently brought into cultivation. In this case *T. dicoccoides* could have arisen prior to the earliest grain cultivation and therefore might first have been cultivated in conjunction with *T. boeoticum* (wild-type einkorn). Some investigators (Sarkar & Stebbins, 1956), however, suggest that the tetraploid wheats are a result of a hybridization involving domesticated-type einkorn, *T. monococcum*, which would require the cultivation and subsequent genetic divergence of einkorn prior to that of emmer, the earliest known domesticated-type tetraploid wheat. Surprisingly, the archaeological evidence at the moment lends some support to the latter hypothesis. At one of the earliest sites on which cereals have yet been found, Mureybit, only einkorn (wild-type) occurs. Spikelets and grain resembling wild-type emmer have been recovered at Jarmo (the ^{14}C dates of which remain uncertain), but at none of the other early sites such as Ali Kosh, Beidha, Jericho, or Hacılar. However, domesticated-type emmer, *T. dicoccum,* occurs at almost every early Neolithic site in Greece, Bulgaria, and the Near East (Renfrew, 1969). This almost total absence of wild-type emmer on archaeological sites could be ascribed to insufficient data from the appropriate sites, but it is also explicable in at least two other ways. It could be

that *T. dicoccoides* enjoyed a much wider distribution in the past than it does today, and that the wild form was brought into cultivation outside the area in which the archaeological data is now concentrated. Alternatively, one might propose that tetraploid wheat originated under cultivation and that all wild emmer today is the feral form of *T. dicoccum*. Again, there is little to recommend any one of these hypotheses over the other, but each is relevant to the interpretation of cereal remains from archaeological sites.

Another problem which, although frequently mentioned by archaeologists, is often ignored, concerns the origins of hexaploid wheat. The earliest representatives of hexaploid wheat yet discovered are *T. aestivum* and *T. compactum* which appear at sites in Crete, Anatolia, and the Near East between 5000 and 6000 B.C. However, when the two forms supposed to be ancestral to all the hexaploid wheats, *T. dicoccum* and *Ae. squarrosa*, are crossed, the resulting hybrid resembles *T. spelta*. This would seem to argue that the earliest hexaploid wheats should have looked like *T. spelta*, which does not in fact appear in the archaeological record until the European Neolithic, long after the earliest occurrences of *T. aestivum* and *T. compactum*. One must conclude either that we have yet to discover the early sites on which *T. spelta*-like wheat occurs, or that the genetics of the origins of hexaploid wheat are not fully understood. If the former, one must postulate an origin more remote in time or space or both than we have become accustomed to think of, as it is unlikely that spelt-type hexaploid wheat would have been missed had it existed on Near Eastern Neolithic sites. If the latter, one must consider the possibility either that the progenitors of hexaploid wheat have been misidentified or that one or both has changed to such an extent since hexaploid wheat arose, that it is no longer possible to synthesize *T. aestivum* from modern forms. These changes may have affected ecological tolerances and hence distribution, which would throw into doubt the accepted calculation of the centre of origin for hexaploid wheat. Furthermore, Riley (1965) suggests that a polyphyletic origin for the hexaploid wheats is not incompatible with genetic evidence. The several species or subspecies of hexaploid wheat may have had separate origins at various times and places, and it may be misleading to consider the problem in terms of a single origin.

A third problem is whether the ancestral form of modern cultivated barley was two-rowed, six-rowed, or both. Zohary (1960, 1969) has greatly influenced archaeologists in his belief that *H. spontaneum* is the sole ancestor to all forms of cultivated barley. The merits of this view lie in its simple explanation of the data presently available. However, Takahashi (1955, 1963) has put forward plausible arguments for a diphyletic origin of two-rowed and six-rowed cultivated barleys. A wild six-rowed barley cannot be considered an impossibility, and a dogmatic statement, such as, 'It is now clear that only a single wild species of barley is closely related to the various cultivated barley forms, and should be regarded as their sole ancestor' (Zohary, 1969), is an overstatement of our certainty in this matter.

CONCLUSIONS

Although the current hypothesis placing the origins of wheat and barley cultivation in the 'Fertile Crescent' about 10 000 years ago seems to explain much of the existing evidence, it has been pointed out that gaps and discrepancies in our knowledge have been glossed over and largely ignored. Emphasis has been placed on the assumptions and preoccupations of other disciplines which do not view the data in ways helpful to archaeology. No one-to-one correlation can be shown to exist between domesticated-type morphology and cultivation, nor can one assume that the distribution of wild cereals has remained the same during the past 10 000 years. In the absence of these assumptions, the additional assumption that because 'primitive' types of cereals have been recovered from Neolithic age sites in south-western Asia, they should not be expected to be found elsewhere at earlier or comparable dates cannot be accepted. This hypothesis may of course withstand future critical examination, even lacking support from the two assumptions discussed here, but alternatives should not be dismissed without full consideration. One must conclude that the greatest criticism is not to be directed at the preferred hypothesis itself, but at the archaeologists who have allowed the hypothesis to govern their research to such an extent that other potentially productive avenues of enquiry have been virtually ignored. Certain areas and methods of study could lead to rewarding results and possibly to a confirmation or rejection of the present hypothesis.

The first priority must be to begin systematic collection of plant remains. Until very recently collection of plant remains has been sporadic at best. Either no attempt at collection has been made by the excavator, resulting in only obvious caches of seeds and other plant remains being recovered; or the systematic approaches have been inadequate in a number of ways. Methods of 'on site' processing are usually either so cumbersome or designed on so small a scale that only a small percentage of deposit can be processed. Since plant remains are not often obvious in the deposit even when they are present in abundance, in any laboratory based processing of soil samples the excavator runs the risk of transporting large quantities of sterile deposit and of missing very rich deposits. Although it is unlikely that efficient 100 percent recovery of plant remains can be achieved or even that it is desirable to do so, it is essential that the sample size and calculation of bias be

subject to the control of the excavator rather than left to the vagaries of chance. The recently developed technique of froth flotation (Jarman, Legge & Charles, II. 1) permits easy 'on site' processing of a minimum of four to five cubic feet of deposit per hour, and allows detection and calculation of the recovery bias. A desired goal might be the use of such a technique on all archaeological sites, but a programme of investigation intended to probe further into cereal domestication can concentrate on particular periods and areas: Mesolithic and Upper Palaeolithic sites in areas which cannot be excluded because of their ecologically unsuitable nature. The entire Mediterranean Basin presents itself as an obvious candidate. In southern Italy, for instance, there are virtually no plant remains from Neolithic sites, much less from Mesolithic or Upper Palaeolithic sites. In northern Italy bread wheat has been discovered on a lake village site tentatively dated to about 4500 B.C. (Barfield, pers. comm.), where the combination of steep, wooded slopes and a waterlogged lake basin would not have favoured cereal cultivation. Certain portions of southern Italy are today far better suited to cereal cultivation, and it would be interesting to discover whether in these areas grain might appear at an early date. Early sites in Greece and western Turkey provide other possibilities, especially as grain is already known from early Neolithic sites in these countries. North Africa could also have provided a suitable environment for early development of agriculture. Helbaek (1959) states that *H. spontaneum* is now distributed across the whole of north Africa to the Atlantic coast. Hester (1968) suggests that his Libyan culture, dated to 5950 B.C. ± 150 years, may have been based on an agricultural economy; and Wendorf (1968) has argued the same for the much earlier Sebilian culture in Nubia. Certainly this whole area merits further exploration and excavation with a view to recovering both plant and animal remains. Other areas from which far more data are needed include Afghanistan, Pakistan, India, and southern Russia and China. It is only when information from these areas becomes available that one can begin to make intelligent generalizations about cereal cultivation.

The second object of future study should be an attempt to consider the nature of plant remains as archaeological artefacts. Their unique properties must be perceived before adequate interpretations of the data can be made. Their properties of preservation differ in an important aspect from that of other types of artefacts, in that their presence on a site relies to a large extent not only upon their being left at a site, but upon a secondary process, that of carbonization. There are, of course, exceptions such as remains from peat deposits, desert areas, and preservation as impressions or silica skeletons, but the bulk of the material is recovered only because it has been previously carbonized

(Renfrew, 1969). A more detailed preliminary attempt at considering the characteristics of particular types of seeds and their preservation in various deposits is made by Dennell (III. 4). The assessment of the degree of reliance placed on plant as opposed to animal products has not been attempted but would yield important information were a method devised.

The technique of site catchment analysis (Vita-Finzi & Higgs, 1970; and I. 3) may help to overcome some of the problems of interpretation of organic remains. Site catchment analysis provides a means of describing the economic potential of a site territory, thereby greatly limiting the possible interpretations which can be placed on the organic remains recovered from that site.

The third, but perhaps most important, objective must be an attempt to see plant husbandry as a spectrum of man-plant relationships developing gradually through time, linked just as inseparably to plant collection as to modern agriculture. These relationships should be defined from an anthropological point of view rather than from a botanical point of view; only in this way can a clearer idea of the economic relationship between man and plants emerge. A study of these relationships could more profitably emphasize processes of change than dates of first occurrences. Flannery (1969) makes an interesting attempt towards this kind of study in his discussion of the forces of population pressure in relation to carrying capacity. But far more must be learned about the role of plants in pre-Neolithic economies, about spatial and chronological variations in their role, and about factors which may control these variations before the change or lack of change in Neolithic economies can be described. One particular question which must be considered is the problem of distinguishing between the spread of techniques of agriculture and the spread of economically superior crop plants into areas where the technology is already known. It should be understood that the objective of this paper is not to criticize present theory, but to open new paths of research which may at the present time appear unprofitable. No hypothesis can be permanent in any subject, and until existing beliefs come under attack, the yearly addition to our information can all too easily become a means of shoring up obsolete models instead of propagating new ones.

3. PREHISTORIC ECONOMIES: A TERRITORIAL APPROACH

E. S. HIGGS AND C. VITA-FINZI

The study of prehistoric economies has long been recognized as an important aspect of archaeology. Nilsson's classification of prehistoric man, which he put forward in 1873 and which can be traced back in essence to the abstract speculation of classical times, was based largely on modes of existence. He postulated four stages in human development: a hunter-gatherer stage, a herdsman or nomad stage, an agricultural stage, and finally civilization. In 1877 Morgan stressed that, while the Three Age system was extremely useful in the classification of ancient art, 'the great epochs of human progress have been indentified more or less directly with the enlargement of the course of subsistence'. Since then, apart from Clark's important volume in 1952, we have made little progress beyond elaborating on the classic view that all men were hunters until the domestication of plants and animals opened the way to pastoralism and arable agriculture. In spite of Clark's admonition that many archaeologists were too artefactually orientated, the field has continued to be dominated by the consideration of artefactual styles and their chronology, and economic concepts have usually served for little more than the classification of cultures into 'hunter-gatherers', 'pastoralists', or 'farmers'. Yet each of these general terms covers a variety of forms of prehistoric economies and human behaviour, which it is the business of archaeology to attempt to understand.

There is evidently scope for an alternative approach in which prehistoric economies, and hence resources and their exploitation, are given prominence from the outset. Moreover, the time is ripe for such a re-orientation in prehistoric studies. The growing interest in modern subsistence economies and associated ecological problems makes it feasible to attempt a more refined analysis of their early counterparts, and also calls for further information on human response to changing environments, on man's contribution to these changes in the past, and on the relationship of human activities to particular factors in the biotope. Ethology is another constant source of inspiration, and it too is lacking in case studies which refer to the distant past or which encompass extensive periods of behavioural change. A third potential source of palaeoeconomic data is the student of organic evolution who wishes to go beyond the psychic factor in the development of mankind to an understanding of how and when somatic changes were supplemented or even supplanted by adaptations of a more devious character.

But it is not enough to shift the emphasis to economy: new techniques are required to ensure that the information latent in the archaeological record is made available for analysis. Hitherto the prehistorian has tended to borrow from other disciplines rather than forge new methods for himself. The typological framework encouraged the view that successive peoples or tribes played out their lives against the background of nature, and the climatic and vegetational zones of the natural scientist provided a ready-made framework into which stylistic entities could be made to fit. Some studies conducted along these lines have undoubtedly proved illuminating and are capable of further elaboration, but there are drawbacks. The chief of these stems from the fact that the populations or attributes that define a particular climatic or vegetational zone do not necessarily impinge on human activities within it, while, if they do, it does not follow that a change in zonal properties will meet with a corresponding change in response. What is more, economic units are primary flexible artefacts, which are rarely confined to single environmental zones and are more likely to draw on the economically complementary resources of a number of different zones. To base the analysis of prehistoric sites on the methodology of the natural sciences is to disregard these difficulties, and could obscure the true relationships that existed between human activities and their environments. An alternative approach based on agricultural or economic zones may be more relevant to our purpose.

More recently there have been attempts to introduce the methods of quantitative geography, notably location analysis, into the subject. It would be a pity, however, if archaeology discarded what is perhaps its most precious resource — time perspective — in favour of a static view of spatial relationships, a drawback also inherent in the unguarded use of ethnographic parallels.

SITE DATA AND ENVIRONMENT: CATCHMENT ANALYSIS

As a first step it might pay to relate the evidence obtained from a site, and in particular its organic remains, to the area 'served' by that site. We shall define a site as a place where there is a deposit or set of deposits which contain evidence of human activity. Clearly there will be other kinds of sites – rock fissures, caves, river gravels – which show no trace of human activity and still yield evidence relating to the environment. In either case a rewarding first step might be to relate the site record to the area served by the site. We believe that the methods proposed here may be applied with profit to non-archaeological as well as archaeological sites, and to species other than man. Human interests, and therefore archaeological sites, are given a first priority for the purposes of this volume; a broader ecological approach would obviously require that both kinds of site be considered.

An important characteristic of the constituents of a site is that they have been brought together by a variety of different agencies; this applies to inorganic as well as organic remains. The area from which a stream draws its water is termed its catchment, and we have extended this term to other physical and chemical agents of deposition, such as wind and ground water, and to the organisms that have contributed to the site's deposits.

Catchments will differ in shape and size from agent to agent. A collection of rodent bones brought to a site by owls will have come from a territory of about 12 hectares in extent somewhere within 10 km of the site; a collection of bones brought to a site by hunter-gatherers will probably be derived from a territory of about 30 000 hectares. The record will be further complicated where two or more agents of transport have intervened. Wind deposits may be redeposited by water; water-worn pebbles may be carried into a cave by flint knappers.

Even in the most general terms it is misleading to associate an archaeological site with a single uniform environment. Sites are commonly located at the junction of very different habitats, the integration of whose resources results in a viable economy. It could be argued that sites that have been occupied are *ipso facto* anomalous. They are preferred locations atypical of the zone in which they are situated. An oasis, for example, has water; a cave has less extreme temperature regimes than its environs. Thus the site record will be a biased as well as a partial sample. The technique of catchment analysis (Vita-Finzi & Higgs, 1970) has a dual purpose: to make the most of the sample, and to provide a critical basis for the drawing of generalizations from several such samples. The generalizations thus arrived at will be helpful in planning further excavation, whether by pointing to major gaps in the evidence or by furnishing a hypothesis in need of testing.

ECONOMY

The technology that prevails will determine the range of resources which can be exploited, and will thus affect the shape and size of the economic catchment or territory of the site. In time the range and character of exploitation will be modified. Consequent upon technological change there was an increase in sedentary economies, perhaps the greatest known change in human affairs and one which led to civilization. It is therefore helpful to divide prehistoric economies into two broad classes, mobile economies and sedentary economies; the need for a third, mobile-cum-sedentary class will emerge later. These classes will not cover all possible situations, but they provide a useful basis on which to work.

MOBILE ECONOMIES

Mobile economies are practised by groups which move from place to place in the course of the year. In the archaeological record it is possible to observe such mobile economies as those practised by eclectic and specialist hunters; and from the ethnological record it is also possible to observe herders, herd followers, such as the Lapps, and pastoralists. The consequences of a mobile way of life, such as the relative scarcity of accumulations of durable wealth, that is durable beyond the lifetime of its creator, are so far-reaching in their social and economic implications that it seems reasonable to include these subdivisions in one class, that of mobile economies, rather than to include pastoralists in a farming category which includes sedentary exploitations. No mobile economy appears to have led on to a civilization. In a mobile economy the length of time a human group can stay at one place is ultimately determined by the amount of the least available necessary resource. This limit may be modified by social customs, food preferences, and the like, but such buffers against over-exploitation are in turn limited in their scope by the resources to hand. In due course movement will take place. In the long run the effect of movement – if successful – will be to coordinate resources, which from the viewpoint of the human group are ill-distributed, into successful economies and to maintain a higher population than could be supported if the resources were being exploited in isolation by specialized groups. Bird migrations, which serve much the same purpose, have been classified into regular (seasonal) and occasional; prehistoric subsistence economies may benefit from being studied in similar terms.

Recent studies of existing mobile economies have stressed that as with many animal populations numbers are often smaller than those which the available resources could support, being kept at that level by both well known social and less well understood physiological protective feed-back mechanisms (Wynne-Edwards, 1962). Yet in the long term a population is unlikely to be so closely adjusted to resources that it will never enjoy periods of scarcity and plenty, and there also are many ethnographic parallels which illustrate this. Viewed graphically the fluctuating curves of available resources and human numbers will at times converge and at others diverge. The fact that the 'curves' interact increases the likelihood of conflicting trends. Thus population is likely to go on increasing after a resource peak has been attained; conversely, physiological and inflexible social brakes on increase may go on being applied beyond a resource trough. The present-day situation, where hunter-gatherer populations are well within the available resources, could well be a short-term effect of this kind which has been heightened by a population decline fostered by external factors such as the disruption of exploitation patterns at their periphery by the intrusion of differently based economies.

The wide variety of plants and animals eaten by hunter-gatherer groups, and the skill with which they exploit their environments, has also been stressed. The eclectic character of the foods exploited is not likely to survive intact into the archaeological record. Yet this need not rank as a liability. Thomson (1939) saw the need for dividing available foods into staples and casual foods such as medicines, relishes, and aphrodisiacs. When studying prehistoric societies it may be wiser and more practical to concentrate on staple foods even when casual resources are documented, since the former were the principal concern of the population and of greatest significance in the choice of those sites with an economic function and in the formation of exploitation patterns.

With mobile economies we face the difficulty that even though a single group may well have occupied several sites at any one time, we have no means of telling which sites were in fact precisely contemporaneous. This problem is an archaeological commonplace, for even in the study of artefactually defined stylistic groups we have to accept the device of considering them as archaeologically rather than absolutely contemporaneous. It is possible, however, to make the working hypothesis that, even though the great majority of sites which existed will have been lost or are unknown to us, sufficient may be known to indicate long-term trends in site location. That this can be so is indicated by differences in the distribution and location of say Upper Palaeolithic and tell sites. We believe that with careful study observations of this kind can be greatly extended.

Other assumptions may need to be jettisoned. Analysis of a site's territory may show that its resource potential is inadequate to explain its location or perhaps its very existence; the search for non-economic factors can then be given its head. On the other hand, it may be found that a site originally regarded as part of a mobile or mobile-cum-sedentary system is sufficiently endowed with resources to have supported permanent occupation. Even this, however, does not preclude the possibility of seasonal movement. It allows the possibility of sedentary occupation to be entertained and makes sedentism the more probable of the available hypotheses.

SEDENTARY ECONOMIES

Sedentary economies are practised by human groups which stay in one place all the year round. They are marked by the development of durable wealth in the form of houses, buildings, roads and the like. The archaeological data does not always enable us to distinguish in marginal cases between mobile and sedentary economies, but it is misleading to assume that sites were occupied by a sedentary population unless there is positive evidence to the contrary. The study of site territories can help in deciding which hypothesis should be preferred. Some sites, such as Kastritsa in Greece (Higgs et al., 1967) or the Mesolithic upland sites of Britain in the Boreal period, are clearly not likely candidates for year-round occupation; others, such as Sheikh Ali in Palestine, would have been most favourably placed for permanent occupation given an agricultural technology. On the other hand, the presence of houses or house foundations, even at tell sites, does not necessarily indicate that the occupants were sedentary, for the building of stone houses by mobile groups is well documented in the archaeological and anthropological literature.

MOBILE-CUM-SEDENTARY ECONOMIES

Mobile-cum-sedentary occupations are those where there is a mobile element associated with sedentary occupation. These economies are commonly found in lowland areas which lie adjacent to uplands. They are sites which take advantage of both the upland and lowland regions, the former commonly providing the animal protein and the latter the staple cereal crops. It is perhaps significant that frequently the larger tells, such as Megiddo and Jericho in Palestine, occupy sites of this kind. Another example is where a rainy season allows an expansion of exploitation into otherwise arid areas.

TERRITORY

The concept of territory is relevant to the present case. Naturalists have found it helpful in analysing aspects of animal behaviour which involve problems analogous to those facing the prehistorian. Although the concept of territory was not used in archaeology until 1967 (Higgs & Vita-Finzi, 1967), Carr-Saunders had applied it to man in *The Population Problem* in 1922 after Eliot Howard (1920) had given prominence to the discussion of bird territories.

Carr-Saunders suggested that human groups were without exception territorial in behaviour. This view has subsequently met with a measure of criticism.

In part the debate is about the word territory itself. The observation that many mammals kept to a particular area for the greater part of their lives had early led to the concepts of 'home range' and 'home region'. In 1939 Nobis defined territory as a defended area, and Burt (1943) drew a distinction between the home range — the area traversed by an individual in the course of food gathering, mating, and caring for his young — and the defended territory. Later work has blurred this distinction, it now being clear that an area which is habitually occupied is sometimes defended and sometimes not.

In an archaeological context it seems advisable to define territory as an area which is habitually exploited. That the concept is applicable to mobile as well as sedentary economies was clear to Carr-Saunders, who believed that unrestricted nomadism had never been practised by human groups. In classifying the pattern of life in western North America, Jennings (1957) wrote: 'The small groups moved regularly from place to place, from valley to upland, in search of the seasonal animal or plant resources which centuries of experience had taught them were to be had. The wandering was not aimless; it was based on intimate and annually renewed knowledge of a relatively well-defined territory.' This may be compared with the assertion that before agriculture 'small wandering bands of people ... led an essentially "natural" catch-as-catch-can existence' (Braidwood & Howe, 1960). The evidence available on both human and animal behaviour indicates that the 'natural' situation is rarely random, and that in order to understand this behaviour, we must assume the sort of patterning provided by economic territoriality.

The study of animal territories shows that there are occasional forays outside the 'lifetime territory' (Jewell, 1966a). We have defined a *site territory* as the area habitually exploited from a single site. The site catchment, on the other hand, embraces the terrain covered by occasional forays in search of raw materials for tools and other purposes. Yet it does not follow that all kinds of sites call for identical treatment: American 'kill' sites, for example, are not necessarily associated with exploitation territories. One may therefore distinguish between preferred sites — the 'home bases' of Flannery (Hole & Flannery, 1967) and Higgs and Vita-Finzi (Higgs *et al.*, 1967) — and 'transit', 'transitory', or occasional sites which bear evidence of only brief occupation. It may well turn out that a preferred site served as a home base for the exploitation of its environs, but this can be decided only after the analysis of the site territory. These analyses may also help to explain why sites such as Laugerie-Haute, Parpalló, and La Ferrassie, were selected for repeated occupation over long periods of time, while others apparently in similarly advantageous situations were only rarely occupied.

The *extended site territory* (Sturdy, III. 5) may sometimes need to be considered. An extended territory is one where an area beyond the periphery of the site territory is habitually exploited. It will occur in circumstances where the distance factor does not apply. Sturdy points out the value of the natural corral in the exploitation of reindeer. Similar situations occur for example in New Guinea, where pigs are kept at some distance from the village in areas bordered by natural barriers from which they cannot escape, and also in other places where domesticated mountain sheep, tied by their behaviour to a small individual territory, need no containing fence or herder to restrict their movements.

Mobile groups commonly occupy more than one site during the year. There are many present-day and recent instances of this response to seasonal and geographical inequality, and it is not unreasonable to postulate that prehistoric peoples responded in a similar manner. Transhumance — both in animals and in peoples who exploit them — is an effective means of combining the resources of upland and lowland in a Mediterranean climate, or those of land and sea in many climatic settings. The resulting '*annual territory*' (Vita-Finzi & Higgs, 1970) may be found to embrace sites formerly ascribed on the basis of their artefacts to two or more cultural entities. By the methods we propose, the typologist will have additional evidence on which to decide whether or not in such circumstances a single human group or two or more human groups were involved. Where a mobile group occupies over the year a number of sites within its annual territory, it is not to be expected that different functions will be carried out in similar proportions at different sites, and indeed such differences may be expected to reflect in the proportions of the different artefacts present.

THE FACTOR OF DISTANCE

At a given technological level some resources will lie at too great a distance from a site to be exploited from that site. Lee's (1969) studies of the !Kung bushmen are a useful guide to the radius that limits the range of a mobile economy. Input-output analysis showed that the threshold was reached at a distance of about 10 km from the site. Von Thünen's classic studies of the 'isolated state' in which he suggested a hypothetical ideal system of land use as a model by which he could examine the effects of variables in order to observe how they modified the ideal pattern of land use, already indicated the importance of such thresholds in sedentary agricultural economies. The work of

Chisholm (1968) on modern subsistence agriculture suggests that a decline in net return becomes significant at a distance of 1 km from the site and oppressive at 3-4 km (Fig. 1). While there are numerous historical and ethnographic instances of this oppression being surmounted, the general tendency would seem a suitable basis on which to form a workable hypothesis; hence our adoption of a radius of 5 km for the analysis of sedentary exploitation territories and of 10 km for mobile economies. As we show later, the actual delineation of the territories is more realistically based on time.

The effect of distance being cumulative, the resources within the territory have to be weighted according to their position. For the sake of simplicity the terrain bounded by successive rings spaced 1 km apart can be regarded as uniform. The result of weighting is illustrated in Table 1; the factor employed was based in part on the figures given by Virri (Chisholm, 1968) for production per hectare at increasing distance from farms in Finland. A further refinement would be to convert land categories to their maximum calorie yield or to nutritional units. Webley (III, 6) illustrates some of the possibilities still to be explored in evaluating soil distributions within territories. One can also envisage the introduction of a measure to express

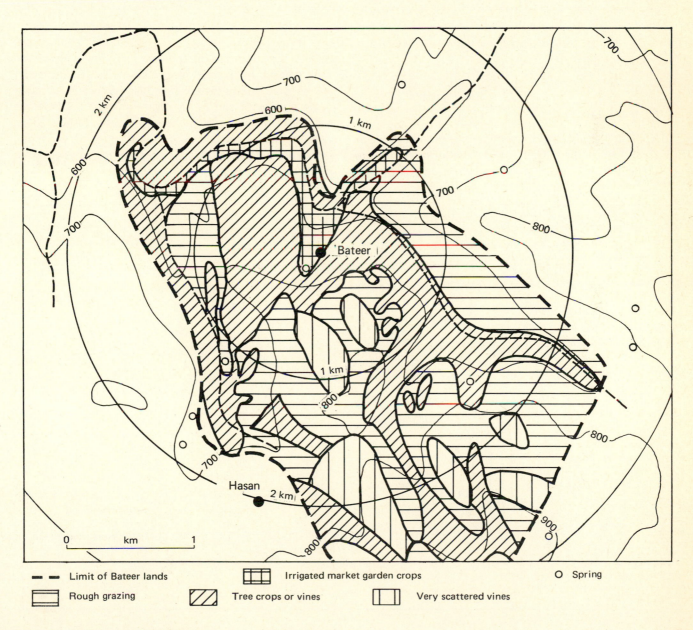

Limit of Bateer lands   **Irrigated market garden crops**   **Spring**

Rough grazing   **Tree crops or vines**   **Very scattered vines**

Fig. 1. A modern Arab village, Palestine.

E. S. HIGGS & C. VITA-FINZI

Table 1. Unweighted and weighted land use classification around the Neolithic site of Megiddo (method of weighting as described in Vita-Finzi & Higgs, 1970)

| | Land classification (percentage) | | | | | |
| | Marsh | | Rough grazing | | Arable | |
	Unweighted	Weighted	Unweighted	Weighted	Unweighted	Weighted
1 km	–	–	38.2	38.2	61.9	61.9
2 km	–	–	57.4	28.7	42.6	21.3
3 km	1.9	0.6	40.3	13.4	57.8	19.3
4 km	14.4	3.6	37.2	9.3	48.4	12.1
5 km	18.5	3.7	26.4	5.3	55.1	11.0

how far the territory departs from the ideal of circularity (cf. Bunge, 1966).

FIELD METHODS

It is a wise precaution to confirm that the proposed scheme is locally tenable by subjecting a modern subsistence site to catchment analysis. At Nahal Oren, where prehistoric sites were being investigated, their present-day counterpart yielded the pattern shown on Figure 2. Note that distortion is introduced by factors other than those immediately obvious from terrain investigation, namely by lack of water to the north-west and by the intrusion of a neighbouring territory to the south. Nonetheless the result inspires some confidence in the method. A sedentary pastoralist economy may be expected to have a territory which approaches in size that of other sedentary site territories.

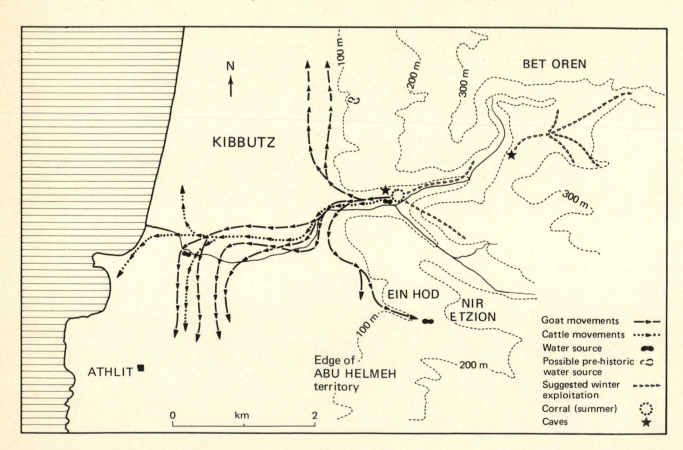

Fig. 2. Modern Arab sedentary pastoral exploitation from the Nahal Oren Cave.

32

As Chisholm points out, distance needs to be translated into the time taken to cover it. A walking distance of 1 hr is a workable basis for drawing the boundaries of agricultural territories and one of 2 hr for hunter-gatherer territories, since under optimum conditions the resulting areas come close to the 5 and 10 km circles proposed earlier. Broken or difficult terrain will evidently distort the shape of the territory so that in practice the ideal circular territory rarely occurs (Fig. 3). It is worth noting that von Thünen based some of his calculations on the speed of horsedrawn carts; but wheeled transport appears to have had little effect on the limiting distance. Four walked radii will commonly suffice for the operation, but more may be needed in hilly country. Since their measurement can be combined with resource evaluation they are a sound investment. Excessive overlap between adjoining territories may invite a reduction in the adopted radius, but it is usually advisable to delay such adjustments until the nature of the economy is better understood since the areas of 'conflict' (like those of 'neglect') may emerge as having a significance of their own.

PHYSIOGRAPHIC CHANGES IN TERRITORY OVER TIME

At some sites geological changes during or since the period of occupation may have altered the character of the successive exploitation territories, either by the addition, transport, or removal of soils and deposits. In exceptional

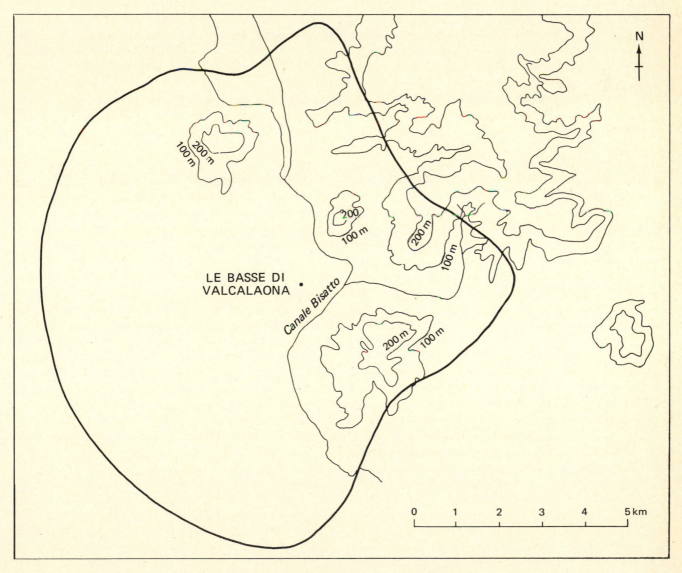

Fig. 3.   Le Basse di Valcalaona, northern Italian Neolithic. Territory distorted by topography.

circumstances the change may be drastic: volcanic eruptions, earth movements, and the like enliven not a few site histories. Pompeii apart, it has been concluded that erosion of the alluvial soils near the site of Beidha stemmed from tilting of the Arabian block, while at Mohenjo-daro silting is attributed to blockage of the lower Indus by localized uplift (Raikes, 1967). In general, however, the processes are more familiar and their recognition demands little beyond practice. Indeed, a lack of formal training in the relevant field, be it geology or pedology, can on occasion prove advantageous since the observer is innocent of the conventional preconceptions. The long-established association between geology and prehistory has meant that the reconstruction of former landscapes is based on stratigraphic criteria. A site in the Thames valley, for example, will be referred to one of the alluvial terraces in the accepted sequence; a period of occupation will be related to some climatic phase or other. We may regard this as the temporal counterpart to the zonal approach; and once again the principal drawback is an undue emphasis on 'the rule' to the detriment of 'the exception'.

Let us first take topographic change. If we wish to discover the character of a river valley during a certain period we may be tempted to extrapolate to that basin the erosional and depositional record of the area as manifested in a type section. But, to put the case at its crudest, there can be no deposition without corresponding erosion, and vice versa. While the overall trends will doubtless become felt at the site, as when a prolonged erosive phase strips the hillsides of their soil and thus modifies their ecological significance, the crux is whether or not the exploited territory is being aggraded or degraded. Hence the alluvial record must be read within the site catchment. Sea-level changes are meaningless unless their interaction with the local coastal topography can be gauged: a vertical cliff may nullify the sharpest of fluctuations, a gently sloping coastal plain may render the mildest of oscillations of profound geographical significance. Climatic changes embody the zonal problem even more acutely. It may be doubted whether glaciation on the Alps impinged very much on the life of Palaeolithic man in North Africa; yet it is to the classic Alpine sequence that the environmental history of this area tends to be referred. Doubtless this stems partly from the days when the only source of geological dating was stratigraphic correlation; radiometric methods have now made this method obsolete and will ultimately render it unnecessary. The omission of climate from this section is intentional; all too often climatic reconstruction is based on evidence which is itself directly relevant to the nature of the catchment, such as soil type, vegetation cover, and stream discharge (Vita-Finzi, 1969a), and represents a loss in definition.

Some of the gross changes that may emerge have been considered elsewhere (Higgs et al., 1967). Palaeolithic occupation in the Louros valley of Epirus (Greece) took place prior to deposition of the valley-floor alluvium and during accumulation of the Red Beds. The site in question – the cave of Asprochaliko – lies in the middle reaches of the valley where the succession was worked out. Hence the sequence is applicable to the entire human catchment of the site; it involves both the alluvial phases in the valley and the corresponding periods of soil loss and soil stability on the slopes. One may therefore reconstruct changes in the form and distribution of the clays and alluvium upon which plant growth is restricted by virtue of the calcareous nature of the country rock.

As we have just seen, topographic and hydrological changes are interrelated. Stream action may be responsible for morphological features which in turn affect the local distribution of surface and underground water. The marshy areas in the coastal plain of Palestine which were drained first by the Romans and then by settlers in the nineteenth and twentieth centuries were largely the product of impeded drainage resulting from the lithification of coastal dunes into relatively impervious calcarenite; the faunas supported by these marshy areas thus have little palaeoclimatic significance.

Evidence which is inadequate for the reconstruction of former climates is often suited to the elucidation of stream regimes and groundwater conditions within individual catchments. The form, lithology, and internal structure of the Red Beds of Epirus, for example, reflect deposition by ephemeral streams, whereas their incision was accompanied by the prevalence of well-drained conditions; the analogous deposits at the foot of Carmel show a similar depositional environment in the upper reaches and the persistence of high water tables well into historical times further downstream. Other deposits may point to the operation of periodic floods or to the prevalence of sustained stream discharges (Vita-Finzi, 1966, 1969b). The Red Beds of Epirus suggest the alternation of periods of flood flow with others of pronounced aridity; the associated Pleistocene glacial features are most economically explained by a reduction in mean temperature which was most marked in summer; hence, although the modern seasonal pattern may have been less pronounced as regards temperature, the persistence of the snow cover would have led to its accentuation by rendering the uplands virtually unproductive in winter. In Palestine (as in Epirus) there is today a pronounced seasonal alternation in the availability of grazing resources between uplands and lowlands; here the Pleistocene situation would appear to have reduced the contrast by virtue of the presence in the coastal plain of marshy areas more accessible to grazing animals during the summer.

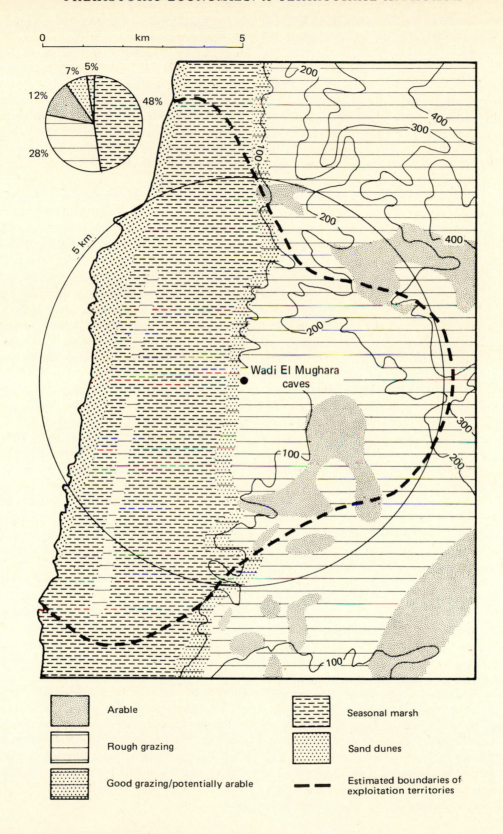

Fig. 4. Classification of land use at Wadi el Mughara.

Were fishing populations under discussion it would be possible to introduce into the map the seasonal pattern of marine resources.

While we have tended to play down the role of palaeo-climatology in catchment analysis in favour of more immediate environmental controls, there cannot be any doubt that certain limiting conditions not now manifested may be found to have applied in the past. The distribution of snowline indicators such as cirques may show that the winter snow cover during the last glaciation was more extensive than at present and that it excluded parts of a site catchment from exploitation during that season. In our experience pollen analysis cannot serve in establishing limits of this kind, since any pollen sequence draws on a wide variety of catchments; but it is of course a valuable adjunct to other indicators of local conditions.

LAND QUALITY

So far we have considered land only in terms of total area. Some measure of its quality is needed if comparisons between catchments are to have any meaning. It is difficult enough to make a map of land potential in terms of the modern soil and of current technological resources; the problems are compounded when soil properties, plant and animal breeds, and land-use methods have to be inferred. The ideal would be to reduce the maximum yields attainable by the available soils to some measure of nutritional value (Stamp, 1958). Until more is known about ancient yields and carrying capacity, however, we have to be content with a more primitive assessment; but this has the benefit of speed and of low 'operator variance' (in that field mapping by workers with a variety of backgrounds gives broadly consistent results).

Figure 4 shows the catchment of the sites of Wadi el Mughara, which were occupied repeatedly from Middle Palaeolithic to Medieval times, broken down into the following categories: seasonal marsh, sand dunes, arable, potentially arable/good grazing, and rough grazing. While clearly open to refinement, this classification embodies certain useful principles.

(1) Land-use categories are employed only where neither environmental nor technological change are likely to call for their alteration for different stages during human occupation, or at any rate where such changes can be allowed for without the need for re-survey. Thus arable could serve as grazing land, but the converse is unlikely; rough grazing indicates a thin or patchy soil which if anything will have been further impoverished by the progress of erosion, but which does not justify the hypothesis that it represents former arable land which has been eroded or depleted during occupation. Note that the intermediate category of arable/grazing is available for areas where there is room for doubt, and that the territory it embraces can be summed with either the arable or the grazing class when the maximum possible extent of one of these is being investigated.

(2) Terrain which is susceptible to drastic changes in value as a result of technical advances or human enterprise is given the most informative physical epithet. 'Marsh', for example, denotes areas for which there is either pedological or historical evidence of swampy conditions. Once it is ascertained what were or are the factors controlling this situation, it is possible to allow for their modification when obtaining totals for different stages in the past, once again without renewed mapping. In Palestine, for example, the coastal marshes will represent a contribution to the grazing total (with a marked seasonal significance) until modern times, when they become part of the arable category.

(3) Bare rock and the like are classified separately as unproductive since we are concerned with biological productivity; if mineral exploitation is at issue, the original survey can be oriented so as to specify the rocks represented within the catchment.

(4) A miscellaneous category (here represented by 'dunes') acts as safety valve for the field surveyor; the interpreter can then pass judgement.

Within these major categories there is scope for subdivision. In subsequent surveys of agricultural sites, for example, arable land was mapped according to its texture, it being argued that of the numerous soil properties that affect yields this factor was likely to have been least modified by cultivation. The value of distinguishing between light and heavy soils will be apparent to students of early agriculture or of Roman agronomical literature.

CONCLUSION

We have seen that prehistoric economies can be classified as to whether they were mobile, sedentary, or mobile-cum-sedentary. The concept of economic territoriality allows us to delimit the habitually exploited area around a site from which any of the above types of economy was practised. Through the use of the technique of site catchment analysis and an assessment of past and present economic potential of the site territory, we may make a start in the study of man's changing relationship with his environment through time. The methods outlined here are capable of considerable refinement and elaboration, but the results already obtained suggest that further research along these lines will prove fruitful.

SECTION II
METHODS AND TECHNIQUES

1. RETRIEVAL OF PLANT REMAINS FROM ARCHAEOLOGICAL SITES BY FROTH FLOTATION

H. N. JARMAN, A. J. LEGGE AND J. A. CHARLES

The increasing attention being given to the study of pre-historic economies demands that more efficient means of collecting ancient plant remains be developed and used. Apart from chance discoveries of sizeable caches of seeds or fruits, the only methods of collection which have been published are dense media separation (called 'flotation') (Helbaek, 1969) and water separation (Struever, 1968). There are several reasons why collection of plant remains has not been more extensively developed and applied. Part of the fault lies with the excavator, who has given the problem a low priority, and part with the climate of thought in archaeology, which has laid down boundaries in time and space outside which early food resources become of peripheral interest. However, it can already be seen that much apparent plant and animal domestication occurs outside the predicted nuclear zones (Helbaek, 1960a; Godwin, 1965; Higgs & Jarman, 1969). Pollen analysts have shown the importance that plant remains can have for the interpretation of prehistoric settlement and economy in areas such as north-west Europe. However, while pollen analyses are in general indicative of regional characteristics, the plant husbandry of particular sites may be better assessed on data which can be directly attributed to the sites themselves.

Plant remains in the deposits can rarely be detected by eye alone, even when shown to be present in abundance by the method described in this paper. For example Struever (1968) noted that in his excavations at Apple Creek, in only one of 600 features were plant remains visible during trowelling, whereas plant remains were recovered from 95 percent of the 200 features which were treated by water separation. It has been our experience, however, that even archaeological features do not provide a guide to the deposition of plant remains. On many sites at which we have worked it has not been possible to distinguish between high and low yielding deposit on the basis of colour, texture, or context of the deposit. Thus the presence of occupation levels or hearths cannot be considered a prerequisite for plant preservation. Helbaek (1969) records similar experience at Ali Kosh where deposit from 'dark patches, ashy layers and other promising or doubtful occurrences' yielded 'negative as often as positive result'.

Another factor discouraging the systematic collection of plant remains has been the inadequacies of present field techniques. If a seed sample is to provide useful data for the interpretation of the economy of a site, it must be representative of the full range of archaeological contexts at that site (Dennell, III. 4). Since one cannot reject deposits for sampling on the basis of a visual inspection, earth processing must proceed on a massive scale. Struever (1968) published a rate of 120 ft^3 in 400 man-hours for his water separation method. This method results in a sample of small bone and plant material and must undergo further dense media separation to separate the two components: an additional investment in time and a greater risk of sample damage discussed below. Nevertheless, this method represents a vast improvement over sorting by microscope; but it would not have coped with the quantities of deposit with which we were faced in our field trials. There are no published figures for the processing rate of dense media separation. However, it was because we found it to be slow, tedious, and obviously inefficient in retrieval, that we began development of the froth flotation technique. Furthermore, the use of water without additives as a separation medium for dense media separation means that seeds denser than water will be missed. The use of soluble salts, such as sodium chloride or zinc chloride, to increase the density of the separation medium, while in part solving the first problem, presents different additional problems. Sodium chloride will leave a white encrustation on plant remains rendering identification more difficult. Zinc chloride is hygroscopic and endangers preservation and storage of remains. To remove the salts the remains must be thoroughly rinsed at the time of processing, which not only increases the risk of damage to the sample but also requires large amounts of clean water. Dense fluids, such as carbon tetrachloride and toluene mixtures, are equally unsuitable for large-scale field work due to their expense and the toxicity of their fumes.

The method of froth flotation developed by the authors has been specifically designed to overcome the limitations of dense media and water separation and to encourage excavators to include the systematic collection of carbonized and other seeds among their priorities.

PRINCIPLES OF FROTH FLOTATION

In froth flotation additions known as 'collectors' made to a suspension of the mixed solids in water selectively coat the surfaces of the required particles, so that they become more water repellent and air avid than the particles with which they are mixed, i.e., hydrophobic and aerophilic. The suspension is searched by rising air bubbles and the formation of a short-lived froth at the surface is facilitated by making additions of a frothing agent (e.g., terpineol) which lowers the air/water surface tension so that bubbles may approach one another without coalescing. When suitably coated particles meet an air bubble they attach to it and are lifted into the surface froth for removal.

The attachment of the particle (e.g., a seed) to the air bubble is a function of the balance of the interfacial forces involved at the point of contact, and is usually described by a contact angle:

$$T_{ws} + T_{aw} \cos \theta - T_{as} = 0$$

$$\cos \theta = \frac{T_{as} - T_{ws}}{T_{aw}}$$

where T_{aw} = surface tension for air/water, T_{ws} = surface tension for water/seed, and T_{as} = surface tension for air/seed (Fig. 1). If the contact angle of a surface is nil, water wets the surface in preference to air and solid/air contact is

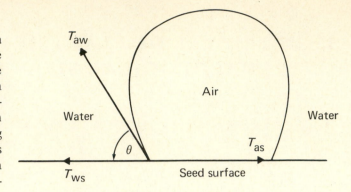

Fig. 1. Contact angle shown as function of interfacial forces at point of air-surface contact.

impossible, that is, it represents a condition of non-flotability (Fig. 2, top). Conversely, a contact angle of 180° would represent wetting of the surface by air to the exclusion of water (Fig. 2, bottom). No solid is known to give a contact angle of more than about 110°, but materials such as paraffin wax with a contact angle of 105° are naturally flotable in water. The contact angle need not, however, be a characteristic of the material itself but of some surface coating, as previously suggested, and in this lies the whole basis of selective mineral concentration by flotation. As a typical example from mineral flotation a fresh galena (PbS) surface has a contact angle of 0°, but if

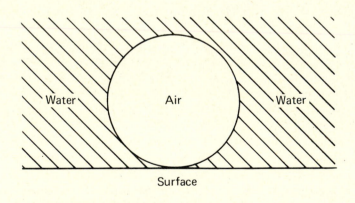
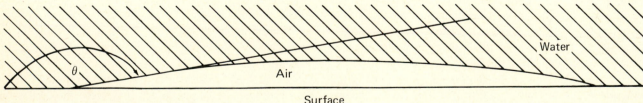

Fig. 2. Flotability. Top: condition of wetting, contact angle as given by tangent at point of contact = 0°. Bottom: condition of non-wetting, contact angle approaching 180°.

potassium ethyl xanthate is added to the pulp (solid/liquid mixture) in only very small amounts, it is selectively oxidized to a sparingly soluble oil, dixanthogen, at the surface of the galena, and the contact angle increases to 60°, enabling flotation. The mechanism by which various collectors provide suitable selective coatings in differing minerals is still not fully understood and need not be discussed here.

The industrial use of froth flotation for removing coal from associated shale etc. suggested its possible application to carbonized plant remains. Non-polar minerals such as sulphur, graphite, and coals are generally easily flotable. Coals are, of course, heterogeneous materials and differ in natural flotability in terms of the rank of the coal as reflecting their composition and structure. Bituminous coals normally have a natural contact angle of about 60°, anthracites about 45°, whereas lignites exhibit no natural flotability with a contact angle of 0°.

It is important to note that since the specific gravity of the desired carbonaceous materials is, relatively speaking, very low (about 1.25), the lifting function of the air bubbles is not such an important requirement. Accordingly, the process can be applied to much coarser pieces of material than is possible in mineral dressing with, for instance, the separation of galena from sand, where the particles may have to be less than 150 mesh (0.104 mm) for satisfactory operation; the size range for coal, however, extends over the whole range likely to be encountered in terms of carbonized seeds. In fact, with coal, several bubbles may be attached to a single particle to give lift.

Coal flotation is largely confined to the treatment of fines associated with earthy materials, which arise from the more widely used primary gravity concentration methods. As mined, coal is a rich deposit and is readily amenable to gravity concentration methods at coarse size. Nor is the application of flotation particularly suited to the separation of a major constituent away from a minor, as must happen when coal is bound to exhibit a higher contact angle than the other oxide solids present. In the case of seeds, however, we require to separate a relatively minor carbonaceous soil constituent away from a large amount of oxide materials, an ideal situation.

Although several of the constituents of bituminous coals may be floated by air bubbles with their natural surface properties, using only a water-soluble frothing agent, it is generally recognized as advantageous to employ a collector of an oily type which appears to coat the coal particles preferentially. Xanthates have been used, but they show no advantage over cheaper materials such as kerosene (paraffin). With non-soluble additives such as this, emulsification may be necessary to reduce the amount required and this can be assisted by the addition of a surface active agent

such as Lissapol (ICI). The combination of kerosene type collectors with cresylic acid or pine oil as frothers seems to have been generally successful in coal flotation.

PRELIMINARY LABORATORY AND FIELD TESTS ON SEEDS

Clearly it was impracticable to carry out preliminary quantitative efficiency tests on genuine excavation material, so various sizes and shapes of seeds (lentils, peas, beans, wheat, barley, and rice) were slowly carbonized by heating in an oven. Counted quantities of these were then mixed with clean sand and the mixture put into the base of a water column through which air could be blown as fine bubbles. It was immediately apparent that whereas some seeds would float naturally, complete collection of all the seeds to a surface froth required the addition of a collector. Kerosene worked satisfactorily, and in view of its low cost was selected as suitable for the field trials.

During the earliest field trials at the Bronze Age to Medieval site of The Udal in North Uist, in the Outer Hebrides (Crawford, in press), the effectiveness of froth flotation in recovering remains of varying densities was demonstrated conclusively. As soon as the deposit had passed through the froth flotation cell, the seed sample was immersed in water and the float fraction separated from the sink fraction. The float and sink fractions were then identified and counted separately. The large seeds from one soil sample of 0.2 m³ totalled 534, including barley, oats, and some emmer and small vetches. It was found that 62 percent of the barley, 58 percent of the oats, 58 percent of the emmer, and 28 percent of the vetches sank in water, yet had been retrieved by the flotation process. In all, 229 seeds floated against 305 that sank in water.

DESIGN OF FLOTATION CELL

The principal aims in design were to create an apparatus which would not only give efficient large-scale retrieval, but would also be portable, easy to operate, and durable under field conditions, anticipating its use in areas where spares and repairs may be difficult to obtain. Two years of field use convince us that these objectives have been substantially met.

A variety of materials could be used to fabricate the flotation cell, but polypropylene sheeting of 6 mm thickness was chosen in this instance, as it is tough, inexpensive, and easily fabricated. The cell was hot-air welded from the sheeting into a cylindrical form. This shape was chosen for rigidity, but field experience suggests a rectangular or square section may have some technical advantages. Further trials with such a model are planned.

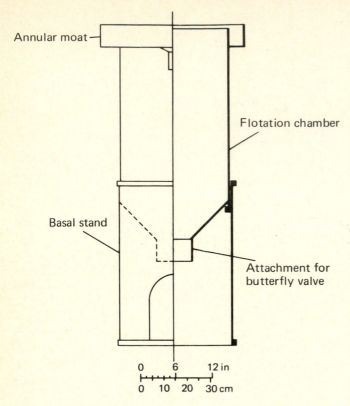

Annular moat

Flotation chamber

Basal stand

Attachment for
butterfly valve

0   6   12 in

0   10   20   30 cm

Fig. 3.   Flotation cell shown in elevation and in section.

A diagram of the flotation cell is given, shown in elevation and in section (Fig. 3). The cylinder is 46 cm in diameter and is constructed in two parts; the basal stand can be removed, reversed, and pushed over the cylinder to facilitate storage and transport. At the top of the cylinder, an annular moat drains to a spout below which granulometry sieves are suspended for seed collection. Sieves of 1 mm and 0.3 mm mesh have been found to be generally convenient, but these may be varied according to the size range of the plant material in the deposit. The base of the cylinder is closed by a cone which tapers from 46 cm in diameter to 15 cm through a vertical distance of 23 cm. The sides of the cone must be at least this steep for complete flushing out of the mud. The cone terminates in a 15 cm diameter spout on to which a butterfly valve is fastened by means of a rubber sleeve and screw clips.

This valve allows the discharge of the mud from the base of the cylinder but retains the water while flotation is in process. The valve (Fig. 4, Plate I) is constructed of corrosion resistant metals, and consists of a short cylinder containing a sealing disc which is mounted across its diameter on a shaft, by means of which it can be rotated to form a tight fit in the metal sleeve when closed. In the sealing disc, two metal plates sandwich a rubber or plastic washer, this assembly being screwed on to a flat on the rotating shaft.

Screws placed at the periphery of the sealing disc allow some adjustment of the fit of the seal by increased or reduced tension. In practice, the life of the seal depends on the nature of the soils processed, occasional replacement of the washer (once every four to six weeks) being necessary in stony deposits. An extension T-bar handle allows the valve to be operated externally to the body of the cell. The base of the valve fits into a wooden chute which carries deposit away from the cell.

The fine bubbles needed for the flotation process are distributed at the base of the flotation cylinder, just above the mud collection cone, by small porous metal bubblers fastened to a framework of metal tubing through which the air is pumped. The most satisfactory material for the bubbler elements has been found to be sintered bronze, which can be obtained pre-formed according to desired shape and porosity. This material resists accidental damage, and can be attached to the metal compressed air pipe by soldering. Good bubble formation and distribution has been attained with a unit (Plates II and III) consisting of twenty-four sintered bronze elements (itemized as flange cones by manufacturers, porosity = 25μ) distributed over a 30 cm × 30 cm frame of brass tubing. Attached to the bubbler unit is a rigid metal pipe for air delivery, which passes out of the water at the top of the cylinder. This supports the bubbler unit at its correct position at the top of the basal cone and allows the easy removal of the bubbler unit when not in operation.

The supply of compressed air to the flotation unit comes from a 2 HP petrol engine driving a rotary-vane air pump.

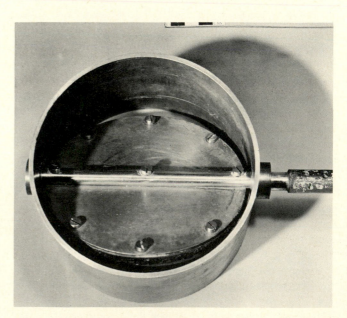

Plate I.   Butterfly valve for discharge of deposit. (The scale shows centimetres.)

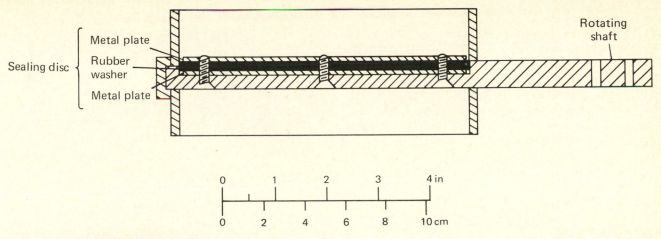

Sealing disc { Metal plate
Rubber washer
Metal plate

Rotating shaft

Fig. 4. Butterfly valve for deposit discharge.

Plate II. Bubbler unit. Plate III. Detail. (The scales show centimetres.)

The advantage of this type of pump is that air delivery at the bubbler elements is continuous, the slight pulsation at the pump having been equalized in the delivery tube. The particular pump used (Pump E. B. 3, Edwards High Vacuum Limited) incorporates in its design a pressure relief valve which allows air pressure, and consequent delivery rate, to be adjusted to suit the prevailing conditions.

In order to ensure more uniform introduction of deposit into the flotation cell, a vibrating feed mechanism run by compressed air and supported above the cylinder will be incorporated in future models.

METHOD OF USE

Due to variations in conditions among archaeological sites, it is not possible to describe in every detail a standard method of use for the flotation cell, and adaptations of the technique may be required. The description set out below gives a guide to use based on the experience of operators to date.

The flotation cell is filled with water to within about 3 cm of the lip and a frother (Cyanamid Aerofroth 65) and a collector (paraffin/kerosene) are added. For the size of cell described above, about 20 cc of frother and 5 cc of paraffin are sufficient for one run.

Before introducing deposit into the flotation cell, it has been found advisable to remove large objects from the earth by coarse sieving. Stones and large lumps of deposit may block or damage internal components of the apparatus. The form of sieve employed is that described by Payne (II. 2, p. 50), the lower fine sieve being replaced by a wooden box, and the upper sieve being of 2.5 cm or 1.0 cm mesh depending upon the deposit. The soil is passed through the sieve as gently as possible to avoid damage to seeds, after which the deposit is ready to be fed into the flotation cell. The petrol engine is started and the bubbler positioned inside the cell. Time must be allowed for mixing of the chemicals and the formation of a good froth bed. The soil should be poured in a steady stream into the centre of the froth bed (Plate IV), the manner of introduction of the soil being highly important to effect good separation. Should large quantities of earth be dumped into the cell, complete wetting cannot occur, and seeds may be carried directly to the bottom. If they are present, seeds and charcoal will begin to be carried over into the moat almost as soon as the soil is introduced and will collect in the granulometry sieves suspended below the spout. Selection of the appropriate mesh sizes allows the sample to be divided into coarse and fine fractions, often approximating to food and weed seeds. This has been found to greatly facilitate subsequent sorting and identification.

Plate IV.   Introduction of soil into flotation cell.

The deposit drops through the height of the cell and collects in the cone below the bubbler. The capacity of the cone is effectively 20 litres (two small buckets), and once this amount has been introduced, the mud must be removed through the valve at the base of the cone (Plate V). More soil can be accommodated by raising the bubbler slightly, but larger quantities of soil are less easily removed. Experience in the operation of the butterfly valve to release the mud is important in the conservation of water. The bubbler unit is removed and gentle agitation of the mud with a pole assists its free flow as the valve is operated. Skilful use of the valve allows a given volume of soil to be processed with the loss of only half its volume of water, and, as much of this water may be re-used, the efficiency is in fact much greater. After emptying, the cell is refilled and the cycle begins again.

When a run of soil has been completed, it is essential that the bubbler unit be removed from the water and allowed to blow dry. It has been found that if this is not done, fine silt or calcium salts will accumulate in the pores of the bubbler elements resulting in eventual clogging. In the case of clogging in calcareous soils, the bubbler unit may be cleaned by brief immersion in 10 percent acetic acid.

The seeds collected are washed from the granulometry sieves with the aid of a small hand spray and wrapped in pre-wetted paper towelling. This is fastened by stapling and allowed to shade-dry for two to three days before packing

Plate V.   Operation of butterfly valve.

in rigid containers. The particular method of packing the seeds may need some modification to suit local conditions. Relatively 'pure' samples, that is, of seeds alone or with small shells only, transport well in the paper towelling. Some more superficial samples, however, may be heavily contaminated by recent rootlets and other organic material. If this is packed too tightly, it will tend to harden upon drying into a mass that cannot easily be separated without the risk of damage to some of the contained seeds. For this type of material the problem is solved by packing into small rigid boxes directly from the granulometry sieves. It is important that the sample be washed from the sieve while it is still wet, as repeated wetting and drying of the remains can result in their total destruction. This is illustrated by the results of tests on a sample of 500 carbonized seeds from a silo deposit at Tell Gezer in Palestine. The sample was collected directly from the silo, without flotation, and subjected to a five-minute immersion with gentle agitation in a solution as is used in the froth flotation process. When dry, examination showed that 4 percent of the grains had broken in half, but remained identifiable. A subsequent wetting and drying destroyed a further 56 percent of the sample, and only 15 percent were left whole. A further repetition of the cycle destroyed virtually the whole sample. The small percentage damaged by the initial wetting has been confirmed in practice, where few seeds in a sample show fresh damage. The slow drying in damp paper

towelling also reduces damage below that shown in the tests.

At least two sets of granulometry sieves are necessary to ensure continuous processing when one set becomes full. This needs careful observation by the operator, as the fine sieve is subject to clogging, for example by large quantities of minute shells, very fine deposit which never sinks below the froth, or large quantities of organic matter as in peat deposits.

The labour involved in the operation of the flotation cell is not great. It is possible for two people to sieve the deposit, operate the cell, and package the seed sample, but the rate of processing is greatly increased if the work is divided between three or four people. In cases where little labour is available and the deposit is difficult to process, about six runs per hour can be accomplished. However, under optimum operation conditions, continuous processing of the deposit is easily possible. Thus in an eight-hour work day between 1 and 2 m^3 may be processed by three people.

COMPREHENSIVE RETRIEVAL SYSTEM

The operations at Nahal Oren in Palestine are described in detail, as they represent not only the use of flotation under testing conditions, but also the use of the flotation cell as part of a system of comprehensive retrieval of artefacts and organic remains. Due to the importance of the succession at

Plate VI. Flotation cell and settling tank at Nahal Oren.

this site, it was imperative that no deposit should be processed solely for plant material at the risk of losing other types of artefacts. Trials in 1969 had shown the presence of seeds in all layers, but in small quantities. Difficulties were presented as much of the deposit was stony, and although water was available in the locality, it had to be carried by hand for some 400 m. This meant that water use had to be limited, as the amount of soil processing and sorting was already placing demands on available labour.

The flotation cell was set up adjacent to the site (Plate VI), with a 180 litre drum for water storage and a settling tank to allow the reuse of water. The settling tank was a trough 1 m wide, 2 m long, and 0.5 m deep. It was divided into three compartments, the first compartment being 1 m × 1 m and containing a large 'wet sieve', with a 2 mm mesh, into which the mud from the bottom of the flotation cell was directed when the cell was emptied at the end of each run. This sieve rested on arms on the top of the settling tank, and could be immersed in the water.

Care was taken in excavation to damage as little as possible the plant remains which might be contained in the excavated deposit. Here it should be noted that some of the traditional aims and techniques of archaeology may be especially harmful to plant remains. For instance, the

tracing of architectural features in tell excavation usually involves trowel scraping of living floors and continual walking on these surfaces which is obviously damaging to the plant remains which often occur in floor deposits. This is a point that excavators might well bear in mind if they are concerned with the securing of adequate samples of plant remains.

Earth from the excavation was coarse sieved to remove large stones, bones, and artefacts. Soil from the sieving was collected and wrapped in plastic sheeting until a sufficient amount had accumulated for processing. The quantity processed was recorded at all stages. After flotation the soil was released into the wet sieve where the sediment was washed by the agitation of the sieve in the water (Plate VII). It was found that satisfactory washing could be achieved even with very muddy water, the residue in the sieve needing only a brief rinse in clean water before sorting, when small bone fragments and artefacts were picked out for bagging.

The fine sediment gradually filled the first compartment of the settling tank, displacing water into the second and third compartments. By the time it reached the third compartment the water was clean and could be returned to the cell. The possibility of contamination was avoided by

Plate VII.   Washing the wet sieve in settling tank.

pouring the water through a fine mesh filter. The mud was periodically removed from the settling tank and discarded. In practice, complete recovery of water is not possible, as some is lost in the discarded mud and through spillage. It was found that with the settling tank in use, a cubic metre of soil (=1000 litres) could be processed with the expenditure of about 200 litres of water. Were water not recycled, two or three times this amount would be needed, and soil washing would require much more.

This system is briefly described as a means of comprehensive retrieval, various classes of data being extracted at different stages in the process. Large finds come from excavation and the coarse sieves, seeds and shells from the flotation, micro-fauna and microliths from the wet sieve. On sites with microlithic industries, or any component of small artefacts, such soil washing and sorting greatly enhances collection (Payne, II. 2, p. 54). The customary disposition of labour on the site involved three excavators, two coarse sievers, one flotation cell operator, one wet siever, and two hand sorters: an average of two persons involved with deposit processing for each excavator. Although such an organization of labour may at first sound strange and perhaps wasteful, it is not so in practice. Excavation itself can proceed more quickly if only the essen-

tials of excavation (i.e., stratigraphy, architecture, and large finds) are dealt with in the trench. Labour which would normally be employed in excavation can be shifted to deposit processing jobs, such as sieving and froth flotation, with no loss in the speed of excavation and with a gain in artefact retrieval.

SAMPLING TECHNIQUES

The froth flotation system provides a means of fast and efficient separation of carbonized plant material from deposit. It has been tested on a number of different sites under varying conditions of operation and deposit types. At many of these sites it was found that the amount of deposit excavated was so great as to demand a heavy expenditure of resources if a policy of total soil processing were adopted. Furthermore, much of the deposit may contain no plant remains or, conversely, such a quantity of plant remains, as in the case of peat, that it would be impossible to sort and identify all the material from an entire site. In these cases some method of sampling must be adopted. The authors have found that each site presents its own particular problems which cannot be solved within the framework of a single sampling plan. However, some guidelines can be established within which common sense will easily suggest a plan of action.

It is evident from the results of Dennell's work in Bulgaria (III. 4) that one of the most important aspects of sampling is to ensure the recovery of remains from a number of different archaeological contexts. It is obvious that a large cache of seeds belonging to a single species, while it gives evidence of utilization by man, will give no information about the range and versatility of plant husbandry at a site, although it may yield information about the quality of husbandry of that particular species. A sample of a scatter of seeds on a living floor, on the other hand, may give a good indication of the variety of plants used and their relative economic importance, but no data on crop purity. Thus in general, the greater the number of different contexts from which plant remains can be recovered, the more accurate and comprehensive one's interpretation of those remains will be.

A second factor of importance is that of sample size. Small samples and even individual seeds do, of course, provide data which can be of interest, but any statistical treatment of the data will necessarily be seriously affected by the limitations imposed by the size of the available sample. The actual quantity and diversity of deposit which must be processed cannot, however, be determined before excavation. At some sites a single 2 m × 2 m trench may produce such an abundance and variety of seeds that only small spot checks are necessary from other areas on the site. However, one may find that abundant remains represent a single species, in which case it would be desirable to test deposits as diverse as possible to eliminate errors due to localized concentrations of species. If remains in one area are sparse, again it is wise to sample a large number of different deposits in order to discover those situations where a greater abundance of remains will yield a larger sample for a smaller input of labour.

Several examples may help to illustrate successful sampling procedure. The method of excavating a separate trial area solely for the collection of plant remains was highly successful at Tell Gezer in Palestine and at Tells Chevdar, Kazanluk, and Ezero in Bulgaria. At these sites a small area of the tell was excavated by a team associated with the operation of the flotation process, and concerned primarily with the retrieval of organic remains. At Tell Gezer the excavation took the form of a 2.5 m × 2.5 m trench dug to bedrock down the face of an existing section. It was possible to choose a location for the trench where layers were uniform and horizontal, and where the succession was not interrupted by major architectural features. Soil was excavated and sieved with as much care for plant remains as possible and with the advantage that a consistent method of excavation was maintained throughout the sample. The plant remains from this one sounding, involving the flotation of 50 m³ of *in situ* deposit, are so numerous that they present a tremendous task of analysis.

At many sites it will not be feasible or desirable to maintain a separate excavation solely for the sake of retrieval of plant remains. At Knossos on Crete sampling was approached in a different manner. In this case, 25 percent of the excavator's deep sounding was processed for seeds and small artefacts. Unfortunately the deposits in this trench proved to be extremely poor in plant remains. Therefore, the sampling system was expanded to include two test runs from every level, whether or not it appeared likely to be productive, of all trenches with deposit of desired age. If test samples produced more than one or two seeds, the remainder of that deposit was processed. In this way the number of seeds collected was greatly enhanced with a minimum of time and labour. Without the flotation cell and its capacity for mass processing, the sample from Knossos would have consisted of a large cache of several hundred wheat grains from the one aceramic level and less than one hundred seeds from the nine remaining Neolithic levels. The sample from the later levels has been increased to several hundred seeds, and the sample from the aceramic level to include remains from non-cereal plants.

At the Neolithic lake-village of Molino Casarotto in north Italy the peaty deposit produced abundant organic material, but identifiable plant remains (excluding charcoal) were found in localized concentrations. As the deposit was of limited thickness and the site excavated in metre squares, a system of processing 10 percent to 20 percent of each square metre throughout its depth was easily applied and ensured that most local concentrations would be sampled.

In conclusion, the authors wish to encourage the use of the flotation cell on all sites of any age or geographical situation. It is easily portable, very durable, and adaptable to use in remote areas. It costs no more than much of the equipment that is now considered essential for excavation, and the returns it yields are high. Not only does it make possible more efficient recovery of badly needed plant remains, but its use in a system of comprehensive retrieval brings nearly complete recovery of remains within the resources of most excavators.

ACKNOWLEDGEMENT

We would especially like to thank Mr K. A. Fern of Cyanamid of Great Britain Limited for all the help and advice he has given us during our experiments with the flotation cell.

2. PARTIAL RECOVERY AND SAMPLE BIAS: THE RESULTS OF SOME SIEVING EXPERIMENTS

SEBASTIAN PAYNE

The present paper is a contribution to the study of data retrieval from archaeological deposits, a topic of vital importance to any detailed analysis of material from excavations. The value of any analysis depends on the quality of the sample on which it is based. The results of experiments designed to test the efficiency of recovery by various means are presented for a number of sites. These show that, even for pottery, for flints, or for animal bones, normal excavation recovers a biased and sometimes misleading sample of what is actually present in the earth. Experiments have been carried out at a number of sites, since it might otherwise be thought that they merely expose the inefficiency of recovery at a particular site. I would like at the outset to thank the directors who have allowed me to carry out sampling tests on their sites, and to state my belief that the results reflect not on the efficiency of individual directors or teams, but on the inefficiency and inaccuracy of methods that are usually regarded as adequate.

A full account of the experiments and their results will not be given here: this will, in due course, be given separately for each site. Instead, I will describe the methods used, and the sort of results that have been obtained. It is hoped that this will stimulate excavators into trying similar experiments at their sites, so that they can see what they are missing, and whether this affects their conclusions. It is my belief that every excavation report should state precisely what methods were used in the retrieval of data. If every archaeological excavation is regarded as an experiment, it follows that precise information should be provided about the conditions under which the experiment was carried out. Conversely, unless an excavation is regarded in these terms it is surely the case, except perhaps in rapid rescue operations, that it should not have been carried out.

A brief review may first be offered of the chief sieving methods that have been used on archaeological excavations.

SIEVING METHODS

1. Dry-sieving

Most of the sieving that has been done in the past has been dry-sieving.

The throwscreen is a mesh set nearly upright, against which the earth is thrown: the larger particles roll down the near side on to the ground, where they are searched through (see, for instance, Coon, 1957, Plate XII). Though frequently used, the throwscreen has little to recommend it: it is not as efficient as a sieve, it is difficult to search through the pile on the ground, and the risk of contamination is high.

Hand-held sieves, of the sort used in the kitchen or the garden, are in some ways better. They are usually a little slow and difficult to work with; the sides are usually so high in relation to the area of the mesh that searching for and picking out objects is difficult. Against this, they are cheap and readily available almost anywhere in a range of mesh sizes. In areas where local labour is used to them (as for instance in Turkey, where women sort through grain in such sieves to pick out small stones), they can conveniently be used.

Much better than either of these are the various dry-sieves that have been designed for archaeological work. Usually these have to be specially built, but they are well worth the extra expenditure of time and money. There are many designs: in Figures 1 and 2 details are given of one such sieve, designed by Dr C. B. M. McBurney, which can be made almost anywhere from locally available materials. It is important that such sieves are designed so that they are as easy to work at as possible. The height and the size of the working surface are important; they should allow the operator to work all over the surface from a single position with as much ease as possible.

In exceptional soil conditions, such as sands or dry loesses, dry-sieving is reasonably efficient, at least down to 2 or 3 mm. However, in most conditions dry-sieving misses a proportion of the finds held by a 3 mm mesh, and the efficiency of recovery is often rather variable, depending on a wide range of factors such as the colour, texture, and moisture-context of the earth, the personnel, the time of day, the weather, the amount of finds coming from the sieve, and the size of any backlog that has accumulated. I have therefore used water-sieving instead of dry-sieving in these experiments.

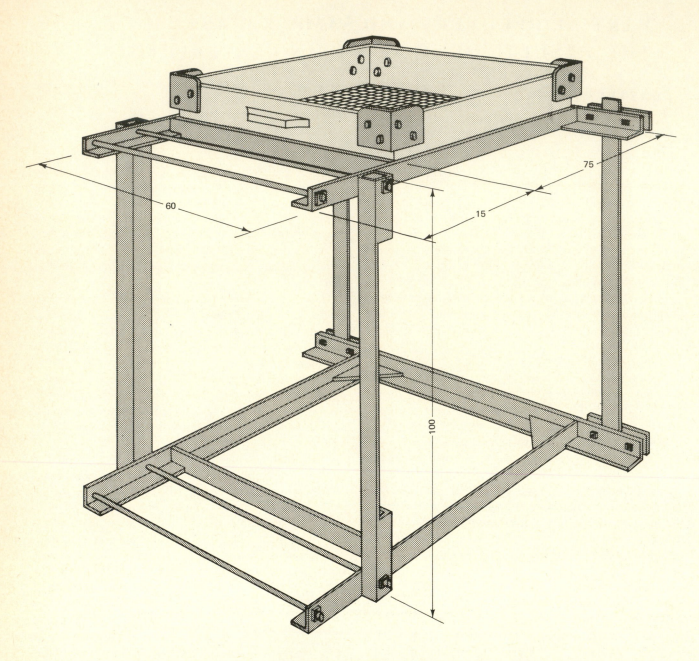

Fig. 1. The shaker. A stack of sieves (of which only one is shown) sits on a shaker-frame. Two of the legs pivot freely; the other two are car springs, bolted firmly at top and bottom. (Measurements in centimetres.)

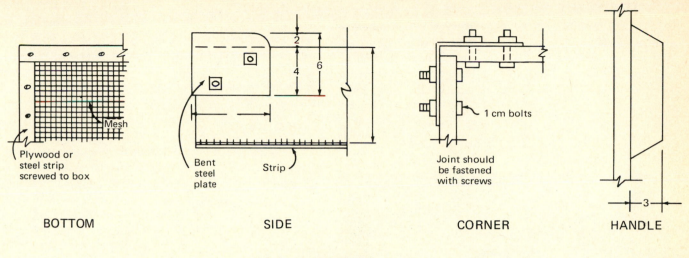

BOTTOM   **SIDE**   **CORNER**   **HANDLE**

SIEVE DETAILS
(2 req'd) outside dimensions are
57 cm × 72 cm

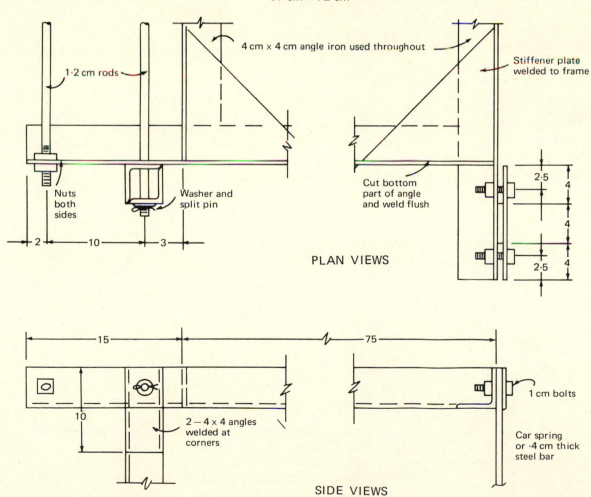

Fig. 2. Construction details of the shaker. (Measurements in centimetres.)

2. Water-sieving

This is a process whereby the earth is sieved in water, so that all the smaller particles are washed away, leaving the fragments retained by the sieve clean. These can then be dried and sorted. I have used a basket made of sheets of mesh (Plate I). This is shaken either in a river, or in a series of tubs of water (Plate II).

The advantage of water-sieving over dry-sieving lies in its accuracy. The residue retained by the sieve is so clean that

Plate I. A water-sieve. The mesh used in this sieve is slightly finer and less durable than that finally used for the experiments reported here, and needed to be supported with chicken-wire.

Plate II. A water-sieve in use.

it can be sorted very efficiently: properly checked, very few finds are missed. If carefully supervised, the work can be done reasonably satisfactorily by unskilled workers: it is far easier and quicker to keep an adequate check on water-sieving simply because the residue is so clean that one can clearly and rapidly see what each fragment is.

EXPERIMENTS

The data used in this paper result from a series of experiments in which particular soil units, after having been normally searched in the trench, were searched by water-sieving. In all cases all the earth in the unit went through both processes. The finds recovered in the trench, and those missed in the trench and later recovered by sieving, were kept separate for comparison. For these units, therefore, we can directly compare what was found by normal excavation with what was missed in the trench and subsequently recovered by sieving. Brief notes on each of the sites and on the experimental units are given in Appendix I (p. 63).

A possible objection to this method is that because the people searching the earth in the trench know that the earth is going to be sieved, they will be less careful than usual. Ideally, of course, the experiment should be so designed that the workers in the trench do not know that the earth is going to be sieved. In practice, it is difficult to organize this, and in these experiments the workers knew that the earth was going to be sieved. It could therefore be argued that these results might make normal recovery look less efficient than it in fact is. I discount this objection for two reasons. First, there is no obvious difference between what was recovered in the trench in units that were chosen for these experiments, and in units that were not going to be sieved later. Secondly, the finds recovered by water-sieving always look very different, mainly in average size, from any set of finds from normal excavation. Also, so far as small-scale tests such as these are concerned, I believe that the effect on those searching the earth in the trench is more likely to be that they are stimulated by this challenge, and therefore look even more carefully than usual.

For all the experiments reported here, a standard wire mesh with square holes of approximately 3 mm (in fact ⅛ inch, as this is what was available) was used. The reasons for using this are the availability of suitable very durable mesh, and considerations of time and eye-strain: below this size it rapidly becomes very difficult and tiring to sort objects without other equipment, such as magnifying lenses. Also, 3 mm is already at or below the size-level of any effective recovery in the trench.

As the standard mesh used is 3 mm, anything that can pass through this mesh is likely to have been lost. *To this extent, all the samples that I have recovered are partial samples*. Clearly, to obtain good samples of land snails, seeds, or rodent bones, it would be necessary to use meshes far finer than 3 mm. I have not attempted to discuss these, as it is already generally recognized that special sampling and recovery methods are necessary. In these experiments, I am simply concerned with those materials, such as pottery, or the bones of the larger mammals for which it is generally assumed that normal recovery in the trench is adequate.

Above 3 mm, I believe the standard of recovery by water-sieving in these experiments to have been extremely high. When the sorted residues were checked through by a second sorter, the resulting finds were almost always negligible: the exception being, rarely, that some very large and obvious object has been missed, as if the sorter had been 'focused too fine'. This high degree of accuracy is possible because the washed fraction is clean: sorting is a matter of identifying each fragment and throwing out what is not wanted, and not of picking out whatever can be recognized from a pile of earth. A few things will probably have been sometimes confused with stones and missed. The obvious examples are some of the carpal, tarsal, and sesamoid bones; all the sorters were made familiar with their appearance, but some were still no doubt missed.

RESULTS

In this paper I have chosen to describe results for three materials: pottery, chipped stone, and the bones of the larger mammals. This is because the samples available for comparison from these experiments are reasonably large.

For each of these three materials, I will show that recovery in the trench was only partial: much of what was there in the earth was missed. I will also show that what was recovered in the trench is a heavily biased sample of what was in fact present in the earth. It is important not to miss so much both because of the new information it can give us, and so that we are not misled by the biased samples that are at present recovered by normal excavation methods.

Other materials were of course also recovered, both in the trench and from the sieves: they will not be discussed in detail. Results for them are in no way less informative than those described here, and are often more striking. This is especially true for some rather scarce categories, for which it would probably be admitted that normal recovery is not very good, but which are not usually the subjects of any special sampling programme. These include smaller animal remains (e.g. birds, fishes, mammalian 'microfauna', crustacea, echinoderms), and many categories of small finds, such as smaller figurines, beads, pendants, small bone tools, and small metal objects. At Sitagroi for instance, the sieving experiments have produced several hundred small beads; normal excavation has not yielded even one, despite the far larger volume of earth treated in this way: among these beads are ones made of copper, which are of great interest: they are the earliest metal objects at the site. At Aşvan, in eastern Anatolia, a site excavated by Dr D. H. French, where dry-sieving is a standard procedure, apart from one large hoard over half the coins have come from the dry-sieves.

Table 1. Efficiency of recovery in the trench of flint or obsidian, in four experiments, in terms of number and of weight of pieces

	Number of pieces			Weight of pieces (g)		
	Recovered in the trench	Missed in the trench, recovered by water-sieving	Percentage efficiency of recovery in the trench	Recovered in the trench	Missed in the trench, recovered by water-sieving	Percentage efficiency of recovery in the trench
Franchthi Cave F/A Baulk, Unit 49, obsidian	7	81	8	34	31	52
Can Hasan III 49L 105.6 + 105.7, obsidian	210	557	27	215	49	82
Can Hasan III 49L 109.1 + 109.4, obsidian	27	620	4	23	46	33
Sitagroi ZA 47, flint	0	453	0	0	155	0

Chipped stone

In Table 1, the amount of flint or obsidian found in the trench is compared with the amount subsequently recovered by water-sieving. The results of four experiments are given. In each experiment it is clear that the efficiency of recovery in the trench is low in terms of the number of pieces. In terms of weight, efficiency is higher; this reflects the smaller size, on average, of the pieces recovered in the sieves.

The classic approach to chipped stone industries has been to concentrate on tools and retouched pieces. The extent to which these are missed in excavation depends on their size as well as on the efficiency of recovery: probably few handaxes are ever missed!

The importance of good recovery on sites with microliths has been pointed out before: workers on Mesolithic sites especially have been aware of the need for meticulous recovery, and have often dry-sieved the earth they have excavated. An example of the extent to which differences in recovery can affect the relative proportions of different tool types is given by the Upper Magdalenian site of La Gare de Couze. Successive excavations using progressively more careful recovery techniques have completely altered the appearance of the industry. Peyrony, in 1912, produced an industry dominated by burins and scrapers: *outillage lamellaire* was only a minor component (4.1 percent) and there were no geometric microliths (Sonneville-Bordes, 1960). Fitte, using dry-sieves, increased the importance of the *outillage lamellaire* to between 27 percent and 45 percent in different levels, and produced a few geometric microliths (Fitte & Sonneville-Bordes, 1962). Finally, Bordes, using wet-sieving, produced an industry dominated by the *outillage lamellaire* (65 percent to 79 percent), in which geometric microliths were consistently present as a minor component (Bordes & Fitte, 1964). These differences become more striking if considered in another way: for every 100 larger tools (i.e. all tools apart from the *outillage lamellaire*), Bordes recovered between 185 and 375 *outils lamellaires*, Fitte between thirty-seven and 122, and Peyrony only four. While it is true that these differences could reflect local variation within the site, it seems reasonable to assume, as did Bordes, that they are chiefly due to differences in recovery technique.

In our experimental units, the total number of tools and retouched pieces is small. In all except Can Hasan III 105.6 + 105.7, the majority of the tools and retouched pieces were missed in the trench. At each site differences in size between the different tool types are such that incomplete recovery to the extent revealed by the experiments would be expected to affect the relative proportions of the different tool types. At each site there are some very small types: few or none of these were recovered in the

trench. At Franchthi Cave, in the Mesolithic layers, there are small trapezes, often less than a centimetre long, and small backed bladelets. At Can Hasan III, there are small obliquely truncated bladelets, often less than 1½ cm long; five of these, from one unit, are illustrated (Plate III): none was recovered in the trench. At Sitagroi, only a small proportion of the tools was recovered in the course of normal excavation: in a longer series of experiments, four tools were recovered in the trench as against 247 from the same earth found subsequently by sieving.

Apart from the changes made in the relative representation of the different tool types, and the fact that poor recovery may mean that some types, even ones that are in fact common, may be totally missed, there is also the consideration that the absolute number of tools in any class is being reduced. Many of the interesting newer statistical techniques require reasonably large samples: often a particular approach cannot be applied, or its results are not significant, because the available sample is too small. Sieving cannot produce more tools than are present in the earth, but it can stop us throwing most of them on the dump, and then complaining that the available sample is too small to give significant results.

Apart from traditional studies, concentrating on the tools alone, there is now increasing interest in the 'waste', from a technological viewpoint. This can give us information about tool use and resharpening as well as about manufacture, and may also tell us something about trade. For all this, a sample of the sort given by sieving is of far more use than the sort of biased and partial sample that is usually produced. Dr R. Tringham, who is working on the chipped stone from Sitagroi, tells me that without sieving, the virtual absence of any debris of flint working might have led one to believe that tools were imported on to the site ready-made, and were not even resharpened on the site; in fact, as the sieving clearly shows, there are large quantities of debris as well as the tools and utilized pieces.

Pottery

In all the experiments, substantial amounts of pottery were missed in the trench. Since many of the sherds found by sieving are small, I have given results for four units in terms of weight, rather than in terms of the number of sherds (Table 2).

Is the pottery that is missed useful, and how much difference does it make? As one might expect, the sherds that are missed in the trench are generally smaller than those that are recovered in the trench. However, among those that are missed are some larger sherds, and even small sherds are not useless: for instance, among the Late Saxon pottery from the two experimental units at Lion Yard, all the Stamford ware came from the sieves, including a rim

Table 2.   Efficiency of recovery in the trench of pottery, in four experiments, in terms of weight

	Weight of pottery (g)		
	Recovered in the trench	Missed in the trench, recovered by water-sieving	Percentage efficiency of recovery in the trench
Franchthi Cave F/A Baulk, Unit 49, mixed Neolithic and post-Neolithic	2164	1834	54
Sitagroi ZA 47, Phase III	30 740	67 912	31
Lion Yard 2a.33a, Late Saxon	109	31	78
Lion Yard 3.14, Late Saxon	67	485	12

Table 3.   Partial recovery of pottery in the trench has a biasing effect on the relative representation of the different wares: this is less marked when percentages are calculated in terms of weight, rather than number of sherds. Data from Franchthi Cave F/A Baulk, Unit 49

	Weight of pottery (g)			
	Recovered in the trench	Percentage of total diagnostic	Total recovered in the trench and by water-sieving	Percentage of total diagnostic
Coarse	881	41.9	1815	48.5
Matt painted	717	34.1	947	25.3
Slipped and burnished	151	7.2	377	10.1
Monochrome Urfirnis	142	6.7	289	7.7
Post-Neolithic	77	3.7	85	2.3
White slipped	36	1.7	76	2.0
Crusted	59	2.8	74	2.0
Burnished Urfirnis	36	1.7	64	1.7
Patterned Urfirnis	4	0.2	16	0.4
Undiagnostic	(61)	(2.9)	(255)	(6.8)
	Number of sherds			
Coarse	39	29.8	291	43.1
Matt painted	43	32.8	98	14.5
Slipped and burnished	19	14.5	86	12.7
Monochrome Urfirnis	15	11.5	146	21.6
Post-Neolithic	3	2.3	7	1.0
White slipped	3	2.3	10	1.5
Crusted	2	1.5	7	1.0
Burnished Urfirnis	6	4.6	25	3.7
Patterned Urfirnis	1	0.8	5	0.7
Undiagnostic	(8)	(6.1)	(209)	(31.0)

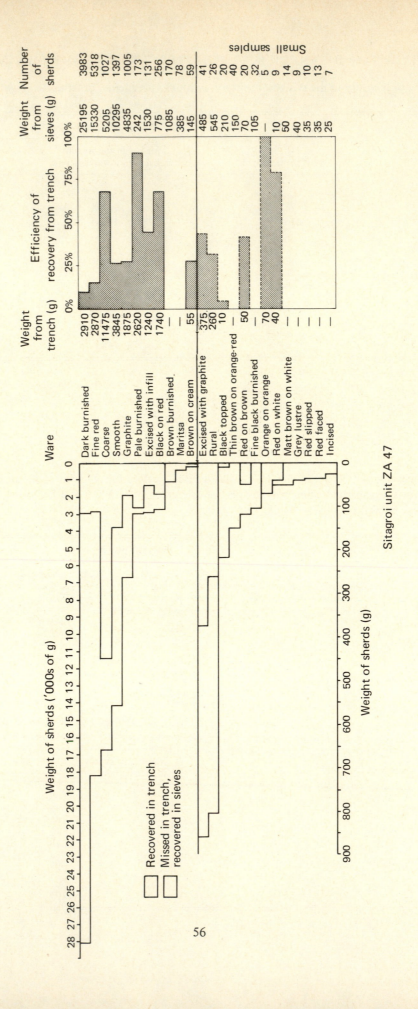

Ware	Weight from trench (g)	Efficiency of recovery from trench	Weight from sieves (g)	Number of sherds
Dark burnished	2910		25195	3983
Fine red	2870		15330	5318
Coarse	11475		5205	1027
Smooth	3845		10295	1397
Graphite	1875		4835	1005
Pale burnished	2620		242	173
Excised with infill	1240		1530	131
Black on red	1740		775	256
Brown burnished	—		1085	170
Maritsa	—		385	78
Brown on cream	55		145	59
Excised with graphite	375		485	41
Rural	260		545	26
Black topped	10		210	20
Thin brown on orange-red	—		150	40
Red on brown	50		70	20
Fine black burnished	—		105	32
Orange on orange	70		—	5
Red on white	40		10	9
Matt brown on white	—		50	14
Grey lustre	—		40	9
Red slipped	—		35	10
Red faced	—		35	13
Incised	—		25	7

Small samples

Weight of sherds ('000s of g)

Weight of sherds (g)

Recovered in trench

Missed in trench, recovered in sieves

Sitagroi unit ZA 47

56

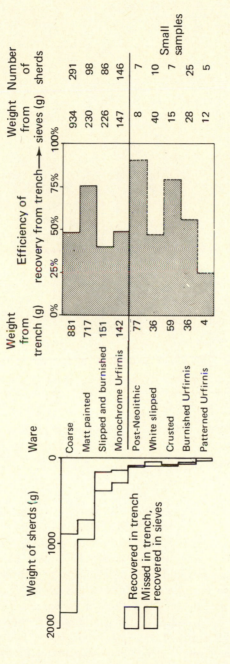

Fig. 3.   Comparison of the efficiency of recovery in the trench of different wares, in terms of weight, in two experiments. (Wares represented by fewer than five sherds are omitted.)

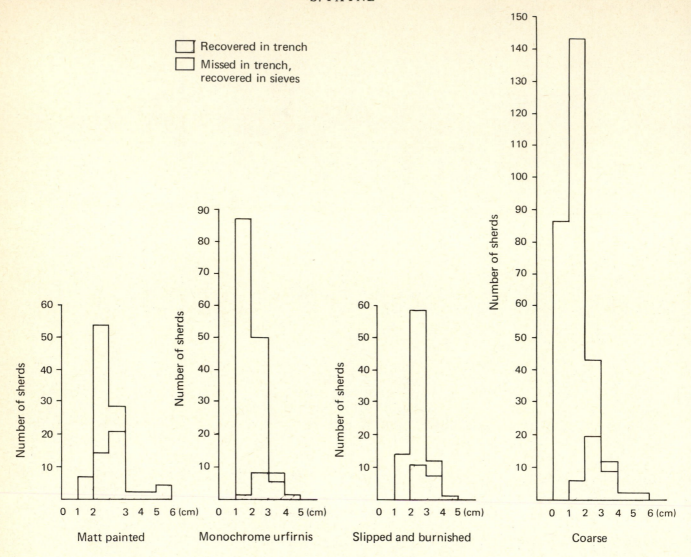

Fig. 4. Size distributions of sherds in four wares, and their relationship to the efficiency of recovery in the trench. Data from Franchthi Cave, F/A Baulk, Unit 49.

from unit 2a.33a, where recovery was otherwise fairly good.

Does sieving change the relative proportions of the different wares? In Table 3, the results of an analysis by ware of one experimental unit are given, in terms both of weight and of number of sherds. This shows that the percentages of the different wares are significantly altered. The changes are smaller if the percentages are calculated on a weight basis than if the numbers of sherds are used. In Figure 3, the efficiencies of recovery (in terms of percentage by weight) of the different wares are directly compared, and similar results are given for another experiment: these again show clearly that the efficiency of recovery in the trench is different for different wares.

This effect can be accounted for in three ways. Recovery is size-related, so that if different wares have different distributions of sherd sizes, wares that tend to break into smaller pieces will be under-represented in partial samples in comparison with wares that tend to break into larger pieces: this can be counteracted or exaggerated by the fact that smaller pieces of some wares are more diagnostic than smaller pieces of other wares. While many of the differences can be explained in this way, a third factor is that differences in colour and surface texture affect recovery.

These points are illustrated by Figure 4. In this, the size-distribution of different wares in the same unit is compared: note in particular the difference between matt-painted and monochrome Urfirnis. Secondly, as Table 4 shows, the efficiency of recovery, *even size for size*, is

PARTIAL RECOVERY AND SAMPLE BIAS: THE RESULTS OF SOME SIEVING EXPERIMENTS

Table 4.   Efficiency of recovery in the trench, as percentage of number of sherds within each size-class. Cells where the number of sherds is less than ten are bracketed

	Wares			
Size	Matt painted	Monochrome Urfirnis	Slipped and burnished	Coarse
<1 cm	(0)	1	0	0
1-2 cm	26	16	19	4
2-3 cm	72	(63)	58	45
3-4 cm	(100)	(100)	(100)	75
4-5 cm	(100)	–	–	(100)
5-6 cm	(100)	–	–	(100)

different for different wares: note especially the poorer recovery of coarse ware.

It is probably true in general to say that fine brittle and coarse crumbly wares tend to break into smaller pieces than medium wares; that small pieces of fine wares tend to be more diagnostic than small pieces of coarse wares; and that recovery tends to be better, size for size, for smooth-surfaced wares than for rough-surfaced wares, and better the greater the contrast in colour with the earth.

These changes in proportion are not in fact enough to cause any very great change in interpretation at present, but may become more important if more sophisticated analytical techniques are applied to pottery. The main effect of importance at the moment is in fine decorated wares: these tend to break very small, small fragments are often completely diagnostic, and often so little is present that efficient recovery is important: for instance, at Can Hasan I, the only stratified Halaf-type sherd found in six seasons

came from the sieves. In Figure 5, the picture given by normal recovery in the trench of the distribution of some wares in eleven units at Sitagroi is compared with the picture given by adding in the pottery recovered by sieving. There can be little doubt, here, of the value of the pottery missed in the trench.

Animal bones: the larger mammals

Most excavators would recognize that normal recovery in the trench would not yield a good sample of the bones of mice or bats. However, they would probably assume that few large bones were missed in the trench, and that they were recovering most of the identifiable bones of the larger mammals, to which this discussion is therefore restricted.

The results of one experiment are given in Figure 6 and Table 5. As these show, sieving substantially alters the relative abundance of the bones of the different animals: the number of cow bones is doubled, pig increases by a factor

Table 5.   Partial recovery of bones in the trench has a biasing effect. Recovery in the trench is more efficient for larger animals and larger bones. Data from Sitagroi ZA 47

	Cow		Pig		Sheep/Goat	
	Recovered in trench	Missed in trench, recovered in sieves	Recovered in trench	Missed in trench, recovered in sieves	Recovered in trench	Missed in trench, recovered in sieves
Single teeth	6	10	1	41	1	128
Mandible and skull fragments with teeth	2	2	5	10	1	6
Long bones and metapodia	12	7	5	21	13	73
Phalanges, carpals, and tarsals	9	13	1	35	0	111

Notes. Only the following bones were counted: teeth, when over half the tooth is present; mandible or skull fragments when more than half a tooth is present; the following parts of long-bones only if at least part of the articulating or fusion surface is present – femur distal, tibia distal, scapula glenoid, humerus distal, ulna proximal, radius proximal or distal, metapodia proximal or distal; all phalanges, astragalus, calcaneum, naviculocuboid (for pig, central and fourth tarsals), ulnar carpal, and the fused second and third carpal (for pig, third carpal). Data are only given for cow, pig, and sheep/goat: other animals were also present.

59

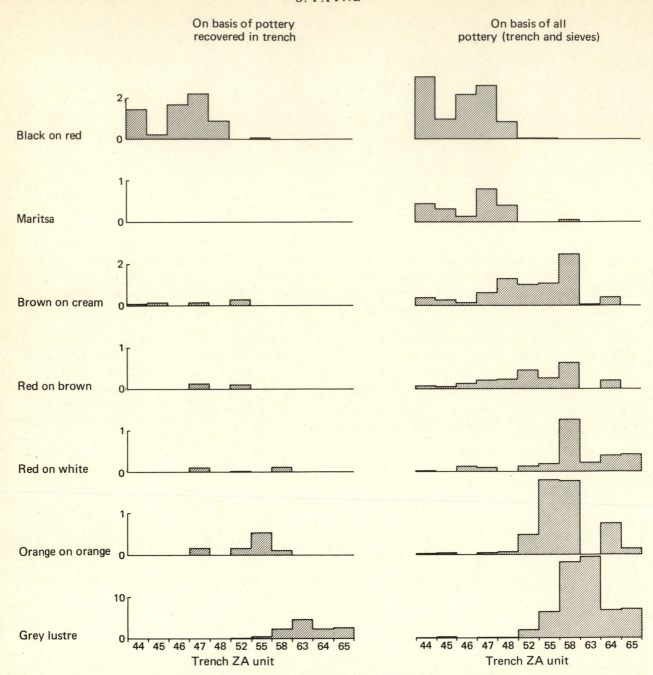

Fig. 5. The frequency of occurrence of seven wares in a series of excavated units at Sitagroi. The frequency of each ware in each unit is expressed as the number of sherds of that ware per kilogram of pottery. Thus, in a sample weighing 40 kg, 20 sherds of a particular ware give a frequency of 0.5. For grey lustre ware, only rims, handles, and bases were counted.

of ten, and sheep/goat by a factor of over twenty. As one would predict, the smaller parts of the skeleton are most strongly affected.

The degree to which this changes one's assessment of the relative importance of the animals depends on the method of calculation used. It is customary to work either in terms of the number of identifiable specimens, or in terms of the

minimum number of individuals for each species: for obvious reasons, the second is less affected than is the first by poor recovery. However, even the minimum number of individuals will be affected if the commonest bone (on which the calculation is normally based) is not efficiently recovered in the trench, and the experimental results suggest that this is not a safe assumption. A correction

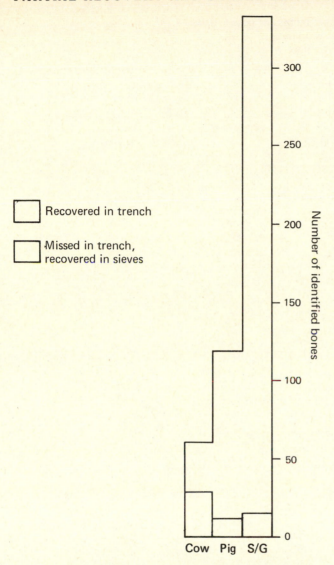

Fig. 6.   The low efficiency of recovery in the trench of the bones of sheep/goat, pig, and cow. Data from Sitagroi Unit ZA 47; see also Table 5 and Figure 7.

trench at Sitagroi to suggest some difference in butchery between cow and sheep/goat, based on the lack of sheep/goat phalanges, carpals, and tarsals. Thus, in a longer experiment at Sitagroi (Table 6), using the sample recovered in the trench, phalanges, carpals, and tarsals comprised 35 percent of the identified cow bones, but there was none of sheep/goat. However, on adding in the bones recovered by water-sieving, phalanges, carpals, and tarsals become 30 percent of the sheep/goat bones, and 37 percent of the cow bones; one would no longer conclude on this basis that there was any great difference.

Two general propositions are clear: that smaller animals will tend to be under-represented in relation to larger animals, and that the smaller bones will be more affected than the larger bones. I have confined the discussion here to large mammals: to cow, pig, and sheep/goat: the effect is even more marked for smaller mammals, such as the smaller carnivores (dog, cat, fox, badger, marten, otter), hare, rabbit, squirrel, beaver, or hedgehog, quite apart from the 'microfauna'.

Again, apart from the effect of changing the relative importance of the different species, another result of inefficient recovery is to decrease the number of any particular kind of bone in the sample submitted for analysis: this will decrease the usefulness of the sample for various kinds of metrical analysis, either making techniques useless, or reducing the significance of their results.

CONCLUSIONS

From the experiments that have been carried out so far, several conclusions emerge.

(1) Even among the usual large find categories, discussed in this paper, far more is missed by conventional methods of excavation than is generally realized. The effect of this is:

(a) The partial sample that is in fact recovered is biased: this bias may affect the accuracy of the results of any analysis, and hence the validity of any conclusion drawn from such analyses.

(b) The available size of sample in any particular category or subcategory, whether typological or chronological, will be reduced, and may therefore limit the analytical techniques that can be applied.

(2) Among the smaller find categories, not considered in this paper, sampling is even poorer: the results of sieving are often dramatic, and the yield in extra information substantial. Such categories include smaller animals (e.g. bats, insectivores, rodents, birds, reptiles, amphibians, fish, marine and terrestrial molluscs, crustaceans, and echinoderms), as well as 'small finds', such as beads, pendants, small figurines, and metal objects (Plate IV).

that can be introduced is to express the results in terms of meat weight: for some purposes this is useful. In Figure 7, for the same experiment, the relative importances of sheep/goat, pig, and cow are calculated in terms both of number of identified bones, and of meat weight, and the picture before and after sieving is shown: in both sets of figures, the effect of sieving is to increase the importance of sheep/goat at the expense of cow.

It has often been suggested that the relative representation of the different parts of the skeleton is a guide to butchery methods (e.g. Perkins & Daly, 1968). However, as the figures given in Table 5 suggest, poor recovery in the trench may give a misleading picture. One might, for instance have been tempted by the samples recovered in the

Relative abundance of cow, pig, and
sheep/goat, on basis of number of
identified bones

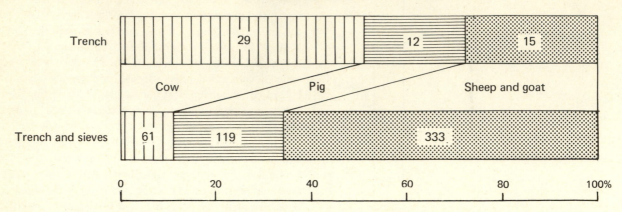

Relative importance of cow, pig, and sheep/goat
in terms of meat-weight, calculated on basis
of number of identified bones

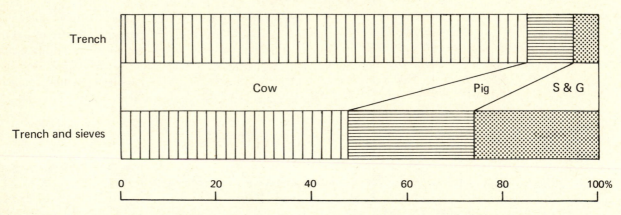

Fig. 7. The effect of partial recovery in the trench on the relative importance of cow, pig, and sheep/goat. Data from Sitagroi Unit ZA 47; see also Table 5 and Figure 6. Estimates used for calculations of meat-weight are: cow 250 kg, pig 70 kg, and sheep/goat 25 kg.

Table 6. Partial recovery in the trench missed the sheep/goat phalanges, carpals, and tarsals. Data from Sitagroi ZA 44-48 and ZA 52

	Recovered in the trench		Total recovered in the trench and by water-sieving	
	Cow	Sheep/Goat	Cow	Sheep/Goat
Phalanges, carpals, and tarsals	40 35%	0 —	98 37%	465 30%
All bones, including phalanges, carpals, and tarsals	115	94	265	1537

Note. The same bones were counted as in Table 5.

(3) The efficiency of recovery at a site is affected by a wide range of factors, including the site and soil, and the nature of the finds, as well as the personnel and conditions of excavation. Efficiency at the same site is often very variable: compare, for instance, the efficiency of recovery of pottery in Lion Yard 2a.33a and Lion Yard 3.14 (Table 2), or the efficiency of recovery of obsidian in Can Hasan III 105.6 + 105.7 and 109.1 + 109.4 (Table 1): in each case the units were dug within a few days of each other (see Appendix I).

Plate III. Obliquely truncated obsidian bladelets from Can Hasan III; these were missed in the trench, but recovered by sieving. (The scale shows centimetres.)

Plate IV. This figurine, from Sitagroi, was missed in the trench, but recovered by sieving. (The scale shows centimetres.)

These results are communicated in the hope that they will encourage excavators to sieve trial units at sites, in the way described in this paper, to test the efficiency of recovery. If they are missing nothing, they will be able to demonstrate it the better: the experiment will not have been wasted. If they are missing too much, they can consider what action can be taken.

Furthermore, it is my belief that if the data that we are at present collecting are to be of maximum use in the future, it is important that whoever works on it should know as accurately as possible how the samples were collected, so that he can know, with respect to the information he wishes to use, whether the sampling method that was used has introduced any bias that may affect the validity of his conclusions. It is therefore desirable that the method of collection should be as objective as possible, and allow precise description. At present, because this information is rarely available, it is difficult to assess material from sites excavated in the past. Sieving, and especially water-sieving, is useful in giving recovery an objective standard.

It should be stressed that I would not argue that all excavations should automatically be sieved with micron-fine sieves. Not only would this be unpractical, but also it would be a waste of time and money. Sampling must be seen in relation to the aims of an excavation. What is important is that the methods of recovery used should be determined by the questions that are being asked, and the samples that are needed to answer them.

APPENDIX I: SITES AND EXPERIMENTS

Can Hasan III.
Aceramic mound, near Karaman, at the south end of the Konya Plain, Turkey. Excavation began in 1969, under the direction of Dr D. H. French. Units used here are —

49L 105.6 + 105.7: pale silty house-floors slowly excavated by trowel under good conditions.
49L 109.1 + 109.4: darker house-floors, slowly excavated by trowel under good conditions.

Franchthi Cave.
Cave with important Neolithic and Mesolithic sequence, in southern Greece. Excavation began in 1967, under the direction of Dr T. W. Jacobsen. Unit used here is —

F/A Baulk, Unit 49N: fairly rapidly excavated with small pick and trowel.

Sitagroi.
Neolithic and Bronze Age mound, in northern Greece. Excavation began in 1968, under the direction of Dr A. C. Renfrew. Unit used here is —

ZA 47: fairly rapidly excavated by pick, in good conditions.

Lion Yard, Cambridge.
Medieval town-site in England. Excavation in 1969 under the direction of Dr J. Alexander. Units used here are —

2a.33a: carefully excavated by trowel, in poor conditions.
3.14: rapidly excavated by pick, in moderate conditions.

At three of the sites (Can Hasan, Sitagroi, and Franchthi Cave), as a result of these and similar experiments, some form of sieving or refinement of sieving technique has been introduced during the course of the excavations. At Can Hasan III, water-sieving to 1½ mm is now standard (though only the fraction above 3 mm is being sorted, the smaller material being stored as an insurance policy). At Franchthi Cave dry sieving to 3 mm is now standard, and selected columns are being water-sieved to 3 mm. At Sitagroi dry screening to 3 cm is now standard, and 1 cm was briefly used in one area. Dr Renfrew has kindly allowed me to carry out a more prolonged experiment at Sitagroi, which will shortly be published.

ACKNOWLEDGEMENTS

I am deeply grateful to the directors of the four sites at which these experiments took place: Dr J. Alexander, Dr D. H. French, Dr T. W. Jacobsen, and Dr A. C. Renfrew. Many people helped in each experiment: my thanks to all of them for their patience in a dreary and monotonous task, and especially to Dr T. W. Jacobsen and Miss J. Marriott for sorting pottery from Franchthi Cave and Sitagroi. Finally I would like to thank Dr D. H. French for continuous encouragement, help and criticism.

3. ON THE INTERPRETATION OF BONE SAMPLES FROM ARCHAEOLOGICAL SITES

SEBASTIAN PAYNE

In recent years, there has been a complete change in our approach to animal bones from archaeological sites. Fifty years ago the approach was essentially palaeontological; the bones were examined by zoologists whose chief interest lay in the animals themselves, in the reconstruction of faunal change and species evolution. Since then, and especially in the past twenty years, a growing interest in prehistoric economies and in the origins of agriculture has made archaeologists more aware of and interested in animal bones. The approach to animal bone samples has changed as new questions have been asked: the interest now lies not so much in the animals themselves as in their relationship with man and the part they played in the economy.

In the attempt to answer these questions, the analytical techniques applied to samples of animal bones have become increasingly sophisticated. The emphasis is now on the statistical treatment of whole samples rather than on the morphology of single specimens. As a result, we are making many more assumptions about our samples, about the way in which they are collected and about the ways in which animal bones accumulate on sites, as well as a number of assumptions about animal and human behaviour. These assumptions are rarely explicitly stated or discussed.

The purpose of this paper is, by questioning some of these assumptions, to re-examine our approach to the analysis and interpretation of bone samples, and our approach to some of the sampling problems involved. I would refer the reader also to a recent thoughtful paper by Higham (1968), in which he discusses some of these problems.

THE BONE SAMPLE

A bone specialist is usually sent a number of boxes or bags of bones from a site, and is asked to produce a report on the animal bones from this sample. If he is to have any confidence in his results, there are certain questions about the sample that must be considered at the outset.

Incomplete recovery and sample bias

The first question is how far the sample recovered is representative of what was in the earth that was excavated.

This problem is discussed in detail elsewhere (Payne, II. 2). As I have argued there, this question adds a further area of uncertainty in the interpretation of bone samples recovered from many excavations in the past: there are already enough problems without adding the further complication of an unknown degree of sample bias produced by incomplete recovery in the trench.

For the future, this is one difficulty that we can eliminate by improved methods of recovery. On ethical grounds, one might argue that nothing short of total recovery can be acceptable, because archaeological deposits once excavated are destroyed. It is, however, doubtful whether total recovery – to pollen grain level, for instance – is either practicable or defensible in the absence of unlimited funds. The important points are:

(1) That the methods of recovery used on an excavation should be adequate to provide samples that will answer the questions that are asked; in particular, that partial recovery should not bias the samples with respect to the data that are required to answer these questions.

(2) That an excavation report should include an accurate description of the methods of recovery used, so that any subsequent worker can assess whether the samples recovered are adequate for *his* purposes – purposes which may not have been considered by the original excavator. The technique of water-sieving is important in this respect, as it allows precise and objective description of the level of recovery attained.

Lateral variation and random sampling

The second question is to what extent the bones in the excavated areas are representative of the bones present in the earth over the whole site. Recently there has been growing interest in the division of sites into different 'activity areas', as shown by lateral differences in deposits, structures, and objects contained within the deposits. If a site shows marked lateral variation, the bones in one area may well be very different from those in another area in contemporary deposits.

Frequently, the excavation of a site is restricted to a limited area. Directors often choose to excavate a single set of closely grouped trenches, for reasons of control, or of correlation, or for architectural plans. The bone sample from such an excavation cannot, however, be assumed to be representative of the whole site, and there is no way of finding out whether it is without further excavation.

If, however, we have samples from a number of trenches widely and systematically distributed over a site, and compare the samples from these *with each other*, we can then try to assess the extent to which our results are representative of the site. Furthermore, the information obtained about any lateral variation may itself be of the greatest interest.

Vertical grouping and phasing

Generally, the bones from any site are grouped according to phases defined by artefacts — usually pottery in Neolithic and later sites. Crudely put, this is the result of an approach to sites as if they were a kind of cultural layer-cake, where the deposits within any ceramically defined phase can, as far as the contained finds are concerned, be regarded as uniform. In other words, it is assumed that any significant change in the bones will coincide with a significant ceramic change — that within a ceramic phase, significant change in the bones is unlikely to occur. Clearly this is not a reasonable assumption. Equally it is wrong to assume that no significant change happened during the occupation of a 'single period' site. It is therefore desirable to treat all the different materials from a site — pottery, bone, flint, etc. — independently. In this way we can see whether changes in these different materials do in fact coincide; also, if, for instance, a significant change in the animal bones occurs in the middle of a ceramically defined phase, it will not be missed. This approach is familiar to Palaeolithic archaeo-

logists (see, for instance, McBurney, 1967), but is not often used for later sites, to which it is equally applicable.

An example is taken from Sitagroi, a Neolithic and Bronze Age site in north Greece. Within a series of deposits in one sounding assigned to the same ceramic phase, there appears to be a significant change in the animal bones (Table 1): as can be seen, in the upper part cow is relatively scarcer and sheep/goat commoner. In the normal course of events, the bones from all these excavated units would have been treated as a single sample. Not only would this change have been missed, but the figures given for the animal bones from this phase would have been misleading, as they would have given a picture that never in fact existed. How can we be certain that either the upper or lower part is itself homogeneous? There are two ways of approaching the problem. The first is to subdivide these parts still further, and to see whether there is any significant difference between the subdivisions. On this basis, the two parts each appear to be homogeneous (Table 1). The second approach is to arrange the data unit by unit after the fashion of a pollen diagram (Fig. 1) and to use this as a basis for grouping and phasing: this is probably preferable. On this basis, the two parts again appear to be reasonably homogeneous: the fluctuations within each part are probably partly the result of small sample size in some units, and partly the result of using a count of the number of identified specimens: the occurrence of a number of bones from a single animal at a particular level could obviously cause a considerable fluctuation of no real significance.

These three questions are basic to the interpretation of any sample from a site: firstly, to what extent is the sample

Table 1. Change shown by animal bones within a ceramic phase: further subdivision suggests that the upper and lower parts are internally homogeneous

| | Number of identified specimens | | | | Number of identified specimens | | |
	Sheep/Goat	Pig	Cow		Sheep/Goat	Pig	Cow
				Units 109-15	93 67%	34 24%	12 9%
Upper part: (Units 109-20)	210 69%	73 24%	20 7%				
				Units 115-20	117 71%	39 24%	8 5%
				Units 121-5	124 57%	50 23%	42 19%
Lower part: (Units 121-30)	260 55%	118 25%	95 20%				
				Units 126-30	136 53%	68 26%	53 21%

Source. The data are taken from successive units from Trench ZB, at Sitagroi: ceramically all these units are included in Phase III. The bones of other species were also present, in smaller quantities.

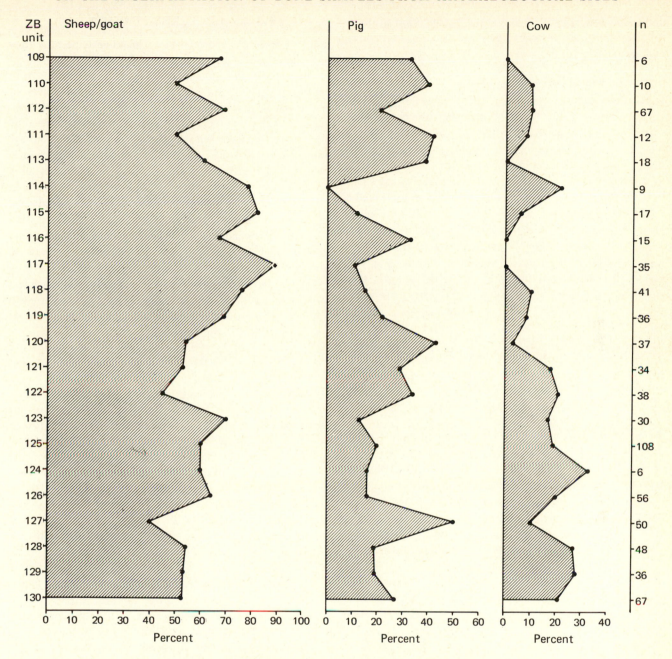

Fig. 1.   The relative abundance of bones of sheep/goat, pig, and cow in a series of excavated units from Sitagroi.

submitted for analysis representative of what was in the excavated earth; secondly, to what extent is the area that was excavated representative of the whole site; and thirdly, is there any significant change within the series of successive units that have been grouped together to make up the sample? These questions apply not only to animal bones, but to everything else recovered from sites, from pottery to molluscs. It would be misleading to suppose that using the techniques I have suggested, one was likely to be able to answer each of them with complete confidence. Using these

techniques and others like them, we can perhaps come to partial answers which will allow us to place more confidence in the representativeness and homogeneity of the samples at our disposal, and thus more confidence in the data with which we are trying to answer our questions.

THE BONES IN THE EARTH
The bone samples we recover are samples of the bones preserved in the earth. Before discussing the analysis and interpretation of these samples, it is worth thinking a little

about the processes involved in the preservation of bones on sites: the ways in which they are brought on to sites, and are removed or destroyed.

Sources of animal bones

Man killing animals for meat may be a major source of animal bones on sites, but is by no means the only source. First, he brings bones back to the site for other reasons as well. He picks up pieces of bone or antler to make tools; he brings back the heads of large animals such as bears or lions as trophies; he kills animals for their skins: if they are small, he may bring the whole animal back to skin at home, and if they are large, though skinning them where they are killed, he may leave some bones in the skin, such as phalanges or the skull. Secondly, other animals living on a site bring back bones as well. Dogs will scavenge bones from carcasses lying out in the fields; cats will bring back the animals they catch. Thirdly, many animals die naturally on a site — not only domestic animals, but also a wide range of animals commensal with man, such as storks, sparrows, mice, and rats. Finally, especially after a site has been abandoned, it is an attractive place for other animals to live — for large predators, for owls and birds of prey, for bats and for burrowing rodents. The bones left on a site are produced by all these animals, and not just by direct human agency.

Removal and destruction of bones

Equally, bones are removed from sites or destroyed in a number of ways. Man is only one of the agents. He softens and destroys bone in cookery and eating, he burns bone as fuel or to get rid of rubbish, he cuts it up and grinds it down to make tools and ornaments. He carts rubbish away from his settlements; if animals die inside a village they are often dragged some distance away. Animals are also active: scavengers such as foxes carry bones away from sites; dogs will chew bones to unrecognizable scraps. Finally, bone that lies around on or near the surface will slowly disintegrate: in some soil conditions bone will decay however deep it is buried.

The bones that are preserved in the earth reflect therefore not only human activities, but also the activities of other animals and the effects of the natural processes of decay. Few, if any, of these agencies can be assumed to act randomly: each must be seen as potentially introducing a fresh bias to the sample. Thus, for instance, the weaker bones, such as ribs and vertebrae, will tend to be more easily destroyed by dogs or by decay than the more solid teeth or phalanges. In the interpretation of bone samples it is important that we consider the possible effects of all these agencies, rather than assume that any feature of a bone sample must be explained in terms of human activities alone.

ANALYSIS AND INTERPRETATION

Bone samples are collected by archaeologists because they may be expected to tell us something about the economy of the people who inhabited the site, the environment in which they lived, and what changes these both show with time. We are trying to form a picture of the part the animals played in the economy in the context of the contemporary environment, and we are interested in the relationship between economic and environmental change. A wide range of techniques and approaches has been used in the analysis and interpretation of bone samples. It would be impossible within the scope of a single paper to discuss all these techniques. Instead, I will take five topics, and discuss them individually, considering whether the assumptions implicit in each approach are reasonable, and how we should interpret the results, especially in view of the foregoing discussion of the nature of bone samples from sites. I have selected these topics because the approach used in each is commonly used and widely accepted, and because each highlights different problems.

The relative importance of the different species present

There are two methods in general use at present to compare the relative abundance of the different species present in a bone sample. One calculates on the basis of the number of identified specimens, the other on the basis of the minimum number of individuals represented in the sample.

Use of the number of identified specimens has been criticized for a number of valid reasons. First, different animals have different numbers of bones: a dog has 52-8 phalanges, a pig 48, a cow 24, and a horse 12. Though this is easy to correct for, it is often ignored. Secondly, all bones are not equally identifiable: for instance, a small shaft fragment of a sheep/goat radius or metapodial is more readily identified than a similar fragment of a pig. This is especially true if only one large animal, such as *Bos*, is present, in which case any fragment of bone too large to be from any of the other animals present can be 'identified' — while similar fragments of smaller animals must remain unidentifiable because several smaller species are present. Thirdly, any consistent difference between the animals in the pattern of the parts of the skeleton present in the sample, caused for instance by differences in the pattern of butchery or preservation, will bias the results: one cannot assume that these patterns are the same for all the animals at a site, and frequently there is evidence that they are not. Finally, difficulty in statistical treatment is caused by sample inflation: a few animals may be represented by a large number of identified specimens. This problem is particularly obvious in the difficulty presented by whole skeletons found in articulation. For this reason, one has to be

Table 2. Comparison of the relative abundance of sheep/goat, pig, and cow, in two samples from Lerna (Lerna II and III – data from Gejvall, 1969)

	On basis of the number of identified bones		On basis of the minimum number of individuals	
	Lerna II	Lerna III	Lerna II	Lerna III
Sheep/Goat	296 53%	340 44%	35 60%	33 43%
Pig	158 28%	254 33%	12 21%	25 33%
Cow	107 19%	176 23%	11 19%	18 24%
	$\chi^2 = 9.66, df = 2,$ $p < 0.01$		$\chi^2 = 3.97, df = 2,$ $0.20 > p > 0.10$	

Note. When the two are compared using the number of identified bones, there is a significant difference at the 1% level, but if the minimum number of individuals is used, the difference is not significant at the 10% level!

extremely careful in the application of some statistical tests to data based on the number of identified specimens. In Table 2 the relative abundance of pig, sheep/goat, and cow in two different samples is compared. In terms of the number of identified specimens, the samples are significantly different at the 1 percent level. However, in terms of the minimum number of individuals, the samples are not even significantly different at the 10 percent level!

Use of the minimum number of individuals (MIND) is not, however, without its problems either. First, it is unusual for authors to state how they arrive at this figure, and it appears that many different methods are in use. Secondly, as has frequently been pointed out, use of MIND tends to exaggerate the importance of the rarer animals: Gejvall (1969) has suggested that at least 300 bone fragments of a species are needed for a realistic estimate of MIND. This may in fact be no more than a salutary reminder of the importance of having sufficiently large samples. Thirdly, any consistent difference between the different animals in, for instance, the pattern of butchery, or preservation, of the commoner bones (on which estimates of MIND are normally based) will cause errors.

Some of the problems involved can be resolved by comparing the representation of the different species independently on a number of different bones, chosen because they come from different parts of the body, are reasonably common in bone samples, and range sufficiently in size to test sample-bias due to poor recovery. Such a selection might, for instance, include the left distal femur, the right distal humerus, the right astragalus, the left ulnar carpal, and the right mandible. If the relative abundance of the different species was similar in all five counts, one

would have some confidence that the figures were a fair picture of the bone sample; if there were differences between the counts, it would probably be obvious whether they fell into a pattern, and, if so, what was then worth counting to investigate further. As an example of this kind of approach, Figure 2 presents data from Lerna, a Neolithic and Bronze Age site in Greece (Gejvall, 1969). The sample clearly shows considerable differences between sheep/goat and cow in the representation of the different parts of the skeleton: the ratio between sheep/goat and cow varies from about 4:1 (for the scapula or the mandible) to about 1:10 (for the phalanges). These differences could be explained in a number of ways; an obvious possibility is that many of the smaller sheep/goat bones were missed in excavation. If this were so, one might suggest that the upper ratio (c. 4:1) was the best available estimate, and that a ratio based on the number of identified bones (c. 4:3) or on the minimum number of individuals (c. 5:2) would underestimate the abundance of sheep/goat in relation to cow.

With this kind of approach, one can determine the relative abundance of the different species in a bone sample. In the past osteologists have often been content to take such figures, sometimes converted to meat weights, and present this as the final result of the analysis. Secondary products, such as milk, wool, or traction, are either ignored or discussed in passing, as of minor importance. The main reason for this is that it is obviously difficult to assess what use man made of secondary products on the basis of a sample of animal bones. After all, one might argue, one cannot tell whether the secondary products were used or not, but one can reasonably assume that the meat was eaten: this is the only safe basis on which to work.

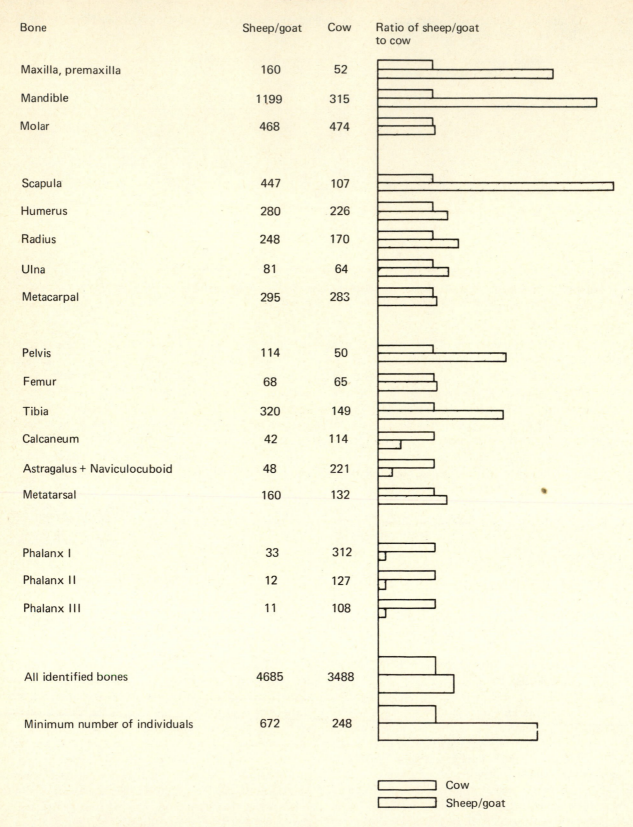

Bone	Sheep/goat	Cow	Ratio of sheep/goat to cow
Maxilla, premaxilla	160	52	
Mandible	1199	315	
Molar	468	474	
Scapula	447	107	
Humerus	280	226	
Radius	248	170	
Ulna	81	64	
Metacarpal	295	283	
Pelvis	114	50	
Femur	68	65	
Tibia	320	149	
Calcaneum	42	114	
Astragalus + Naviculocuboid	48	221	
Metatarsal	160	132	
Phalanx I	33	312	
Phalanx II	12	127	
Phalanx III	11	108	
All identified bones	4685	3488	
Minimum number of individuals	672	248	

Cow
Sheep/goat

Fig. 2. Variation in the relative abundance of sheep/goat and cow from Lerna when calculated from different bones.

An example shows how misleading this can be. Many of the bones lying round the modern Turkish village of Can Hasan are horse bones, and according to this argument, one would on this basis conclude that horse was an important source of meat. One would be wrong: for religious reasons horses are not eaten. When they die they are left to rot, after being dragged out of the village if they die there. The villagers also keep dogs, and these strip the carcases, bringing bones back to the village to chew; it is for this reason that there are so many horse and donkey bones lying around. Horses are important to the villagers as draught animals, and it is this importance that is reflected by the bones lying round the village. Thus meat supply is no simpler to assess than secondary products.

The very term 'secondary products' is itself misleading: they are often far more important than the meat or hide produced when an animal is killed. Thus, for instance, the food value of the milk produced by a cow during its life is of the order of ten or twenty times the food value of a dead cow. Traction can be even more important: the food value of the grain produced each year from the ground cultivated with two bullocks is of the order of twenty-five times the food value of the bullocks themselves. Many other secondary products are important, but, as they are not eaten, cannot be directly compared with meat in this way; for instance wool, transport, or dung (as a fertilizer, or for heating). A vital aspect of these secondary products is that they are produced more or less continuously: often they play an important part in daily subsistence, while the large quantity of meat produced by killing an animal is an occasional luxury. One has only to look at modern peasant economies to see that secondary products are generally far more important than meat: the one major exception to this generalization is the pig, which though important as an efficient converter of vegetable foods (especially acorns, maize, or barley) into fat and meat, produces little in the way of useful secondary products.

It seems reasonable to suggest that secondary products were equally important in the Bronze Age or the Neolithic, and that the origins of domestication are intimately linked with the exploitation of secondary products. The moral of this, in terms of the analysis of bone samples from archaeological sites, is that these samples must not be interpreted simply in terms of meat, without consideration of secondary products. A bone sample represents a number of potential resources, all of which must be considered in interpretation if one is to arrive at an understanding of the part each animal played in the economy.

The interpretation of groups and clusters

In considering the bones of a single species (or of a number of species that are difficult to distinguish, such as sheep and goat) from a sample, bone specialists frequently make use of histograms or scatter diagrams to demonstrate that the bones can be divided into more or less distinct groups or clusters.

Kollau, for instance, discussing the reindeer remains from the Ahrensburgian occupation at Stellmoor, demonstrated that there were gaps in the distributions of the lengths of several bones (Fig. 3). He interpreted these as due to the absence of reindeer of certain age-groups, and inferred that the site was seasonally occupied (Kollau, in Rust, 1943).

The distribution of the lengths of ibex metapodia from the Grotte de l'Observatoire shows two peaks. This was interpreted by Boule as the result of sexual dimorphism (Boule & Villeneuve, 1927).

The caprine metapodia from the Greek Neolithic site of Nea Nikomedeia fell clearly into two clusters: I have suggested that these should be identified as sheep and goats (Payne, 1969b).

The presence of different size-groups among the bovine bones from Seeberg Burgäschisee-Süd (Stampfli, in Boessneck, Jéquier, and Stampfli, 1963) has been interpreted in various ways (Grigson, 1969). Two basic causes are considered: sexual dimorphism and difference in size between wild *Bos primigenius* and domestic cattle; the only difference between the various interpretations is exactly how each group should be identified, and whether there is a group of animals of intermediate size or not (Fig. 4).

The problem is one of interpretation: when a scatter diagram or histogram shows convincing clusters or peaks, there are many possible reasons.

First, the presence of two or more separate populations within the sample considered is an obvious explanation. The populations might be kept from interbreeding by genetic barriers (e.g. sheep and goat), by behavioural barriers, or even by human intervention: this is how many breeds of domestic animals are kept separate.

Secondly, if the sample contains only the bones of a single interbreeding population, there are at least four kinds of explanation for grouping in the sample.

(a) **Age grouping**: if for some reason the sample was drawn mainly from certain age classes, and intervening age classes are scarce or absent, grouping may be observed. In many situations an animal is either killed towards the end of immaturity, when it shows the best return in meat for the grazing it has used, or is left to join the adult flock or herd, and only killed when its output of secondary products starts to decline. This would obviously produce two distinct groups in the bone sample.

Another possible reason for this kind of grouping is the seasonal occupation of a site (as invoked by Kollau for the

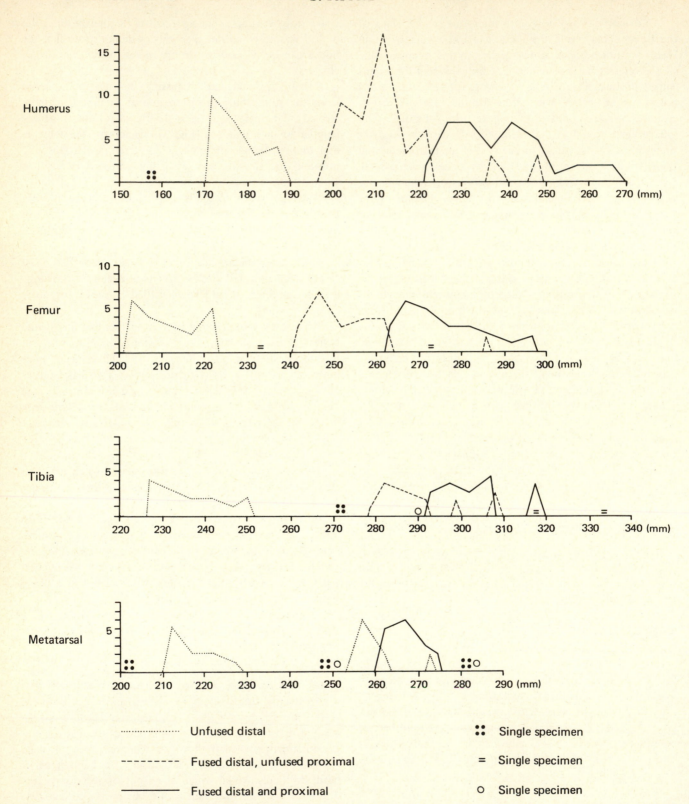

Fig. 3.   Length distributions of reindeer bones from Stellmoor (after Kollau, in Rust, 1943).

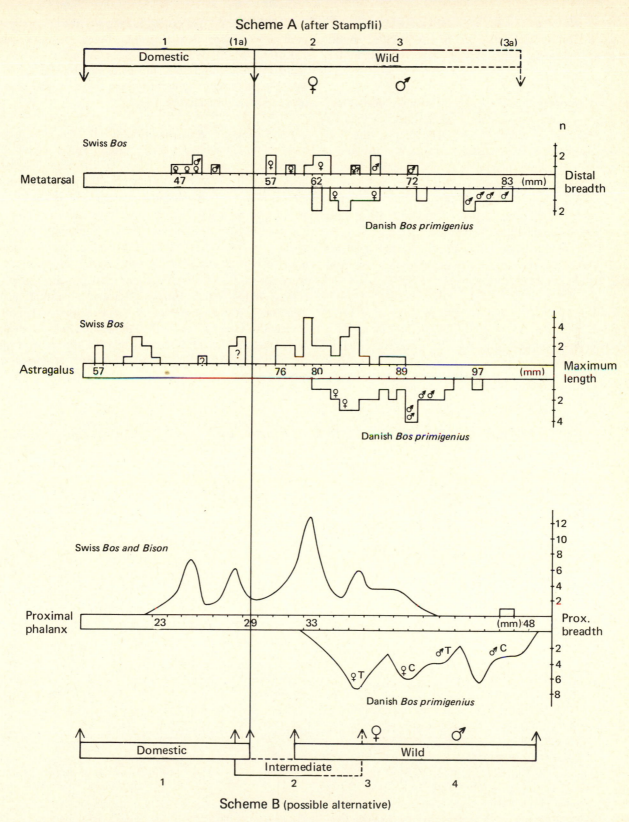

Fig. 4. Alternative interpretations for the *Bos* measurements at Seeberg Burgäschisee-Süd (after Grigson, 1969).

reindeer at Stellmoor), or the seasonal killing of an animal. In Greece, for instance, pigs are normally killed in the winter, as the meat is regarded as a health risk in the summer.

(b) **Sex grouping**: Many species are sexually dimorphic: in mammals, males tend to be larger and heavier than females. Frequently, especially in artiodactyls, there is sufficient difference for measurements to fall into two distinct groups. Castrates may also form a separate group; castration has been an important part of some patterns of exploitation: wethers have been important in wool production, and bullocks are used for draught and for meat production. Occasionally a further complication may be provided by intersexes: in some breeds of dairy goat, for instance, the incidence of pseudohermaphrodites may be as high as 10-15 percent (Asdell, 1964).

(c) **Phenotypic grouping**: If groups from one interbreeding population are kept in different conditions, they may differ very considerably. Pigs, for instance, raised on different diets show very considerable skeletal differences (McMeekan, 1940, 1941; McMeekan & Hammond, 1940).

Such differences — for instance if some of the goats kept in a village were kept in or around the houses the whole year, and others were taken up into the hills in the summer — could well lead to grouping in a bone sample. Similarly one would expect considerable differences between pigs kept in sties and pigs herded in the open.

(d) **Genotypic grouping**: Genetic differences can also cause grouping within a single interbreeding population. The simplest case is the expression of different alleles at a single gene locus: blue and brown eye is a familiar example in man. Though it is generally true that size and shape are affected by so many different loci that variation is more or less continuous, and there is no clear grouping within a single population, there are many exceptions: hornlessness is an obvious example. Perhaps the most interesting case is the otter sheep. This was a curious breed of sheep kept in Massachusetts, which had very short legs, rather like a dachshund; it was easily herded and enclosed. The otter characteristics arose suddenly, and behaved in breeding as a single recessive allele: on crossing with sheep of normal appearance, the offspring were either otter or normal; no intermediates were produced (Landauer & Chang, 1949).

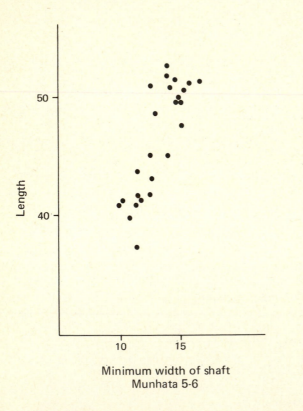 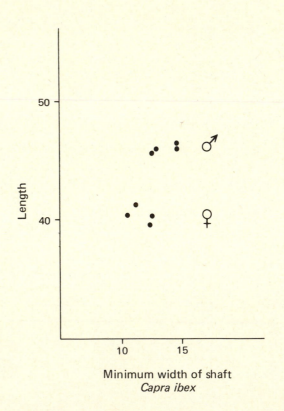

Fig. 5. Grouping in measurements of caprine first phalanges from Munhata 5-6 (after Ducos, 1969) and figures given by Bosold (1966) for male and female *Capra ibex*. (The four figures shown for each sex are means for inner and outer phalanges of the fore and hind legs.)

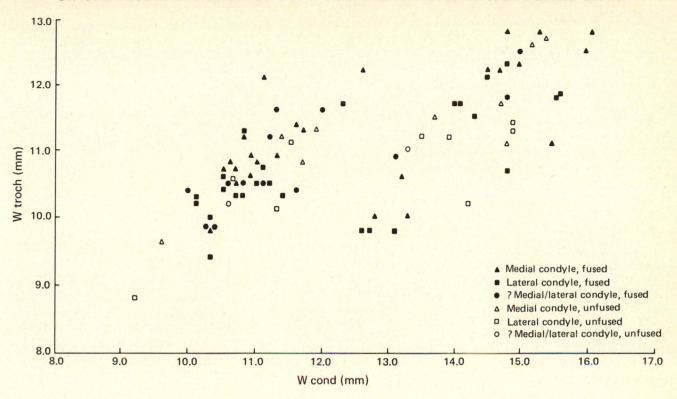

Fig. 6. Grouping in measurements of caprine metacarpals from Nea Nikomedeia.

When grouping or clustering is observed in a sample from an archaeological site, there is an unfortunate tendency among authors to present one interpretation without stating or discussing any alternatives. Ducos, for instance, gives a scatter diagram for Caprinae first phalanges at Munhatta 5-6 (Fig. 5), and states that on that basis, 'it is clear that two species of large Caprinae are present' (Ducos, 1969). It could, however, be argued that an equally plausible interpretation is that the two groups are males and females: compare, for example, figures given by Bosold (1966) for male and female *Capra ibex* (also shown on Fig. 5). Frequently, once stated, some alternative explanations can be discarded on the basis of the available evidence. It was, for instance, possible to show that the groups observed in the Caprine metapodia at Nea Nikomedeia (Fig. 6) were not simply different age groups from the same population on the grounds that each group contained both fused and unfused specimens.

The situation is complicated by the possibility that the explanation may lie not in any single cause, but in a combination of causes. I have already mentioned the bovines at Seeberg Burgäschisee-Süd, where grouping is explained by sexual dimorphism and the presence of two populations.

It is sometimes possible to increase or decrease the effects of one of the possible causes, and this may help in interpretation. The most obvious case is age grouping. Some measurements can only be taken on the bones of individuals over a certain age, and therefore cannot give data for animals below that age, either because the bone is unfused and therefore the measurement cannot be taken, or, in the case of teeth, because they have not yet erupted, and cannot be measured. If one wishes to minimize the possible effect of the presence of different age groups, it is advisable to use measurements that can only be taken on adult or nearly adult animals, such as the length of the calcaneum, or the length of the fully erupted tooth row. If, however, one is interested in the possibility of age grouping, one should use a measurement that can be taken on all age classes, such as the length of the astragalus, or the proximal breadth of the metacarpus. Kollau, for instance, measured both fused and unfused bones and added a constant to the measurements of the unfused bones to allow for the missing epiphyses (Kollau, in Rust, 1943).

The main value of histograms and scatter diagrams is that they provide an objective way of dividing bones into groups, at the level where normal morphological distinction becomes difficult or too subjective. They are useful, for instance, in distinguishing sheep from goat, or males from females. It is, however, important that the measurements used are carefully chosen, and that one should consider all the possible reasons for an observed grouping, rather than assume immediately that any particular explanation is the correct interpretation.

The relative representation of different age classes

Considerable attention is currently paid to data about the ages of the animals represented in bone samples. Interest in this subject dates from over twenty years ago, when Coon used a high percentage of immature individuals in a sample of sheep bones from Belt Cave as a criterion for the recognition of domestication (Coon, 1951).

The problems associated with age breakdowns are of two kinds: first, how to establish a reliable age breakdown for a particular species in a bone sample, and secondly, how to interpret the results. It is important to make two points straight away. First, if an age breakdown is to be reasonably useful, the results must be based on bones from a single population: if, for instance, we are told that 45 percent of the sheep/goat metapodia are unfused, this in itself is of limited value to our understanding either of the sheep or the goats. Secondly, a simple distinction between adult and immature is inadequate: we need a breakdown into a number of age classes. Fortunately the tendency in recent publications has been in this direction.

Age breakdowns are generally based on data on epiphyseal fusion, and the eruption and wear of the teeth. Fusion and eruption sequences are variable — probably even more variable than the published figures suggest. As yet, most of the available information applies to improved breeds, kept in good conditions. We know already that tooth eruption dates and epiphyseal fusion dates differ very considerably between individual breeds within a single species. There is also evidence that nutrition has a significant effect on tooth eruption (Wiener & Purser, 1957). Most of the work done so far on ageing in living animals has concentrated on the teeth, and especially on the incisors, as this is of most practical use to the farmer or veterinary surgeon. Less is known about epiphyseal fusion, and much of the available information is based on radiographic evidence of epiphyseal closure; Silver (1969) points out that an epiphysis that is radiographically fused may still separate from the shaft after the cartilage has been broken down by cooking or decay. This is a field where, if archaeologists want more information, we will probably have to collect it ourselves: it is of little practical value to anyone else.

A further difficulty that is not usually discussed is how one should in fact calculate from the kind of data normally available from a bone sample. For instance, in Table 3 information is given about the distal tibiae of sheep/goat in a bone sample from Greece. From this, depending on what one chooses to count, the percentage of unfused specimens

Table 3. Data for fused and unfused sheep/goat distal tibiae in a sample from Sitagroi (ZA 44-48 and 52, ZB 121-131), to illustrate the problem of how one should calculate the 'percentage unfused'

	Complete	Nearly complete	Half	Small fragments
Fused ends	17	7	2	8
Unfused shafts	4	–	–	7
Unfused epiphyses	2	2	1	7

could *justifiably* be given as anything from 14.3 percent (4 in 28) or 39.3 percent (22 in 56).

Once we have decided on how to calculate from the data, how should information about the relative representation of different age classes in a bone sample be interpreted? The obvious question is whether we can take the sample, in this respect, to be representative of the kill-off. This would involve the assumption that none of the factors intervening between the kill-off and the bone sample (as discussed earlier) have biased the sample, and this seems an unreasonable assumption. The most obvious objection, is that if there has been any substantial destruction of bone by dogs, or by decay, the softer and more fragile bones of immature animals will be likely to suffer most. Examination of the figures in Table 3 will show that a higher proportion of the unfused shafts and epiphyses are small fragments than of the fused ends: this is perhaps a reflection of the greater fragility of unfused tibiae. It is not, however, safe to assume that the immature bones will always be under-represented, and that we can take the figure for the percentage of immature specimens as a minimum figure. An obvious case to the contrary is the probable selection of fused bones for making into tools: this might result in the over-representation of unfused specimens in the bone sample, especially if the osteologist does not include the bone tools in his sample.

These problems can be overcome in part by counting and calculating independently on a number of bases, and testing whether these give consistent results. Probably one should be cautious of any bone commonly used as a tool (often this applied to the distal metapodia), and also any bone that is unexpectedly scarce, on the grounds that if a higher proportion has been destroyed, it is probable that the results will be more heavily biased. Having arrived at a reasonably consistent picture, this can then be used with the proviso that young animals, and especially very young animals, may well be under-represented.

A further problem is that a bone sample does not only

consist of kill-off, but also may include animals that died of natural causes. In some circumstances a sample may even consist only of such animals, without any kill-off component, as for instance would be the case for the horse bones in the village of Can Hasan — though here, the absence of any cut-marks on the bones might arouse suspicion, and in some circumstances cut-marks can provide a good cross-check. Recognizing these difficulties, and the need to bear them in mind in interpretation, it still seems worthwhile to collect information about the relative representation of the different age-classes in the sample, because the relative representation of the different age-classes in the kill-off is obviously related to the way in which man uses an animal, and this is one of the things we want to know. Even when, for the sake of argument, one has assumed that the sample gives a fair picture of the kill-off, there are other assumptions that workers have in the past been content to make that are of doubtful validity.

It has, in the past, often been assumed that hunters will tend to kill wild animals randomly. This is, for instance, implicit in Bökönyi's statement that 'there is certain evidence for animal keeping on a prehistoric settlement if: 1) the proportion of age groups of a domesticable species is not the same as found normally in the wild population . . .' (Bökönyi, 1969a). Higgs & Jarman (1969) have commented that a hunting culture may in certain situations kill a high percentage of young animals. In fact, very little is known about what hunters do kill, and it is exceedingly unlikely that any hunter would in fact succeed in killing randomly, even if he were trying to. Anyone who doubts this point has only to talk to an ecologist about the problems associated with trying to assess the relative representation of the different age groups in a wild population! What a hunter in fact killed would depend on a variety of factors, including the behaviour of the animals, the hunting methods used, and the preferences of the hunter.

Equally, when the man-animal relationship has become closer — when the animal has become to some extent dependent on man, as well as man being dependent on the animal, for this is one way of looking at domestication — and when man can in theory choose exactly which animals he will kill, what he in fact kills will again depend on a number of factors. Among other things, it will depend on the products for which the animal is being kept, on the seasonal availability of fodder and water, on the fertility of the animals, on whether the owner wishes the herd or flock to increase in number or to stay at the same level, on how much is known about the management and reproduction of the animal, and on whether selective breeding is practised. A change in any one of these might cause a considerable change in the kill-off.

Useful though it would be, one cannot simply distinguish a limited number of different kinds of man-animal relationship, or patterns of exploitation, each distinguished by a characteristic kill-off pattern. The same pattern can be the product of a number of different situations, and we must use other evidence to distinguish between them.

Problems in demonstrating and interpreting size change

The literature is full of comparisons of size between animals from different sites or from different phases at the same site, in order to document changes in size that have occurred in the past. Interest has been particularly directed to size changes, as it has often been said that domestication frequently causes a decrease in size, and therefore that size decrease can be indicative of domestication.

In theory, there are few problems in establishing that a size change has occurred. One measures, for example, the lengths of the bovine astragali from two successive phases at a site, compares the results, and arrives at the conclusion that the bovine astragali in Phase B are significantly smaller than those in Phase A. One therefore concludes that the cattle have grown smaller between Phase A and Phase B. This conclusion is open to criticism for a number of reasons.

Two assumptions made are that each of the samples is drawn from a single population, and that the population represented by the sample in Phase A is ancestral to the population represented by the sample in Phase B. Frequently these are not safe assumptions: the problem, for instance, of distinguishing between the bones of the various *Caprini* (e.g. *Ovis, Capra, Ammotragus*) or of the *Bovini* (e.g. *Bos, Bison, Bubalus*) even at generic, let alone at specific level, in the fragmentary state in which they are usually found on archaeological sites, is well known. Thus an observed change may simply be caused by a change in the relative frequency of bones of different species or populations, or by the replacement of one species by another. Higgs, for instance, reports a size decrease in the caprine bones from Haua Fteah between the Capsian and the Neolithic, and relates this to the introduction of sheep and goat, and a relative decrease in representation in the bone sample of the larger *Ammotragus* (Higgs, 1967a).

Even assuming that one is dealing with samples drawn from single populations, and that the earlier population is in fact ancestral to the later population, there are still difficulties. Let us return to the example given above — the bovine astragali in Phase A and Phase B. A number of possible reasons could explain their difference in size without there having been a size change in cattle between Phase A and Phase B.

First, sample B may contain a higher proportion of astragali of immature individuals than sample A: thus the average length of the astragali would be smaller. For this reason, in investigating size change it is unwise to use a measurement like the length of the astragalus: as has already been pointed out, the astragalus is measurable from birth, and grows substantially thereafter. It is clearly better to take a measurement that cannot be taken on the bones of younger animals, and thus more closely reflects adult stature — for instance, the length of the fused calcaneum (the calcaneum fuses only when the animal is almost fully grown).

Secondly, even if there is a difference between the lengths of the calcanea in the two samples, this does not prove that a size change has happened. If, for instance, sample B contains mainly cows, and sample A bullocks, the average length of the calcanea in sample B would be smaller.

If one can establish that there has been a size change, there are several possible explanations: one should not immediately assume that there has been a genetic change, and still less that the change is the result of deliberate selection. The change may simply be phenotypic, the result of a change in the animal's environment. An obvious possibility is a change in nutrition: Steffensen (1958) has for instance related changes in height in Icelanders in the past eight centuries to changes in nutritional level, using the frequency of famine years as an index of nutritional level. Other factors may also be important.

If the change is in fact genotypic, it may be the result of the immigration or introduction of new breeding stock, or of change within the population caused by genetic drift or by selection. Man is simply one selective agent — often a very effective one. It must be remembered that man, as well as selecting deliberately, can, in the course of his management or exploitation of an animal, select unintentionally — sometimes in an undesirable direction. If, for instance, in a flock or herd, most of the young males are killed off for meat, and if the larger individuals are chosen for killing because they give more meat, the end result will be selection for smaller size. Similarly, if bullocks are used for haulage, and the largest bull calves are castrated because they will make the strongest bullocks, again the effect will be selection for smaller size. There is however no particular reason to assume that the effect of a closer man-animal relationship is to select for smaller size; also the fact that a size decrease has not taken place is no real evidence that there has been no change in the man-animal relationship.

Natural selection can be assumed to operate the whole time, in domestic as well as in wild populations. Populations are not static; they are continually adjusting both to the current environment, and to the effects of new mutations and gene recombinations. It is sometimes assumed that changes in the size of wild animals occur predictably in obedience to Bergman's rule; that when the climate grows warmer, a species can be expected to become smaller, and conversely that when it grows colder, a species will become larger. There is often a tendency to assume therefore that once the Postglacial climate has stabilized, the size of wild species remained more or less stable, and we can safely interpret any size decrease during the last ten thousand years as the result of domestication. This is not a safe assumption: in north-west Europe, for instance, bears and wildcats have decreased in size during the Postglacial, foxes have stayed the same size, and badgers and otters have grown larger (Kurtén, 1968; Jarman & Wilkinson, II. 4).

Our conclusion must be that there are many possible reasons for size change. The subject is of interest, because one can plausibly suggest that changes in size may be related to the way in which an animal is kept, bred, and used, but there are other possible factors that must be considered.

Season of occupation

Recently, there has been increasing interest in determining the season or seasons of the year during which sites were occupied. Faunal samples offer various possible approaches to this problem.

First, the bones of migrant species can be used, especially birds. Some species of fish are anadromous, and at the breeding season swim up rivers from the sea where they live normally, to lay their eggs. Many mammals migrate seasonally.

Secondly, direct seasonal data can be derived in various ways. Antler, for instance, grows and is shed in an annual cycle. In many situations, species breed only during a short period of the year, and thus the bones of late foetal or very young individuals can be used to give an indication of season. Birds' eggshell survives well on some sites, and again in many species and situations gives seasonal information.

Thirdly, size grouping in histograms can sometimes be interpreted in terms of a seasonal killing pattern (see, for instance, Fig. 3, where Kollau's interpretation, as already discussed, seems entirely reasonable). Age breakdowns, especially on the basis of tooth eruption and wear, can be used in the same way, to see whether they show grouping: using this kind of evidence, Ewbank et al. (1964) were able to suggest that autumn killing of sheep was not practised at the English Iron Age site of Barley.

Finally there are various structures, such as fish otoliths and the shells of marine molluscs, that show growth rings that can be used to give seasonal data as well as for age determination. Recent work indicates that mammalian teeth may also be able to provide this kind of information: more experimental work needs to be done, but this is of great potential interest, as it could be used for adult specimens.

In using such techniques, there are various problems of which we should be aware. First, we should use a little caution in the way in which we use detailed information about species at present to interpret the past, the ranges and habits of species can change considerably over short periods — note, for instance, the spread of breeding stations of the fulmar petrel (*Fulmarus glacialis*) in Britain in the past century, or the spectacular spread of the collared dove (*Streptopelia decaocto*) in the last few years. Although in general terms the situation has probably not changed greatly in the past seven thousand years, before then one should be correspondingly more careful. It might, for instance, be tempting to use seasonal data about reindeer in Lapland today to interpret Magdalenian samples from France — but a major difference between Lapland today and France then is the number of daylight hours at different times of the year: France was never the land of the midnight sun. As the number of daylight hours can be of critical significance to breeding cycles, the seasonal pattern of reindeer breeding in Lapland today cannot be directly applied to Pleistocene France.

A related problem is one of geography. Seasonal data that may be of great interest and use in Britain or Denmark, may be valueless in areas where the seasonal patterns are less well-marked, or different in areas with different patterns. It is however, difficult to generalize or predict. In Britain, for instance, or the United States, goats conceive most commonly between mid-September and mid-November, and only rarely outside the period August-January. In India, the Jumna Pari goat mates most frequently from July to October, but a dwarf breed, the Bar Bari goat, breeds at any time of the year. In New Zealand, surprisingly, feral goats breed throughout the year! (Asdell, 1964).

A third problem is one of interpretation. Antler, for instance, can be traded, or kept and carried around as a convenient piece of raw material, and seasonal indications could be misleading, especially as antler is only seasonally available. Consider, for instance, a reindeer hunter's summer camp. If the hunters use antler tools, and keep any spare antler around, this will give autumn or winter indications, as summer antler is soft and useless; for this reason also, the antler of the animals killed during the summer, if brought back to the site at all, will be very prone to decay, and may have vanished completely. In this case the apparent cross-check provided by the presence of abundant reindeer bones on the site is misleading. As already discussed, a bone sample is the product of many agents besides man — and this must apply to seasonal data as well. Eggshell, for instance, may reflect birds nesting in deserted houses as well as men eating eggs. This kind of problem can

often be resolved once the question has been asked. On the question of eggshell, for instance, it is possible to identify it within limits, and, if preservation is good, hatched and unhatched eggshell can be distinguished (C. Tyler, pers. comm.).

It is probably unwise to rely too heavily on any one strand of evidence, and one should remember that some seasons have many more indicators than others. If, for instance, there is positive indication in the form of neonate animals, and eggshell, for spring or early summer occupation, one should then try to think of what positive indication one would accept for winter occupation, before arguing that the site was occupied *only* in the spring and summer. One should always remember that seasonal use of some resources may give what appears to be a seasonal pattern at a site in fact occupied all the year round: I have already mentioned the seasonal consumption of pigs in Greece. While it may be possible to argue convincingly that a site was occupied at some seasons, it is far more difficult to try to show that it was unoccupied at any season of the year, or that it was occupied by fewer people during part of the year.

Having made these points, nevertheless it seems to me that it is possible, with care, to build up a reasonably convincing dossier on the season of occupation at any site, as long as the information used is as broadly based as possible, and one is careful to make as few assumptions as possible.

THE USE OF DATA FROM PUBLISHED BONE REPORTS

So far, I have assumed that one is dealing with an actual bone sample. Further problems arise when one tries to use the data provided about a bone sample in a published report either for comparative purposes or in an attempted reinterpretation.

Any bone report is simply one man's view; there is no such thing as a definitive bone report. Two different osteologists, working on the same samples, may well come to different conclusions, and the basic data they produce will almost certainly differ. This does not mean that either is incompetent, but simply that they work in different ways. The data they collect and present will naturally reflect the particular questions they are interested in and the ways in which they try to answer them.

Especially over identification, there are wide differences in opinion and practice, not only on the validity of particular criteria, but also on whether any individual fragment is identifiable or not. Most fragments are only identifiable within limits, and published identifications usually rely largely on reasonable presumption. Take, for instance, a broken calcaneum listed as 'sheep/goat', from a Neolithic site in Europe. On morphological grounds alone, a number of other identifications are probably equally possible: depending on the state of the specimen, these might include ibex, chamois, saiga antelope, and roe deer. In the absence of indications to the contrary, most authors would probably list the bone as 'sheep/goat', rejecting the other possibilities because they seem less likely, usually because there is abundant positive evidence for the presence of sheep/goat in the sample, and only little or no positive evidence for the presence of the other species. Other authors might list the bone under a broader heading, such as 'sheep/goat/roe deer', or 'small artiodactyl', or even regard it as unidentifiable and not list it at all. Problems like this are tackled in different ways by different workers, but are rarely discussed.

As a result, great care is needed in the use or reinterpretation of data extracted from published bone reports. If we use the data in a way which was not envisaged by the author of the report, we may be unaware that the way in which it was compiled makes it unsuitable for such use. Secondly, as a corollary, it is desirable that osteologists, as well as producing data and conclusions, should give more information in their reports about the way in which they have produced the data — how they have worked, what they have counted, and what criteria they have used. Thirdly, bone samples from sites should not be thrown away after the report has been written.

CONCLUSION

In the analysis of a sample recovered by excavation one should begin by asking three questions:

(1) To what extent is the sample submitted for analysis representative of what was in the excavated earth?

(2) To what extent is the area that was excavated representative of the whole site?

(3) Is there any significant change within the series of successive units that have been grouped together to make up the sample?

I have suggested various ways in which we can try to answer these questions. Two aspects are of particular importance.

Firstly, sampling should be determined by the aims of an excavation, the questions that are asked, and the samples that are required to answer them. Therefore, when bone samples are one of the objects of an excavation, it is desirable that the osteologist should be a member of the excavation team from the start, and should play a part in helping the director to decide on the strategy of investigation.

Secondly, if the samples recovered by an excavation are to be of maximum value in the future, it is important that precise and objective information should be provided about the way in which the site was excavated and the samples were recovered. The same consideration applies also to reports on material from sites: unless working methods are described it is difficult to assess the data presented, or to compare it with data for other sites.

The bone samples we recover from sites are samples of the bones preserved in the earth. If our interpretations of these samples are to be realistic, we must consider carefully the processes involved in the preservation of bones on sites: the ways in which they come on to the sites, and the ways in which they are removed, destroyed, or buried.

In this light, in the second part of this paper I have discussed some of the analytical techniques commonly applied to animal bone samples, and the conclusions one can draw from them. It is my belief that many of the assumptions that are generally accepted in the interpretation of such samples are difficult to justify, and that some are definitely misleading. Much that is currently regarded as established is in fact open to question and to reinterpretation. Too often, a single interpretation is advanced and accepted for data that could equally reasonably be interpreted in other ways, of which no mention is made. It is important that the various possible interpretations of any data should be explicitly stated, for this is the only way in which we can ask the right questions to be able to choose between them. Often, if the right question is asked, the information is available.

It is important that particular interpretations should not become immovably enshrined in the literature and in archaeological thought. If an alternative hypothesis is advanced, we should try to judge impartially between the two on the basis of the evidence, rather than require that the old interpretation be disproved before we are prepared to consider the new. At present, preconception often prevents an impartial view of the evidence. For instance, evidence that we would readily accept as showing that the sheep at a Neolithic site were domesticated might as readily be rejected if the site were Mousterian, or the animal gazelle.

Finally, I believe that more importance should be attached to effective collaboration between the various specialists concerned in the investigation and interpretation of archaeological sites. First, there must be more effective communication between the excavator and each specialist. It is vital that the specialists should know what questions the archaeologist wants to answer, and should understand something of the limitations of archaeological data; otherwise their reports will reflect only the preoccupations of their own disciplines, and be of limited value archaeologically. Secondly, there must be more communication between the different specialists. No aspect of a site can be viewed meaningfully in isolation, and the work of the different specialists should become an integrated approach, in which each makes full use of the information provided by the others.

EDITORIAL NOTE

The difficulties and limitations outlined in this paper need to be stated. They might well be compared with the sources of error outlined so carefully by Faegri and Iverson in their *Textbook of Modern Pollen Analysis*. Such a statement is necessary as a preliminary to the formation of a sound method of analysis.

In contrast to pollen analysis samples of organic remains from archaeological sites are commonly collected by a variety of methods by operators with very varied degrees of skill, knowledge of their materials and expertise, and with few resources allocated to them. Such samples have a very limited value in the study of the past record of the relationship of man to his environment. The members of this project have largely confined their studies of organic remains to material collected by themselves by uniform methods. They have been encouraged to find that many directors of excavations have not only agreed to cooperate but many more have requested us to do so.

4. CRITERIA OF ANIMAL DOMESTICATION

M. R. JARMAN AND P. F. WILKINSON

Several contributors to this volume have noted inconsistencies and inadequacies in the criteria in general use by which, it is thought, prehistoric wild and domestic animals may be distinguished. Some authors have suggested alternative conceptual and methodological approaches to the investigation of past man-animal relationships, and the aim of this paper is to consider critically the way in which the archaeological data is customarily approached at present.

No universal agreement exists upon what precisely is meant by the term 'domestication', but Bökönyi (1969a) has offered a definition which may fairly be taken as representative of a large body of archaeological and zoological opinion: 'I would define the essence of domestication as: the capture and taming by man of animals of a species with particular behavioural characteristics, their removal from their natural living area and breeding community, and their maintenance under controlled breeding conditions for profit'. We hope here to show that current zoological techniques are not capable of recognizing all such relationships. Further, we shall argue that such relationships, even when they can be confidently recognized from the archaeological record, represent only one aspect of a wide range of close man-animal relationships, most of which receive little attention. It seems to us inappropriate to the interests of economic prehistory to focus attention on a single major dichotomy such as that which the wild-domestic classification envisages, and we feel that many relationships which are classified as 'domestic' are in no fundamental way different from others classified as 'wild'.

Many analyses of prehistoric domestication rely upon the detailed consideration of modern domestic animals and their relationship to modern wild animals. This is to be expected, of course, as the modern situation permits experiments and observations which are obviously out of the question as far as prehistoric data are concerned; and much valuable information has arisen from such studies. It is generally easy to discuss modern domestication and domestic animals, as there is usually a clear distinction visible between contemporary populations of wild and domestic animals of the same species, both as regards their morphology and their relationship with man. Even today, however, there is a number of marginal cases, notably some reindeer economies and game-cropping experiments, in which the distinction is far from clear-cut. Although it is tempting to do so, it is dangerous simply to transpose classifications based on contemporary situations and practices into prehistoric contexts, where our information is so much more scanty, and to which they may be inappropriate.

The zoological definition of domestication, emphasizing man's creation of reproductively isolated populations, has recommended itself particularly because it offers a precise conceptual dividing line, whereby the 'wild' class can be conveniently and consistently separated from the 'domestic' class. This concept is especially appropriate to zoology, the existing taxonomic structure of which already incorporates important considerations of interfertility and breeding barriers. It is becoming increasingly apparent, however, that this classification is not suitable for studying effectively the range of past human economies. Even if we assume for the purpose of argument that reproductive isolation took place and would have caused recognizable changes in the animals concerned, it is clear that these changes would have occurred only at some unspecifiable stage after the creation of the new animal groups. Opinion as to the probable length of time involved is divided: Herre (1968) and Bökönyi (1969a) suggest that a relatively short period of only a few generations would suffice, whereas Ducos (1969) takes the view that a longer time would be necessary. Data from experiments in animal domestication are inconclusive. In the case of highly inbred and protected animals, such as the mink and chinchilla, striking changes have occurred after only a few generations, whereas the eland in Russia has apparently remained unchanged for as long as records have been kept — more than eighty years of inbreeding and protection.

The criteria which have been used to show prehistoric domestication can be divided conveniently into two main classes. The first employs physical characteristics of the animals involved, such as their size, morphology, and colour, for example. The second concerns the demography and ecology of the exploited animal populations and the evidence of the way in which they were cropped, including analyses of distributions, sex ratios, mortality and survival patterns, and the ecological fitness of the animals to the local biotope. Artefactual and artistic data are a further source of potentially informative evidence, but they are notoriously ambiguous and difficult to interpret. We shall discuss each type of evidence in turn in order to assess its relevance to analyses of human patterns of economic exploitation. Recent studies (Drew, Perkins & Daly, 1971) concerning the possible existence of biochemical means of distinguishing wild and domestic animals are not discussed here; we feel that more experimental evidence is required before the significance of these techniques can be assessed.

ARTISTIC AND ARTEFACTUAL DATA

Both of these forms of evidence have an obvious potential for studies of early domestication, but they have rarely been employed successfully except in chronologically late contexts, for which there is usually abundant evidence for the existence of close man-animal relationships from other sources. A brief comment upon a few examples will serve to indicate some lines of argument which are largely neglected.

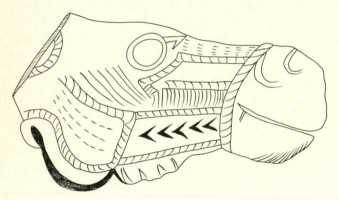

Fig. 1.   Representation of a horse's head from St Michel d'Arudy (after Cheynier, 1965).

An important depiction is that of a horse's head from St Michel d'Arudy (Fig. 1), which Piette (1906a) interpreted as indicating the presence of a bridle. Similar examples exist from Espelugues, Mas d'Azil, Laugerie-Basse, Isturitz, and Raymonden-Chancelade (Piette, 1906b; Leroi-Gourhan, 1965; Zervos, 1959). None of these finds is ^{14}C dated, but their Upper Palaeolithic age is not in dispute. Piette pointed out that this constitutes strong evidence for the domestication of the horse during the Palaeolithic and suggested (1906b) that the well known *bâtons de commandement* may have formed the rigid portion of such bridles. Whether in fact we believe that the *bâtons* were bridle pieces, arrow-straighteners, or that they have some other significance, it is appropriate to note here that close man-animal relationships do not demand an advanced artefactual technology, nor in many cases one that differs in major respects from that of a hunting group (Higgs & Jarman, I. 1; Wilkinson, 1971a). In addition to the manifest economic importance

of the horse at such sites as Le Solutré, a close association with man in the Upper Palaeolithic of western Europe is suggested by some cave paintings. For example, several paintings apparently depict horses which are dappled or piebald, such as that from the Aurignaco-Perigordian levels of the Grotte du Pech-Merle (Zervos, 1959, p. 65), a characteristic often believed to be associated with domestication. In his discussion of palaeolithic representations of horses, Zeuner (1963a) concluded that their variability could best be explained by either artistic inaccuracy and stylization, or by the existence of several ecotypes of *Equus caballus* within western Europe, although he offers no opinion as to which of these explanations is the more probable. A choice is thus presented. If we take the view that the representations display more imagination than reality, then they cease to be relevant to the present discussion. If we assume, however, that they depict a substantially real situation, then the observed degree of variability is worthy of attention, and in addition to the explanations offered by Zeuner there is the possibility that the variability of Upper Palaeolithic horses had much in common, both in its nature and its sources, with that of modern domesticated horses. Comparable variability in colouring and in horn shape can be seen in paintings of cattle from Lascaux and elsewhere. Some (e.g. Windels, 1948) have interpreted this as the depiction of two species of wild *Bos*, others (e.g. Zeuner, 1963a) as the representation of natural variability, including sexual dimorphism and semi-albino individuals. The number of paintings of cattle with albino or otherwise aberrant colouring would seem to be excessive in comparison with the number likely to occur in nature. Again, there is a choice of explanatory hypotheses: artistic distortion of reality; particular attention by the artists to abnormally pigmented individuals, for psychological reasons; or the results of long-term human selective pressure upon the genotype of cattle and thus upon aspects of the phenotype.

It seems fair to conclude that in the present state of knowledge artistic and artefactual data from chronologically early contexts are intriguing but inconclusive. They are consonant with a variety of explanatory hypotheses, yet offer no opportunity for arriving at firm conclusions.

SIZE

It is frequently stated that modern domestic animals differ in size from related wild populations where these still exist, and that they tend as a general rule to be smaller than their wild counterparts. There are, of course, exceptions to this generalization, including many recently domesticated species and older domesticates such as the camel and the Indian elephant. Nonetheless, archaeologists and zoologists studying archaeological material have generally assumed that where size changes can be observed in animals now commonly domesticated, and within an archaeological context considered appropriate to animal domestication, then they may be taken as good evidence for the domestication of those animals. The work of Degerbøl (1962, 1963; Degerbøl & Fredskild, 1970), Jewell (1962, 1963), and Flannery (Hole & Flannery, 1967) on cattle, and that of Boessneck (Boessneck, Jéquier & Stampfli, 1963) and Reed (1961) on pigs, is characteristic of this approach. For both these animals clear evidence has appeared that, in many areas of south-west Asia and Europe, Neolithic individuals were on the average smaller than their Late Palaeolithic or Mesolithic predecessors. It was believed as a corollary of the apparent link between domestication and size decrease that wild animals could, in the same way, be distinguished in the archaeological record if they were unchanged in size from wild populations of the species today. Many variable samples of bones have thus been divided into a wild and a domestic group on the basis of their absolute size, such as the cattle and pigs of Burgäschisee-Süd (Boessneck, Jéquier & Stampfli, 1963).

The size decrease associated with domestication is usually attributed to human selection for small size, aiming to produce a more easily controlled animal than the supposedly ferocious wild individuals, or to the poor care and low standard of feeding of early domesticated populations by their captors. The latter is a particularly widespread belief (Herre, 1963; Zeuner, 1963b; Reed, 1969; Grigson, 1969; et al.), but neither it nor the former explanation have much to recommend them.

As is well known of modern breeds of livestock, neither small individuals nor small breeds tend to be more easily handled or docile than large ones (Mason, 1963). Experience with elk and musk-oxen suggests that the contrary may often be the case, for in both these species it is the larger mature males that are most tractable. Furthermore, size changes of the order of magnitude observed in the prehistoric record and attributed to domestication would not have made the animals involved notably easier to restrain physically. The ability of man to control economically-worthwhile numbers of large animals must have always depended, as it does now, on behavioural adaptations in the human and animal populations; modern domestic cattle would have no difficulty in wreaking havoc on most fencing, but their adaptation to what Zeuner called 'the social medium of man' results in a high degree of complacency towards restraint and the other conditions of domestication. The experience of one of us (PFW) with wild musk-oxen indicates that such tolerance is not alien to most young wild calves, and that others can acquire it within a few hours of capture. Elk calves seem to be identical in this respect (Knorre, 1961), and Youngson wrote (1970, p. 469) of experimentally reared red deer, that 'after the initial phase of timidity and shock, calves developed an absolute confidence in their handlers'. The same is true of adult individuals of recently domesticated species; neither free-grazing elk nor eland show any tendency to abandon their captors, even when their wild counterparts co-exist in the same areas.

The second explanation is equally suspect, at least in the form in which it is commonly expressed. Zeuner's (1963b) picture of the capture of immature crop-robbers, followed by their almost total neglect and near-starvation is an unconvincing model for the intensification of man-animal relationships, and there is certainly no direct evidence that it occurred. Modern experience with wild animals suggests that the period immediately after capture is very critical, especially with calves, which are vulnerable to disease and to death from shock, and which must be well cared for if they are to survive and later thrive. People closely involved with and dependent upon animals cannot afford the luxury of ignorance concerning their stock's (wild or domestic) requirements and preferences, and there is in fact a large body of ethnographic evidence to suggest that most 'primitive' peoples have a good understanding of these matters. If newly domesticated animals were fed so poorly as to lose condition, this cannot have escaped the attention of their herders, nor would the remedy have been beyond their grasp. While we can conceive of animals with the status of pets or scavengers sometimes suffering neglect in this way (as do, for example, dogs in many contemporary Eskimo communities, where their importance as work-animals is seasonal, or where they have been largely replaced by the use of motorized sleds and aircraft), it is difficult to imagine why an early domesticator would forgo his successful hunting of wild animals for the exploitation of undersized, undernourished tame ones, or why pastoral economies should have spread so successfully if they were so inefficient. It is of course true that some early domestic animals may have been no more than pets, but they normally appear in quantities too great for this to have been the case. We should remember also that in many instances modern, and presumably also past, domestic animals forage for themselves. In such a situation any size changes which took place can be seen as part of an evolutionary mechanism relating the animal biomass to the food resources available to it; this process may, but need not, be directly related to or influenced by human activities.

Zeuner (1963a) took the view that in its early stages animal domestication was not primarily an economic process, but an 'almost inevitable' outcome of the social interaction of man with other animal species. This is an expression of belief rather than an explanation of the available data, and there are cogent reasons for at least considering the alternative hypothesis, that domestication was from the first principally an economic relationship. This enables us to view the undoubted size changes which have affected certain domestic animals within a different framework. Indeed, economic considerations often impose a high selective value on reducing the size of animals or maintaining small body size even at the present time, and it seems not unlikely that the same was true of some prehistoric situations.

Modern British mountain sheep illustrate the case in point very well, and the reasons for preferring small sheep are not at all complex: 'One sheep weighing a hundred pounds has only one head and one set of legs; two sheep, weighing a hundred pounds together, have two heads and two sets of legs, so that they can be in two different places to hunt the scanty herbs, and for this reason in conditions where the sheep of fifty pounds can just live, a hundred-pound sheep must necessarily starve' (Hagedoorn, 1945). One of the changes associated with the rise of close man-animal relationships may have been attempts to raise the stock-carrying capacity of given areas, thus increasing the pressure of the animals upon the available food resources. Even in the early stages of domestication, it would have been advantageous to carry the maximum number of individuals possible over the lean period of the year, when food resources were at their lowest, which would have favoured the development of large herds of relatively small individuals, which could survive periods of crisis yet quickly pick up condition when food once more became more abundant. Thus it seems highly probable that some size decreases were associated with early attempts at domestication, although there is no need to follow Zeuner and to explain them in terms of indifference, ignorance and mismanagement.

It is important to note, however, that similar changes can occur in evolutionary situations not dominated by man (see below, pp. 86-7). Zoo-archaeological interpretations of size changes in prehistoric animals seem to have adopted an over-simplistic viewpoint, and we should emphasize that man is only one of the agencies capable of causing size-changes, even in animals that are now domesticated. The changes in newly domesticated populations of animals are likely to reflect in part human economic pressures and the pressures of natural selection, and in any given case it is difficult to distinguish the one from the other, for there is every reason to believe that human selection was diversified in prehistoric times, as it is today.

There are several further aspects of size change in animals which need consideration. These may show the operation of factors which are unconnected with human behaviour, and which bring the study of prehistoric domes-tic animals more in line with the principles of modern animal ecology and ethology than is currently the case. It is a remarkable fact that the period customarily thought to have witnessed man's first experiments in animal domestication coincides with the end of the last glaciation and the first stages of the Postglacial period. Far-reaching climatic and environmental changes were taking place in what are now north-temperate latitudes and to a lesser extent in the Mediterranean/south-west Asia area; indeed, Heusser (1961) has suggested that many climatic fluctuations are more or less synchronous on a global scale, although their precise manifestations may vary from area to area. These changes are not generally discussed when considering animal domestication, other than to note the gross changes in the faunal composition of the various ecosystems, and sometimes to suggest that the climatic changes might have provided a direct or indirect 'stimulus' to domestication.

The relevance of Bergmann's rule, for instance, has received insufficient attention. This principle states that 'body size in geographically variable species averages larger in the cooler parts of the range of a species' (Mayr, 1963), the largest races being up to double the weight of the smallest. Size changes through time can be explained in a similar way when climatic changes have occurred. Kurtén (1959) has shown this factor affecting the size of carnivores in north-west Europe, and the diminution in size observed in many North American mammals (Edwards, 1967) in the Late Pleistocene can probably be explained in part by the same mechanism. The importance of this in considering size changes in domestic animals is obvious: until the possibility has been considered of the operation of an evolutionary process(es) unconnected with human exploitation, it is unjustified to label particular instances of size change as being necessarily the result of domestication. This is particularly relevant when we consider species such as cattle, which, though believed until recently to have been first domesticated in the Fertile Crescent, have been studied primarily in north-west Europe, where the surviving evidence is much more abundant. In an area such as Denmark, for instance, the effects of climatic change operating in accordance with Bergmann's rule could have been very considerable, and indeed Degerbøl (1933) has noted Postglacial size changes in several Danish mammals during this period. This is discussed at greater length by Jarman (1969).

Kurtén (1965) suggested that size reduction among certain Late Pleistocene carnivores in Palestine may indicate a response by the populations involved to impoverishment of the habitat and food resources, the severe selective pressures resulting in a drastic reduction of body size, a mechanism whereby a species may maintain viable populations in the face of a deteriorating ecological niche. In this connection it is interesting to note the considerable body of evidence for density-dependent growth rates in many species. Thus, in *Daphnia* raised in tanks of uniform volume it was found that 'the total biomass of all the cultures increases at roughly the same rate, and attains roughly the same maximum volume, regardless of whether there are 8, 16, 24, or 32 individuals per ml present' (Frank, Boll & Kelly, 1957). In this experiment, the possibility of direct nutritional dependence was eliminated; maximum size and growth rates were both correlated negatively with numerical density. Wynne-Edwards (1962) has suggested that the same mechanism may explain the small size of some mammalian populations, but it is difficult in field situations to separate density-dependent from nutrition-dependent phenomena.

It is apparent, therefore, that a simple temporal correlation between a size change and the apparent introduction of a new method of exploiting the animal concerned does not necessarily imply that the two are linked by a relationship of cause and effect, although this may sometimes be the case; conversely, the occurrence of size changes does not always or necessarily imply the initiation of a new man-animal relationship.

NEOTENY AND ALLOMETRY

Zeuner (1963a) suggested that domestication often causes the retention of juvenile characteristics, involving the absolute size of the various limbs and their relative proportions, as well as certain behavioural characteristics. There is no evidence to support this claim with respect to behaviour, for the characteristics often selected for by domestication, docility, and tractability, seem to characterize mature and large animals captured from the wild at least as much as juvenile animals. Herre & Roehrs (1971) have discussed this and the related problems of allometric changes in great detail. They concluded that it is a gross oversimplification to speak simply of a retention of juvenile characteristics, but that allometric changes may be caused in many cases by inbreeding or selective breeding. This approach is, therefore, potentially relevant to archaeological investigations of the origins of selective breeding, but the fragmentary nature of most surviving bones from archaeological sites precludes its use in most cases; and there is rarely any data on the range of variation of these features within contemporaneous wild species and populations.

SIZE AND ISOLATION

Grigson (1969) has provided a succinct statement of present archaeological beliefs with regard to size changes:

'interbreeding forms that are interfertile cannot diverge if they are able to breed freely, so that groups of animals of smaller stature than the main members of the population could only be set up if they were isolated from that population in one way or another. The main kinds of isolation are geographical, distance, ecological, and biological, but domestication by man might mimic the effects of natural isolation'. Such arguments depend upon the hypothesis that adjacent populations of wild animals, and those that are not prevented by major physical or geographical barriers from interbreeding, do in fact form single interbreeding units, and that the phenotypic similarity between the members of the many populations that constitute a species is the result of gene flow between these populations. Evidence is accumulating, however, that populations of a single species often form more or less closed breeding units, and that phenotypic similarity is maintained more by the operation of similar selective pressures on the different populations than by gene flow among them (Ehrlich & Raven, 1969). This conclusion is based on the simple observation that many populations which are separated by large distances, and between which gene flow must be minimal or absent, show striking phenotypic similarity (e.g. in *Pseudosinella hirsuta*, *Euphydras editha*, and *Clarkia rhomboidea*), whereas some closely adjacent populations, between which some gene flow is known to occur, show striking phenotypic differences (e.g. in *Maniola jurtina*). The situation with respect to mammals has been less well studied, but investigations of epigenetic variation in closely adjacent populations of mice (Weber, 1950; Berry, 1964), mountain goats in North America (Cowan & McCrory, 1970), and grey seals (Berry, 1969a) have shown that significant differences in the type and frequency of many characteristics exist between populations between which there are no physical barriers to interbreeding. Neel (1970) has indicated the existence of a high degree of genetic variability between adjacent villages of some human populations. Epigenetic polymorphism is 'assumed to arise as an expression of a mutation *that has become part of the genetic complement of a local population*' (Cowan & McCrory, 1970, our italics). This statement implies that interbreeding between local populations is in many cases at least highly restricted. As our knowledge of the social controls and regulators of reproductive behaviour in terrestrial mammals increases (e.g. Ewer, 1968), it becomes clearer how reproductive isolation may be achieved and maintained despite the absence of physical barriers to free interbreeding. Roberts (quoted in Payne, 1968) has described an example of such 'ethological isolation' which is of particular interest to economic prehistorians in that it concerns the relationship between a population of domestic sheep and one of wild sheep. A flock of wild mouflon was introduced from

Corsica and Sardinia to Lambay Island, County Dublin, which already possessed a population of domesticated sheep. Despite the lack of physical barriers to interbreeding, no crosses between the two populations occurred for some twenty years, by which time the wild ewes had become extinct.

Table 1. Insular isolation and size change (after Foster, 1964)

	Smaller	Same	Larger
Marsupials	0	1	3
Insectivores	4	4	1
Lagomorphs	6	1	1
Carnivores	13	1	1
Rodents	6	3	60
Artiodactyls	9	2	0

When considering the likely manifestations of man's isolation of chosen breeding populations, it is tempting to see them as closely analogous to those resulting from the insular isolation of animals. A general pattern of size change seems to characterize mammals in such situations, which has been summarized by Foster (1964) and which we present in Table 1. There is little reason to assume that the observed size changes are a product of isolation as such; they are likely to be at least partly the result of the altered selective pressures on islands, related perhaps to differing climatic regimes, limitations in food supplies, the frequent absence of large predators on islands (Foster, 1964; Ehrlich & Raven, 1969). Inbreeding might be thought to be important if the original group was small, but the white Park cattle of Chillingham, England, have been inbred for c. 700 years without a significant size change resulting. Comparable size changes are also known to occur among mammals in non-insular situations, including such animals as prehistoric cave bears and the modern dwarf pig, *Sus salvanius* (Herre, 1961), and MacPherson (1965) has considered the likelihood of such occurrences and their possible consequences in Canada. There are, too, examples of artiodactyls in isolated insular situations which appear not to have undergone size-reductions, but may even have become larger. The musk-oxen of Nunivak Island, Alaska, which were introduced into Alaska originally from east Greenland, and which have been isolated on the island for thirty-five years provide one good illustration of this, although the time-period involved may be too short for firm conclusions to be drawn.

Much archaeological thinking concerning the likelihood of changes in size associated with prehistoric domestication has been conditioned by the belief that early herders would have placed a high priority on preventing interbreeding between wild and domesticated animals of the same species. There are many known instances, however, where modern pastoralists encourage or tolerate interbreeding between domesticated and wild/feral forms (Higgs & Jarman, I. 1, p. 6).

VARIABILITY

It is often argued (e.g. Roehrs, 1961; Herre, 1963) that human protection and selective breeding of chosen groups of animals will result in an increased variability of size and morphology within populations. One might question the validity of the assumption that early (or for that matter modern) pastoralists are likely to find it economically worthwhile to protect poorly adapted animals; with occasional exceptions such as modern fur farmers. Even where desirable, the protection of large numbers of animals demands at least the provision of large quantities of food, and often depends upon a high level of technological competence. Belyaev (1969) has, however, suggested one mechanism by which domestication might result in increased variability: 'the mutation processes in mammals depend largely on hormone balance, particularly between the adrenocorticotropic and sexual hormones. A decrease in the function of the suprarenal glands ... increases the frequency of mutations', and it appears that selection for docility promotes such changes in at least some mammals. The increase in variability appears to affect principally 'unstable' characteristics, such as coat colour and horn shape, and some of these will be referred to later in the section on morphology. One of us (PFW) has shown elsewhere in this volume (III. 1) that marked phenotypic changes appear to have accompanied only a few modern domestication experiments, notably those involving the smaller, fur-bearing carnivores, and that in every case the observed changes were the product of conscious selection on the part of their domesticators. The factors controlling skeletal size are not fully understood, but they are developmental as well as genetic.

Size variations within modern wild populations have rarely been studied, but it has been firmly established for the musk-ox (Tener, 1965) that statistically significant size differences do exist between different wild populations and may be explained at least in part by variations in food supplies, and perhaps also with reference to human hunting pressures. It is known, however, that wild populations of black-tailed deer (*Odocoileus*) and mountain goat (*Oreamnos*) in North America show considerable variation in some morphological features, and variability in island populations of deer mouse (*Peromyscus*) is apparently greater than among mainland populations occupying territories of similar size (Foster, 1964). Indeed, Cowan and McCrory were led to state that 'epigenetic variation is more frequent and more varied in *Oreamnos* than in any other mammal in North America'. If, as seems to be the case, some of the factors controlling certain aspects of variability operate to an equal or greater extent in wild populations than in domestic ones, arguments which associate increased variability with domestication are considerably weakened. Once again, we are not suggesting that domestication never produces the effects which it is claimed to, but only that these effects can also be produced by other agencies and that they do not always and inevitably result from what archaeologists and zoologists call domestication.

In view of the many complications in the use and interpretation of techniques for studying variability, it is worth quoting at some length from a standard textbook on zoological statistics (Simpson, Roe & Lewontin, 1960):

> discernment of the meaning of a value of V is largely a matter of experience. Its interpretation on functional zoological grounds depends on nonnumerical biological knowledge. We have compared hundreds of V's for linear dimensions of anatomical elements of mammals. As a matter of observation, the great majority of them lie between 4 and 10, and 5 and 6

are good average values. Much lower values usually indicate that the sample was not adequate to show the variability. Much higher values usually indicate that the sample was not pure. . . . If the sample is adequate and reasonably unified, then different values of V generally represent in a clear and useful way inherent differences in variability.

The samples of bones available to archaeologists are rarely suitable for employing such techniques, for neither hunters nor pastoralists tend in general to exploit their prey randomly with respect to age and/or sex, and it is often impossible to determine the age and sex of many of the animal bones commonly recovered by excavation. Table 2 presents data on the variability of some measurements of bones found in archaeological contexts, together with comparative measurements from samples of modern bovids. It is apparent that their interpretation poses difficulties. In the case of the least frontal breadth from the presumptively wild *Bos primigenius* samples from Denmark and Britain, the variability is so low as to suggest that the samples were inadequate. The astragalus length for the wild bovids approaches the 'good average values' of 5 to 6, whereas the domestic bovids show lower values. This is, of course, the reverse of the situation that is predicted for domestic animals, but one must remember that the development of

Table 2. Coefficients of variation

Species	Origin		Dimension	C.V.
Bos primigenius	Britain	Wi	Least breadth of frontal	1.33
,, ,,	Denmark	Wi	,, ,, ,, ,,	1.428
,, ,,	Britain	Wi	Length astragalus	4.281
,, ,,	Denmark	Wi	,, ,,	4.961
,, ,,	Hungary	Wi	,, ,,	4.808
B. taurus	Red Danish	D	,, ,,	3.02
,, ,,	Aberdeen Angus	D	,, ,,	4.52
,, ,,	,, ,,	D	,, ,,	4.72
,, ,,	Red Danish	D	Maximum distal width metacarpal	3.03
,, ,,	Aberdeen Angus	D	,, ,, ,, ,,	4.10
,, ,,	,, ,,	D	,, ,, ,, ,,	3.28
,, ,,	Kalmyk	D	,, ,, ,, ,,	5.0
,, ,,	,,	D	,, ,, ,, ,,	4.38
,, ,,	,,	D	,, ,, ,, ,,	6.37
Sus scrofa	Holland	Di	Length M^1	2.912
,, ,,	,,	Wi	,, ,,	4.876
,, ,,	,,	Di	Length M_3	14.65
,, ,,	,,	Di	,, ,,	16.43
,, ,,	,,	Wi	,, ,,	4.23
B. taurus	Holland	Di	Length M_3	1.55
C. elaphus	Switzerland	Wi	Length M_3	4.895

Key. D – domesticated; W – wild; i – inferred.

Source. Data from Grigson, 1969; Boessneck *et al.*, 1963; Clason, 1967; Higham, 1969.

breeds may in fact lead to a reduction of variability. From the point of view of archaeologists, a study of within-breed size variation would prove most useful. The M^1 Length of the Dutch pigs does not permit their subdivision into wild and domestic groups on the basis of variability, and the supposedly domestic individuals show a range of variation so narrow that it is difficult not to assume that the sample was inadequate. The variability of the M^3 Length of the Dutch pigs on the other hand is so great that one cannot exclude the possibility that the sample was heterogeneous with respect to age, sex, or perhaps both.

To summarize our discussion of size, it is quite clear that the relationship between size and domestication is a complex one. On the one hand, size changes may be caused by factors other than domestication, whilst on the other, domestication does not always or inevitably result in size changes. Finally, the nature of archaeological samples is such that if statistical techniques are to be used, they require very careful selection.

MORPHOLOGY

Criteria of morphology have been used in a very similar fashion to those of size, and they suffer from many of the same limitations. They are also difficult to express in quantitative terms. It is known that in some species captivity and selective breeding may have a marked and relatively swift influence on the size and shape of certain bones such as jaws and teeth. Other organs and features such as coat colour (Richter, 1954; Belyaev, 1969; Herre & Roehrs, 1971) are similarly influenced but in archaeological deposits such evidence rarely survives. Ryder's (1969) work on changes in the structure of fleeces and fibres in sheep is of particular interest to archaeology. These studies have shown major changes over a period of several millennia, but the assumption that modern populations of 'wild' sheep used for comparative purposes were in fact wild rather than feral or wild/domestic crossbreeds is questionable (Payne, 1968). In our discussion of the criterion of size, we referred to the analysis of epigenetic polymorphisms. This approach is of potential value to archaeologists, for it may permit them to recognize whether the animal remains of a single species from an archaeological site were derived from one or more populations, and it is possible also that inbreeding, selective breeding, or reproductive isolation from wild populations might affect the frequency of some characteristics and that others might develop only within such isolated populations. This approach is handicapped by the small size of many archaeological samples of bones and the fragmentary nature of most of these bones (especially skulls, on which the technique is most effective).

Morphological features are related to environmental selection as well as to genetic background, and morphological changes in animal populations take place at varying rates, depending among other things on the nature and severity of this selection. Some changes occur with great rapidity. The work of Kettlewell (1961) on industrial melanism in lepidoptera illustrates well a quick response to changing selective pressures. Perhaps an even more striking example is that of the independent development of DDT resistance on several different occasions by house flies within two years of its introduction as a household insecticide. Relatively simple environmental changes can quickly effect major morphological changes in many mollusca and fish. The polymorphic snail *Cepaea nemoralis* varies pronouncedly in colouration, a feature which seems to relate to micro-environmental factors. These variations in colour appear to be linked with other traits; thus laboratory populations of the five-banded form were found to lay twice as many eggs as the unbanded or single-banded forms (Ruiter, 1958). In the sea-trout, *Salmo trutta*, the number of vertebrae is affected by different temperature conditions (Tåning, 1952). Experimental factors have been observed to exert a similar determining influence on tail length in mice (Sumner, 1909).

As is frequently the case, however, less is known about mammals from this point of view; they present difficulties as laboratory animals, and are usually difficult to study in the field. Nevertheless, instances of morphological change can again be related both to simple mutations and to environmental change. Kurtén (1967) has discussed such occurrences in some European carnivores. He suggests that in *Ursus*, for example, a mutation in the genes controlling dental morphology may have been responsible for the appearance of the ancestral *U. arctos* form in populations of *U. spelaeus*. In the badger population of Zealand a mutation for long talonid teeth seems to have spread within 1000 years in the Postglacial period. In the fox, on the other hand, continental or cold climate appears to be correlated with the absence of a subsidiary cusp on the lower carnassial. This feature, rarely predominant in any population, is absent in modern western Europe, but is present in Sweden and becomes more frequent in Finland and Poland. In Britain this feature is absent in contemporary foxes and in those from Eemian contexts, but occurred during the Saale and Würm glaciations. Similar examples exist for many herbivores; indeed, much of the classical taxonomy of the herbivores is based on the high degree of variation in their cranial morphology. Thus: 'the genus *Bison* constitutes a closely related group, the members of which differ principally in their horn core growth' (Skinner & Kaisen, 1947). There is, for instance, a decrease of about fifty percent in average horn core size between Degerbøl's *B. bonasus arbustotundrarum* of Late Glacial and Postglacial Denmark and the modern *B. bonasus* (data from Degerbøl & Iversen, 1945). Red deer are notable for variability in the size and form of their antlers, which seem to be profoundly affected both by nutrition and genetic factors. The red deer of New Zealand are said to have greatly increased the size and quality of their heads when first introduced from Scotland, largely due to improved forage conditions in forested areas. 'Hummels' (stags naturally without antlers as a result of a genetic anomaly) and other abnormal antler types occur in certain Scottish populations, particularly in isolated areas. The 'cromie' antlers of Jura, for example, are apparently a particular characteristic of that island (Whitehead, 1964). Another case of interest is the occurrence of hornless females in the mouflon, *Ovis musimon*, of Sardinia and Corsica (Zeuner, 1963*a*), although it is possible that this feature arose under the influence of human selective pressures and that the populations concerned have since become feral (Payne, pers. comm.).

Here, as with the criterion of size, the situation is rather more complex than most students of prehistoric domestication have acknowledged. Modern population ecology has long since discarded the concept of static, uniform species. A high degree of metrical and morphological variation within and between populations of animals is common, although its precise extent in the higher mammals is only beginning to be determined (Long, 1969), and variation through time can occur very quickly in response to changes in selective pressures. Human interference is only one such pressure, and there is as yet no infallible means for the zoologist or prehistorian to distinguish the effects of human interference from that of other agencies.

ZOOGEOGRAPHICAL DATA

It has been rightly pointed out (Dyson, 1953; Reed, 1960) that animals can have been domesticated only in those areas in which they naturally occurred, and that domestication is likely to have caused alterations in their distributions. Indeed, the Fertile Crescent came into prominence as a probable 'hearth' of domestication because it was believed to be one of the few areas in which the distributions of the progenitors of the major domesticates (both plant and animal) overlapped. Whilst geographical considerations are relevant to the study of early domestication, it seems to us that the situation as regards their application is more complex than has generally been acknowledged.

It is difficult, and often impossible, to specify accurately the past distribution of many animals. Students of domestication have attempted to infer these distributions from the present distribution and the preferred habitats of contemporary, supposedly 'wild' representatives of the same species. This approach does, however, ignore several possibilities: that the modern 'wild' populations are in fact feral animals, whose distribution is as much the product of human activities as of other selective pressures; that the wild populations are in fact wild, but that their distribution has been so altered by the selective pressures of the past millennia (including man), that it no longer corresponds to their distribution in the Late Glacial and early Postglacial period; that the distribution of the wild or feral animals represents only a fraction of their former distribution, and that they have been displaced or become extinct over much of their former range. Attempts to reconstruct the distribution of past animal populations on the basis of faunal remains from archaeological or palaeontological contexts encounter similar obstacles. In the case of remains from archaeological contexts, there is little certainty that the distribution of the animals concerned (whether they were wild or domesticated) was not in important respects a product of human activity. Palaeontological collections on the other hand are generally too rare to provide sufficiently accurate data.

Further difficulties arise from the fact that man is only one of several agents capable of altering the distribution of animals. Climatically induced vegetational changes are an obvious example of a mechanism which can stimulate alterations of distribution, and MacPherson (1965) has discussed such changes since the end of the last glacial in the Canadian Arctic and Sub-Arctic. It is not even necessary to invoke such relatively catastrophic changes as glacial-interglacial changes, for animal distributions are likely to alter with vegetational successions, and populations may grow or decline in response to alterations in any one of the many prevailing selective pressures operating to maintain a balance between the components of the biotope. Peterson (1957) described important changes in the distribution of mammals in Ontario since the end of the last glacial, and Snyder (1957) provided similar data for the avifauna, whilst Telfer (1967) demonstrated that major alterations in the distribution of moose and deer had occurred in the space of only a few years in Nova Scotia independently of human activity. Since students of animal domestication have concentrated their attention on the Late Glacial and early Postglacial period, a time when major climatic changes were occurring in many areas and when many animals were becoming extinct or undergoing distributional alterations quite independent of human activity (Guthrie, 1968; Lundelius, 1967), it is dangerous to assume that changes in the distribution of those animals that are today domesticated were caused by human intervention rather than by other factors.

Our criticisms should not be taken as implying that zoogeographical data are valueless. It seems to us that it is unjustified to attribute localized changes in animal distribution to man's activities unless it is possible to eliminate the operation of all the other likely agents of such changes. On the other hand, it is undeniable that on a broader scale studies of changes in animal distributions can be highly indicative of man's increasing manipulation of his staple resources (although this need not necessarily involve domestication as traditionally defined). Once again, we are not arguing that the techniques employed by archaeologists and zoologists are incapable of achieving their stated objectives, but simply urging that adequate consideration be given to alternative interpretations of the available data and to the dangers in misapplying or overinterpreting fundamentally sound techniques.

POPULATION STRUCTURE

Lurking behind much contemporary archaeology and anthropology of considerable apparent sophistication is the romantic nineteenth-century idea of prehistoric and modern primitive man as the 'noble savage'. This idea is seldom expressed overtly but finds support in the drastic impact which modern industrial societies are having upon their environments. These effects are frequently so rapid, far-reaching, and injurious, that they encourage the idea of a division between natural man, in harmony with Nature, and industrial man, who is unnatural, divorced from, and out of harmony with his environment. This is inherent in the widespread belief that Pre-Neolithic man, as a hunter, exploited his prey randomly; whereas, with the beginnings of domestication which came with the Neolithic, man began to exploit animals selectively with respect to age and sex. It is at this stage, therefore, that human exploitation is thought first to have had an important effect on animal populations. Bökönyi (1969a) expresses this view: 'And this (i.e. domestication) is a real difference in comparison to the wild, hunted animals, for in connection with the latter, primitive man had only one purpose; to kill as many of them as possible.'

The firm belief in this fundamental exploitive dichotomy forms the basis of the third major group of criteria used for separating prehistoric wild and domestic animals: that of the demographic characteristics of the exploited segment of the population. This criterion has become increasingly popular with many workers as doubts have arisen concerning the ability of other criteria to recognize the early stages of domestication. Ducos (1968) states the position clearly:

Dans le cas où ils [i.e. the animals] ont été chassés, cela signifie qu'ils ont été pris ou tués plus ou moins au hasard parmi l'ensemble des animaux qui vivaient en liberté à proximité du groupe humain . . . Il ensuit que le butin de chasse . . . est plus ou moins à l'image de l'environnement animal du groupe humain. Les proportions des différentes espèces parmi les animaux tués tendent à se rapprocher des proportions de ces mêmes espèces dans la nature; les proportions des sexes, les fréquences des diverses classes d'âge tendent, en particulier, à se rapprocher des proportions des sexes et des classes d'âge dans les populations naturelles.

For domestic animals, however, the situation is quite different:

L'une des caractéristiques de la domestication réside dans le fait qu'il est possible de choisir avec précision l'animal qui doit être tué et consommé. Cela est même nécessaire: il convient de laisser dans le troupeau suffisament de jeunes, suffisament de femelles, d'éliminer les animaux malades ou faibles. Dès lors, si l'on considère l'ensemble des animaux tués de la sorte pendant une période assez longue, les proportions des sexes et des âges envisagées ci-dessus s'éloigneront de celles des populations naturelles.

The mortality curve is used in this way particularly frequently as the rates of tooth eruption and wear, and characteristics of epiphyseal fusion, provide a readily available and sufficiently accurate guide to age at death in those species for which these rates have been studied. Perkins' claim (1964) for early domestic sheep at Zawi Chemi Shanidar on the basis of the high proportion of immature animals is well known, and similar arguments are frequent in the literature (Ducos, 1968, 1969; Clason, 1967, etc.). Sex ratios have been employed in this fashion less frequently, largely because it is difficult and often impossible to work out techniques for separating the sexes in samples of prehistoric bones. Some progress has been made in studies of sex ratios in the exploited segments of prehistoric animal populations, notably in Higham's studies of cattle (1969). Flannery (Hole & Flannery, 1967) noted of the Ali Kosh goat population that not only was the age curve different from that of a wild population, but that 'Judging by the discarded horn cores, mostly young males were eaten, presumably to conserve the females for breeding'. The study of the incidence of castrates has considerable potential value in the field of economic prehistory, for this can give useful and unequivocal data on certain aspects of man-animal relationships. It is, however, a question which has been very little studied.

The use of demographic data does have advantages over the approaches discussed previously, and the data upon which it is based can be of great significance in assessing man-animal relationships. There are, however, difficulties inherent in their use as wild-domestic discriminants; in particular we must question the belief first in the existence of a single natural demographic pattern for each species, with which divergent 'unnatural' patterns can be contrasted, and secondly in the random operation of primitive hunting.

Demographic characteristics are not static in time and space. They vary from population to population, from year to year, decade to decade, and century to century. Population size, pressure on available resources, interspecific competition, and the degree and nature of disease and predation can all have an important effect, while periodic catastrophes (whether humanly induced or not) also leave their mark. By far the majority of available data on this is from human populations, as these are both the easiest to study and have an obvious practical application in medical and sociological studies. Catastrophic events such as wars, epidemics, and climatic freaks all have effects which are unlikely to be random; a war, for instance, will probably eliminate differentially males of certain age groups, while there is also some evidence that it may also raise the ratio of male to female births (Colombo, 1957). Different diseases affect different populations in different ways, affecting age groups and occupation groups differentially. Figures 2 and 3 show geographical and temporal variations in human survival curves.

The same is true for animal populations, although it is less well documented. At the extremes the difference is, of course, self-evident; thus, the mortality curve and demographic structure of a flock of sheep infested with liver fluke will be different from those of a healthy flock or one infected with milk fever. Of greater interest here, Julander,

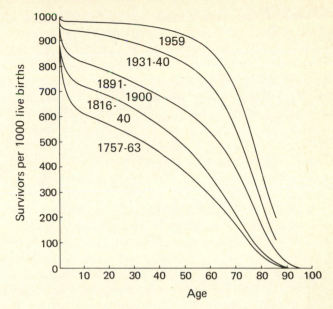

Fig. 3. Temporal variations in human survival curves in Sweden (after Clark, 1967).

Robinette, and Jones (1961) showed that ovulation rate, birth rate, and fawn mortality in mule deer all showed a strong variation between two nearby ranges, being greatly influenced by the pressure of the deer population on the available forage. Spencer & Lensink (1970) have shown that some of the musk-ox cows on Nunivak Island, Alaska, calve annually, in contrast to the biennial pattern of calving typical of most musk-ox populations. This unusually high rate of calving is probably attributable to the easy availability of winter fodder, which permits calves to cease suckling in time for their mothers to breed annually. Tener (1965) suggested that certain features of the size of musk-oxen in parts of Ellesmere Island and some characteristics of their population structure may reflect human hunting pressures about the turn of the century. Table 3 presents data on fluctuations in the composition of the population of sheep on St Kilda for a six-year period (Jewell 1966b). Klein & Olson (1960) showed that predation by wolves on deer in Alaska produced a different herd structure from that found in areas free of wolves. Peek, Lovaas & Rouse (1967) noted a general increase in the mortality rate over a

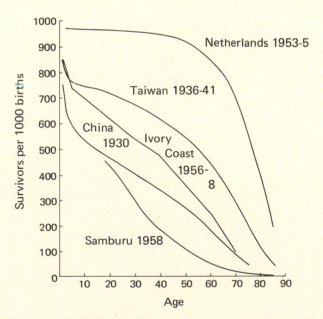

Fig. 2. Geographical variations in human survival curves (after Clark, 1967).

Table 3. Population structure of St Kilda sheep (after Jewell, 1966b). Figures expressed as percentages

	1959	1960	1961	1962	1963	1964
Lambs	34.1	14.1	45.8	20.9	32.9	23.6
Ewes	53.7	73.4	45.8	59.1	51.4	65.0
Rams	12.2	12.5	8.4	20.0	15.7	11.4

period of nearly twenty years in a herd of *Cervus cana-densis*. The effect of natural catastrophes has been studied by Blair (1957), who showed that not only do such catastrophes sometimes affect different species selectively, but that within single species certain age and/or sex groups may be affected differentially. Whilst these data are scanty, they suggest very strongly that it is misleading for archaeologists to adopt as a criterion for comparing patterns of economic activity, a now outdated and inadequate concept of static animal populations. Animal populations are as prone to change as are man's patterns of economic exploitation of these populations.

We must now consider the proposition that in animals and in primitive man, predation will tend to be random. Predator-prey relationships are not uniform; all predators do not exploit their prey in the same way, to the same degree, or with the same effect. The relative abundance of the two species, their body size, methods of predation/evasion, social organization, and other similar factors, all play their role in determining the nature of the mutual impact of predator and prey. For this reason we should not necessarily expect that predator-prey relationships will be standard within a single species, or indeed within the associations of any two species.

Exiguous though our information may be, we do have evidence of selective predation in invertebrates, birds, and mammals. Thus the American whelk tingle, *Urosalpinx cinerea*, preys selectively upon oysters of a particular size (Hancock, 1959) and age group (Haskin, 1950). The many records of selective predation in birds (e.g. Rudebeck, 1950, 1951; Baker, 1970) are strikingly exemplified by the oystercatcher, *Haematopus ostralegus*. Dewar (1915) and Drinnan (1958) observed instances of selection for particular sizes of mussel, while Hancock & Urquhart (1965) and Davidson (1967) have shown age and size selection of cockles.

Turning to mammalian predators we find a similar situation; where the question has been studied instances of selective predation are not uncommon. Wolves have been relatively well studied and have been observed to prey selectively on bison (Fuller, 1962), moose (Allen & Mech, 1963), caribou (Crisler, 1956), deer (Klein & Olson, 1960), and Dall sheep (Murie, 1944). Between them these instances reflect selective predation on young and old age groups, on handicapped individuals, and on adult males relative to females. The wild dog, *Lycaon pictus*, is another predator which has been shown to act selectively with regard to the species, age groups, and sex of its prey (Estes & Goddard, 1967). Lions (Wright, 1960), cheetahs and leopards (Schaller, 1968), and tigers (Schaller, 1967) have also been observed in similar relationships with their prey. This is not an exhaustive catalogue of such cases; nor

should it be construed as an argument that all predation is selective, at least to such an obvious degree. It should further be noted that we are not imputing conscious or mentally controlled selection to the predators discussed. Selective predation can clearly arise from the predators' following the easiest course open to them. The wild dog was never observed to have the slightest difficulty in obtaining any of its prey; but in input:output terms the most efficient and economic strategy involved selective predation on adult males of Thomson's gazelle. The small size of this species is probably significant, for while the ratio of Thomson's gazelle to Grant's gazelle in the area was about 7:3, the ratio of kills was about 7:1.

An important conclusion to emerge from the studies quoted above is that predation cannot be considered as a simple, static process. It is a relationship between members of different species which must necessarily fluctuate and adjust as other factors in the ecosystem change. In particular, the relative densities of predator and prey, and the degree to which the predator depends upon a single prey species will affect profoundly the nature and intensity of the pressure exerted by the predator.

Turning to the evidence of human predation, we are faced with a scarcity of sufficiently detailed information. Modern hunting for sport is almost always selective, whether this be for the purposes of game management or for obtaining trophies. Table 4 illustrates this well and serves also to emphasize our earlier point that other causes of mortality, catastrophic and otherwise, are also often selective. In most instances of selective human hunting males are usually the preferred prey, breeding females and young animals being conserved. In some cases this is probably encouraged by the fact that males are apparently more vulnerable than females, as for instance in some deer. It is important to emphasize once again that for the purposes of discussing the existence of selective hunting by past human groups, it is not relevant whether or not the selection is conscious. Bulmer (1968) illustrates this point well in a modern context: 'Although few of New Guinea peoples are conscious conservationists, ritual restrictions on hunting or diet probably have conservational effects in many parts of New Guinea'. Obviously, the behaviour of the prey species will have a profound effect on the type of predation possible: old male musk-oxen, for instance, which no longer breed or associate with a herd are probably the only individuals easily susceptible to predation by wolves, for the defensive semi-circle of musk-oxen in herds generally constitutes an adequate defence against wolves. Similarly, it has been suggested that one of the reasons for selective predation on Thomson's gazelle may be the reluctance of territorial males to move outside their territories (Estes & Goddard, 1967).

Table 4.   Musk-ox mortality, Nunivak Island, Alaska (after Spencer & Lensink, 1970)

Cause	Adult			Yearling			Calf			Age/sex unknown
	M	F	U	M	F	U	M	F	U	
Unknown: old age/winter kill etc.	35	13	1	2	6				4	22
Falls from cliff	1			1						2
Lost on sea-ice/drowned	6	5							3	
Mired in bogs/drowned	2	2		1		1			1	1
Injured	2	1							1	
Shot	11	3		1		1				
Transplant mortality		1				1	2	4		
Removed for transplant						1	20	35		

Key. M – male; F – female; U – unknown.

Many herbivores split into sexually segregated groups for part of the year, and this often has the effect of making a particular segment of the population vulnerable to predation, possibly influencing the nature of the crop available to predators in different areas. This reaches an extreme in some cases like the caribou. Hoare (1930) wrote of migrating caribou in the Thelon Game Sanctuary, Canadian North-west Territories, that 'in about three weeks we saw several thousand animals going northwest and did not notice a single female among them'. Gubser (1965) notes that the Nunamiut Eskimos are fully aware that the spring migration of caribou follows a fairly rigid pattern: cows and calves in the first herds, followed by young bulls and then by mature bulls. Therefore, when Woodburn (1968) says of the East African Hadza's exploitation that 'adult males are preferred', it is not of particular importance to our argument whether this is, as he says, 'only because they are generally larger'. The evolutionary effect of predation on prey populations (and thus on prospects for future predation) will depend upon the actualities of predation, not on its rationalizations.

Studies of recent hunters record some instances of selective hunting, although we must bear in mind that such studies are handicapped by the fact that they are short-term studies and that there is no certainty that hunting groups surviving to the present day (many of whom occupy what can only be called 'marginal' environments) resemble in important respects prehistoric hunters. Speaking of the Tungus' hunting, Shirokogoroff (1935) records that 'the females, especially when pregnant, must not be killed at all, the very young fawns of elk, *Cervus Elaphus, Cervus Tarandus* must be spared too'. Stefansson (1946) records that the Indians of the Mackenzie River area showed a preference for larger caribou, especially males. Roe (1951), on the other hand, mentions that the Plains Indians preferred female bison, and that males were taken only in times of shortage.

In the past there is good evidence of selective exploitation of several species of deer: *Cervus elaphus* and *Capreolus capreolus* in the Neolithic of Europe (Jarman, 1971), and almost certainly prior to the Neolithic as well (Jarman, III. 3); *Odocoileus* in both historic and prehistoric periods in the United States (Elder, 1965). The red deer in particular has evidently been exploited in a sophisticated fashion, selective both with respect to age and sex. At Burgäschisee-Süd the pigs identified as wild (Boessneck, 1963) were exploited, on the basis of the small sample available, at a rate of two males to eight females. Even so apparently unpromising a species as the rhinoceros, *Dicerorhinus kirchbergensis*, was selectively exploited at Taubach, where more than 70 percent of the specimens were from immature animals. Not only were prehistoric animals exploited selectively with respect to age and sex, but there are many instances in which prehistoric hunters appear to have concentrated their predation on only a limited portion of the total faunal community available to them. Some examples of this practice have been discussed elsewhere (Higgs & Jarman, I. 1).

SUMMARY AND CONCLUSIONS

Most modern domestic animals are morphologically and behaviourally very closely adapted to their environments, which are usually dominated by man. This, and the increasing role of intensive selective breeding for particular characters has resulted in the present situation in which most modern domestic animals are clearly different from their closest wild relatives. It is obvious, however, that we cannot expect that the distinction will have been so clear-cut in the past. In the present state of knowledge it does not seem possible to arrive at firm conclusions as to the speed and magnitude of the changes associated with early domestication, but evidence from modern experiments suggests that rapid and striking phenotypic changes do not characterize most newly domesticated animals, occurring only where they are specifically sought.

It has been the practice to label changes occurring in those animals which are now domesticated as the result of domestication, when they occur in what is considered a suitable geographical and chronological context. Many of these phenomena could have been caused by non-human factors, however, or by a combination of human and non-human factors. Some changes were undoubtedly the product of human agencies, but it is more difficult than has generally been acknowledged to distinguish between these and the results of other evolutionary mechanisms. A situation which may frequently have arisen is that of human selection adopting and intensifying a favourable change which was initiated by non-human agencies.

It has further been customary to argue that prehistoric animals which are unchanged osteologically relative to a supposed 'wild' type are necessarily wild, hunted animals. This hypothesis rests on two propositions: that domestication will necessarily involve selection for new characteristics; and that changes will take effect quickly because of the reproductive isolation imposed by the human domesticator. One might equally view domestication as the end-product of a series of gradually intensifying man-animal relationships (Higgs & Jarman, 1969; I. 1), and it seems likely that in the early stages of such relationships at least animals were exploited for qualities they already possessed rather than with a view to inducing selective changes (Wilkinson, 1971a). Furthermore, the role of reproductive isolation in causing and maintaining physical change is of uncertain significance, for not only would complete isolation have been difficult or impossible to achieve in many cases, but it may even not have been desired.

A feature of archaeological research over the past few decades has been the increasing extent to which specialists from other disciplines have collaborated in an attempt to evolve a unified 'interdisciplinary' approach to the subject. Most of the criticisms that we have voiced, however, arise from the uncritical view which each principal discipline involved has taken of the assumptions and hypotheses of the other. Archaeology has suggested that in some respects a firm dividing line can be drawn between Neolithic and Pre-Neolithic societies. Zoology has accepted this as a basis for studying prehistoric animals and, through them, prehistoric economies. Thus there has been an almost total neglect of Pre-Neolithic economies, all of which have been lumped together as hunting-fishing-gathering economies, from which, it was felt, there was little to be gained by closer analysis. Zoological evidence for domestication has been sought only in those areas and periods considered by the *archaeologist* to be suitable. On the other hand, the archaeologist has accepted the zoological species classification as a useful framework for interpreting human economic behaviour (Higgs & Jarman, I. 1, p. 4), in spite of the fact that they are clearly concerned with very different problems. Similarly, the archaeologist has accepted a zoological definition of domestication, based largely on the breeding characteristics of the animal populations concerned. Such a definition is admittedly adequate for studies of most contemporary domesticates, and the zoological techniques applied to studies of early domestication are undoubtedly capable of recognizing such relationships in some circumstances. The economic prehistorian, however, is at least as interested in the fashion in which prehistoric animal populations were cropped as in the ways in which they were bred, and it is not always strictly relevant to his interests whether they were tamed or reproductively isolated.

It has also been accepted without demur that animal predation, and thus 'natural' Pre-Neolithic human predation, will be substantially random in its impact upon prey populations. This is no longer sound zoologically, and it certainly does not provide a useful model for human predation at any stage in man's development. Similarly zoologists have proposed that isolation may have been a contributory cause to certain physical changes in domestic animals, and indeed it may have been so on occasion. However, this has tended to develop into a general hypothesis that isolation was an early characteristic of *all* domestic populations, which could thus be studied by means of the resulting physical changes. This hypothesis is implausible in view of the well-known anthropological data (Higgs & Jarman, I. 1, p. 6).

The contribution of zoological techniques to economic prehistory has been and will clearly remain considerable. On the other hand we believe that the economic prehistorian should extend his studies to examine the ways in which man has exploited animal (and plant) populations through time and space and that he must develop his own set of techniques and hypotheses to this end. These techniques should integrate in the most profitable way those aspects of zoology, ethology, and ecology which are directly relevant to archaeological interests. They should not be seen as replacing the traditional zoological methods, but as complementing and adding to them. Elsewhere in this volume hypotheses and techniques are put forward which, we feel, may prove a fruitful step in this direction.

5. CAVE CLIMATES

A. J. LEGGE

The choice of location for human habitation sites in pre-history was a highly important factor for group survival, and although the archaeological contents of occupied caves and shelters have received extensive study, the advantages of particular types of habitation have rarely been considered. Man encounters virtually the full range of climatic extremes found in the world, yet only occasionally does he have to tolerate very high or low temperatures, owing to the creation of the special micro-environments in which he lives. Thus the widespread distribution of man depends not simply on mobility, but on those aspects of his technology and behaviour that permit the substantial modification of local climatic regimes.

It is clear that certain caves and rock shelters can be regarded as highly preferred sites. These were repeatedly occupied from the Middle Palaeolithic onwards and even up to the present day, a phenomenon that has received little attention in archaeology. Other sites apparently equally suitable for habitation may show only relatively rare or occasional occupation over a long period of time. Highly preferred sites may be expected to show features in common with each other to account for this situation, and the most important of these may be taken as the proximity of good food resources and the offer of efficient shelter as a means of protection against the external environment. A recent attempt has been made (Binford & Binford, 1966) to classify occupied caves and shelters under the headings of base camps, work camps, and transient camps, according to the nature of the archaeological deposits, and thus to imply that each type of settlement fulfilled a particular purpose within the territory of a human group. Yet the choice of the base camp (the 'home base' of Higgs *et al.,* 1967) may well be determined as much by its suitability for long-term habitation as by the disposition of the resources available to the occupants, and an evaluation of the microclimate offered by the particular types of habitation is an important factor in the understanding of settlement distribution.

The measurement of cave climates by the method described in this article was used first in Epirus, north-western Greece. Higgs *et al.* (1966, 1967) have shown that the sites of Asprochaliko and Kastritsa contain a succession of Upper Palaeolithic industries, with occasional subsequent use in Classical times continuing to the present day. Surveys of this part of Epirus have shown that many natural caves and shelters are virtually devoid of settlement of any period, and that Asprochaliko and Kastritsa may thus be regarded as highly preferred home bases. For a number of reasons, the hypothesis has been advanced that the two sites are economically complementary and represent seasonal occupation of the upland and lowland zones by the same human group (Higgs *et al.,* 1967). At first sight, this hypothesis would seem to be open to other interpretations, as the nature of the two sites is so different. Asprochaliko shelter faces south, and lies at the foot of a low cliff overlooking the Louros river gorge, about 200 m above sea level and adjacent to the coastal plain. Although protected from northerly exposure by the cliff, the shelter is apparently exposed to the east and west. In contrast, Kastritsa is a fully enclosed cave, well protected on all sides except the north-west, to which it faces, and overlooking the Ioannina lake basin at some 500 m above sea level. It would thus appear that the deeper Kastritsa cave would be more suited to winter occupation than the shallow Asprochaliko shelter. On the other hand, consideration of the faunal evidence suggested that Kastritsa was probably the summer occupation site of a group which moved to the warmer coastal regions in winter. One piece of evidence from excavation seemed to support this view. Removal of the talus at Kastritsa revealed evidence of extensive frost shattering on the rock walls, whereas excavation at Asprochaliko showed no trace of such effects at any level. A possible explanation of this is that the winter climate at Kastritsa in the Late Glacial had been considerably more severe than that at Asprochaliko. In consequence it was decided to measure the physical environments offered by the shelter and the cave in both the summer and winter seasons to determine which of the sites would have been more suitable for winter and which for summer occupation.

METHOD OF ASSESSING LIVING ENVIRONMENT

Casual observations on climate generally refer only to air temperature as a measure of human comfort, although other factors contribute strongly to the heat balance of an individual. For example, a temperature that is comfortable in still air may give rise to considerable heat loss when associated with a high air movement, causing discomfort and consequent demands upon the body metabolism. Similarly, if one enters a cave after exposure to strong sun, one feels the effect of the radiant heat loss to the colder rock walls, but without a discernible change in air temperature. Thus heat may be lost (or gained) by the body via a number of channels: convective exchange (depending on air temperature and air movement), conduction due to contact of the body with a surface at a different temperature, evaporation of body water, and radiant heat exchange with the surroundings.

In the caves, the radiant and convective components of the thermal environment were measured by means of a Globe Thermometer (Burton & Edholm, 1945), which has been used in studies of human physiology to measure the demands of the thermal environment upon individuals under testing conditions. This thermometer consists of a 15 cm diameter hollow sphere made of thin copper, painted matt black, with the bulb of a mercury-in-glass thermometer at its centre. The high heat absorbtion/emissivity of its surface renders the sphere comparable to a man in its infra-red heat balance. From a record of the temperature within the sphere, the adjacent shade air temperature (also measured by a mercury-in-glass thermometer), and the rate of air movement, the demands of radiant and convective heat losses or gains may be calculated.

The sphere was suspended 0.5 m from the ground, approximating the body position in sedentary work and resting. Readings of the thermometers were taken at hourly intervals, together with observations on wind speed, cloud cover, sunshine, and precipitation for a twenty-four hour period at each cave.

RESULTS

The results of these readings at Kastritsa and Asprochaliko are given in Figure 1. As would be expected, the two sites show pronounced differences in climate during the summer and winter seasons, each showing an approximate depression of 20°C in the winter as compared with summer temperature. Asprochaliko is also 6-7°C warmer than Kastritsa in both seasons, a factor that can be largely attributed to the different altitudes and geographical locations of the two sites.

From the readings taken, it is possible to consider the particular advantages of both sites as places of habitation in the summer or winter season, and also to consider the way in which a shelter compares, in this respect, with a true cave. In the situation of the two sites in question, some bias is introduced by the different amounts of direct insolation received by each site. This is partly due to the orientations of the cave and shelter, in which respect the shelter has a more favourable aspect; it is however also due to the smaller amount of sun admitted into the more enclosed cave. In consequence, Asprochaliko is exposed to the full force of the sun from the time of local sunrise above the opposite side of the gorge until it passes over and behind the cliff in which the shelter is situated. In the summer this provides more than six hours of sunshine fully within the shelter, with sunlight falling nearby for a longer period, while at Kastritsa the sun falls within the cave only during a three-hour period in the late afternoon. During the winter the degree of cloud cover prevented exact observations on the amount of sun received by each site, but it was evident that the shelter would still be more favoured in this respect.

During the period of direct insolation in the summer season experience gained in excavation showed that some part of the interior of Kastritsa cave remained in the shade throughout the day, while at Asprochaliko the sun could not be avoided. Although this represents some inconvenience during the day, the night-time climate within the shelter is greatly modified by the amount of stored heat in the bare rock wall. During the night this heat is released, causing a considerably slower fall in temperature than was seen at Kastritsa. The temperature curves show that the effect of the heated rock is to maintain the temperature of the black bulb thermometer *above* that of the air at Asprochaliko (showing a heat gain to the sphere) while at Kastritsa the black bulb temperature remains *below* that of the air. At Kastritsa, the black bulb temperature is, in fact, below air temperature at all times except during the period of direct insolation into the cave, while at Asprochaliko the black bulb temperature remains above that of the air throughout the twenty-four hours.

During the period of the winter recordings, there was almost complete cloud cover at both sites with only a short period of afternoon sun at Kastritsa to cause a sharp, but short-lived, rise in radiant temperature (Fig. 2). The effect of the cloud cover is to reduce the gain of radiant heat from the sun during the day, but also to limit the loss of heat at night by the same channel. Yet even without the effect of insolation during the day, the shelter retains an advantage, as the night-time radiant temperature (black bulb) is again above that of the air, while in the cave it remains below air temperature. It might be expected that the shelter, with only a small rock overhang to reduce radiant heat losses to the sky, would show a disadvantage on clear nights, but it seems likely that the heat storage properties of the rock wall would probably outweigh this. It can be seen that during the winter period in question, the *maximum* daytime temperature at Kastritsa exceeds the *minimum* night-time temperature at Asprochaliko by only 0.4°C and is in fact considerably colder through much of the twenty-four hour cycle (Fig. 1). It might also be expected that the shelter would have the disadvantage of higher wind speeds

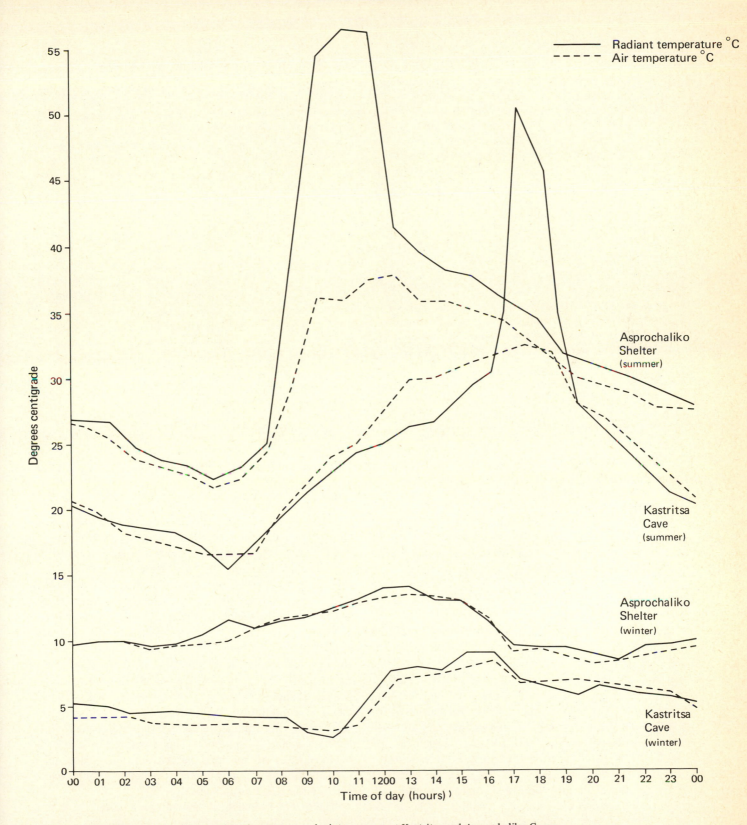

Fig. 1. Radiant and air temperatures in the summer and winter seasons at Kastritsa and Asprochaliko Caves.

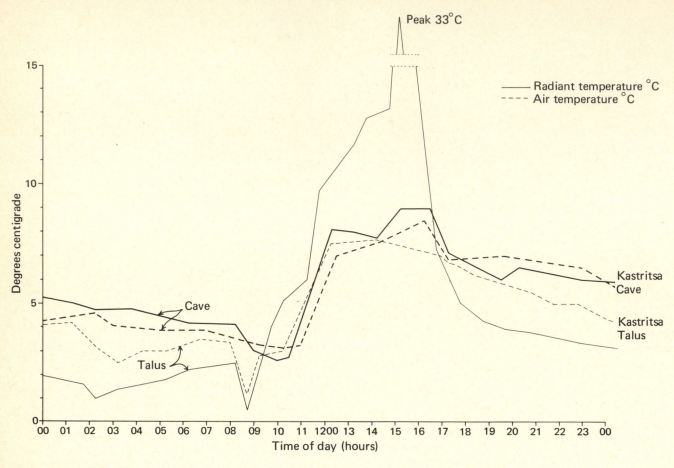

Fig. 2. Radiant and air temperatures in the winter season within Kastritsa Cave and on the talus.

due to its more exposed nature, but very little difference in this was found between the two sites. At Asprochaliko, the wind tended to blow past the overhang, leaving the air inside the shelter little disturbed.

DISCUSSION

As the temperature readings recorded in these observations refer to the present-day situation, and the occupation of the sites was during the colder Late Glacial period, the relevance of modern readings to a past situation must be established. It should be noted that the readings from Kastritsa and Asprochaliko show similar fluctuations at the same period of the day in both seasons, and that although the mean temperature is substantially ˙lowered in the winter, the shape of the curve for both sites remains similar to that of the summer season. This suggests that the effect of the glacial temperature depression would be to alter only the mean temperature at each site, while the relative features of the temperature curves remained unchanged.

The fact that human settlement has extended into the

Arctic Circle may be construed as indicating that man could have ignored the type of climate likely to have been met in Epirus during the Late Glacial, and that either cave could have provided adequate shelter in either season. Yet this is not likely to have been the case if all aspects of human settlement are considered. It has been shown (Higgs *et al.*, 1967) that in the region of Kastritsa and Asprochaliko the distribution of grazing resources available in the summer and winter seasons favour a transhumant economy as practised in the area by the Vlachs today. The situation in the Late Glacial, with a more severe winter climate than today and an economy based upon red deer, renders a similar mode of exploitation highly likely. Thus Kastritsa represents the upland summer habitation, and Asprochaliko the lowland winter habitation. The measurements of the micro-climates of the two habitations shows that their particular location is favourable to occupation according to such a pattern of transhumance.

The extent to which the inhabitants of a cave may have sought to modify the interior and consequently the climate in which they lived remains unknown from the majority of excavations, which have seldom been designed to recover traces of construction. A few notable exceptions exist, such as the Grotte du Renne (Leroi-Gourhan, 1961) where a setting of wooden posts extends around the inner rock wall of part of the cave as well as across its mouth (layer X, Chatelperronian), and which may be interpreted as a structure designed to support an insulation of some organic material. This would have the effect of preventing the entry of cold air from the exterior as well as reducing the losses of radiant heat, as the artificial wall of the structure would assume a temperature intermediate between that of the interior and exterior air temperatures. Yet the absence of such structures cannot always be attributed to less skilled excavation, as at Kastritsa only small structures were found outside the cave in spite of excavation with such features in mind. In this case it may be argued that such attempts to improve the cave climate were not required in a situation of summer occupation.

Cave excavation does, however, bear abundant witness to the use of fire, which presumably was used for modifying the environment as much as for any other purpose. At the Abri Pataud (Movius, 1966) and at Asprochaliko hearths were found to have been arranged against the rear wall of the shelter, which is another way in which the heat storage and radiant properties of the rock wall were used to advantage. The efficient use of fire demands that some of the heat produced in combustion be retained in this way, and in light and poorly insulated structures with low heat capacity, such as skin tents, this is less easily achieved. Stefansson (1943) recorded that in such structures used by the Athabascan Indians, the interior remained cold in spite of the use of a large fire, and frost would rapidly form on surfaces not exposed to the direct radiant heat. Thus although a tent prevents exposure to direct wind cooling, the amount of heating within may be very limited. In this respect, the circumpolar peoples show marked behavioural and physiological adaptations. The Eskimo snow house, even at very low environmental temperatures, can be maintained at a high temperature on the inside due to the unique design employed. The structure itself has very good properties of insulation, and the position of the door below the level of the living and sleeping area prevents exposure to the entering air until it has been heated by oil lamps. Although fuel is not abundant, the small internal volume of the house contributes to the maintenance of a high temperature, and Stefansson (1943) wrote, 'Most Eskimos known to me live in a tropical or sub-tropical environment'. The temperature inside a snow house was measured by Stefansson at 26-32°C, with an outside reading of −45°C, maintaining a 75°C temperature gradient across the house wall. Where such well insulated structures are not used, other cold-exposed peoples attempt to reduce heat loss

from their dwellings by the use of a double-walled construction. The large skin houses of the Siberian Chukchi contain an inner sleeping compartment, also of skin, which contains a fire in the winter season. Yet in spite of restricted movement to and from this sleeping area at night, Borgoras (1904) measured only a −11°C interior temperature with −45 to −50°C on the outside. This type of construction is similar in some respects to the house plans known from the Upper Palaeolithic of Russia (for example Kostienki IV, horizon 2 (Klein, 1969)) some of which are very large, even if taken to represent several overlapping structures. At some sites, it is possible to see that the area of dense habitation is smaller than the apparent outline of the house which may indicate a double-walled construction after the manner of the Chukchi dwelling.

There has been a tendency in the archaeological literature to regard the cave as an inferior type of dwelling and consequently to represent the building of houses as a more advanced cultural manifestation. Yet abundant examples show that house building is not confined to the Postglacial and that the construction of artificial shelters is as old as man in the archaeological record, being claimed by Leakey in Bed 1 of the Olduvai Gorge, from the Grotte du Lazaret (Lumley, 1969) at Nice in the Acheulian, and in Russia from the Middle Palaeolithic onwards. It would seem that the building of artificial shelters has been widely practised in all periods of prehistory whenever the settlement of an area cannot depend upon the use of suitable natural caves. Unless the house is constructed almost entirely below ground or built of some substance such as snow, with a high insulation value, the natural cave would appear to offer a habitation with considerable advantages. It has been shown that the cave modifies the effects of the external environment due to the heat capacity of the enormous amount of rock with which it is surrounded. Such large masses are not subject to the short term oscillations of daily climatic change, and even the seasonal difference in temperature is modified to a considerable degree. Thus as long as the cave is not subjected to excessive air exchange with the outside, the interior temperature will be higher in the winter, and lower in the summer than that prevailing in the external environment. The same cannot be said of light shelters constructed from organic materials which, in spite of good wind-proofing, will be subject to short term changes in temperature according to the daily cycle.

The capacity of the cave to modify the effects of the external environment is no less important in hotter and more arid regions, and man has taken advantage of this fact throughout the middle latitudes of the world. Some of the inhabited caves in this region may be at such an altitude that considerable winter cold might be experienced, though the probability of migration of the inhabitants at such a time renders this of less importance. Many large caves in Palestine show extensive occupation, beginning in some cases as early as the Lower Palaeolithic and extending to the Upper Palaeolithic or Mesolithic (Natufian). It would appear that in all of these periods a considerable amount of settlement was situated outside caves, and is represented by scatters of surface artefacts, local concentrations of which suggest more than a transient settlement. Knowledge of these open settlements in Palestine is limited, and from the later periods only Ain Mallaha has been extensively excavated. This Natufian settlement consists of a number of small houses represented by low stone walls, with the attendant artefact types suggesting a relatively long stay or repeated occupation at the site. However, it remains possible that similar settlement types may be a feature of considerably earlier culture groups whenever local resources permitted a sufficient length of stay. Suggestions that Ain Mallaha and similar settlements represent the imminent appearance of settled villages or proto-urbanization must be considered in the light of our incomplete knowledge of settlements from earlier periods in the same country. However, although occupations dating from the earlier periods of prehistory are best known from cave deposits, such habitations become less common subsequent to the Natufian. The Pre-pottery Neolithic is rare within caves, and occupation in the later periods, such as the Bronze Age material in Shuqbah and Tabun, is sporadic in time and not extensive. It could, however, be argued in this instance that this shift in settlement distribution is associated with a period of profound economic change, when the needs of arable cultivation required the settlement of the plains.

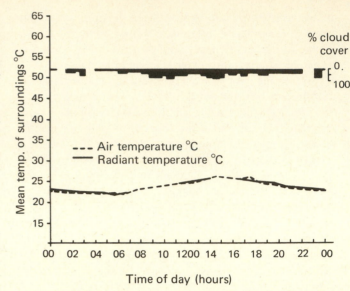

Fig. 4.   Radiant and air temperatures within an Arab stone house, Sorief (summer).

Such sporadic occupation as occurs within caves in Neolithic and Bronze Age times, and even later, is doubtless associated with a continuance of a herding economy, when natural caves would have provided shelter for man as well as, in the larger caves, for domestic animals from both the summer heat and winter rains.

Temperature readings were also taken in a number of caves in Israel, giving particular emphasis in the larger caves to measurement at several different locations within the interior. Kebarah Cave on Mount Carmel is representative of a group of large caves, and shows the typical modification of the external climatic regime towards the depths of the cave (Fig. 3). The temperature curve for Kebarah shows only some 6°C change during the twenty-four hour cycle in both the black bulb and air temperatures, with the radiant temperature consistently 2-3°C below that of the air, thus allowing a steady heat loss to the cooler rock walls. This results in an environmental situation in which comfort is maintained. The climate within the Kebarah cave may be compared with that found within an Arab stone house in the village of Sorief in the Jordan (Fig. 4). This type of house is constructed of large dressed stone blocks, giving a wall thickness of some 45 cm. The local building stone is of light colour, giving added advantages in the reflection of solar radiation. The heat capacity of such a comparatively massive structure results in a similar damping of daily temperature changes as was found at the Kebarah Cave, and the temperature curves from the two habitations show similar small changes. The house walls are evidently somewhat closer to air temperature in the stone house, and consequently no significant difference exists between the

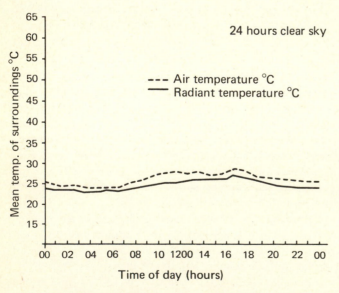

Fig. 3.   Radiant and air temperatures in Kebarah Cave, at rear (summer).

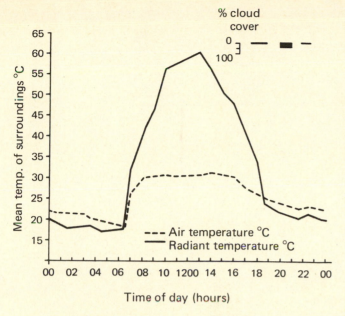

Fig. 5. Radiant and air temperatures in the open air at sea level near Haifa (summer).

frequently seen panting rapidly. In parts of Greece it is apparent that such artificial shelters are constructed only where insufficient caves exist to meet the needs of the local domestic animal population.

It is evident, however, that the use of a light organic covering over a wooden frame cannot prevent a rise in temperature within the house to intolerable levels unless a very high rate of air exchange with the exterior is maintained. In the skin tents of the desert Bedouin the walls of the tent can be readily re-arranged or removed to exclude direct sun, but at the same time to permit maximum air movement. As a house used for long-term habitation, even if for one season only, will be the centre of much human activity during the day, it seems questionable whether light structures would be suited to summer occupation. It may thus be argued that the type of house found at sites such as Ain Mallaha are appropriate for occupation only in seasons that do not demand the avoidance of heat or cold.

The estimation of the microclimates of the sites of Asprochaliko and Kastritsa suggests that the rock shelter may offer advantages as a focus of human settlement, and this suggestion is supported by the large number of densely occupied shelters in the Palaeolithic of south-western France. The postulated seasonal use of the two sites in Epirus is shown to be advantageous from the micro-climates offered as well as in the distribution of other resources. Yet the habitation within caves is a feature of hot climates, no less than in the cold conditions of Late Glacial Europe. Even areas close to the coast in the east and south Mediterranean may experience conditions of winter frost and even snow, and the avoidance of summer temperature extremes also makes the available caves favoured sites for occupation. The measurements obtained at sites in Palestine suggest that the conditions found within a large cave such as Kebarah Cave are difficult to equate with any construction other than the large stone house of the present day Arab villages. The construction of houses such as those at Ain Mallaha may be a feature of even earlier times, and the significance of this type of settlement must be treated with some reserve. It may be suggested that patterns of human settlement within an area, and the types of settlement revealed, need consideration with a broader view than has been used to support some interpretations that have been made.

radiant and air temperatures. The climate prevailing within the deep cave and stone house may be contrasted with that measured in an unshaded open air situation near Kebarah (Fig. 5). The radiant temperature rises to a high level during day-time insolation, but falls below air temperature during the night to a level that may cause discomfort even in summer. It would therefore seem that for the summer season at least, the construction of houses with a large mass is able to provide an environment closely similar to that of the natural cave. On the other hand, it is evident that lighter structures do not possess similar advantages and are liable to extreme overheating during the day-time period of high radiant heat gain from the sun. In some Mediterranean countries domestic sheep and goats are provided with day-time shelters roofed and even walled with a thick layer of reed or straw thatch. The high insulation of such a structure contributes to the maintenance of a tolerable environmental temperature within, but observations suggest that animals thus enclosed endure a greater degree of heat stress than is met by those sheltered in natural caves and are

SECTION III
FIELD AND CASE STUDIES

1. CURRENT EXPERIMENTAL DOMESTICATION AND ITS RELEVANCE TO PREHISTORY

P. F. WILKINSON

If progress is to be made in understanding the origins of agriculture, the validity of the techniques and hypotheses used to interpret archaeological data must be tested empirically wherever possible. Modern experiments in the controlled exploitation of animal populations offer an important opportunity for such testing, but have been largely ignored by archaeologists. The present paper reviews briefly some of these experiments and considers the degree to which they suggest modifying the current conceptual and methodological framework of archaeological investigations into the origins of agriculture.

Musk-ox (Teal, 1958, 1970; Wilkinson, 1971*a,b*) (Plate I): musk-oxen have been tamed and selectively bred under farm conditions since 1953 by the Institute of Northern Agricultural Research. Breeding farms have been established in Alaska, Quebec, and Norway and smaller, commercial village-farms will be started in each of these areas when enough animals become available. At present, musk-oxen are exploited solely for their fine underwool (*qiviut*), which is being used to establish a uniquely arctic textile industry in an effort to combat the widespread poverty and un-employment of the native peoples of the Arctic, but future plans include their use for milk and possibly for meat and as draught animals. Taming newly-captured and selectively-bred calves proved easy and relatively permanent, and experiments in Vermont have demonstrated that musk-oxen will remain tame despite a minimum of contact with humans. The naturally sedentary annual cycle of musk-oxen, their gregariousness, and their relative immunity to predators obviate the need for close herding and the animals need be gathered together only for calving and wool-collection.

Selective breeding plays an important role in this experiment and is directed towards improving the quality and quantity of the annual wool yield, promoting increased docility and tractability, and creating a medium-sized, naturally polled animal. To date only three crops of selectively-bred calves have been born, so that the success of the breeding programme cannot be judged; despite some inbreeding there is no evidence for increased phenotypic variability. The first documented occurrence of twinning in musk-oxen was reported in 1970 from the Alaskan herd,

Plate I.   Domesticated musk-oxen (photo by Robert Koweeluk).

although neither calf survived (Wilkinson, 1971c). The successful spread of domesticated musk-oxen throughout the Arctic is facilitated by the fact that they do not compete for food with reindeer and caribou, and because the activities associated with their maintenance can be integrated easily and profitably into the economic and social structure of contemporary Eskimo life. Domesticated musk-oxen will not be moved outside their native arctic habitat, for they would not thrive and would be unable to compete economically with the traditional domestic animals in other areas.

Elk (Knorre, 1961; Yazan & Knorre, 1964): tamed and selectively-bred elk have been raised on the Pechora-Ilych State Reservation, U.S.S.R., for over twenty years. They are used successfully for milk, meat, and traction. Castration, selective slaughter, and direct mating have all been practised, but the literature makes no reference to increased phenotypic variability or to marked divergence from the wild phenotype as a result of inbreeding. It has proved possible to 'attach' elk to chosen localities by teaching them to associate these places with food and breeding, so that free grazing can be practised and the animals lose their tendency to undertake annual migrations. Elk are by nature gregarious only in autumn and winter, but under the conditions of domestication the herd instinct can be strengthened and herds maintained throughout the year. The elk experiment emphasized the importance of training as opposed to selective breeding, for milk yields and performance as draught animals both improved significantly with training. Although wild and domesticated elk coexist in the same areas, the domesticated animals tend to attract their wild counterparts rather than to run with them as is reported for reindeer (Leeds, 1965). The exploitation of domesticated elk is complemented by a programme of selective hunting of wild populations in the same area, and some management of the staple food species of the domesticated elk is considered desirable if herds are to be maintained in the same areas over long periods.

Eland: (a) Africa (Posselt, 1963; Talbot *et al.*, 1965): despite its promise, domestication of the eland in Africa has not progressed beyond the stage of a small-scale experiment. Capturing and taming wild eland calves proved simple, and the animals showed no tendency to wander when allowed to graze without supervision, despite the presence of wild eland in the area. Castration has no apparent effect on rates of live weight gain or on the mature weight of males. The females quickly became accustomed to being milked and their yield per lactation increased markedly with training.

(b) Russia (Treus & Kravchenko, 1968): four male and four female eland calves were brought from Africa to the Askaniya-Nova Zoological Park, in the Russian Ukraine, at the end of the nineteenth century. Since then 408 calves have been bred from them, but, despite the high degree of inbreeding inevitable, there are no reports of increased phenotypic variability. Free grazing is practised in summer, but food and shelter have to be provided in winter. The eland in Russia are exploited principally for their milk, which is rich and is said to show outstanding preservative qualities. Training and continued milking have increased milk yields by over 400 percent in some cases. Castration, selective slaughter, and controlled mating are all practised in order to 'improve' the herd from the point of view of its exploiters. The reproductive pattern of the eland appears to have been affected, either by the altered conditions of its maintenance or because it has been moved to an environment quite different from its African homeland: in Africa, eland calve in March to May and November to December, whereas those in the Ukraine calve throughout the year, with a peak in February and March.

Mink (Belyaev, 1969): unlike the previous examples, the domestication of the mink places considerable emphasis on replacing natural selective pressures with others more advantageous to man, and the animals in question have been rendered totally dependent on man for food, shelter, and reproduction. Within the past thirty-five years over one hundred complex colour mutations have arisen, many of them accompanied by such reduced fertility and vitality that they can survive and reproduce only with human protection. Much of the variation is apparently controlled by recessive mutations, which have been retained in the wild presumably because the heterozygous state is at a selective advantage, although the reasons why this should be the case are rarely clear.

Norway rat (Richter, 1954): the relationship between man and the Norway rat resembles the man-mink relationship in its emphasis on the production and preservation of mutations. Unlike the mink, however, it serves an experimental rather than a commercial purpose. The Norway rat is one of the few animals in which the effects of taming, captivity, and selective breeding have been studied. The observed changes include a size-decrease affecting the adrenals, the preputial glands, the liver, heart, spleen, brain, and pancreas; a size-increase of the hypophysis and thymus; an increase in the number of Peyer's patches in the intestines; and a decrease in the number of fungiform papillae on the tongue. The metabolic rate of the experimental animals was also lowered, and their food-intake per unit body-weight decreased. Observed behavioural changes included a loss of aggression towards humans in some animals and the disappearance of certain patterns of vocalization. Tameness in rats is apparently controlled by the frontal poles of the brain, but the manner in which these were affected by domestication remains unclear.

Fox (Belyaev, 1969): foxes have been selectively bred in captivity in parts of Russia for over seventy years and have shown phenotypic changes similar to those observed in minks. Captive, selectively-bred foxes show considerable variation in temperament, but tame forms are not uncommon. Changes in the reproductive cycle are apparently related to temperament, for docile animals tend to breed earlier in the season than timid or aggressive individuals, but such changes may be slow to develop and some docile forms have retained their wild reproductive patterns for over sixty years.

Indian buffalo (Loeser, 1968): (*a*) South America: two farms on Marajo Island, off the mouth of the Amazon, have a total of 48 000 buffalo, exploited principally for meat. Taming has proved simple and the buffalo are superior to cattle in their ability to utilize the coarse local grasses and to withstand catastrophes such as floods. Buffalo require only one herder per 300 animals, as opposed to the cattle of Marajo Island, which require a ratio of 1:50. A similar low ratio characterizes elk and musk-oxen.

(*b*) Melville Island, Australia: buffalo have been introduced very successfully to Melville Island, where their exploitation has been based on hunting feral animals. Selective breeding and stricter supervision have been introduced recently, and in 1965 17 000 animals were harvested. A similar pattern of exploiting feral animals is recorded for the cattle of parts of the Argentinian pampas (Strickon, 1965), which were hunted for their hides until the development of fast, refrigerated transport opened up the European market to Argentinian beef and placed stricter supervision of the animals and better management at an economic premium.

Ostrich (Loeser, 1968; Zeuner, 1963a): the ostrich was domesticated in Algeria and parts of South Africa c. 1860, when its feathers were fashionable. Taming was important, although apparently not permanent, and in some cases eggs were incubated artificially. Importing ostriches into Australia proved unsuccessful (Rolls, 1969), and ostrich farming declined as the demand for feathers fell; more recently, a renewed demand for meat has led to a minor revival of ostrich farming in South Africa.

Reindeer (Scotter, 1965; Loeser, 1968): reindeer have been under close human control probably for many millennia, but one new variation on this old relationship is worth recording, for it illustrates well the dynamic nature of many man-animal relationships. In 1951 a fence 350 miles long and 7 ft high was constructed in northern Finland to define the northern limit of the annual migration of the reindeer. Close herding has been discontinued, and the animals are rounded up only when they return south in autumn, leaving the former herdsmen free to participate in other activities required by the modern cash-economy.

Similar changes in patterns of reindeer exploitation are reported from Norway and Russia.

Kangaroo (Rolls, 1969): kangaroos in Australia have been protected and selectively hunted for some years. The growing demand for pet-foods has led to consideration of their potential for increased productivity through selective breeding and maintenance under farm conditions.

Saiga antelope (Gervais, 1855; Loeser, 1968): concern for the survival of the saiga in Russia towards the end of the last century led to the introduction of protective legislation. The population of saiga antelopes has increased to over two millions as a result, of which some 10 percent are harvested annually by professional hunters, although a much higher rate of exploitation could probably be tolerated. In fact, experiments in the controlled exploitation of saiga appear to pre-date 1855, when Gervais (1855, vol. 2, p. 207) wrote: 'on élève aisément les Saïgas en domesticité lorsqu'on les prend jeunes. Ceux qui ont été ainsi apprivoisés courent librement au dehors sans se joindre aux individus sauvages, et ils reviennent à la voix de leur maître auquel ils ne manquent pas de faire quelques caresses'.

Zebra (Bigalke & Neitz, 1954; Loeser, 1968): in South Africa zebras have occasionally been tamed and used as draught animals, with considerable success. Some have been transplanted to the Soviet Union, where they are reported to be thriving.

Tapir (Gervais, 1855): members of the Institute of Northern Agricultural Research have recently been contemplating taming and selectively breeding tapirs as a source of meat, but this is by no means a new idea, for Gervais reported (1855, vol. 2, p. 157) experimental rearing of tapirs over one hundred years ago: 'en captivité le Tapir est doux, tranquille, assez propre et souvent assez familier, et les naturalistes ont inscrit ce genre sur la liste des animaux dont la domestication offrirait le moins de difficultés, et en même temps le plus d'avantages. Lorsqu'on a pris les Tapirs encore jeunes, on peut les laisser vivre au milieu des habitations'.

African buffalo (Bigalke & Neitz, 1954): there are reports of the taming and breeding of African buffalo, apparently quite successfully, but none seems to have progressed beyond the purely experimental stage.

Chinchilla (Zimmermann, 1961): eight male and four female chinchillas were taken from South America to California in 1922-3, and almost all domesticated chinchillas are descended from them. Wild chinchillas apparently show little fear of man, so that taming was unnecessary. Selective breeding and intensive management have been practised, as with the mink, and important changes have affected coat colour and the endocrine system. After ten to fifteen generations the average body weight of some populations had increased by 50 percent, whilst in others the females were consistently 20 percent heavier than the males.

Cassowary (Bulmer, 1968): in parts of New Guinea cassowary chicks are captured, tamed, and raised for trade, slaughter, and for their plumes. Other animals sporadically raised and tamed in New Guinea include several species of cuscus, ringtail possums, hornbills, white cockatoos, parrots, and feral dogs and pigs.

Galapagos tortoise (Dorst, 1970): feral rats were threatening the survival of the Galapagos tortoise by overpredation of eggs and young. The eggs are now being protected, and the young tortoises are released only when they are old enough to defend themselves. Young pheasants are similarly protected in parts of England (Taylor, 1968).

Grass carp (Hickling, 1965): the Asian grass carp is a good converter of aquatic vegetation into edible protein. They have been introduced into some African waterways in order to keep them relatively free of vegetation and more suited to human transport requirements; at the same time, by clearing aquatic vegetation, the grass carp can also create conditions more suitable for light-demanding fish, which can also be exploited by man.

Manatee (Bertram & Bertram, 1968): the manatee, like the grass carp, is an efficient exploiter of aquatic vegetation, which lives predominantly in coastal and estuarine waters, although there is one landlocked species in the Amazon Basin. Manatees have been introduced into some waterways in Guyana to keep them open for transportation. Like the grass carp in Africa, the manatee has failed to breed in its new home, so that stocks have to be renewed by further transplants. The dugong has a similar potential to the manatee in Pacific waters, and both can, of course, be exploited also for meat.

Oyster (Pinchot, 1970): oyster farming has a long history and a wide geographical distribution. Laws relating to oyster farming in Japan were formulated before the time of Christ, and both Aristotle and Pliny make reference to oyster farming. Traditionally, oyster farming has involved clearing chosen areas of predators, providing 'cultch', or smooth, clean surfaces such as shell or ceramics, to which the young oysters can attach themselves, maintaining the growing oysters safe from predators, and in some cases removing them to special areas for fattening shortly before marketing. Recently, however, the Japanese have pioneered the method of suspension farming, the traditional way of raising mussels. This method has many advantages, principally that it is possible to locate the growing oysters at depths where the food supply is richest.

Milkfish (Pinchot, 1970): milkfish are farmed in ponds in the Philippine Republic, and the yield from untreated ponds reaches 78 tons of meat per square mile, contrasted with a yield of only 6-17 tons per square mile from coastal waters. In Taiwan, where the milkfish ponds are fertilized, the yield per square mile reaches 520 tons, and in parts of Indonesia, where raw sewage is diverted into the ponds, yields as high as 1300 tons per square mile have been attained.

Mullet (Pinchot, 1970): mullet are farmed commercially in Hawaii, China, India, and Israel. Milkfish and mullet are the only salt-water fish farmed on a large scale and, unfortunately, both of them breed only at sea. Attempts at breeding mullet in the laboratory have now succeeded, and it may prove possible to breed them commercially.

The above list is not exhaustive, and Table 1 lists some other examples of the special management of animal populations by man. The game-cropping experiments are worthy of special comment, for they are of increasing economic importance, especially in Africa, and seem to offer important advantages over more traditional forms of animal husbandry. Game-cropping is a sophisticated approach to selective hunting, which attempts to exploit animal populations so as to maximize the benefits to the exploiters without endangering the survival or regenerative capacity of their prey, and at the same time takes advantage of the high number of large game animals that can be supported by many of the vegetationally diverse African grasslands. Marine farming, which has been discussed recently by Pinchot (1970), offers highly encouraging prospects for the creation of new and productive relationships between man and a variety of fish and marine mammals, and, for example, whale farming is no longer impracticable, although it remains to be seen whether the benefits to be derived from it would justify the expense involved. Within the more traditional sphere of animal husbandry, the past twenty years have witnessed a major alteration and intensification of many long-established man-animal relationships, of which battery-raising of chickens provides an outstanding example.

Data from the type of experiments that I have quoted have two main limitations from the point of view of archaeologists: in only two cases, the Norway rat (Richter, 1954) and the musk-ox (Wilkinson, 1971a,d), have they been studied from a point of view directly relevant to archaeological interests, and even then the time-span involved is so short that it detracts from their value. Secondly, with the possible exception of the cassowary (Bulmer, 1968), the experiments have occurred in technological and social contexts which differ in important respects from those which may be assumed to have existed in prehistoric times. Nonetheless, the experiments discussed above cast light on the range of man-animal relationships, on the practical difficulties of initiating such relationships, on certain of their manifestations which may leave visible traces in the

CURRENT EXPERIMENTAL DOMESTICATION AND ITS RELEVANCE TO PREHISTORY

Table 1.   Man-animal relationships

Relationship	Species	Location	Reference
Game-cropping	elephant	Kenya	Stewart, 1963
	hippopotamus	Uganda	
	kob	Uganda	
	blesbok	S. Africa	
	springbok	S. Africa	
Experimental rearing and taming	topi	Uganda	Hutchison, 1970
	kob		
	dik-dik		
Fish ponds, protection, feeding, breeding, hybridization, transplanting	bluegill sunfish	U.S.A.	Black, 1968
	largemouth bass		
	crappie		
	bullhead catfish		
	swingle		
	warmouth bass		
	red-ear sunfish		
	channel catfish		
	carp		
	brook trout		
	rainbow trout		
	musky		
	northern pike		
	lamprey		
Selective breeding	quail	U.S.A.	Black, 1968
	partridge		
Protection and/or selective hunting	bullfrog	various	various
	musk-ox		
	polar bear		
	seal		
	whale		
	walrus		
	bighorn sheep		
	mountain goat		
Distribution altered	pheasant	various	Black, 1968; Scott, 1958; Zimmerman, 1963; Niethammer, 1963; Lindemann, 1956
	beaver		
	turkey		
	rabbit		
	rat		
	muskrat		
	raccoon		
	fallow deer		
	kangaroo		
	macaque		
	grey squirrel		
	red squirrel		
	marmot		
	dormouse		
	coypu		
	silver fox		
	marten		
	brown bear		
	badger		
	muntjak		
	axis deer		
	wapiti		
	maral		
	sika deer		
	mouflon		

archaeological record, and they suggest new approaches to recognizing the nature of past man-animal relationships.

PATTERNS OF EXPLOITATION

It is immediately apparent that many of the man-animal relationships described above do not fall within the range of the accepted definition of 'domestication', which is based on the removal of chosen groups of animals from 'their natural living area and breeding community, and their maintenance under controlled breeding conditions for profit' (Bökönyi, 1969a), often accompanied by taming. The usefulness of this definition has been discussed elsewhere (Higgs & Jarman, 1969; Wilkinson, 1971a) and is considered at greater length elsewhere in this volume (Jarman & Wilkinson, II. 4). The principal criticism of this definition is not that it is possible to find exceptions to the classification that it proposes, for this is simply to acknowledge the impossibility of a perfect taxonomy (Johnson, 1970). More important, the criteria of tameness, isolation, and selective breeding were adopted originally by zoologists and agriculturalists to describe the contemporary situation, with special reference to traditional (largely western European) agricultural practices. The term 'domestication' is, therefore, largely inappropriate to the interests of economic prehistorians, and it seems in danger of becoming outmoded as a classification of contemporary agricultural practices as man extends the range and nature of his exploitive patterns to feed the growing population of the world.

One legitimate focus of archaeological attention, which falls within the scope of contemporary investigative techniques, is the search for patterns of economic exploitation. By this, I mean the varying strategies adopted by human populations through time and space to integrate technology and resources into coherent, successful economies. Through time there must have been a strong selective pressure favouring the development of increasingly efficient patterns of exploitation. Efficiency in this sense has been defined elsewhere (Wilkinson, 1971a) as exploitive strategies consonant with a given technology, designed to increase and, in the long run, to maximize the yield obtained from the available resources without endangering the survival of these resources or (in the case of organic, renewable resources) exceeding their regenerative capacity. Domestication as traditionally defined is one means of attaining this objective in some circumstances, but even a superficial consideration of the patterns of exploitation described above suggests that it is appropriate only to a limited number of environmental and technological contexts. The same purpose of increased efficiency may be achieved by means other than taming and selective breeding.

111

The precise form of efficient exploitive strategies in different situations is likely to be determined by a complex interaction involving such variables as technology, the behavioural and physiological attributes of the animals in question, and the limitations imposed upon particular economic strategies by the demands on time, space, and labour of other economic activities with a higher priority in the total subsistence pattern. Restrictions such as those imposed by religion or fashion are likely to be important on an archaeological time-scale only if they have important direct or indirect economic consequences, and they cannot always be safely excluded from archaeological interpretations. Although I do not consider that a taxonomy of man-animal relationships is the major priority of economic prehistory in its present, early stage of development, the experiments described in the first part of this paper share a limited number of features, which may form a useful basis for investigating the nature of past economies: (*a*) they permit the efficient exploitation of a previously inaccessible resource; (*b*) they increase the productivity of a previously exploited resource, either by reducing the expenditure of energy involved in exploiting it, or by increasing the productivity of the resource in question; (*c*) they permit the localization or concentration of the desired resource near areas favourable to human settlement, or permit human occupation of previously marginal or uninhabitable localities.

Animals falling into the first category include the musk-ox, elk, eland, and zebra, for it is impossible to exploit animals for milk, wool, or traction without dispelling their fear of man and accustoming them to close contact with humans. The manatee and grass carp may also be included here, for neither can be used to remove the vegetation from waterways that are important to man unless man can control their distribution. One feature common to all the experiments is that they attempt to increase the range, quantity, or quality of resources available to man, although the precise fashion in which this aim is achieved may vary greatly. Selective hunting, as in the African game-cropping experiments, increases the harvestable portion of herds by eliminating young, infirm, and old animals, which contribute least to group defence and propagation and are, in the case of young animals, the most easily replaced segment of the population. Game-cropping experiments also concentrate on exploiting male animals, thus providing an opportunity for breeding females to thrive, thereby increasing the exploitable (young) segment of the populations. In the case of the mink, fox, and cassowary, captivity achieves a similar end by stabilizing the location of the animals, reducing the labour expended in exploiting them, and in some cases by providing an opportunity of improving the quality of their products through selective breeding. All the new relationships with large mammals increase the concentration of available resources, and some of them, for example with the moose and the musk-ox, permit increased human control over the seasonal location of the animal populations in question, facilitating the colonization of new areas or stabilizing occupation in previously marginal habitats. The huge increases in the yield of milkfish from fertilized ponds in Taiwan and Indonesia is a striking illustration of man's ability to increase the quantity of certain resources without striking social or technological innovations. The preceding discussion highlights the complexity of modern man-animal relationships, both in terms of the nature of the relationships themselves and the animal species to which they can be applied successfully. There seems to me to be no compelling reason to assume that this complexity of relationships is necessarily of recent origin, and it is certainly inadequate and probably quite misleading for archaeologists to try to interpret past economies in terms of a simple, bipartite classification of animals as 'wild' or 'domesticated'.

CULTURAL DEVELOPMENT AND DOMESTICATION

There is little evidence to support the current hypothesis that 'the changes in men necessary to bring them to a state of readiness to domesticate animals must have been cultural' (Reed, 1969). Our knowledge of relationships based on the classical criteria of domestication does not permit us to specify with any certainty the time or place of their origins and precludes anything but speculation as to the motivation of these relationships. Historical data and the evidence of modern experiments in utilizing animal populations, on the other hand, suggest very strongly that new and complex man-animal relationships may occur in a wide variety of 'cultural' contexts as widely divergent as Japan in the pre-Christian era and the modern Arctic.

ENVIRONMENTAL AND GEOGRAPHICAL LIMITATIONS

Nor do these data support the widely-held archaeological belief that close man-animal relationships have developed only with a very limited number of species, notably a few artiodactyls. Taming and selective breeding have been extended to birds, insects, rodents, carnivores, and even to some of the marine mammals, and equally intimate relationships not involving taming and selective breeding link man and a wide variety of non-artiodactyl species. Close man-animal relationships have been initiated in many differing environmental contexts, and it seems facile to seek for a purely external, environmental stimulus to explain the

Table 2.   The spatial and temporal diversity of man-animal relationships

Species	Location	Period
pigeon	Mesopotamia	c. 4500 B.C.
lion, baboon, monkey, oryx, antelope, ibex, gazelle, buffalo, fallow deer, hyaena, fox, donkey, cat, hare, mongoose, hippopotamus, crocodile, Lepidotos, frog, Oxyrhynchus, vulture, falcon, kite, crane, stork, heron, ibis, goose, duck, quail, ostrich, cheetah, bee	Egypt	Old Kingdom and later
silk moth	China	c. 3000 B.C.
jungle fowl	India	pre-2500 B.C.
moose	Siberia	Neolithic
guinea pig	Peru	pre-1800 B.C.
ferret	Palestine	pre-1000 B.C.
peacock	India/Burma	c. 1000 B.C.
guinea fowl	Africa	pre-500 B.C.
pheasant	Caucasus	pre-500 B.C.
oyster	Japan	pre-Christian
rabbit, dormouse, ostrich, moray eel, mullet, wrass, carp, oyster	Rome	Classical
cormorant	Japan	c. A.D. 400
goldfish, paradise fish	China	c. A.D. 800
canary	Canary Islands	? A.D. 800
salmon	Pacific N.W.	?
milkfish	Java	A.D. 1500
bison	Siberia	c. A.D. 1750
cassowary, cuscus, parrot, ringtail possum, hornbill, white cockatoo, feral dogs and pigs	New Guinea	?
ostrich	Algeria, S. Africa	c. A.D. 1860
zebra	S. Africa	c. A.D. 1860
fox, eland, moose, saiga, mink, zebra	U.S.S.R.	A.D. 1890
Norway rat, chinchilla	U.S.A.	A.D. 1919
eland, blesbok, springbok, kob, buffalo, topi, grass carp, elephant, hippopotamus	Africa	20th century
Galapagos tortoise	Galapagos Islands	A.D. 1969
manatee	C. America	A.D. 1968

origin of such relationships in prehistory, although environmental/ecological factors may play a role in limiting the range of potential relationships between human and animal populations.

Table 2 presents some of the data on which these conclusions are based, and suggests also that new man-animal relationships initiated within the past 6000 years have arisen in a variety of different localities, rather than in a single centre as is sometimes postulated for the domestication of the goat, sheep, pig, and cattle, for example. The oyster provides a good illustration of a relationship that appears to have arisen in several areas quite independently at different times, for oyster-farming was practised in Japan before the time of Christ, in Classical Greece and in Rome. In this case, there is no need to postulate the diffusion either of oysters or of the idea of oyster-farming.

TECHNOLOGICAL DEVELOPMENT AND DOMESTICATION

The relationship between technology and animal domestication has received considerable discussion in the archaeological literature, and the consensus of opinion seems to favour the belief that domestication is unlikely to have occurred until a high (but unspecified) level of complexity of artefactual technology had been achieved and that the intensive management of animals requires a suite of artefacts recognizably different from that associated with hunting economies. The experimental data do not on the whole support these assumptions, and I have discussed the logistic aspects of musk-ox domestication in detail elsewhere (Wilkinson, 1971a). Capturing the young of most species is easy, provided that adults of that species can be killed, for young calves tend to remain with the bodies of their slaughtered mothers, and commonly show little fear of man. The archaeological record demonstrates man's ability to kill even large and fierce animals since the time of the appearance of the primitive hominids, and there seems to be no reason to assume that capturing young animals would have ever proved a serious obstacle to initiating close man-animal relationships.

Taming, too, requires little or no technological sophistication and may be achieved quickly through feeding and constant human contact after capture. It is true that domesticated reindeer tend to run with caribou, their wild counterparts (Leeds, 1965), but the reindeer appears in fact to be exceptional in this respect. The musk-ox, elk, saiga, and tapir suggest that taming may be more or less permanent during the lifetime of the animal. In many of the experiments quoted the animals developed a strong attachment to the places where they were raised (as many of them do in the wild) and to their handlers, and free grazing proved practicable, so that neither intensive labour nor technological ingenuity was required to permit the successful management and exploitation of the animals in question. Free grazing is known to be practicable for elk, musk-oxen, saiga, eland, and tapir; indeed, it is even reported (Knorre, 1961) that domesticated elk tend to attract their wild counterparts, rather than vice versa.

Selective breeding (not necessarily an important feature of many otherwise close man-animal relationships) may be achieved by any combination of direct mating, castration, and selective slaughter, none of which requires a complex technology. Ethnographical data (Cranstone, 1969) support this conclusion, and I have discussed its relevance to some aspects of the introduction of agriculture into Britain elsewhere (Wilkinson, 1971d). The essence of the type of experiment discussed in this paper seems to me to be that they are labour-saving rather than labour-intensive. Certain of them, notably the game-cropping experiments, differ in no important respects from traditional hunting economies, although they do achieve an objective similar to that of many more intensive relationships.

CHANGE IN SELECTIVE PRESSURE AND ANIMAL FORM

Archaeologists have also overstressed the role of change in domestication, leading them to the conclusion that interbreeding between wild and domesticated representatives of the same species is necessarily deleterious and contrary to the desires of most pastoralists. The experimental data, however, suggest that most attempts at the intensive exploitation of animal populations tend to take advantage of natural selective pressures, attempting to intensify rather

than oppose their effects. The musk-ox illustrates this well, for natural selection in its Arctic environment operates strongly in favour of the optimal development in the quality and quantity of its underwool, so that it is unlikely that human selection will notably increase either of these (although this is an objective of present breeding programmes). The ethnographic data support this conclusion and many pastoralist groups actively encourage interbreeding between wild/feral and domesticated animals (Higgs & Jarman, I. 1, p. 6). Taking into account the preceding discussion and the interests of economic prehistorians, it is salutary to recall Spurway's (1955) assertion that 'the adjective "domestic" describes human behaviour'.

I do not propose to discuss at length the effects of taming and selective breeding on animals, and the ways in which they can be recognized archaeologically (see Jarman & Wilkinson, II. 4), other than to say that the available experimental data fully support Berry's (1969b) statement that 'it is not possible to recognise any traits which inevitably accompany domestication, and, even worse, most of the criteria by which domestication has been claimed to be recognisable may occur as a result of processes which have nothing to do with domestication'.

DEVELOPMENTAL STAGES IN DOMESTICATION

Some authors (e.g. Zeuner, 1963a; Bökönyi, 1969a) have postulated a number of stages leading to the development of 'full' domestication. These are, however, largely hypothetical stages, for there are few examples of societies in such transitional stages. A possible instance is that of some groups of Yanomamö Indians on the upper Orinoco River, who are said (Chagnon, LeQuesne & Cook, 1971) to be in the process of domesticating the tree, *Anadenanthera peregrina*, although the authors do not specify the meaning of the term as they use it, other than to say that it involves transplanting seedlings. The experiments described in the present paper provide no support for the belief that domestication arose through a series of stages, although they cannot, of course, be taken as proof that these stages did not occur in prehistory.

The pre-adaptation of gregarious animals to domestication has also in my opinion been overstressed (Zeuner, 1963a). Whilst gregariousness may be advantageous in some relationships involving close control, it is unnecessary and even disadvantageous in others, such as game-cropping and the intensive raising of fur-bearing carnivores. Most important, the Russian experiments in elk farming have demonstrated that many aspects of animal behaviour are relatively plastic and can, within limits, be moulded by man in accordance with his preferences. Herd behaviour is presumably at a selective advantage where basic food resources are concentrated and abundant, and man is capable of creating such conditions artificially, thus promoting a selective pressure in favour of its development. Conversely, herd behaviour is also an important defence against predators for some animals, and the extermination of predators by man may lessen selective pressures favouring gregariousness.

Much confusion has arisen from the unthinking misapplication of pseudo-evolutionary theory to the study of man-animal relationships, and many prehistorians appear to consider relationships based on taming, restraint, and selective breeding as some sort of evolutionary pinnacle. Modern experiments in the efficient exploitation of animal populations suggest very strongly that this is not the case, but that such relationships are advantageous only in a limited number of situations. A misleading corollary of the evolutionary approach to the study of man-animal relationships is the belief that, once domesticated, species tend to remain so. There is, however, considerable evidence contradicting this hypothesis, of which the history of the relationship between man and the elk provides an outstanding example. Cliff- and rock-drawings from the basins of the Lena, Angora, and Yenisei Rivers, dating to the Siberian Neolithic, depict elk being pastured, ridden, corralled, and pulling sleighs (Knorre, 1961). Locally, such relationships may have persisted as late as the seventeenth century, but over much of this area they were replaced by reindeer pastoralism between the sixth and tenth centuries. Sporadic use of elk for draught and riding has been frequent in Scandinavia and the Baltic area in the past two centuries (Turkin & Satunin, 1902), and is recorded in the United States in the present century (Knorre, 1961) (Plate II), but it has never developed into a major economic activity, despite its importance locally. The gazelle, which was once herded by the Egyptians (Smith, 1969), the Romans (Zeuner, 1963a), and perhaps very much earlier in other parts of the Near East (Legge, III. 2) provides another striking illustration of the dynamic nature of man-animal relationships. Zeuner (1963a) has suggested that a close relationship may have existed between men and foxes in the Swiss Neolithic, and the data quoted earlier in this paper (Loeser, 1968) showed that foxes can be tamed and will thrive in captivity. Foxes are frequent in some Russian Upper Palaeolithic sites. At Mezin, for example, the fox is the animal most frequently found among the faunal remains (Frenzel, 1960), perhaps arguing for a close man-fox relationship at this early date. Ethnographic data, although sparse, suggest that the relationship between some hunters and their prey may be equally dynamic. The nineteenth-century Polar Eskimo, for example, neither hunted caribou nor fished for salmon, although both were available, until the people from Pond Inlet visited them and reintroduced both practices (Taylor, 1966).

Plate II. Wapiti used as draught animals.

GEOGRAPHICAL CONSTRAINTS

Considerable importance has been attached by some authors to movements of animals (and plants) beyond the limits of their natural distributions as an early indicator in the archaeological record of close relationships: 'starting with a relatively stable configuration of plant and animal species at 10 000 B.C., early cultivation took two genera of cereal grasses and two genera of small ungulates out of their habitat . . .' (Flannery, 1969). In fact, it seems to me that such movements are likely to be difficult to recognize archaeologically, for the distributions of plants and animals in prehistory are rarely known with any exactness. In general, the movements of animals associated with the experiments discussed earlier have tended to involve the redistribution of animals within their natural habitats to bring them into conformity with human requirements, rather than movements of animals outside their natural habitats, although the introduction of the eland and the zebra into Russia (both of which have encountered only moderate success) provide a striking exception to this generalization. Movements of animals outside their natural habitats have not been undertaken on an economically significant scale largely because the new habitats tend to possess better-adapted indigenous species, and introduced species do not always thrive. Of the twenty-two attempts at transplanting large ungulates listed by Niethammer (1963), only three were successful on a large scale, although the situation with smaller mammals, especially the carnivores, was very different. Although some movements of animals and plants (for example, the staple, contemporary domesticates) have been outstandingly successful on a global scale, there is reason to believe that in some cases, such as the African grasslands, they may be less productive than the indigenous game fauna, and that, in the long run, introduced animals are likely to cause serious damage to the vegetational communities on which they depend. In many cases, transplanted animals encounter serious problems in acclimatizing, and they often require supplementary feed and shelter, which are uneconomical.

MODERN EXPLOITATION STRATEGIES – AFRICAN AND ARCTIC

Modern experiments in the efficient exploitation of animal populations are relevant to archaeological interests, for they provide a means not only of evaluating current techniques of investigation, but they suggest new approaches to the study of prehistoric economic patterns. One feature common to all the experiments discussed is that they represent an optimal integration of the requirements and potential of the human and animal populations involved, although the precise manner in which this integration is achieved may vary considerably according to the maintenance-requirements of the animals, the technological abilities and other economic activities of the humans, and the use to which the animals are put. Given a knowledge of the probable population dynamics and seasonal distribution patterns of animal populations in the past, it should be possible for the prehistorian to predict a limited number of optimally productive economic strategies for past human groups in relation to their observed technologies, to forecast the types of human distribution that they would demand, the size-limits of the populations that they would support, and the types of trace that they would leave in the

archaeological record. I have discussed some of the limitations to this approach and attempted to consider the prehistoric colonization of North America in its light elsewhere (Wilkinson, 1972); for the present, I wish to illustrate the feasibility of this approach by contrasting optimal contemporary strategies for the exploitation of African and Arctic ungulates respectively. The peoples exploiting these areas share one overriding objective with one another and, we may assume, with prehistoric man: the need to develop a non-destructive economic strategy to satisfy the demands of a population pressing on the extractive capacity of the contemporary resources, and to ensure an adequate supply of resources at all seasons.

Three factors are particularly important in moulding the nature of man-ungulate relationships in Africa: the complexity of many of the natural grassland communities, which can be exploited to maximum advantage only by equally complex communities of herbivores; the high reproductive rate of most African ungulates; the important physiological fact that African ungulates carry little fat (2-5 percent) and do not therefore undergo the large seasonal fluctuations in weight characteristic of most ungulates in temperate and northern latitudes (Talbot et al., 1965). The high rate of reproduction obviously permits a high rate of exploitation, and the lack of seasonal weight-fluctuations, combined with the abundance of different species and their high densities, permits great freedom of seasonal movements for human groups, which tend to regulate their seasonal movements more in accordance with seasonal variations in the location and abundance of favoured fruits and vegetables (Lee, 1968; Woodburn, 1968). Tolerable levels of exploitation for some African ungulates quoted in the literature, although high, are probably lower than the maximum levels possible. Table 3 gives some of these estimates. The lowness of some of these rates of exploitation may be partly attributable to the infrequency of twinning in many of the species involved, but the abundance and variety of species available and the fact that

Table 3. Rates of exploitation (percent) for some African mammals (data from Dasmann & Mossman, 1961)

Species	Rate p.a.	Species	Rate p.a.
Wildebeest	25	Impala	25
Zebra	20	Steenbuck	20
Warthog	50	Kudu	30
Duiker	30	Giraffe	16.6
Buffalo	16.6	Waterbuck	20
Klipspringer	30	Bush pig	50
Eland	25		

there is no season at which meat is critically scarce compensate for the low rates.

In the complex vegetational and faunal communities of the African grasslands, certain patterns of exploitation may be excluded on the grounds of inefficiency or impracticability. Economic emphasis on a single species, with close restraints on the movements and breeding patterns of the animals involved is one such inefficient strategy, for it is incapable of making full use of the complex, natural grazing successions of the African grasslands and must in the long run yield to better-adapted pastoral practices. It is often argued that European domesticated animals and agricultural practices introduced into Africa have been successful and make the above argument untenable. The time-period involved is, however, short relative to the periods studied by prehistorians, and there is growing evidence that the introduced animals are in fact having a harmful effect on the vegetational communities on which they depend, and also that they are less productive than the indigenous fauna. Indeed, the recent trend towards game-farming after some 300 years of traditionally European pastoral practices illustrates well that, in the long run, selective pressures will favour the development of optimally adjusted exploitive strategies. A major feature of intensive management is to permit the localization and concentration of resources near human settlements at that season during which they are maximally productive and/or most needed. In temperate areas, with relatively simple grassland communities (Hartley, 1964) and comparatively few large herbivores, and where animals show marked seasonal fluctuations in weight, the close control of a single species or of a few species offers an optimal exploitive strategy, which in the long run is likely to be selected for. In the African grasslands under discussion, however, the slaughter of selected segments of the populations of a wider range of game-animals, with less emphasis on close control and with human selection achieved by selective slaughter rather than by castration and direct breeding, offers a much more efficient economic basis. Loeser (1968) has aptly termed this the '*gestalt*' approach to domestication.

In contrast to those of Africa, the vegetational communities of the Arctic and the herbivores that they support are relatively simple in terms of the variety of species. The factors shaping optimal patterns of exploitation in the Arctic include: the low density of the musk-ox, one of the two large Arctic herbivores; the seasonally large aggregates and high densities of the other large Arctic herbivore, the reindeer; the large seasonal weight fluctuations of both these species; the slow regenerative rate of some of the staple foods of the Arctic herbivores, such as lichens, which require twenty to thirty years to recover from heavy grazing (Klein, 1970); the general poverty of vegetable foods

suitable for direct human consumption, with the seasonal exception of berries in some areas; and the richness and diversity, often seasonal, of fish and marine mammals in coastal waters. Optimal Arctic adaptations must follow one of three main patterns, as the ethnographic evidence bears out: concentration on a single resource such as the caribou, for musk-ox populations are too sparse to form the basis for successful economies; concentration on marine resources; or varying seasonal emphasis on a combination of the two. Only the first will be considered here.

The variables involved in the exploitation of caribou include taming some or all of the animals (or none), the use of draught and riding animals, castration, direct mating, and selective slaughter, free grazing, or close herding. Although the frequency, distribution, and manifestations of these different strategies are of some ethnographic interest, I do not feel that they alter the productivity or nature of the man-animal relationship in a fashion that is relevant to the interests of economic prehistorians. In cases such as this, I feel that the application of the standard archaeological dichotomy of hunters and pastoralists serves no useful purpose, and in most cases it is doubtful that current archaeological techniques would be capable of distinguishing between the two. The point is well-illustrated by comparing the so-called reindeer 'herding' Chukchi (Leeds, 1965) with the reindeer 'hunting' Nganasan of the Taimyr Peninsula, who did in fact maintain small numbers of tamed and castrated animals for draught purposes (Chard, 1963).

CONCLUSIONS

The experiments described in the first part of this paper represent optimal economic strategies within the context of present environments, technologies, and demographic pressures, and it is my belief that selective pressures would in the long run have favoured the development of such optimal adjustments at all levels of technological development and at all periods of prehistory. There is no suggestion that modern experiments in animal domestication have been initiated by a unique set of environmental, cultural, or social stimuli, such as are postulated for the origins of domestication in prehistory, and it seems to me inconceivable that close man-animal relationships, approximating in at least some respects to those characterizing modern pastoralists, are not of considerable antiquity. Indeed, there is already abundant evidence that man has exploited his prey selectively in a fashion similar to that described for the modern African game-cropping experiments since the Lower Palaeolithic. Progress in the study of man-animal relationships has been marred by the preconceptions of prehistorians and zoologists, which have discouraged the examination of patterns of economic activity in sites outside the traditional period and area of early domestication. As these prejudices are re-examined critically and replaced by others more suited to contemporary preconceptions, it is appropriate that economic prehistorians develop a methodology better suited to their interests, together with a new conceptual framework to guide their investigations.

The conceptual framework offered here is that, given a knowledge of the physiological and behavioural attributes of animals in prehistory, and of the technological competence of past human populations, it is possible to predict with a sufficient degree of accuracy optimal patterns of exploiting these resources, and to forecast the types of traces which these would leave in the archaeological record. The data recovered by excavation may then be tested against the predicted pattern and the significance of observed divergences assessed. Granted that the purpose of all economies, past and present, is the provision of an adequate supply of resources spread evenly throughout the year, I feel that selective pressures would favour one of two major patterns of exploitation. In ecologically complex areas, such as the tropics, and where food preservation is difficult, the optimal pattern is likely to be based on the exploitation of a large number of plant and animal species at different seasons, exemplified today by game-cropping and swidden agriculture. In ecologically less diversified areas, there is likely to be a stronger tendency towards the intensive exploitation of a smaller number of resources, as for example in reindeer-based economies and to a large extent in modern, western European agriculture. Relationships based on taming, isolation, and selective breeding form an important sub-class within these categories, but they do not in my opinion deserve the monopoly of archaeological attention which they command at present.

Vita-Finzi & Higgs (1970) have suggested the foundations of an appropriate methodology with the concept of 'site-catchment analysis'. In accordance with the objectives suggested in the present paper, the following procedures are suggested. The excavation of single sites provides a picture of the resources available at the time the sites were occupied, the technology available for their exploitation, and the approximate number of people supported by these resources. Given the knowledge of the available resources and the technology, it is possible to specify an optimal exploitive strategy, the probable population density that it could support, the length and seasonality of the occupation of known sites, and the probable location of complementary, undiscovered sites. The data may then be compared with the predicted pattern and the significance of observed divergences assessed. For example, assuming that economic activities were concentrated within a six mile or two hour radius of sites, as Vita-Finzi and Higgs have very

plausibly suggested, it may in some cases be apparent that the observed population could have been supported only if man had artificially intensified the density of the staple food-sources. Data on the seasonality of occupation of sites should be compared with what is known or may justifiably be assumed concerning the seasonal movements of the animals represented, for this may also suggest human interference in the annual cycle of the animals concerned. Transposing two of the modern experiments into prehistoric contexts, such a pattern would occur, for the seasonal movements of elk and musk-oxen have both been modified by human interference. Special emphasis should also be given to the plant and animal *communities* associated with prehistoric man, which should be compared with such communities not influenced by man, for one of the chief results of human interference with plants and animals is often to create new associations of species, either by introducing exotic animals or by eliminating certain components of undisturbed communities. This approach is offered tentatively and remains untested in this form, but it seems appropriate to answer some of the questions of interest to economic prehistorians.

In summary, the emphasis in archaeological studies of past economies should, in my opinion, be given to the objectives achieved by these economies, their successes and failures, rather than to the means by which these ends were achieved, for current archaeological techniques seem incapable of recognizing confidently these techniques in most instances. The two following quotations demonstrate very strikingly that the end which archaeologists tend to attribute exclusively to intensive agricultural systems may be inherent in some ecosystems and may be achieved with neither a complex technology nor a highly developed social system: Sahlins (1968) quotes a Jesuit referring to the prodigality of the Montagnais Indians as if 'the game they were to hunt was shut up in a stable'. In his discussion of the !Kung Bushmen, Lee (1968) writes that 'the mongongo nut, because of its abundance and reliability, alone accounts for 50% of the vegetable diet by weight. *In this respect it resembles a cultivated crop such as maize or rice*' (my italics).

ACKNOWLEDGEMENTS

I am indebted to E. S. Higgs, John J. Teal Jr, and to Michael and Heather Jarman for their comments and advice.

My research is financed by the Emslie Horniman Royal Anthropological Scholarship Fund and the Institute of Northern Agricultural Research, to the Trustees of both of which I am grateful. This is Institute of Northern Agricultural Research Publication 72/2.

2. PREHISTORIC EXPLOITATION OF THE GAZELLE IN PALESTINE

A. J. LEGGE

Throughout the prehistoric record there are instances of the association of man with a particular animal species which formed an important part of the diet. This situation becomes increasingly common from the Middle Palaeolithic onwards, and sites are found where the prehistoric inhabitants pursued economies which specialized in herd animals such as reindeer, horse, red deer, and gazelle. Yet such pre-Neolithic archaeological faunas have provoked little comment beyond the classification of some examples as 'specialized hunting', and even this term has been given only to final Pleistocene and early Holocene situations. Thus the whole spectrum of prehistoric animal exploitation has been arbitrarily divided into 'hunting' and 'herding' separated by only a short period of economic change.

The problem of interpreting patterns of early animal domestication is made more difficult by the fact that Pleistocene faunas have been studied within the framework of palaeontology, while only material from the Postglacial has been treated in a way designed to test its economic implications. This is due in part to the structural divisions within archaeology, in which the Palaeolithic is separated from later periods by its own methods and problems. However, it is also a result of the small number of sites where Neolithic levels overlie extensive earlier occupations. Thus a comparison has seldom been made between the Neolithic and preceding economic systems by the same method of study, and the current hypothetical framework of domestication has been created without consideration of earlier patterns of animal exploitation.

The importance of the gazelle in the Natufian economy in Palestine has long been known, although detailed information on its particular relationship with man is not available. It is intended to assess this relationship in the Neolithic and earlier periods. The data from existing site reports is summarized below.

MUGHARET EL WAD (Garrod & Bate, 1937)

Garrod's excavations at the cave of el Wad, situated on the fringe of Mount Carmel in Palestine, first showed the importance of the gazelle in the Natufian economy. The gazelle is present throughout the sequence at el Wad and the other Wadi Mugharah caves, and was shown by Bate to increase sharply in importance in the Upper Palaeolithic layers, and to replace other animals almost completely in the subsequent Natufian occupation. Although the percentages of the animals found at el Wad are not given, the remarkable predominance of gazelle is clearly indicated. In the Natufian of layer B, gazelle bones number 2000, while no other animal exceeds eighty.

Bate used the fluctuating percentages of gazelle and fallow deer to interpret climatic changes in the past, although this view was criticized by Hooijer (1961), as the faunal analysis of the excavations at Ksar 'Akil did not show similar fluctuations in the species present during a contemporaneous occupation. It has been suggested by Higgs (1967b) that the environmental settings of Ksar 'Akil and el Wad are sufficiently different to account for this disparity between the two faunal assemblages in spite of their common coastal setting. This favours the hypothesis that the composition of a site fauna will be determined by the availability of particular animals, but it cannot be assumed that the species represented will be present in the same proportions as they occurred in the site territory, as some species may have been more worthy of exploitation than others.

KEBARAH CAVE (Turville-Petre, 1932)

The extensive excavations at Kebarah Cave have never been published in detail, and information on the fauna can be gained only from comments by Bate (1940), where the close similarity to that of the Natufian occupation at el Wad is confirmed. It is noted that the predominance of the gazelle is 'still more marked' in the Kebarah Cave.

SHUQBAH (Garrod, 1942)

Shuqbah is the type site of the Natufian culture and is a large cave overlooking the Wadi Natuf in the Judean Hills.

Editorial note. The term 'Pre-pottery Neolithic' is used throughout this article because it is in general usage. The industries, however, are also Mesolithic in character.

The Natufian layer is underlain by Levallois-Mousterian and overlain by traces of Bronze Age and later occupations. The quantity of animal bones from the two principal layers is not large, and is given in the report by the number of bones only.

	Gazella sp.	*Bos* sp.	*Dama mesopotamica*
Natufian	303	40	12
Levallois-Mousterian	112	40	99

Besides these animals, the presence of goat is recorded in the Levallois-Mousterian, and roe deer, hartebeest, and pig in the Natufian, but in very small numbers.

EL KHIAM (Neuville, 1951; González Echegaray, 1964)

Neither the original excavations of Neuville, nor the more recent work of González Echegaray have produced much faunal material from this site. Vaufrey's claims for domestic cattle, pig, and goat (Vaufrey, 1951) in the Natufian occupation rest upon samples too small in number to support such a contention. More recently, Ducos (1968) has identified small goats in the 'Pre-pottery Neolithic' of el Khiam, which he interprets as being domesticated. However, the sample size on which this claim is based is again small in number, and the lack of information available on the stature of Late Pleistocene goats in Palestine renders any such interpretation of doubtful validity.

Although gazelle and goat are present in the Natufian levels of el Khiam, the scarcity of faunal remains gives little indication of their relative abundance.

AIN MALLAHA (Perrot, 1960)

At the open site of Ain Mallaha, gazelle is numerically the most important animal, representing 44.6 percent of the fauna, and is approached in frequency only by a combined total of red, roe, and fallow deer, representing a further 33.4 percent, with pig and cattle 14.2 percent and 3.3 percent respectively (Ducos, 1968). Of the species present, only the gazelle remains are tested to determine the pattern of exploitation. The ages of the animals represented are calculated on the state of eruption and degree of wear shown by a sample of seventy-five teeth, but in the absence of details of the particular teeth employed, the size of the animal population represented in the test cannot be calculated. Ducos' analysis shows a distribution of age-classes that is interpreted as corresponding to a hypothetical wild population, with the exception of a deficit of animals less than one year old.

HAYONIM (Bar-Yosef & Tchernov, 1966)

The faunal remains from the current excavations at Hayonim contain few bones of the larger mammals, although the gazelle would appear to be the predominant animal.

JERICHO (Kenyon, 1957)

The exact status of the Natufian layers at Jericho remains in some doubt, as the number of diagnostic artefacts is only two (Kenyon, 1969). According to a recent report (Clutton-Brock, 1971), no animal bones were found in the Mesolithic levels, the earliest material recovered being from the 'proto-Neolithic'. In this layer, the presence of cattle, pig, fox, and gazelle is recorded, but no percentages are given. In the subsequent 'Pre-pottery Neolithic A' the quantity of animal bones is sufficient to indicate the predominance of the gazelle over other animal species in the collection. Clutton-Brock states that the gazelle provided 36.91 percent of the 'total meat source', although it appears that this calculation included the large number of fox also identified (Clutton-Brock, 1969). It may be taken that in terms of meat supplied, the gazelle was of greater importance than a simple statement of percentages would indicate.

In the 'Pre-pottery Neolithic B' the gazelle is outnumbered by a sharp increase in the frequency of goat. Although evidence on morphological grounds that these animals were domesticated at this time is slight, their relative scarcity in earlier levels gives support to such a suggestion.

NAHAL OREN (WADI FELLAH)

The recent Cambridge University-Israel Museum excavations at this site gave a high priority to the use of careful sieve recovery for artefacts and animal bones, as well as the use of a new technique of flotation for the recovery of carbonized plant remains. All the excavated soil was first passed through a 1 cm mesh sieve, then subjected to flotation, and finally water-washed through a 2 mm mesh sieve. The resultant residue was then hand sorted for the extraction of small artefacts and bones.

The fragmentation of the bones recorded by Bate (Garrod & Bate, 1937; Bate, 1940) at el Wad and Shuqbah Caves was also found at Nahal Oren. The only bones of the larger mammals found whole were the astragali and phalanges, which were well represented at the site suggesting that the relatively meatless limb extremities must have been discarded intact. Separation of these parts from the carcass seems to have been accomplished by breaking the metapodials, as the distal ends of these bones are also well represented, while even fragments of the proximal ends of the same bones are rare.

Excavation in the talus below the cave has shown the following succession to be present:

(1) 1 m of Kebaran, in red/brown soils resting on a weathered bedrock;

(2) 1 m of Natufian, in a layer of black soil;

(3) 1.20 m of Pre-pottery Neolithic, in a light brown soil extending to the present surface.

Although the thickness of the layers varies in the area excavated, a substantial occupation of each culture has been shown to exist. Analysis of the faunal material to date has shown that the gazelle is the predominant animal throughout the sequence. In the basal Kebaran, the fallow deer is present at a frequency intermediate between that of layer C (Upper Palaeolithic) and layer B (Natufian) of the adjacent el Wad cave, while in the Natufian, as at el Wad, fallow deer are much less common. The importance of the gazelle increases in the 'Pre-pottery Neolithic' to some 90 percent of the fauna, and the goat also increases at this time from a mere indication of its presence in the earlier layers, to some 6 percent of the faunal remains. The small collection of goat bones includes two horn core fragments that may be referred to *Capra aegagrus*. The sample of goat bones, in common with cattle, deer, and pig, is so small that any numerical or morphological test for the pattern of exploitation would have little meaning. In the case of the gazelle, however, the population represented in the site fauna is considerable, and it is possible to collect data on the age of the animals at death. With the current recognition of the limitations implicit in the use of morphological changes for the identification of domestication in animal species, the analysis of the slaughter pattern shown in a faunal assemblage is being increasingly used in archaeology for the recognition of early domestication, and is widely held to be a reliable test (Perkins, 1964; Bökönyi, 1969*a*; Chaplin, 1969; Ducos, 1969; Hole, Flannery & Neely, 1969). The metapodia are commonly used to provide this information, although a clear statement concerning the part of the bone used is rarely given. If the shafts of the metapodia or other bones are included, the juvenile animals are likely to be severely under-represented due to the lesser degree of ossification, and consequently the greater chances of destruction before or during deposition. However, even the unfused epiphyses of the metapodials survive well due to the greater bone density of the articular surfaces, and in this case there is less chance that the juvenile animals will be under-represented. The metapodia were chosen to provide the data for this test on the bone collection from Nahal Oren, as no other bone that fuses relatively late in the growth period is well-represented.

In the immature animal, the distal unfused epiphysis is rarely found intact, as the two condyles separate on the decay of the organic part of the bone. In deriving the totals for the percentages of immature animals, the number of separated condyles was halved to provide a figure comparable to the intact distal articulations of the adult metapodia. It scarcely needs mention that the small size of these bone fragments dictates the need for exceptionally careful sieve recovery by both washing and sieving the deposits.

The results of this analysis are given below:

Nahal Oren: percentage of unfused and fused gazelle metapodia

	Sample	Unfused (%)	Fused (%)
'Pre-pottery Neolithic'	129	50.3	49.7
Natufian	164	54.7	45.3
Kebaran	140	54.4	45.6

This data may be compared with that from a number of recently excavated sites where this method of faunal analysis has been employed, Beidha (Perkins, 1966), Shanidar (Perkins, 1964), and Ali Kosh (Hole, Flannery & Neely, 1969).

Percentage of immature animals

	Shanidar	Beidha	Bus Mordeh phase at Ali Kosh
'Pre-pottery Neolithic'	54.2	54.5	55.4
Mesolithic	44.3		

In each of these sites given above, the high percentage of immature animals has been cited as evidence of the domestication of the species concerned, which are sheep at Shanidar, goat at Beidha, and unspecified ovicaprines at Ali Kosh.

The age of metapodial fusion in the gazelle remains to be demonstrated on recent skeletons of known age. Ducos (1968) quotes some data on the degree of tooth wear found in the gazelle at different ages, using information from recent *Gazella subgutturosa*, and shows that by three years of age the fourth pre-molar had had more than half its original height removed by attrition. In a small number of recent *Gazella gazella* and *Gazella dorcas* examined in the British Museum (Natural History) bone fusion, including the metapodia, was complete when wear on the fourth pre-molar corresponded to an age of two years as given by Ducos. From this, there is some evidence that metapodial fusion is complete in the gazelle by an age of two years, a figure comparable to that given by Silver (1969) for unimproved hill sheep.

BELT CAVE (Coon, 1951)

Gazelle were also more numerous in the Mesolithic levels of Belt Cave, a site overlooking the Caspian Sea in Iran. Layers 11-16 contain Coon's 'Upper Mesolithic', and only at this time are faunal remains abundant. Coon calculates the age of death for all the large mammals present in the site fauna, and also compares 'animals with secondary products' (sheep and goat) to those 'without secondary products' (seal, gazelle, and pig) on this basis. He recognizes the fact that animals able to provide milk and wool may be expected to show different patterns of exploitation by the human population, from those able to supply only meat. Although Coon's publication of the excavations at Belt Cave shows considerable theoretical innovation, it is unfortunate that the basis for ageing the large mammals is not given in detail, and the results obtained are thus open to some doubt. It would appear that all bones are used to calculate the percentage of immature animals without regard for the fact that these may show very different fusion ages.

The complete list of bones given in the site report shows that the gazelle is represented by 664 horn cores, but only 122 other bones. Of these bones, 3.3 percent are classified as immature, but no details are given on which bones of the body these are. It is evident that some 86 percent of the faunal remains of gazelle are horn cores. However, the female of *Gazella subgutturosa* rarely has horns, and it follows that the majority of the bones represented in the fauna of Belt Cave must be derived from male animals. This heavy representation of male animals, combined with the very low percentage of juvenile animals, can hardly be regarded as the product of 'random hunting' if the collection of bones published by Coon is taken to represent the assemblage present at the site. The fragmentation of the bones at the site recorded by Coon may, if similar to the situation at Nahal Oren, be responsible for the over representation of the large horn cores, and the very small percentage of juvenile animals present. However, that the gazelle was important in the Mesolithic of Belt Cave cannot be doubted, and Coon's description of the setting of the site suggests very similar environmental resources to the Natufian sites of Mount Carmel in Palestine.

DEH LURAN PLAIN (Hole, Flannery & Neely, 1969)

At many of the later prehistoric sites of the Near East the gazelle is present in the faunas in sufficient numbers, but is invariably regarded as being killed by hunting, while other species present are tested in detail and interpreted as being domesticated. The sequence excavated by Hole, Flannery & Neely (1969) on the Deh Luran Plain in Iran shows the gazelle increasing in importance through the first three phases of occupation, from 24 percent of the faunal remains in the earliest (Bus Mordeh) phase, to 34 percent in the Mohammed Jaffar phase. Yet in spite of the adequate samples of bones available, the particular exploitation is not tested in the detail applied to the sheep and goats, or even to the numerically much smaller sample of cattle. If different modes of exploitation are to be postulated for the species present at the site, a demonstration of this based on the pattern of slaughter for each would be more revealing than comparison with largely hypothetical 'wild' populations.

BEIDHA (Kirkbride, 1966)

At Beidha, Perkins (1966) has shown that some 30 percent of the gazelle present in the Natufian layers are immature, and suggests the possibility that these animals were domesticated at this time. However the available sample was small in number.

OTHERS

Other observations on the maturity of gazelle from archaeological sites are virtually non-existent, with the exception of the late fifth millennium site of Toukh in the Nile Valley, North of Luxor, where Gaillard (1934) observed that the majority of gazelle remains from this site were of young individuals.

DISCUSSION

The very high frequency of immature gazelle at Nahal Oren, and the fact that their predominance is greater in the 'Pre-pottery Neolithic' than in any earlier level, raises the question of the extent to which the gazelle can be regarded as a 'domestic animal' at that time. It has been shown that an analysis of slaughter pattern has been used, where morphological tests are inapplicable, for the demonstration of early domestication in the sheep and goat. We can hardly apply the pre-condition that only present-day practices were likely to have occurred in prehistoric economies, nor can we assume that only those species that are now domesticated would have been appropriate for such exploitation. On the other hand, it must be noted that herd ungulates often have a high rate of mortality in the young males, and many of these live and die with little contribution to the breeding pool. The exploitation of domestic animals relies on this surplus, but under human manipulation the expendability of the young males is intensified to its highest degree. In herd animals subject only to the predation of carnivores, females generally outnumber males as a result of the higher mortality of the latter. Under the control of man, however, males represent a selected minority and may comprise as little as 5 percent of the herd.

The random hunting so often postulated in archaeological interpretations rarely can have existed (Jarman & Wilkinson, II. 4) as man, no less than any other predator, will almost invariably have chosen to kill some particular part of the herd on the basis of age or sex. The particular adaptation shown by man lies in the exploitation of the reciprocal predator-prey relationship to its fullest possible extent, and this situation is indicated in the consistent pattern of the selective cropping of immature animals shown at Shanidar, Beidha, Ali Kosh, and Nahal Oren. What we call domestication today is this same response in a complex and conscious form, which ultimately relies upon the management of the maximum reproductive potential of the herd. This may or may not demand behavioural modification in the domestic animal, and may or may not demand close herding, but all such adaptations do require some control practised over the herd structure. It must be stressed again that some form of selection will be inherent in any form of predation, and man, no less than any other force, has played a part in the shaping of animal species throughout the Pleistocene.

The gazelle can certainly be tamed and made the subject of a herding economy. Paintings and carvings from Dynastic times in Egypt show a wide range of animal species apparently tamed, including gazelle and other antelopes wearing collars for their restraint and being fed from mangers. Even under such conditions of artificial restraint, it is recorded that gazelle rapidly become tame and continue to breed freely each year (Clot, 1840). Yet can such close herding be shown to be necessary for, or even relevant to, the production of the maximum protein output from an animal herd? Reasons for close herding which are common to all husbandry practices include the greater security of the herd against competing carnivores, both human and non-human, and the degree of handling required for the extraction of milk and services such as traction. Protection from predators would be as relevant in the case of the gazelle as in any other animal species, and large predatory mammals are well known from the prehistoric deposits of the caves in Palestine.

Yet at this point interpretation is inevitably restricted by the lack of comparable data. As yet no standards have emerged in archaeology for the recovery of animal bones, still less for their subsequent treatment and publication. Until more data are forthcoming from new excavations the extent of such selective exploitation of animals in prehistory must remain unknown, but may be expected also to have occurred earlier in the Pleistocene.

In spite of the long-standing success of the gazelle-based economies in Palestine, they are replaced comparatively rapidly by the exploitation of other animal species that have persisted under domestication to the present day. It is unfortunate that the replacement of the gazelle cannot be followed in detail at any sites in Palestine other than Jericho. Indeed, the available data for this period are so incomplete that Reed (1969) has recently commented that '. . . animal domestication cannot be demonstrated for much of Palestine and Southern Syria prior to the late fifth millenium B.C.', a statement that remains substantially true for the modern domesticated species, if the criteria customarily used to determine the presence or absence of domestication are accepted.

The faunas of the 'Pre-pottery Neolithic' in Palestine are known in any detail only from Jericho (Clutton-Brock, 1971), Munhatta (Ducos, 1968), and Nahal Oren, with some data from el Khiam. It has been shown above that in the earliest 'Pre-pottery Neolithic' both Jericho and Nahal Oren had an animal economy based on the gazelle. Although the extent of such economies in Palestine is not well known, similar patterns have been discovered in adjacent regions, where a 'Pre-pottery Neolithic' occupation has been found with a fauna predominantly of gazelle at Taibe in Syria (Ducos, 1968), and possibly also the Site B of the Wadi Dhobai in the Jordan (Waechter & Seton-Williams, 1938). On the other hand, the goat is known from the 'Pre-pottery Neolithic' only at Beidha, where it is the predominant animal from the Kebaran onwards, and possibly at el Khiam. From the data available, the species of domestic animals common in later periods do not predominate with the first identification of 'Neolithic' technologies, and it appears that the goat has not been extended beyond its preferred habitats at this time. The only interpretation that can be made is that the 'Pre-pottery Neolithic' shows an economic continuity with earlier periods in that the animal species most suited to local conditions of climate and vegetation continued to be those exploited.

The fauna of Kenyon's 'Pre-pottery Neolithic B' is known only from Jericho (Clutton-Brock, 1971) and Munhatta (Ducos, 1968). At Jericho, it is evident that the economy of the 'Pre-pottery Neolithic B' was based on the exploitation of the goat, and the gazelle, though still present, is now a small part of the fauna. The goats at Jericho in this period cannot be separated on morphological grounds from *Capra aegagrus*, and the only evidence for their domestication is the abrupt replacement of the gazelle at this time. Recent work at Nahal Oren has confirmed a similar sharp increase in the frequency of goat bones in the 'Pre-pottery Neolithic B' levels.

At Munhatta, the gazelle appears to undergo a more gradual replacement, and the combined fauna of the four 'Pre-pottery Neolithic B' levels is composed mainly of sheep/goat (51.8 percent) and gazelle (42.8 percent) (Ducos, 1968). Even at this period, the limited faunal collections permit only the morphological tests for domestication, with the consequent uncertainties. However, at this time, Perkins (1966) has claimed domestic goats at Beidha, only some hundred miles to the south of Jericho, and it seems likely that this practice would have been more general, although this cannot be demonstrated. Certainly the data available from 'Pre-pottery Neolithic' sites in Palestine do not support the interpretations that have been made of the innovation of the widespread herding of sheep and goat at this period.

The earliest 'Pre-pottery Neolithic' of Jericho is derived from the underlying Natufian (Kenyon, 1969), particularly as the Natufian has new types of artefacts identified as mortars and sickles, which have been widely interpreted as showing a heavy reliance on the use of plant foods. Recent excavations in Egypt have shown identical traits in the artefacts of Upper Palaeolithic industries dated to 15 000 B.C. from sites which lie well outside the postulated distribution of wild cereals, and although such artefact types may well indicate the use of plant foods, this data cannot be used to ascertain the degree of such dependence. The Natufian period in Palestine is often seen as a time when progress was being made towards sedentary life, which is held to be established in the 'Pre-pottery Neolithic'. If a move to sedentism is indeed taking place recent excavations at Nahal Oren have shown that this would seem to have been accomplished with remarkably little change in site location or in the economic basis of the community from Kebaran to 'Pre-pottery Neolithic' times. Yet the year-round occupation of archaeological sites remains difficult to demonstrate from the data obtained from excavation. If a trend towards sedentism existed, it would more probably be in the direction of plant cultivation to provide the necessary storeable staple foods. Vita-Finzi & Higgs (1970) have shown that sites with extensive Natufian occupation usually are situated in locations where there is a minimum of opportunity for cereal cultivation. By the Bronze Age, settlement is concentrated in the many large tells that are situated in areas now favoured for arable cultivation.

During the Nahal Oren excavations and in an experimental sounding at Tell Gezer (Legge, in litt.; Dever, 1968), a careful record was made of the quantity of each of the classes of archaeological material recovered in relation to the volume of soil excavated. By similar flotation methods the deposits of Nahal Oren produced about four seeds or fragments in each cubic metre excavated, while at Tell Gezer, a yield of some thousands of carbonized seeds were recovered from the same volume of soil. The quantity of animal bones present shows a complete reversal of these figures, from some twenty to thirty identifiable pieces per cubic metre at Tell Gezer, to five or six hundred at Nahal Oren. A change of this magnitude could be taken as an indication of the evident economic change. Such a method of comparison may eventually help to show the part that the 'Pre-pottery Neolithic' and the Neolithic played in that change.

3. EUROPEAN DEER ECONOMIES AND THE ADVENT OF THE NEOLITHIC

M. R. JARMAN

It is an archaeological belief so widely accepted as to excite no comment that the Neolithic saw the appearance in Europe of communities whose subsistence was based primarily upon plant and animal husbandry, in particular upon the exploitation of cereals, and of sheep, goats, cattle, and pigs. It is seldom discussed why such a uniformity should occur (for despite the individual variations in relative proportions the overall similarity of many Neolithic faunal communities over wide geographical areas is outstanding), or whether indeed it is capable or worthy of explanation. An additional feature has received even less attention; over much of the area which they occupied, Neolithic groups succeeded communities with economies based primarily on a similarly restricted range of species. From the beginning of the Postglacial period until the appearance of the Neolithic, most of Europe south of the Baltic was occupied by human groups which exploited in particular red deer and pigs, with cattle and roe deer as common subsidiaries. This is not to ignore the existence of exceptions nor the fact that many other species do appear in Mesolithic faunal assemblages. Coastal sites, for instance, frequently give evidence of a concentration upon marine resources; birds, carnivores, and other herbivores appear often in small numbers, occasionally in large numbers. The same is true of Neolithic sites. This does not alter the fact that from Star Carr in Yorkshire to Sidari in Corfu a very few species provided the bulk of animal protein and were apparently staple foods of diverse 'cultural' groups for several millennia, and that the red deer was commonly the most important of these species.

We should not allow this evident selective interest to influence us too greatly in our studies, however. A barrier to the successful analysis of past human economies has been a tendency to approach them solely from the point of view of the exploitation of individual species. It is perhaps legitimate to study in this way the zoological and evolutionary histories of the animals found at archaeological sites, but the primary interest of the archaeologist is in the human relationships with the animals, and it is economic rather than zoological factors which are of the first importance to him. The principles arising from the study of synecology are of some help to us here, presenting the model of interacting communities of plants and animals exercising considerable influence upon each other, rather than one of individual species acting in isolation. It is thus possible to view many human economies as exploiting not an assortment of individual species but rather integrated associations within balanced communities, of which man is a part and to which he must adapt himself if he is to be able to maintain the whole complex system in a state which is advantageous to the human population.

THE NATURE OF THE DATA

Many hazards intervene between past human behaviour and its perception by the archaeologist, and the quality of data varies widely both in its preservation and in its treatment by the excavator. Archaeological information is at best imperfect; and when considering broad questions involving different areas, excavators, and methods of excavation, it is necessary to be conscious of the dangers of over-interpretation. Payne (II. 3) has discussed the effects of some of these factors, ways in which they can be assessed and their impact minimized. But in order to pursue a study on any other than a purely descriptive level it is often necessary to make *a priori* assumptions about the available data. In what follows it has been assumed firstly that there is a close relationship between faunal remains on archaeological sites and the animal economies of the human groups concerned, and secondly that the published data can be accepted as a basis for analysing this relationship as a whole, in spite of the distortions which doubtless affect the picture at individual sites to a greater or lesser degree. Where relative proportions of different species are quoted they have been calculated on the basis of number of identified specimens, unless otherwise stated. This is not due to a belief that this method is superior to others currently employed, but simply a reflection of the mode of expression of most of the available data. The assumption has been made that, while this may have inflated the proportions of large relative to small species in some cases, this will not be a sufficient distortion to negate the general conclusions; sites whose faunas have been analysed on the basis of minimum number of individuals seem on the whole to support this assumption.

In dealing with faunal remains inevitable difficulties arise over species attributions. Apart from the well-known diffi-culties in distinguishing between *Ovis* and *Capra, Bos* and *Bison*, on the basis of fragmentary osteological remains, the taxonomic labels of many species have changed greatly over the years, and even now the usage varies from author to author. Thus *Meles meles* and *M. taxus* both occur com-monly for the badger, *Lutra lutra* and *L. vulgaris* for the otter, *Lepus europaeus* and *L. timidus* for the hare, and so on. Such distinctions are ignored in this paper. In addition I have assumed that only one species of *Sus* and one of *Bos* is present. The case for more than one wild species of either in Postglacial Europe remains tenuous, and quite apart from the difficulty of separating satisfactorily the wild and domestic forms of these species according to the available criteria, this distinction is not relevant to our present purposes. Equids are rather more difficult to deal with; both *E. caballus* and *E. hydruntinus* concern us, and there seems to be some indication that they may have had differ-ent habitat preferences. At many sites, however, no dis-tinction has been made between the two, and the attri-bution has simply been 'Equus sp.' For this reason, while Figure 1 shows data for the two species separately, and ignores equids not identified to species, Figure 2 combines all records of Equidae, including '*Equus* sp.' Figure 2 also combines in the same way the *Capra ibex* and *Capra/Ovis* categories, and the *Lepus* and *Oryctolagus* categories.

Appendixes 1 and 2 list all the Mesolithic sites which have contributed data to this paper, with some of their faunal statistics. The assumption has been made that *Bison* is unlikely to have been present in significant quantities in Postglacial Europe; consequently citations such as 'large bovid' and '*Bos* or *Bison*' have been included with *Bos*. It is, of course, nothing approaching a full list of relevant sites, and no doubt important ones have been omitted. However, a wide geographical and chronological range has been in-cluded, and it is unlikely that additional sites would greatly affect the conclusions which have been drawn.

MESOLITHIC FAUNAL COMMUNITIES

Faunal representation on European Mesolithic sites com-monly incorporates a large number of species. Even leaving aside small rodents and other micro-mammals, which can seldom if ever have been of great economic significance, and non-mammalian species, which can only have been so in special instances, a wide range appears, with hare, rabbit, marmot, beaver, and many species of carnivore appearing in addition to herbivores. Two factors allow us to perceive some pattern in this apparently amorphous picture. On a simple presence/absence basis some species occur far more frequently than others; and some species habitually occur in large numbers, consistently forming a high proportion of

the total assemblage, while others are usually rare even when present. The carnivores as a group are represented at many sites, but usually in small numbers of each species. The fox, cat, and badger among the carnivores are especi-ally widespread. The beaver is common, but largely con-fined to sites near water; the hare and rabbit are patchy in their occurrence. Of the herbivores ibex, chamois, elk, bison, and equids are of localized occurrence both geo-graphically and chronologically, and reach economically significant proportions only in special instances. Roe deer and cattle occur at many sites, often in considerable numbers, but only rarely in such proportions as to suggest economic concentration upon their exploitation. Two species which are notable above all the others are the red deer and the pig, which are present together in almost every European Mesolithic site yielding faunal collections of any size, and which between them usually account for the preponderance of the faunal remains.

Figures 1 and 2 analyse in presence-absence terms the occurrence of the more common mammalian species at 165 European Mesolithic sites. All figures and tables exclude marine mammals, insectivores, and rodents other than the beaver and marmot, and percentages have been calculated on this basis. Particularly in southern Europe, the dis-tinction between final or Epi-Palaeolithic and Mesolithic industries is by no means clear-cut, and there is consider-able industrial and economic continuity between the two 'periods'. Consequently some sites have been included which might well be classified as 'Late Palaeolithic' on a strictly chronological basis. In many cases the absence of ^{14}C dates makes precise chronological relationships a matter of inference.

The herbivores can be considered as falling into three groups. Red deer and pig are clearly the most frequently occurring species, present in almost all the sites reviewed. Roe deer and cattle form another group, appearing at about 60 percent of the sites; the remaining herbivores falling into a third group which range from *E. caballus* at about 20 percent to reindeer at 2 percent. Figure 2 shows that when the equids are considered as a group, and the caprines as another, they form together a fourth group of intermediate importance, occurring in from 35-41 percent of the sites. No single carnivore appears in as many as half the sites, and they range from the commonest, the fox (at 41 percent of the sites), to the least common, the *Mustela* group (at 6 percent of the sites), with no obvious groups within the range of variation. The beaver occurs at about one quarter of the sites, the hare, rabbit, and marmot less frequently.

Table 1 illustrates the relative numerical importance of nine herbivore species in fifty-two sites from which the information is available. The similarity of the pattern pro-duced here with that in Figures 1 and 2 is of some interest;

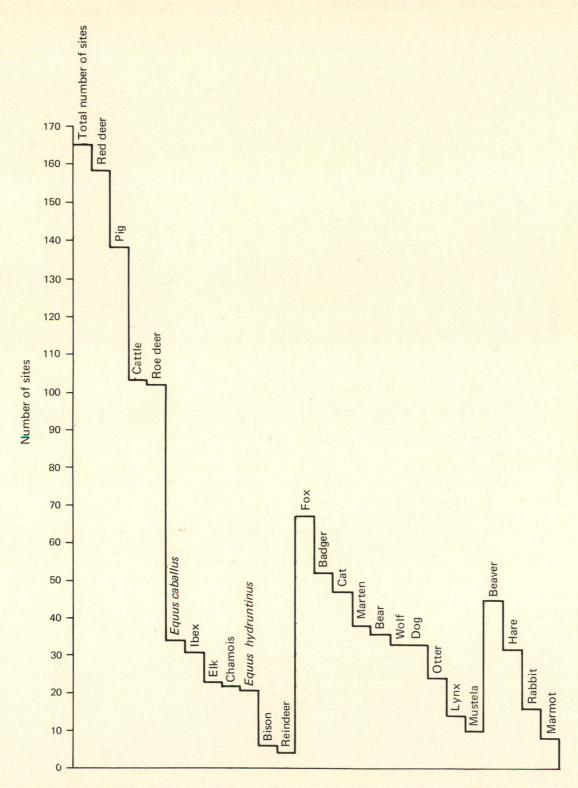

Fig. 1.   The presence of animals at 165 sites.

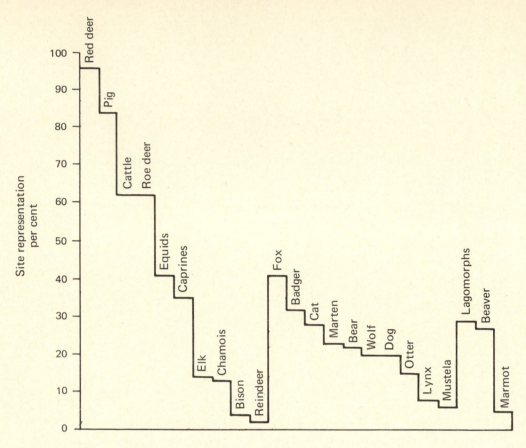

Fig. 2.   The presence of animals at 165 sites expressed as percentages.

the mean proportions of red deer and pig again place them clearly as the predominant elements, and the slightly greater importance of red deer over pig visible in Figures 1 and 2 is clearly re-emphasized in Table 1, where the mean value for red deer is double that for pig. Table 1 also shows the number of sites at which each species was the commonest of the nine species considered. Here again, red deer is conspicuously the pre-eminent species, dominant at thirty-three sites, with pig second. Cattle and red deer each account for 30 percent of the remains at Hesselbjerggaard, and thus the figures in this column total fifty-three from the fifty-two sites.

As is evident from Appendix 2, other species than these do indeed appear prominently on occasion, but none displays the widespread dominance of red deer and pig. Cattle and roe deer again fall into intermediate positions, occurring widely as significant but secondary species; neither occurs commonly as a dominant species. The elk is almost entirely limited to the Baltic region during the Postglacial, and there seems to be evidence that it was less well able to withstand human exploitation in this period than were other species. As is well known its importance declines

sharply in Denmark between the Maglemose and Ertebølle cultural periods, and it seems to have declined similarly elsewhere in Europe; thus while it is an important faunal element in the Upper Palaeolithic deposits of the Vicenza region of northern Italy, there is no sign that it survived long into the Postglacial. Similarly, its prominence during the Allerød oscillation and in Early Mesolithic sites in England, such as Star Carr, is not sustained in later sites.

Equids present a more complicated picture. *Equus caballus* occurs sporadically throughout most of Postglacial Europe, but at only a small proportion of the sites and never in large numbers (1-21 percent). *Equus hydruntinus* is confined to parts of southern Europe, and is particularly prominent along the Mediterranean coast of France and southern Italy, and in Greece. The dating of many of the relevant sites is by no means secure, but the evidence of Kastritsa and Romanelli suggests that the peak of exploitation of *E. hydruntinus* may have been in Late Glacial rather than Postglacial times. It is unquestionable however that it continued to be exploited until, and in some cases after, the appearance of pottery-using communities. On occasion this species attains the predominance of a staple

Table 1. Proportions of herbivores at fifty-two European sites

Species	Number of occurrences	Mean percent in total number of sites	Mean percent in sites at which species occurs	Number of sites at which species is commonest
Red deer	51	38.5	39.3	33
Pig	48	17.6	19.1	12
Cattle	38	8.9	12.2	4
Roe deer	39	8.1	10.8	1
Elk	16	2.2	7.0	–
E. hydruntinus	7	2.0	14.7	1
E. caballus	10	1.3	6.6	–
Ibex	6	1.7	14.3	2
Chamois	6	0.9	8.2	–

resource, as at Grotta Mangiapane (49 percent), but it is not clear whether or not this is of Postglacial date. Ibex and chamois each occur at only a small number of sites. Ibex only appears in large numbers at one site, chamois in none, and both are confined to alpine and high plateau areas as species of economic significance.

THE NEOLITHIC TRANSITION

The appearance of pottery-using cultures saw the end of the Mesolithic in Europe. It is widely accepted that this took place at different times in different areas, but what is less clearly seen is that the change-over took place in a very different manner in different areas. In some areas the appearance of pottery-using groups coincides with an obvious economic change; in particular caprines appear in large numbers, and small-sized cattle and pigs are present. In many cases there is in addition evidence for the practice of cereal agriculture. Recent reviews of the data have shown that there are important variations of this general theme, however; different species vary in their importance, and the change-over from the Mesolithic economy varies from a clear-cut change to a long drawn-out development. Thus one may contrast the situation in parts of the north German plain with that in sub-alpine Italy: in the former case an economy based on sheep/goat, pig, and cattle became established with no apparent intermediate stages from the Mesolithic economy, whereas in the latter the transformation was very slow, lasting two to three millennia. The more detailed description of some individual sites will indicate more clearly the degree and nature of this variation.

Late Palaeolithic and Early Postglacial sites in Greece are characterized by economies depending to a large degree on deer, especially the red deer (*C. elaphus*), which accounts for about 80 percent of mammalian specimens at the Late Glacial site of Kastritsa (Higgs *et al.*, 1967) and about 75 percent in the Postglacial levels at Porto Cheli (Payne,

1969*a*). Other commonly occurring species are *E. hydruntinus* and *Bos*. This may be contrasted with the faunal assemblages from the Early Neolithic sites of the area, Argissa (Boessneck, 1962), Nea Nikomedeia (Higgs, 1962*a*), Porto Cheli (Payne, 1969*a*), Knossos (Jarman & Jarman, 1968), which are uniformly dominated by caprines (65-85 percent), the remainder of the fauna being almost exclusively cattle and pigs. Equids are absent, deer are absent or extremely rare.

In northern Yugoslavia we find a rather different situation; at Lepenski vir the two 'pre-Starčevo' deposits are dominated by red deer, with cattle and pig as minor constituents (Bökönyi, 1969*b*). In the Starčevo deposit red deer is still the commonest animal, but has decreased relative to cattle, and caprines appear for the first time. Table 2 shows that in spite of variation in individual percentages, the total percent of red deer + cattle + caprines is almost identical for all three deposits: I (74 percent), II (78 percent), and III (76 percent); this suggests the possibility that the three species were behaving to some extent as mutually dependent variables, with the reduction in importance of red deer directly linked to the increase in importance of cattle and caprines. Other Starčevo sites, such as Divostin show possible developments of this situation, with deer in small numbers only, cattle and caprines forming the overwhelming majority of the specimens.

In sub-alpine Italy, and in ecologically comparable situations elsewhere in the Alpine area, red deer and pig are the primary Mesolithic faunal constituents, as in the lower levels of Birsmatten (Schmid, 1963) and at Vatte di Zambana (Alessio *et al.*, 1969). The first pottery-using communities seem in many cases to have continued a similar subsistence pattern for the most part; sites such as Molino Casarotto in north Italy (Jarman, 1971) and Seeberg Burgäschisee-Süd in Switzerland (Boessneck, Jéquier & Stampfli, 1963) illustrating the continuing importance of red deer (c. 45-50 percent), associated mainly with pig at the former site and with both pig and

Table 2. Proportions of faunal elements at Lepenski vir (Data from Bökönyi, 1969b)

Species	Level I		Level II		Level III	
	no.	%	no.	%	no.	%
Red deer	115	66	111	73	862	44
Cattle	14	8	7	5	549	28
Caprines	–	–	–	–	81	4
Pigs	10	6	6	4	219	11
Others	36	20	28	18	248	13
Total red deer + cattle + caprines	129	74	118	78	1492	76

cattle at the latter. Similarly, the typologically Mesolithic, but chronologically late, upper level at Birsmatten shows the long-lived importance of deer-pig economies in this area.

The Ukraine is remarkable for the consistently high proportion of pigs throughout the Postglacial; at Tash Aïr and Zamil-Koba they fluctuate between 60 percent and 80 percent of the specimens (Dimitrieva, 1960). At neither site are there obvious signs of important change in economy coincident with the appearance of pottery; the importance of pigs is unchanged, the only other animals of significance being red deer (which decline with time at both sites), roe deer, and at Tash Aïr, cattle.

Along the Mediterranean coast of France and in much of coastal Italy a different picture emerges. Sheep are present in the Tardenoisian levels at Chateauneuf-lez-Martigues and occupy an increasingly important position through the Neolithic layers (Ducos, 1958). Red deer, cattle, and pigs occupy secondary roles, the percentage of red deer again showing a tendency to decrease with time. An important feature at this site is the high proportion of rabbit, which occurs in all levels; it is by far the dominant species in the Tardenoisian level (about 95 percent), and continues at a high level (59 percent) in the earliest Neolithic. It should not, of course, be overlooked that these figures grossly exaggerate the economic importance of rabbit, whose low body weight would lower its value relative to sheep by a factor of about twenty to thirty. At other sites in this area, equids occur in important proportions, as at Grotta Mangiapane in Sicily (Vaufrey, 1928), where *E. hydruntinus* constituted almost 50 percent of the faunal remains; the succeeding Neolithic economies of the area relying primarily upon caprines. However, a high degree of continuity between the Mesolithic and Neolithic economies is evident in this area at sites such as Grotta delle Prazziche (Borzatti von Löwenstern, 1969), where *E. hydruntinus*, red deer, pig, cattle, and fox all appear in significant proportions throughout, the abrupt appearance of caprines with the Neolithic being the only new element.

North of the Alps on the north European plain the red deer-pig economies of the Mesolithic are followed by Neolithic communities depending almost exclusively upon the sheep-goat-pig-cattle combination. Red and roe deer do occur but are very rare. In the area bordering the North Sea the Mesolithic is again dominated by red deer, with pig, roe deer, cattle, and elk as important subsidiaries. Certain sites of the Ertebølle-Ellerbek group, while customarily classified as Mesolithic, do contain small amounts of pottery and rare bones of caprines, while retaining an economy primarily based upon red and roe deer, cattle, and pigs. Taxonomically Neolithic sites show dependence upon the sheep-goat-pig-cattle combination, and while red deer occurs on many sites it is usually in very small percentages.

While this series of isolated examples does not cover fully the whole range of European Postglacial animal economies, it does serve to highlight the great variation in the nature of the transformation between what we usually call 'Mesolithic' and 'Neolithic' communities. The stereotype of immigrating Neolithic peoples using pottery and exploiting the sheep-goat-pig-cattle complex is by no means valid everywhere. In particular we may note the perseverance of substantially Mesolithic economies in conjunction with Neolithic artefacts, as at Seeberg Burgäschisee-Süd and Molino Casarotto, and the strong continuity shown between Mesolithic and Neolithic animal economies in many areas.

DEER ECONOMIES

A clear feature in the pattern is the importance of deer in economies over much of Europe for a very long period of time. This is a phenomenon worthy of further consideration in itself. In many cases the deer exploitation is coupled with that of large pigs, but more often than not red deer is numerically the most important constituent, and the importance of the other species varies considerably according to geographical, ecological, and chronological factors. The great longevity of the man-deer relationship suggests that it was of considerable importance, as does the high degree of economic dependence by the human upon the deer population. Over much of the continent, after all, human groups exploited deer populations consecutively for 5000 years or more.

Indeed, over large areas of southern Europe the relationship lasted more in the region of 50 000 years. Red deer is the dominant species throughout the succession in Greece at Asprochaliko (Higgs & Vita-Finzi, 1966) and Kastritsa (Mousterian to Mesolithic). Similar evidence is available from southern Italy, where at Grotta Ulluzzo (Borzatti von Löwenstern, 1965) a very high degree of dependence upon red deer is evident throughout the Middle and Upper Palaeolithic layers, as is also the case for the Mousterian and Mesolithic levels of Grotta delle Prazziche. In Spain red deer occur at Mousterian sites such as Cova Negra (Fletcher, 1956) and throughout the long Upper Palaeolithic sequence at Parpallo (Pericot, 1942). They range from 49 percent to 60 percent in the Upper Palaeolithic levels at Aitzbitarte IV (Altuna, 1963). In the Mesolithic levels at Marizulo it is the dominant species at 60 percent (Altuna, 1967). A further point which is often overlooked is the large number of Neolithic sites which show a high degree of economic dependence upon red deer. In northern Italy they are the most important species at Molino Casarotto (46 percent) and occur in large numbers at Isolino (Barocelli, 1953) and Pescale (Malavolti, 1951-2), while at many sites in Liguria red deer and pig predominate. In central Italy, at Valle Ottara, they account for more than 60 percent of the Neolithic faunal remains (Acanfora, 1962-3). The high percentage of wild animals in the Swiss Cortaillod sites is well-known, and red deer are commonly the most frequently occurring of these. They commonly account for 10-40 percent of the finds, but occasionally rise above this level, as at Seeberg Burgächisee-Süd (47 percent) and Col des Roches (87 percent) (Reverdin, 1930). In France they reach 50 percent in the Lagozza levels at the Grotte d'Unang (Paccard, 1952), 40 percent at the Abri Sous-Balme (Vilain, 1966), and are common at Roucadour (Ducos, 1957) and Videlles (Basse de Ménorval, 1966). Elsewhere in Europe they reach important proportions in Holland with 33 percent at Vlaardingen (Clason, 1967), in Spain with 58 percent at Marizulo, and in Romania with 59 percent at Săpături (Dumitrescu, 1965). In some areas this importance continues into the Final Neolithic and Bronze Age.

Although the archaeological evidence cannot prove it, it is a reasonable hypothesis that most areas in Europe were continuously occupied during the Postglacial within the scope of a seasonal or repetitive multi-annual cycle, and that broadly speaking the same individual human populations and their descendants exploited continually the same individual red deer populations and their descendants. As has just been discussed, for much of Europe this situation

seems to have obtained for much of the Upper Pleistocene as well. This in itself implies strongly that a mutually favourable relationship was achieved between the two species; it is not likely that so successful and so well-balanced a relationship could survive for such long periods if it were simply a case of a parasitic predator exploiting a prey population to the latter's detriment. Studies of predator-prey relationships have shown the common existence of complex and delicately balanced associations in which the predator and prey both profit to some extent; and Wynne-Edwards (1962) has pointed out the rigorous evolutionary pressure on predator populations to regulate their exploitation to the capacity of the prey population to withstand it, and suggests that all long-lasting predator-prey relationships must be organized on these lines. Thus the crucial selective pressures will in general be not for a super-successful predator or a super-successful prey, but for the most efficient relationship which can continue to maintain itself within the ecosystem. There is no reason to suppose that human relationships with animals will in principle differ from this pattern, and we may thus suspect that there may be more to be said about the European deer economies than simply that man was hunting deer. We should not of course expect the relationship to have been static in time and space; its precise nature will have depended on what is profitable and practicable in individual situations, and these factors depend in turn on a host of internal features of the human and deer populations and external features in the economy and ecosystem.

PATTERNS OF EXPLOITATION

Turning now to direct evidence of deer exploitation patterns we find that data are scarce but most suggestive. First, as we have already noted, red deer are conspicuous by their economic importance both in terms of the numbers killed at many sites and the period over which they were successfully exploited. In the rare instances where they have been studied in sufficient detail to provide the data, there are signs that the exploitation was not a simple case of parasitic hunting. At Star Carr (Clark, 1954) and Seeberg Burgächisee-Süd, for instance, a strong bias was noted in favour of male individuals, 70 percent of the sexed sample in the latter case. There is further evidence of the operation of a close man-animal relationship in the mortality curves of the deer from Seeberg Burgächisee-Süd and Molino Casarotto. Small samples make it difficult to interpret the results with precision, but a higher proportion of the kill consists of young individuals than would be expected were they culled randomly. At Molino Casarotto about 75 percent of the total kill comes from the 0-3-year-old age group; at Seeberg Burgächisee-Süd this peak is present but less exaggerated, the calves (36 percent) particularly being exploited. At Vlaardingen (Late Neolithic) in Holland a pattern exists which diverges widely from that of a wild herd, and also from those just described, the emphasis being heavily upon mature adults.

In assessing the possible significance of this information some features of red deer populations themselves are of great significance. While the sex ratio at birth is high, with more males born than females, the differential is not great. The male red deer, as is the case in many other mammals, experiences a higher mortality rate than the female, and consequently the sex ratio in the herd as a whole is generally low, with females sometimes outnumbering males by as much as 2:1. The social organization, too, is of significance in considering their exploitation; not only are red deer territorial, often with strongly marked seasonal movements depending on food supply, insects, and weather, but also the mature males spend much of the year in segregated groups away from the hinds and their followers (calves, yearlings, and two-year-olds), social interaction between mature males and females being virtually confined to the rut. We have noted that at two sites for which there is evidence available considerably more males than females were killed; this contrasts with the probable pattern in the basic herd, in which males were almost certainly outnumbered. There are several hypotheses which might account for this state of affairs. Jéquier (1963) has suggested that the males were more vulnerable to hunting than females, and consequently fell prey to hunters more easily. Conscious selection by hunters could produce the same result, as could unconscious selection, for instance the chance exploitation of male rather than female territories. Furthermore, we should not overlook the possibility that deer may have been herded and husbanded in the past. Although it is usual to consider the deer as essentially a wild animal, there is no reason to believe that this was necessarily always so; indeed, there is much evidence to the contrary. In Britain today there exist many herds of park deer which have long histories and pedigrees, are selectively bred for antler-shape and other characteristics, and are the subjects of careful and sophisticated management; they are, in fact, farmed on a commercial basis and are often termed 'semi-domestic'. There is ample evidence that this is not a recent practice, although how far back it goes is not known. Certainly from the period of the Norman conquest deer were favoured with elaborate measures of husbandry and management in Britain, and we must note, too, the evidence for Roman and Ancient Persian management of fallow deer. Reed (1965) describes a Sassanian hunting representation showing the intentional release of a specially marked fallow doe, an account reminiscent in many ways, of the hunting of 'carted deer' in England. There would be

no difficulty in establishing a close economic relationship with red deer, which respond well to winter feeding and can become fully tame. Indeed in the eighteenth century the Third Earl of Orford is recorded as having had four stags trained to draw his phaeton, while much earlier Abbot Thokey bore the body of Edward II in a stag-drawn chariot (Whitehead, 1964). From the period of the first literary records onwards in much of Europe there is good evidence for the existence of a close relationship between man and red deer. A further consideration is of importance. All these records concern a period in which the economic importance of deer was very low, indeed negligible in most cases. The staple crops in most of Europe by this time were much as they are now, cereals and the common farm animals, and the deer were on the whole hunted for sport by an aristocratic minority, or as vermin, and were of trivial economic significance. This is evident from many literary records, and has been inferred from medieval faunal material from Germany (Müller, 1959). As we have seen, the situation is very different at the prehistoric sites we are considering, at which the red deer was a crucial economic resource. It seems in no way improbable that Mesolithic and Neolithic man may have pursued a rational course and husbanded his herds of deer in a way not dissimilar to that in which they are now treated in deer parks, or to the way in which Neolithic man treated his sheep.

We can go some way towards placing these alternative explanations in order of likelihood. There is certainly evidence to confirm Jéquier's suggestion that female red deer are more wary than the males. As Darling points out, the individual and group personalities of the sexes are widely different. We should note, however, that females are more curious than males, too, a factor which could be manipulated by human exploiters to increase the vulnerability of females. More important, whereas the males tend to behave more erratically and unpredictably, and each to keep guard for himself, the females form firmer patterns of movement, and much of the group vigilance is taken over by the lead hind and her deputy; Darling (1956) describes an occasion when four hinds fed on maize a few yards away from him while the lead hind ignored the food, moving nervously around until she located him. It may also be noted that in order to produce the situation seen at Seeberg Burgäschisee-Süd (7 males:3 females) from a probable 1:2 ratio in the basic herd, the males would have to be about five times more vulnerable than the females, a differential which seems too great to be wholly accounted for in Jéquier's terms. Some slight corroboration of this may be seen in the figures given by Picton (1961) for the results of 'random' modern hunting of wapiti, the red deer of North America, which show about 4 males:6 females in kills from two different herds in Montana. We cannot, of course, interpret our data directly in the light of Picton's figures, owing to differences in the geographical and chronological situations, in the subspecies, and in the hunting techniques involved. They nevertheless serve as an indication that some further factors may have been of importance.

It is always very difficult to distinguish between the operation of conscious and unconscious selective measures by past human populations, and most of the arguments one way or the other which appear in the literature are in fact based more on assumptions regarding the cultural or technological status of the human groups than on real ability either to distinguish the effects of the two processes in the archaeological record or to eliminate the likely operation of one or the other mechanism. It is, however, difficult to build up a convincing case for unconscious selection of males in this case if we eliminate the question of their greater vulnerability discussed above. Male and female territories in red deer are separated socially more than geographically; they overlap and cross-cut each other extensively, even though the groups remain separated for most of the year. These territories vary in size according to population size, topography, and other features, but they are frequently not more than a few kilometres in maximum radius. It has been shown (Vita-Finzi & Higgs, 1970; Jarman, Vita-Finzi & Higgs, in press) that the exploitation territories of human subsistence economies are commonly within 5-10 km in radius from the site, and on this scale the human exploitation territories would be very likely to intersect with neighbouring territories of both male and female deer; it would certainly be impossible for the human exploiters to be unaware of the local social organization of the deer, and of the presence and location of female territories. Unconscious selection is perhaps made still less likely as a significant factor in increasing the proportion of males in the kill when we remember that the males range more widely, more erratically, and in less stable groups, while the females behave more predictably and tend to establish favourite feeding and resting grounds.

This leaves us with two possibilities: conscious selective hunting, and a herding economy. Here again there is a difficulty, in that the two relationships can be very close to each other in both their behavioural connotations for the human group practising them and in their economic effect in terms of the crop they yield. As has been considered in detail elsewhere (Higgs & Jarman, I. 1; Jarman & Wilkinson, II. 4) the archaeological evidence resulting from the two economic practices might be very similar or indeed identical. The artefacts, which might on occasion offer clues to economic practices, do not help us here. What can, however, be said with confidence is that the man-deer relationship was one which tended strongly to produce a husbanded herd. The combined influence of the bias in

exploitation upon males and young individuals can be seen as having the effect of removing as crop primarily those animals which are least essential to the preservation of a successful breeding herd. Young animals, too, are those which can be most quickly and cheaply replaced. By the time it reaches full maturity a herd animal represents a considerable investment in terms of forage, and care in the case of a humanly husbanded herd. It is thus more economic to crop heavily from the young, less valuable animals which have absorbed less outlay, and will be replaced more quickly by herd reproduction. Hinds do not generally calve until they are 3 or 4 years old, breeding at 2½ to 3½ years (although evidence from New Zealand (Daniel, 1963) suggests that they can breed earlier than this in exceptionally rich environments), and stags are not effective in the rut until they are older than this. At both Seeberg Burgäschisee-Süd and Molino Casarotto the majority of the kill was from the non-breeding part of the herd. At Seeberg Burgäschisee-Süd 70 percent of the crop was male, which as has often been pointed out serves to raise the yield without imparing herd viability. To put it another way, in any herbivore, and especially in a species like red deer in which almost all the hinds are in any case served by mature dominant stags, a large proportion of the younger stags can be considered as an economic surplus whose elimination from the herd will have no effect of endangering future herd survival and thus the continuance of the successful economic relationship. The high percentage of males at Star Carr as well as Seeberg Burgäschisee-Süd suggests that this practice may be widespread among European deer economies, but the detailed information is not at present available to demonstrate this.

Figure 3 illustrates a hypothetical age/sex distribution of the Seeberg Burgäschisee-Süd crop. Jéquier gives age data on fifty-three individuals, and a sex ratio of 7:3 for several different anatomical elements. If we assume that both these sets of information are valid for the collection as a whole, then one can envisage the situation illustrated; other combinations of sex and age classes are of course possible, but

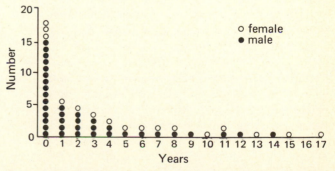

Fig. 3. Hypothetical age/sex distribution of the Seeberg Burgäschisee-Süd crop.

something approaching the one depicted has several features which recommend it to our attention. The high proportion of males to females in the younger age classes is, as we have seen, encouraged by several factors; the high sex ratio at birth, the greater biological vulnerability of male calves, and the greater temperamental vulnerability of male yearlings and two- to three-year-olds, and the economic advantages of cropping heavily the sexually immature males. After this other factors intervene which would select strongly for a different cropping pattern. For the mature age groups females would predominate strongly over males. Furthermore there would have been a degree of incentive not to overcrop the mature males; Darling notes that it is the mature, best antlered stags which come into rut first and sire the majority of the calves: 'if too many mature stags are shot . . . breeding is left to the later young stags, and the result is that the extra high winter-mortality factor, working normally on a very small number of late calves, operates on a greater proportion of the calf crop, thus seriously diminishing natural increase'. The position of mature females is somewhat different. If the herd is required to increase in size, then the maximum number of adult females will be maintained in the population, and the kill of adult females will be largely restricted to unhealthy or barren individuals; but assuming that in the long term the herd size is to be maintained stable in numbers, then a proportion of adult females may be surplus to the requirements of herd maintenance. The great importance of an experienced lead hind to the success and well-being of the hind group, and thus the herd as a whole, is well known, and it would be vital for any human economy dependent upon the exploitation of red deer to foster a succession of mature and experienced lead hinds; but with this exception it would be advantageous to maintain a relatively young hind stock which is more productive than one with a high proportion of hinds in late maturity. The rarity of bones from very old or senile deer at prehistoric sites is indeed notable, and it is perhaps significant that such beasts represent a poor economic return in relation to their cumulative range and forage requirements and their increasing liability to predators and disease. In addition, it has been shown (Dzieciołowski, 1970) that body weight of animals older than twelve shows a decline, on the average, relative to mature adult individuals (8-11 years).

A brief discussion is also necessary of the situation at Vlaardingen, which as we have seen, presents a very different picture. Clason was unable to calculate the sex ratio of the deer crop, but the age curve shows a very much higher proportion of mature beasts relative to immature; only 35 percent are from 0-3-year-olds, in contrast with 57 percent to c. 75 percent at Seeberg Burgäschisee-Süd and Molino Casarotto. This means that an unusually large proportion of the crop came from a relatively small percentage of the herd. It is possible, of course, that a disproportionately large number of the immature and more fragile specimens was missed in excavation or was not preserved, but this can hardly account for the low numbers of yearling and two-year-old individuals. Most of the bones which can be aged with precision appear to come from the time of year between calving and the rut, May to November, and it is possible that local factors operated so as to increase the accessibility of the mature age groups to human exploitation at this time of year; but it is difficult to see exactly how this could have come about. Furthermore it may be noted that Molino Casarotto was almost certainly primarily a summer occupation site, too, and displays a very different age curve.

We should not, of course, assume that every individual site will yield evidence which is readily explicable in terms of simple economic pressures, but some further factors which may have influenced the situation may be noted. Firstly we should not rule out the possible effect of different techniques of exploitation — whether this involved hunting with bows and arrows, trapping, herding, corralling, and so on. The coastal-marsh environment of Vlaardingen at the time would have lent itself well to the technique of driving deer into water or miring them in marshes, practices noted as aiding capture in Britain. It is difficult, however, to see in what way such a technique would necessarily select the mature animals. Indeed one might think on the contrary that the younger, weaker, and less experienced individuals might more readily be taken this way. Probably more important is the effect of the long term economic history of the areas concerned.

Both Seeberg Burgäschisee-Süd and Molino Casarotto are in areas occupied apparently continuously since the end of the Würm glaciation, and are the successors to animal economies which are virtually identical to those practised at these sites. Furthermore, in both areas subsequent to the occupation of these sites, the record shows but a slow adaptation towards a classic 'Neolithic' economy with sheep-goat, pig, cattle, and cereals; in the Molino Casarotto area, for instance, red deer are still an important food animal 1000 years later at Rivoli, and a 'typical Neolithic' economy is not visible until the Bronze Age at Monte Tondo and Torri (Jarman, 1971). The situation at Vlaardingen is very different. The site occupies an area which was submerged under the North Sea previously, and only became available for terrestrial exploitation, due to fluctuations in the relative level of land and sea, at about the time of first occupation of the site. It would at this period be a most unsuitable area for a typical 'Neolithic' economy, being situated near the junction of tidal clays and peat deposits; if it was occupied mainly during the summer and autumn, as was suggested above, this may have been because it was still too wet for winter occupation, although here it should be noted that Clason (1967) argues for year-round occupation. Hekelingen, a few kilometres away, was probably occupied a century or two later (Vlaardingen [14]C 2380±100 B.C.-2240±70 B.C.; Hekelingen [14]C 2250±120 B.C.-2130±85 B.C.), when peat had formed over much of the tidal clays, and the surrounding land was in general drier. A little to the north the sites of Langeveld and Vogelenzang, occupied about 1000 years later, show a continuation of this process, while the pre-Roman Iron Age and Roman sites at Vlaardingen (c. 400 B.C.-0 B.C.) are predominantly surrounded by fen peat, with some sandy and clayey tidal deposits. It is most instructive to place against this picture of a (broadly speaking) slowly drying environment around Vlaardingen the faunal record from the various sites. Whereas at the earliest Vlaardingen site red deer and pig are by far the most important animals exploited, their importance has slightly declined by the period of occupation of Hekelingen. At the Bronze Age and Iron Age-Roman sites the importance of red deer is negligible (Table 3). We have thus a situation in which an area was colonized by a human group and by deer as soon as it was available for exploitation, probably both species under pressure from the well established farming economies further inland. Within 1000 years or so, and in all probability in half that time, the environment had significantly altered, while the population pressure continued to exert its influence. The deer economy was a very short lived one, being born of a particular combination of circumstances which were ephemeral viewed against a prehistoric time scale. This being so it is perhaps not surprising that we should find a different, and almost certainly less efficient, pattern of economic exploitation of the deer; with such a rapidly changing environmental situation neither the human nor animal populations are likely to have achieved stability. It is possible that the human population was unable in the time to acquire the necessary expertise to exploit the deer to maximum advantage, but it must also be considered a possibility that over so short a time scale it was unnecessary for them to do so.

MECHANISMS OF ECONOMIC DEVELOPMENT

We have examined in detail some aspects of European prehistoric economies, and have noted that in most of the areas discussed there is a basic change at some time from deer-pig based economies to sheep-goat, pig, cattle, and cereal based economies, although the period and manner of the change-over varied widely from place to place. It is evidently a question of considerable significance what primary reasons can be seen for this development, which is remarkable by reason both of its uniformity over large areas and of its long term importance – the latter economy remains after all the agricultural basis upon which we now rely. The usual view is to see the economy as basically culturally controlled; following the invention of the techniques of agriculture by Neolithic peoples in the Near East, Neolithic cultures spread thence across Europe bringing with them the new economy. Many (Bökönyi, 1969a; Murray, 1970) see the variations within this broad pattern equally as the result of the operation of cultural choice. Murray (1970) writes that, 'Sheep are ... the basic animal in the Impressed Ware economy', and that, 'The Linear Pottery farmers were essentially cattle breeders', while at most Cortaillod sites 'hunting is still a valuable part of the economy'. Similarly, although 'cattle breeding and wheat cultivation remain the basis of the subsistence-economies until the end of the neolithic period' in central Europe, yet, 'There were, however, one or two societies which preferred to breed pigs to cattle'. This attitude implies the belief that economic practices can be treated as essentially culturally-dependent variables, subject to human whim and fashion in very much the same way as pot decoration. There is much evidence, archaeological and otherwise, to the contrary. At Knossos, in Crete, for example, the pattern of animal husbandry remains very largely unchanged in its basic species representation pattern for 6000 years; from the

Table 3. Proportions (percentage) of the main species at some Eneolithic to Roman sites in Holland (Data from Clason, 1967)

Species	Vlaardingen Eneolithic	Hekelingen Eneolithic	Langeveld Bronze Age	Vogelenzang Bronze Age	Vlaardingen Iron Age	Vlaardingen Roman
Red deer	34	32	2	–	–	–
Pig	37	26	4	17	11	4
Cattle	14	22	64	65	70	67
Sheep/goat	1	2	8	–	16	24
Horse	–	–	18	6	2	4
Others	14	18	4	12	1	1

earliest Neolithic to the Roman levels, encompassing a vast range of cultural variation, the animal economy is based on sheep, with goat, pig, and cattle in subsidiary positions. Similarly, as Bökönyi himself points out (1970), phase III at Lepenski vir, while belonging to the Starčevo-Körös cultural group, is very different from the normal Starčevo-Körös site from the point of view of its animal economy. Starčevo-Körös sites are in general characterized by dependence upon caprines and cattle, with caprines commonly accounting for the majority of the fauna. At Lepenski vir III not only is red deer by far the dominant species, but cattle bones outnumber those of caprines by 4:1. Higham (1967) has documented comparable variations within the Swiss Michelsberg Culture. The cultural interpretation of economic patterns unfortunately has done little to provide a predictive or explanatory framework for changes which can be seen to have behaved in a conspicuously regular and uniform way when viewed in the long term. One reason for this is that when faced with apparent exceptions and disparities it has been the custom to explain them in terms of some undefined 'local influence' or to the fact that the site concerned is not on the primary route of development of the culture in question; a device which can account for any conceivable pattern in the data without going very far towards explaining the causative mechanisms involved. In addition, such a model fails to take account of external environmental factors or intrinsic economic mechanisms which must surely have had profound and far-reaching effects. Whatever attractions it may have for the study of archaeological cultures, from the point of view of economic prehistory the alliance of culture with economy is an archaeological marriage of convenience in which both partners are ill at ease.

One of the factors which exerts a great influence upon the nature of economic practices might be termed the background environment. The basic fertility of soil, its structure and depth; the broad features of the climate, in particular the amount and distribution of rainfall, the annual temperature curve, and the length of the growing season; and the combined effects of these with that of topography, often introduce severe limitations into the theoretically unrestricted field of choice open to man. Even in the area under consideration, notably lacking in violent environmental extremes for the most part, circumstances will in some places encourage arable agriculture, in others dairy farming; in yet others sheep farming will be the only viable economy. This cannot, however, be the sole major determinant of economic practices; many instances exist where economic change cannot be related to major environmental shifts, even though local ecological adjustments may be involved. Thus Clark (1947) pointed out the trend to increase in sheep relative to pig from Neolithic to Iron Age in

much of Europe, and discussed probable causative factors of this phenomenon. This is of course a commonplace of long term economic development, but as Payne (II. 3, p. 66) has demonstrated, economic changes can equally occur in the middle of unbroken 'cultural' phases.

There is evidently another factor or set of factors involved, and here we do well to consider the influence of mechanisms and pressures built into the very structure of the system of relationships between human populations and their surroundings. One aspect of these is the impact of human economic practices upon the functioning of the local ecosystem, and a related factor is the ever-present goad of population pressure. Many modern examples of land improvement and intensive livestock production are best seen in this light; but it is perhaps worth considering in more detail an example of the operation of these factors in prehistoric Europe. Jarman (1971) traced the pattern of economic change in a small area of sub-alpine Italy between c. 4500 and 2000 B.C., providing basically a picture of the gradual development from an economy based on deer, pigs, and aquatic and woodland plants to one based on sheep, goat, pigs, and cattle, with cereals. The earliest site, Molino Casarotto is interesting in that it provides the earliest ^{14}C dates for a Neolithic site in inland north Italy, with an abundance of bocca quadrata pottery. A notable feature is the presence at this site of both sheep and small (morphologically 'domestic' according to traditional criteria) cattle in very small percentages. Red deer is the commonest animal, and with pig it accounts for over 90 percent of the animal remains. There is no sign of large scale exploitation of hazel nuts, the only considerable source of plant protein likely to have been available. The utilized plants are dominated by water chestnut, a plant of limited nutritional value; but, as with the animals, it is most interesting to note the presence of cultivated wheat in a highly developed form. At Rivoli, about a millennium later, cattle and caprines have increased in proportion at the expense of deer, a broad trend which is maintained at the Bronze Age sites of Monte Tondo and Torri. A recently excavated site at Fondo Tomollero, a few hundred metres from Molino Casarotto and in a similar lakeside situation seems to confirm the trend, although the collection has not yet been fully analysed. Again the plant data correspond closely to the animal; at Fondo Tomollero the absence of water chestnut is striking, whereas cereals are relatively abundant.

A conventional explanation of this situation might be to call the occupants of Molino Casarotto Neolithic hunters with some slight acculturation from local 'fully Neolithic' cultures. From then on a picture of culture change might be invoked with decreasing 'Mesolithic' influence as the inhabitants of the area opted increasingly for Neolithic agricultural techniques. Even apart from the difficulty that

Molino Casarotto itself is by far the earliest known Neolithic site in the area, this is not a very satisfactory explanation of the evidence. Farming economies based upon modern domestic species had spread successfully from Yugoslavia to Holland in about 1000 years by c. 4500 B.C. 'Cultural choice' or adherence to tradition seem insufficient in themselves to have delayed this process by more than a millennium in northern Italy unless some positive evidence is available that other factors did not influence the situation.

A basic clue to the possible nature of other mechanisms involved here comes from a consideration of the modern economic situation in the area. Most of the sites are in the Berici Hills, a small discrete area of low, steep-sided hills just south of the Alps, while Rivoli is slightly to the west in the Adige valley just north of Verona. Neither of these areas can be considered attractive from an agricultural point of view. Today the Berici Hills can be considered in three sections with regard to their exploitation; the valley floors, the steep hillsides, and the flatter basins and small plateaux that occur in some areas on top of the hills. The valley floors, often primarily lacustrine in origin, are under intensive agricultural exploitation, with maize and fodder crops forming the basic rotation. Except on alluvial fans close to the hill sides this exploitation has only been made possible by recent drainage schemes, often within the last century, and the vast majority of the valley floors, now the most productive area of the hills, was evidently unsuited to any form of agriculture during prehistory, most of it being marsh. The hills are not high (maximum altitude c. 450 m) but are extremely steep-sided. Today the slopes are uniformly covered with thick deciduous scrub, greatly cut back and with very few mature trees. In many places this is growing almost directly on loose limestone scree with negligible soil content, and it is evident that any effort to clear and cultivate would be fruitless and would increase the movement of large stones downhill on to the arable land. The hill tops consist partly of continued steep scrub-covered slopes, and partly of agricultural land in small basins and pockets, and a few wider plateaux. The exploitation of these latter areas is based upon maize and fodder crops as below, but with a large proportion of pasture (cut for hay) and some vines, these latter practices generally utilizing the steeper, stonier areas. The limiting factor upon agriculture in this area is again the local topography, and the soil cover which is dependent upon this factor. The pressure of human population upon the resources is evident in the cultivation and grazing of the smallest areas — sometimes only a few metres across — of available soil; colonization is continuing today and is expanding into situations which are increasingly marginal and unfavourable in terms of the relationship of input of effort to expected profits.

The Rivoli situation is somewhat different, with both wider areas of arable exploitation and more rugged cliffs with much limestone exposed; however, the pattern of exploitation is similar to that of the Berici Hills, and the limiting factors are evidently the same.

Against this background it is possible to achieve a new understanding of the changing economy, presenting a picture not accessible to an approach which ascribes economic configuration purely to cultural choice. The Mesolithic and earliest Neolithic economy is based upon deer and pig, both of which do well in deciduous woodland. The low-lying areas of the Berici Hills were very poorly drained at this period, with considerable open lakes, the marshland affording another habitat suitable to pigs. Open areas would probably have been few, although mature forest with well-grown trees tends to less underbrush than the severely cleared woods of the area today. Also human action may have encouraged and enlarged natural glades and open areas which provide optimum browsing conditions for deer. All in all, however, in spite of the availability and knowledge by 4500 B.C. of the economic practices of caprine husbandry and cereal growing, there can have been very little opportunity to exploit those techniques; sheep do not exploit thick woodland successfully, and even assuming that it were cleared the area suitable for arable agriculture was very limited. In such a situation the red deer-pig economy is the most profitable practicable within the limitations of the technology and resources. By the Late Neolithic of Rivoli the economic pattern has changed; in particular with the reduction of deer and the increase of cattle and caprines. There is also evidence of cereals. The Bronze Age sites essentially represent the continuation of this development. Two interrelated factors seem likely to be involved here; the evolution of superior modes of economic organization and the impact on the area of a prolonged period of population pressure.

A feature of the economy which emerges in the Late Neolithic and Bronze Age is its high productivity relative to that which it succeeds. This increase in productivity is achieved in two ways; a greater productivity of individual elements within the economy per unit area exploited; and a better overall integration of the individual elements into a coherent system. Sheep and cattle are both more productive than deer, acre for acre, assuming that it is possible to clear the thick woodland, which can certainly not have been a problem; fire and the browsing of the animals themselves would be potent controllers of forest regeneration. Deer carrying-capacities vary according to the nature of the available browse, but commonly range between 1:15 and 1:45 acres. Sheep could be expected to run at about 1:3 acres on hill pasture, and as high as 5:1 on good lowland pasture; while for cattle about 1:20 on hill pasture, and 1:2

on lowland, seem average figures. In addition to their lower stocking rate, the reproductive rate of deer is commonly about 60 percent, whereas for sheep it might be expected to average about 100 percent. It is difficult to place too much significance on these figures, however, as both birth and survival rates can vary widely from population to population, being in particular closely related to population pressure upon food resources. Pigs might be expected to come under more intensive management at this stage, too, particularly as the expansion of cattle and sheep in the economy would have greatly reduced the available woodland, an important source of food for the pig. An additional incentive to management would be the destructive effect of wild pigs upon agricultural land, particularly in areas where the amount of forest is decreasing. In modern Poland hunting regulations permit an especially high kill of wild pig in small forests, in an effort to lower the pig population and reduce their destructive influence (Taber, 1961). Under conditions of increased control and supervision, and with systematic cropping, a higher rate of breeding and survival might be expected to occur. Similar advantages attend the practice of cereal cultivation; under favourable conditions it is one of the most productive forms of land exploitation, and can be expected to produce in the order of seven to ten times the calorific value of any animal exploitation per unit of area.

An important aspect of the economy outlined above — essentially the mixed farming typical of so much of Europe even today — is its flexible yet highly integrated structure. It is well known that not all herbivores compete directly with each other, feeding on different plants and on different parts of the same plant. For this reason the most efficient economic use of pasture is often to run two or more different species on it. This has been shown to be so to some extent for deer and cattle, and even more so for sheep and cattle, as sheep will graze pasture successfully after cattle have eaten it as close as they are able. The cultivation of cereals, too, is closely involved. They would of necessity have been grown as part of a rotation, with fallow periods or some fodder crop, or both, interspersed with the cereal crop. Fallow, stubble, and fodder crops would all have been grazed by the stock either directly or cut as hay; and the animals would play an important part in maintaining soil fertility by manuring the fields. A close relationship would necessarily link the area cultivated, the proportion under cereals, and the size of herds, forming in the simplest instance a closed, or nearly closed, system in which the cereals provided seed grain and a surplus for human (or animal) consumption, with the cultivated area not under cereals providing winter fodder for animals which might well be fed on permanent pasture during the summer. The human group would subsist on the combined plant and animal (meat and dairy) surplus of this system. The pig is to some degree the odd man out in this scheme, as it would probably be fed to a large extent in the woodlands and upon kitchen refuse. Yet even here there is an element of feedback from the exploitation of pigs to the rest of the system in that the destructive effect of pigs upon woodland growth and regeneration was probably an influence in the maintenance and extension of more open areas suitable for pasture. Pigs are both economically and ecologically very flexible, and their ability to withstand a very high cropping rate (as high as 50 percent sustained yield in hunted populations of wild pigs in Poland (Taber, 1961)) means that they are appropriate to a variety of economic situations. They are frequently associated with impoverished situations as the main or sole animal protein source for human populations under considerable stress. On the other hand they can be similarly employed by relatively affluent societies to raise their intake of animal protein, a nutritional element which is maximized by the majority of human groups.

The important feature of this system, as we have noted, is its high productivity relative to that which it succeeded. It should perhaps be pointed out that while productivity per unit area of land is rising, productivity per unit of human effort does not necessarily do so, as the more sophisticated methods very frequently require a greater investment of human labour — both more men and more hours per day — than those previously employed. Pastoral exploitation varies very greatly in its labour requirements, but under both intensive and extensive management arable exploitation is generally more expensive of labour than pastoral exploitation. Similarly, the grazing requirements of cattle and sheep are likely to have absorbed more labour than the deer and pigs which preceded them, particularly as these latter species were part of a long-existing ecological community in the area, whereas cattle existed only in smaller numbers, and sheep were almost certainly only able to exist there at all due to the exertion of human selective pressure. The point is readily seen that the system has changed from low to high productivity only at the expense of becoming a *labour intensive system*, requiring the expenditure of much input of labour to maintain the high productivity necessary to maintain the high human population.

Here we return to our proposition that two closely linked factors — superior economic organization and a maintained population pressure — can be seen as at least partially responsible for the changes which might otherwise be labelled simply 'cultural', and inexplicable or requiring no further explanation. Here it is of importance to note the inherent tendency in economic development to increased complexity of organization and to increased returns, even be this at the expense of huge expenditure of capital, in the form of human effort. A reason for this may be seen in the population pressure which, over a prehistoric time scale, will always tend to give selective advantage to the more successful economy over the less successful. A community whose food supply has increased and whose population has risen in consequence to a new level, cannot allow the supply to decrease again without seriously lowering the standard of living of its members. In this position there are two basic alternatives; successful economic adaptation to the new population level, in which case a new 'plateau' may result; or economic failure, which may either result in vulnerability to other, more successful economies, or cataclysmic decrease in population to the level the available resources can support; the decrease may well take place through any of a number of occurrences apparently not directly connected with economics (e.g. epidemics, wars, emigration, decline in the birth rate, etc.). For this reason, the trend of economic change has in the long run been invariably in one direction, in order to accommodate the ever increasing demands of an ever increasing population. In our example of northern Italy, the evidence of Molino Casarotto shows the knowledge and presence somewhere in the locality of highly productive techniques of plant and animal husbandry. The Berici Hills were unsuited ecologically to this form of economy at the time, but the long term effect of population pressure led eventually to the slow adoption of more profitable techniques which both required and could accommodate a larger population. Once the changes were initiated they would have a strong tendency to self-perpetuation and development, for quite apart from the continued population pressure the new practices would tend automatically to create conditions more suitable for the further development of the new system and would destroy the ecological conditions necessary for the pursuit of the old. This is indeed a process which can be seen continuing today, as increasingly poor sites are colonized under the modern population pressure, in addition to the growing rash of weekend and holiday occupants from large urban areas. The deer are still on the retreat from the dwindling cover and browse, and from the increasing disturbance which comes with dense human population; having long since abandoned the Berici Hills, they are now only found to the north, in the Alps proper, at higher altitudes.

CONCLUSIONS

This paper has examined some attitudes to the study of prehistoric economies, in particular highlighting some aspects which although of great significance have received

little attention hitherto. Interpretations relying upon artefactual phenomena to explain economic data ignore the evident influence of environment upon many economic practices. We may note that the 'Impressed Ware people' and Neolithic inhabitants of the Balkans may have been sheep breeders not simply because they wished to be so, but because this was — and is — the most profitable form of economy open to them. It is often necessary, in order to obtain the basic data for analysis to consider economies in terms of their individual components; to consider individual species of animals and plants as separate entities. It is frequently left at that, resulting in a rather static zoological or botanical view of the situation, but long-established concepts of ecology and ethology suggest other and more complex facets to the picture, introducing the important principle of the dynamic biotic community, with complex interrelationships linking individual species in their behaviour. For the archaeologist, of course, it is impossible to study the totality of such communities in the past, but he can attempt at least to deal with the elements which do survive in terms of this overall framework. We may thus think of the development of economies not in terms of inventions or choices with regard to individual species, but more in terms of the evolution of the complex system of which they form a part. Particular forces of great significance arise, however, from the human factor in the biotope, operating through processes of economic change which may be to a large extent autonomous and not directly dependent upon other factors in the ecosystem. An example of the operation of two different kinds of mechanism may be seen in the Late Neolithic and subsequent prehistoric occupation of the coastal areas of modern Holland. The spread of the Neolithic Bandkeramik Culture from the Balkans to north-west Germany and south Holland was notable for its rapidity; a large factor in its success appears to have been the functioning of a highly productive and well-integrated economy based on cattle, pigs, caprines, and cereals. Occupation of the Dutch coastal area was delayed 2000 years or so by environmental factors, a critical change permitting settlement at c. 2400-2300 B.C. After about 2000 B.C., however, changes in the background environment appear to have been of less significance, and the subsequent economic development can be viewed largely in terms of responses in human economic behaviour to sustained population pressure from the centres of high population supported by more productive economies to the south-east. Thus in a sense it is wrong to regard such sites as the first occupation at Vlaardingen as 'backward' or 'impoverished'. This is only true to the extent that it is true of the modern Welsh sheep farmer relative to the market gardener supplying Birmingham. Fitness for the individual situation is a criterion upon which it seems justifiable to judge the success or failure of exploitation patterns.

We have noted that at any time a human population may be presented with a variety of possible modes of economic behaviour; a range of choice. From the range of what is possible one pattern will be the most successful in terms of the contemporary situation, the remaining alternatives being less successful to varying degrees. We have further noted that in the long term, the selective pressure imposed by population increase will ensure that it is those communities which take the successful economic routes which flourish while those which do not are inevitably assimilated or overrun in the long term. For this reason undeniable trends are visible beneath the welter of apparent confusion of random variation. Fluctuations occur, in part because of local economic factors such as changes in the relationship of population to resources, but we should not allow the fact that short-lived and local fluctuations have occurred to deter us from recognizing, for example, that the proportion of arable land in Europe has risen steadily over the last 1000 years, and indeed over the last 5000 years. The interdependent factors which we may associate with this trend are the steady trend towards forest clearance, drainage of marshes, and so on; the improvement of agricultural technology; and the ever-present promptings of population pressure. Murray has given us a picture of economic patterns dominated by cultural tradition, as deduced from artefact (largely ceramic) typology. Slicher van Bath (1963), on the other hand, writing of the early historic period of western Europe, holds that the form of the economy is very closely shackled to necessity, there being very little room for manoeuvre. To some extent both viewpoints can be justified, but it is possible to gain a clearer insight by consideration of the time scale with which one is concerned. Slobodkin (1962), dealing with animal populations, found it necessary to distinguish between physiological time (appropriate to short-term changes), ecological time (approximately ten generations), evolutionary time (appropriate to long-term changes), and geological time. Similar distinctions can obviously be usefully applied to human populations. In particular we are concerned here with a distinction between short- and long-term phenomena. In the short term unpredictable fluctuations can and do occur in the relations between both individual and population resources relative to the demands placed upon them. This short-term variability ensures that there will be periods when resources are in excess of subsistence demands, producing an affluent society; and under such circumstances personal and cultural choice can be exercised with comparative freedom, though one should perhaps point out that this choice tends to operate more upon the manner in which the economic surplus is expended than directly upon the methods whereby it is achieved. At the other end of the scale of short-term variation is a situation more closely approximating to van Bath's model; population pressure on available resources high, with near poverty the general rule, and little leeway left for choice of any description. The economic system is under severe stress, and unless relief comes in the form of population decline or economic advance then choice in the economic or any other field is a practical impossibility. In the long term, the constant potential for rapid population increase, and the biological mechanisms tending to stabilize population at the optimum — i.e. highest safe — level for a given level of available resources, between them ensure that neither the extremes of affluence nor of poverty are likely to last long on a prehistoric time scale.

APPENDIX 1

EUROPEAN MESOLITHIC FAUNAS; PRIMARY ECONOMIC SPECIES. SITES ARRANGED BY COUNTRY, AND ALPHABETICALLY WITHIN COUNTRIES

The following table records the presence (×) of primary economic species at each Mesolithic site, arranged by country (Sweden and Denmark shown on this page).

Species	Ageröd I. H+C	Ageröd I. D+B	Ageröd V.	Rörvik	Rötekarrslid	Sjöholmen	Soldattorpet	Aamølle	Aasted	Bloksbjerg	Braband Sø	Drøsselholm	Dyrholmen	Ertebølle	Faareveile	Gudumlund	Hallebygaard	Havnø	Hesselbjerggaard	Holmegaard	Jaegerspris	Kildegaard	Klintesø	Kolind	Kongemosen	Langø	Maglemose	Magleø	Muldbjerg I	Øgaard	Sølager	Strandegaard	Svaerdborg	Tingbjerggaard	Vinde-Helsinge	Virksund	Visborg
Oryctolagus																																					
Lepus																											×				×						
Marmota																																					
Castor						×				×		×		×		×		×	×		×		×			×	×	×	×	×		×		×	×	×	×
Mustela													×																								
Martes						×	×			×	×		×	×	×	×		×			×		×				×	×			×			×	×		×
Meles							×		×	×			×	×				×				×			×		×		×		×			×	×		×
Lutra					×	×	×		×	×		×	×	×	×		×			×			×		×		×		×		×			×	×		
Felis							×		×	×	×	×	×	×		×		×			×	×				×	×		×		×			×			
Lynx												×		×																		×		×		×	
Vulpes							×		×	×	×	×	×	×		×	×	×	×		×		×		×		×		×		×			×			
Canis familiaris	×	×				×	×		×	×	×	×	×	×	×		×	×	×		×		×		×		×		×		×			×	×		
Canis lupus									×		×			×	×																×			×	×		
Ursus	×	×	×			×								×	×											×			×					×			×
Equus sp.																																					
E. hydruntinus																																					
E. caballus										×						×	×		×	×			×			×					×						
Sus	×	×	×			×	×		×	×	×	×	×	×	×	×	×	×	×	×	×	×	×	×	×	×	×	×	×	×	×	×	×	×	×	×	×
Ovis/Capra									×	×						×				×		×		×													
Capra ibex																																					
Rupicapra																																					
Bison																																					
Bos	×	×				×	×		×		×	×		×	×	×	×	×	×	×					×		×	×	×	×				×	×	×	
Rangifer																																					
Alces	×	×	×	×		×			×	×		×	×				×	×						×	×		×				×	×					
C. capreolus	×	×	×		×	×	×		×	×	×	×	×	×	×	×	×	×	×	×	×	×	×	×	×	×	×	×		×	×			×	×	×	
C. elaphus	×	×	×		×	×	×		×	×	×	×	×	×	×	×	×	×	×	×	×	×	×	×	×	×	×	×	×	×	×			×	×	×	×

SWEDEN
Ageröd I. H + C.
Ageröd I. D + B.
Ageröd V.
Rörvik
Rötekarrslid
Sjöholmen
Soldattorpet

DENMARK
Aamølle
Aasted
Bloksbjerg
Braband Sø
Drøsselholm
Dyrholmen
Ertebølle
Faareveile
Gudumlund
Hallebygaard
Havnø
Hesselbjerggaard
Holmegaard
Jaegerspris
Kildegaard
Klintesø
Kolind
Kongemosen
Langø
Maglemose
Magleø
Muldbjerg I
Øgaard
Sølager
Strandegaard
Svaerdborg
Tingbjerggaard
Vinde-Helsinge
Virksund
Visborg

APPENDIX 1 (continued)

	Cushendum	Glenarm	Mother Grundy's Parlour	Oban	Oronsay	Star Carr	Thatcham	Westward Ho!	Abri Cornille	Abri Dumas	Abri Edward	Abri Genière	Abri Pagès	Abri du Sault	Abri de Sous	Abri Sous-Sac	Abri Trosset	Baume de Ronze	Borie del Rey	Perigordo-Tardenoisian	Sauveterrian	Tardenoisian	Chambre des Fées	Chateauneuf-lez-Martigues	Chinchon No. 3	Chinchon No. 2	Chinchon No. 1	Colombier	Cuzoul: Sauveterrian	Cuzoul: Tardenoisian	Grotte de la Combette	Grotte des Escabasses	Grotte des Hoteaux	Grotte de Poeymaü	Azilian	Arudian	Grotte de Souhait	Grotte d'Unang	Hoëdic	La Montade	Le Grand Cave	Le Havre: Campignian
Oryctolagus							×			×							×			×	×		×	×	×	×				×								×		×		
Lepus						×															×		×		×	×	×	×										×				
Marmota																				×									×													
Castor						×	×					×				×				×	×		×	×	×	×							×				×					
Mustela																×																										
Martes						×	×									×																×				×	×			×		
Meles			×			×	×					×		×		×									×	×						×				×	×			×		
Lutra				×												×			×																							
Felis				×			×																×						×	×												
Lynx					×																		×							×		×										
Vulpes						×	×		×	×				×			×							×				×	×	×								×				
Canis familiaris			×			×	×																×								×											
Canis lupus							×									×										×					×						×					
Ursus																×																	×									
Equus sp.																									×																	
E. Hydruntinus									×		×	×																														
E. caballus		×					×							×						×	×				×	×	×															
Sus	×		×	×	×	×	×		×	×	×	×	×	×	×	×				×	×	×	×	×	×	×	×	×	×	×		×	×			×		×	×	×	×	×
Ovis/Capra									×	×	×					×							×									×	×	×	×	×		×				
Capra ibex																													×	×		×	×		×	×	×	×				
Rupicapra																×																×	×			×			×			
Bison		×										×																														
Bos			×	×		×	×		×			×	×			×	×			×	×	×	×		×	×	×				×	×				×	×	×	×	×		×
Rangifer																	×						×																			
Alces						×	×																																			
C. capreolus			×			×	×		×					×		×				×				×				×	×	×	×				×	×		×		×		
C. elaphus	×	×		×	×	×	×		×	×		×	×	×	×	×				×	×	×	×	×	×	×	×		×	×	×	×	×		×	×	×	×		×	×	

Le Martinet
Sauveterrian
Tardenoisian
Le Roc Allan
Tardenoisian
Mas d'Azil
Azilian
Arisian
Rochedanne
Soubeyras
Sous-Balme
Téviec

GERMANY
Borneck
Bregentwedt-Förstermoor
Duvensee
Ellerbek
Falkensteinhöhle
Hopfenbach
Pinnberg

SWITZERLAND
Balm bei Günzberg
Birseck Hohler Felsen
Birseck Schlossfelsen
Birsmatten
Sauveterrian
Tardenoisian
Col des Roches
Ettingen
Höhle bei Soyhières
Höhle von Oberlarg
Liesbergmühle
Wachtfelsens bei Grellingen

CZECHOSLOVAKIA
Kůlna-Höhle: Layer 3
Sered'

POLAND
Janislawice

ROMANIA
Baile Herculane
Ciumesti
Cuina Turcului II
Erbiceni
Icoana

PORTUGAL
Mugem

143

APPENDIX 1 (continued)

	SPAIN										ITALY																													
	Aitzbitarte	Cocina	Cueva de la Riera	Cueva del Rey	La Chora	Lumentxa	Marizulo	Santimamiñe	Urtiaga	Valle	Addaura	Arene Candide	Arma di Nasino	Arma dello Stefanin	Capo d'Acqua	Ciclami	Fontana Nuova de Marina de Ragusa	Levanzo	Grotta Azzurra	Grotta della Campane	Grotta del Castello	Grotta del Cavallo	Grotta Cipoliane	Grotta Corrugi de Pachino	Grotta dei Fanciulli	Grotta de Golino	Grotta Jolanda	Grotta Mangiapane	Grotta de Monte Pellegrino	Grotta della Mura	Grotta di Niscemi	Grotta Polesini	Grotta la Porta	Grotta delle Prazziche	Grotta del Prete	Grotta de San Teodoro	Praia a Mare	Riparo Blanc	Riparo Tagliente	Ripoli
Oryctolagus		×																						×																
Lepus						×																×		×		×	×	×				×							×	
Marmota								×					×	×							×														×			×		
Castor																																								
Mustela														×											×															
Martes						×																															×			
Meles			×			×		×						×		×				×				×		×	×		×					×	×		×			
Lutra																																								
Felis						×		×																		×	×	×									×			
Lynx																											×				×									
Vulpes	×		×		×	×		×	×						×			×			×			×	×	×	×		×					×		×		×		×
Canis familiaris																									×															
Canis lupus	×		×			×										×										×					×	×							×	
Ursus	×				×	×		×	×			×														×														
Equus sp.		×																			×		×							×										
E. hydruntinus					×						×								×				×	×	×		×	×	×	×	×				×					
E. caballus	×		×	×	×	×		×	×	×									×	×						×				×										
Sus	×	×	×	×	×	×		×	×	×		×	×	×	×		×		×	×	×		×	×	×	×	×	×	×	×	×		×	×	×	×	×			×
Ovis/Capra																										×														
Capra ibex	×	×	×	×	×	×		×	×	×		×	×	×						×					×		×						×			×				
Rupicapra	×		×		×	×		×	×	×										×					×														×	
Bison					×																																			
Bos	×		×		×	×		×		×	×	×		×			×	×			×	×	×	×	×				×	×										×
Rangifer																									×															
Alces																																								
C. capreolus	×		×		×			×	×	×		×	×		×	×			×				×		×	×			×	×			×	×	×			×	×	×
C. elaphus	×	×	×	×	×	×		×	×	×	×	×	×	×	×	×	×		×	×	×	×	×	×	×	×	×	×	×	×	×	×	×	×	×	×	×	×	×	×

Romanelli
San Corrado de Palazzo Acreide
Ulluzzo
Valle Ottara
Vatte di Zambana

YUGOSLAVIA
Crvena Stijena
Lepenski-vir I+II

GREECE
Asprochaliko
Porto Cheli

U.S.S.R. (UKRAINE)
Murzak Koba
Tash Aïr I
Zamil Koba II

APPENDIX 2

PERCENTAGES OF NINE HERBIVORE SPECIES FROM EUROPEAN MESOLITHIC SITES (x = trace)

	C. elaphus	Sus	C. capreolus	Bos	Alces	E. caballus	E. hydruntinus	Rupicapra	Capra ibex
Ageröd I. H + C.	33	19	13	16	6	–	–	–	–
Ageröd I. D + B.	43	18	6	8	4	–	–	–	–
Ageröd V.	62	5	2	–	8	–	–	–	–
Soldattorpet	54	15	8	15	–	–	–	–	–
Bloksbjerg[1]	42	23	23	x	x	–	–	–	–
Drøsselholm[2]	46	12	36	–	–	–	–	–	–
Dyrholmen	35	36	14	6	2	–	–	–	–
Ertebølle	13	12	33	1	1	–	–	–	–
Hallebygaard	64	10	5	2	–	–	–	–	–
Hesselbjerggaard[2]	30	11	11	30	7	1	–	–	–
Kildegaard	78	15	7	–	–	–	–	–	–
Maglemose	11	34	11	12	23	–	–	–	–
Magleø	50	17	21	1	1	–	–	–	–
Øgaard[3]	45	18	15	10	4	–	–	–	–
Svaerdborg	10	26	18	8	14	–	–	–	–
Tingbjerggaard[2]	47	16	11	1	4	–	–	–	–
Vinde-Helsinge	30	13	4	3	17	1	–	–	–
Star Carr[1]	49	2	12	13	17	–	–	–	–
Thatcham[1]	33	25	14	2	1	1	–	–	–
Abri Pagès[4]	43	1	–	1	–	6	1	–	–
Abri Sous-Sac[4]	17	25	–	3	–	–	–	5	–
Chambre des Fées[2]	–	81	–	6	–	–	–	–	–
Chateauneuf-lez-Martigues[5]	26	6	–	8	–	–	–	–	–
Soubeyras[1,5]	7	1	3	7	–	21	–	–	45
Sous-Balme[1]	26	30	3	–	–	+	–	3	–
Duvensee[2]	90	–	10	–	–	–	–	–	–
Pinnberg[2]	84	–	11	–	–	–	–	–	–
Birseck Hohler Felsen[1,2]	47	22	2	9	–	–	–	–	–
Birseck Schlossfelsen[1]	30	24	16	5	–	–	–	–	–
Birsmatten									
Sauveterrian	26	50	5	1	–	–	–	–	–
Tardenoisian	45	36	2	2	–	x	–	–	–
Col des Roches[2]	72	–	–	–	–	–	–	–	–
Höhle bei Soyhières[2]	3	9	6	–	–	–	–	–	–
Höhle von Oberlarg[1]	16	5	–	78	–	–	–	–	–
Cuina Turcului[4]	6	3	3	6	3	3	–	12	21
Icoana[6]	21	31	10	1	–	–	–	5	–
Aitzbitarte	58	x	3	8	–	4	–	19	4
Marizulo	60	13	21	–	–	–	–	–	6
Capo d'Acqua	50	1	5	41	–	–	–	–	2
Grotta Mangiapane	40	1	–	7	–	–	49	–	–
Grotta delle Mura[1]	6	6	–	63	–	10	8	–	–
Grotta delle Prazziche[7]	35	2	2	33	–	–	9	–	–
Grotta de San Teodoro	77	17	–	4	–	–	1	–	–
Riparo Blanc	2	34	31	–	–	–	–	–	–
San Corrado de Palazzo Acreide[2]	56	11	–	–	–	–	22	–	–
Uluzzo[1,7]	5	x	–	22	–	19	13	–	–
Valle Ottara[2]	76	–	–	11	–	–	–	5	8
Lepenski-vir I + II.	69	5	2	6	–	–	–	–	–
Porto Cheli[1]	75	3	–	12	–	–	–	–	–
Murzak Koba	32	14	14	–	–	–	–	–	–
Tash Aïr I.	17	76	3	–	–	–	–	–	–
Zamil Koba II.	11	82	5	–	–	–	–	–	–

Notes
[1] Approximate figures.
[2] Sample smaller than fifty bones.
[3] Figures based on astragalus and calcaneum only.
[4] Figures based on the minimum number of individuals.
[5] Excluding the bones of rabbit, which constitute 94 percent of the bones from the Mesolithic levels at Chateauneuf-lez-Martigues, and an unspecified proportion at Soubeyras.
[6] Figures for *Bos* and *Rupicapra* approximate.
[7] Assuming *Dama* to have formed an insignificant proportion of the Cervid category.

APPENDIX 3

REFERENCES TO SITES INCLUDED IN APPENDIXES 1 AND 2

Ageröd I and V (Althin, 1954), Rörvik, Rôtekarrslid (Murray, 1970), Sjöholmen (Thomas, 1954), Soldattorpet (Althin, 1954), Aamølle (Winge, 1900), Aasted (Murray, 1970), Bloksbjerg (Westerby, 1927), Braband Sø (Thomsen & Jessen, 1902-7), Drøsselholm (Degerbøl, 1943), Dyrholmen (Degerbøl, 1942), Ertebølle (Winge, 1900; Althin, 1954), Faaraveile (Winge, 1900), Gudumlund (Murray, 1970), Hallebygaard (Degerbøl, 1943), Havnø (Winge, 1900), Hesselbjerggaard (Degerbøl, 1943), Holmegaard (Broholm, 1926-34), Jaegerspris (Murray, 1970), Kildegaard (Degerbøl, 1943), Klintesø (Winge, 1900), Kolind (Degerbøl, 1942), Kongemosen (Jørgensen, 1956), Langø (Broholm, 1928), Maglemose (Sarauw, 1911; Althin, 1954), Magleø (Degerbøl, 1943), Muldbjerg I (Troels-Smith, 1953), Øgaard (Degerbøl, 1943), Sølager, Strandegaard (Murray, 1970), Svaerdborg (Johansen, 1914-19; Althin, 1954), Tingbjerggaard, Vinde-Helsinge (Degerbøl, 1943), Virksund, Visborg (Murray, 1970), Cushendum, Glenarm (Movius, 1942), Mother Grundy's Parlour (Garrod, 1926), Oban (Anderson, 1895), Oronsay (Bishop, 1914), Star Carr (Fraser & King, 1954; Degerbøl, 1961), Thatcham (King, 1962), Westward Ho! (Churchill & Wymer, 1965), Abri Cornille (Escalon de Fonton, 1966), Abri Dumas (Combier, 1967), Abri Edward (Gauthier & Paccard, 1962), Abri Genière (Gaillard, Pissot & Côte, 1927), Abri Pagès (Bouchud, 1956), Abri du Sault (Gaillard, Pissot & Côte, 1928), Abri de Sous (Vilain, 1966), Abri Sous-Sac (Vilain, 1966; Hescheler & Kuhn, 1949), Abri Trosset (Gaillard, Pissot & Côte, 1928), Baume de Ronze (Combier, 1959), Borie del Rey (Coulonges, 1963), Chambre des Fées (Poulain-Josien, 1964), Chateauneuf-lez-Martigues (Ducos, 1958), Chinchon No. 3 (Gagnière, 1966), Chinchon Nos. 1 and 2 (Gagnière, 1959), Colombier (Combier, 1967), Cuzoul (Lacam, Niederlender & Vallois, 1944), Grotte de la Combette (Gagnière, 1966), Grotte des Èscabasses (Méroc, 1967), Grotte des Hoteaux (Vilain, 1966), Grotte de Poeymaü (Laplace-Jauretche, 1953), Grotte de Souhait (Vilain, 1966), Grotte d'Unang (Paccard, 1952), Hoëdic (Péquart & Péquart, 1954), La Montade (Escalon de Fonton, 1956), Le Grand Cave (Vilain, 1966), Le Havre (Cayeux, 1960; Graindor, 1965), Le Martinet (Coulonges, 1928, 1935), Le Roc Allan (Coulonges, 1935), Mas d'Azil (Laplace-Jauretche, 1953), Rochedanne (Millotte, 1967), Soubeyras (Paccard, 1956), Sous-Balme (Vilain, 1966), Téviec (Péquart, Péquart, Boule & Vallois, 1937), Borneck (Herre & Requate, 1958), Bregentwedt-Förstermoor (Murray, 1970), Duvensee (Requate, 1958), Ellerbek (Murray, 1970), Falkenstein-höhle (Peters, 1934), Hopfenbach (Herre & Requate, 1958), Pinnberg (Requate, 1958), Balm bei Günzberg (Heschler & Kuhn, 1949), Birseck Hohler Felsen, Birseck Schlossfelsen (Sarasin, 1918), Birsmatten (Schmid, 1963), Col des Roches (Reverdin, 1930), Ettingen (Sarasin & Stehlin, 1924), Höhle bei Soyhières, Höhle von Oberlarg (Sarasin, 1918), Liesbergmühle (Wyss, 1957), Wachtfelsens bei Grellingen (Heschler & Kuhn, 1949), Kůlna-Höhle 3 (Valoch *et al.*, 1969), Sered' (Barta, 1957), Janislawice (Jażdżewski, 1965), Baile Herculane (Nicolăescu-Plopşor & Păunescu, 1961), Ciumesti (Păunescu, 1964), Cuina Turcului II (Bolomey, 1970), Erbiceni (Păunescu, 1964), Icoana (Bolomey, pers. comm., 1971), Mugem (Obermaier, 1924), Aitzbitarte (Altuna, 1963), Cocina (Pericot García, 1945), Cueva de la Riera (Conde de la Vega del Sella, 1930), Cueva del Rey, La Chora (Madariaga, 1963), Lumentxa (Aranzadi & Barandiarán, 1935), Marizulo (Altuna, 1967), Santimamiñe (Aranzadi & Barandiarán, 1935), Urtiaga (Barandiarán & Sonneville-Bordes, 1964), Valle (Obermaier, 1924), Addaura (Bovio Marconi, 1953), Arene Candide (Cardini, 1947; Taschini, 1964), Arma di Nasino (Anfossi, 1967), Arma dello Stefanin (Anfossi, 1958-61), Capo d'Acqua (Tozzi, 1966), Ciclami (Legnani & Stradi, 1963), Fontana Nuova de Marina de Ragusa (Bernabó Brea, 1950), Levanzo (Graziosi, 1962; Taschini, 1964), Grotta Azzurra (Radmilli, 1963), Grotta della Campane (Palma di Cesnola, 1962), Grotta del Castello (Vaufrey, 1928), Grotta del Cavallo, Grotta Cipoliane (Palma di Cesnola & Borzatti von Löwenstern, 1963), Grotta Corrugi de Pachino (Bernabó Brea, 1950), Grotta dei Fanciulli (Graziosi, 1928), Grotta de Golino (Vaufrey, 1928), Grotta Jolanda (Zei, 1953), Grotta Mangiapane (Vaufrey, 1928), Grotta de Monte Pellegrino (Bovio Marconi, 1954-5), Grotta delle Mura (Borzatti von Löwenstern, 1964), Grotta di Niscemi (Taschini, 1964), Grotta Polesini (Radmilli, 1953), Grotta la Porta (Taschini, 1964), Grotta delle Prazziche (Borzatti von Löwenstern, 1969), Grotta del Prete (Alessio *et al.*, 1970), Grotta de San Teodoro (Vaufrey, 1928), Praia a Mare, Riparo Blanc (Taschini, 1964), Riparo Tagliente (Alessio *et al.*, 1970), Ripoli (Radmilli & Cremonesi, 1963), Romanelli (Graziosi, 1928), San Corrado de Palazzo Acreide (Bernabó Brea, 1950), Uluzzo (Borzatti von Löwenstern, 1965), Valle Ottara (Acanfora, 1962-3), Vatte di Zambana (Alessio *et al.*, 1969), Crvena Stijena (Benac, 1962), Lepenski-vir I + II (Bökönyi, 1969b), Asprochaliko (Higgs & Vita-Finzi, 1966; fauna unpublished), Porto Cheli (Payne, 1969a), Murzak Koba (Tringham, 1969), Tash Aïr I, Zamil Koba II (Dimitrieva, 1960).

ACKNOWLEDGEMENTS

I am grateful to all the many people who have helped me in the collection of data for this paper; in particular Alexandra Bolomey, who permitted me to use her unpublished material from the site of Icoana.

4. THE INTERPRETATION OF PLANT REMAINS: BULGARIA

R. W. DENNELL

This paper is concerned with the interpretation of botanical samples from archaeological sites. Although much outstanding work has been done in this field for over a hundred years, it has suffered from the disadvantage that, with the techniques available, only a limited amount of botanical material could be recovered from excavations. Because of this, our knowledge of prehistoric crop agriculture has until recently been derived from two principal sources: pottery or clay impressions, and such carbonized or dessicated remains as were visible to the archaeologist in the course of excavations. The possibility that the composition of samples of plant remains might vary according to their contexts could not be investigated, nor could the validity of the conclusions drawn from these restricted and possibly unrepresentative types of samples be examined. These problems can now be faced because of the increasingly common use of more sophisticated means of recovering plant remains. The advantage of these techniques is not merely that less material is lost during excavations, but that a wider range of deposits can now be examined. Thus the contents of various samples can now be compared with each other and a more accurate assessment be made of the plant husbandry on a prehistoric site.

In the summer of 1970, the author was permitted to investigate three sites in Bulgaria in conjunction with Bulgarian and Russian archaeologists. With the aid of a froth flotation technique, a large amount of plant material of Karanovo I and Early Bronze Age date was recovered. As a necessary preliminary to the understanding of prehistoric agriculture, one of the main objectives of this work was to investigate the differences between plant samples from different types of deposit. The problems encountered in this work are common to the interpretation of all plant samples recovered from excavations, and thus the results obtained are felt to have wide implications for archaeobotanical work in general.

PRELIMINARY CONSIDERATIONS

When only a limited amount of botanical material could be recovered from excavations, it has frequently been assumed that the composition of plant samples accurately reflected the percentages of the different crops that were grown. Thus changes in the composition of plant samples through time were assumed to indicate a change in the economy. Although in the past there was no means of investigating either of these assumptions, they can now be examined more closely.

Because of the means by which plant remains become incorporated into an archaeological deposit and the specific characteristics of each type of plant, samples of plant remains need not necessarily reflect the percentages of the different crops that were grown. These factors will be considered in turn.

CIRCUMSTANCES OF PRESERVATION

The plant remains on an archaeological site are likely to result from specific human activities. The amount and type of preparation a crop will need before it is ready for storage, either as food or as seed for the following year, will depend upon the type of crop and the technology available. With some crops, several separate processes such as threshing, winnowing, sieving, and parching may be needed before the crop can be stored. Each of these processes is likely to leave some trace that could be recovered on excavations. It is thus possible that several plant samples, each with different relative proportions of plants, could be recovered from the same archaeological horizon and yet be part of the same crop at various stages of processing. This has two important implications for the archaeologist. First, plant samples must be considered within the context of agricultural techniques likely to have been practised. For example, sieved and unsieved emmer crops would contain different proportions of weed seeds and small grain seeds, such as einkorn. Secondly, the changes in composition of plant samples through a stratified sequence need not represent economic change, for unless crop processing activities were carried out at the same point on the site throughout its occupation, excavated samples may contain crops at different stages in their preparation. It is thus important that as wide a range as possible of these crop preparation activities be traced before any conclusions are drawn on possible changes in the plant husbandry.

The seeds of plants that are weeds, and thus unconsciously reaped, can provide useful information about the local conditions of the time. They may also reflect the method of harvesting, since weeds that are shorter than the level at which the crop is cut are less likely to be gathered. Therefore, a change in weed seed representation could be caused by changes in the method of reaping rather than by environmental or economic changes. Weed seeds may also yield information on crop purity, but the means and efficiency of cleaning the crop after harvesting will remove some weeds more than others. For example, the grains of darnel (*Lolium temulentum* L.) are similar in size and shape to those of wheat and were difficult to remove from the crop in Medieval times (Salisbury, 1961).

PRESERVATION ON ARCHAEOLOGICAL SITES

Plant samples can be recovered from many contexts that are likely to represent different activities. These contexts can be classified as follows:

A. Storage jars, silos, and storage pits that contain samples of grain, seeds, or fruits

Plant remains from these contexts are likely to have been stored either as seed for the following year or for consumption, but need not indicate the actual importance of the crop to the economy. They may however be good indicators of the quality of the stored crop.

B. Plant material in or associated with ovens or hearths

These plant remains are likely to have been taken from a storage place (A context) and burnt when being cooked or, in the case of some crops, carbonized when being parched. Such material can give a minimum estimate of the purity of the crop, as it is likely to have been contaminated either by other plants added as fuel or by other material already in the deposit.

C. Floor deposits

Plant material in this type of deposit is likely to result from a wide range of human activities. It is sometimes found in distinct concentrations in this context and can often be the 'spill' from stored (A) contexts. In this case, one would expect the composition of the 'spill' to be similar to that in the stored sample from which it came. On the other hand, plant material on floors can be scattered, and if the composition of such samples differs from that in either a storage place or an oven, it could have been deposited during some other stage in the preparation process.

D. Middens or rubbish pits

The plant material from this context is probably no more than refuse. It may thus represent the least valued parts of the diet, and is unlikely to indicate the relative importance of the crops which were grown. It is important, however, in that it indicates the part of the plant food which was not eaten and which was intentionally thrown away. The part of the crop which is thrown away is likely to differ according to the stage in preparation at which it was discarded. Wheat in such a context could, for example, have been lost during winnowing, or have been thrown away before or after sifting or parching. Possible ways of determining this will be discussed below.

E. Impressions in pottery, burnt clay, or tauf

Plant material incorporated in these substances is unlikely to result from food production. Their presence could be wholly incidental or the result of tempering.

This is certainly true in the case of ovens and other large clay fictiles. On the other hand consistent results have been obtained by Helbaek from the identification of grain impressions on sherds. If the sample is assumed to be adequate some indication may be obtained both as to change in time and variation in space. Under conditions in which potting can be assumed to have been a domestic craft and in which pots were shaped by the same hand that ground the daily ration of grain, it is not unreasonable to presume that impressions on pottery may give a broad indication of what cereals were cultivated and eaten. It is perhaps significant that cereal impressions are rare or even non-existent where pottery was manufactured in quantity as a specialized craft.

F. Fill deposits

This term, beloved by excavators, is used here to describe a wide range of deposits from the debris between features to the contents of ditches, and includes plant material which was derived from elsewhere and of which the original context is unknown.

The above classification is applicable to most types of occupation sites from which plant remains have been recovered. However, different types of context may occur in peat and cave deposits, and faecal remains have also yielded some plant material. Different types of plant remains could be expected from each of these contexts.

Deposition of plant remains in the various contexts will take place at different rates. Thus the grain in a storage jar will represent the activities of a single year, the floor under it perhaps five or fifty years, and the destruction above it perhaps only half an hour. Clearly these factors will affect the relative percentages of plant remains from different deposits. Within any of these deposits, the distribution of plant remains is not random. At Ali Kosh in the Mohammed Jaffar levels, for example, it was noted that in a large ash deposit 'some samples of ash were almost entirely *Prosopis*, others included cereals and tinier legumes' (Hole, Flannery & Neely, 1969).

It is also possible that a plant sample from some of these contexts could result from more than one kind of activity. A rubbish pit, for example, could contain material discarded after winnowing and sieving grain, as well as grain which was thrown away after it had been parched or stored. If parching were used as a means of facilitating threshing, a grain sample from an oven might represent either this activity or grain that was being cooked. Similarly, different types of deposit could yield plant samples of a similar kind. A sample of emmer, for example, which was being parched before storage would be similar to a sample of emmer which had been parched and stored. It would thus seem desirable to consider each plant sample in relation to the others so that the differences between these samples can be more accurately interpreted.

DIFFERENTIAL PRESERVATION

Although all plant remains are preserved accidentally, some plants are more likely to be preserved than others. Because einkorn, emmer, and spelt require parching to free the kernels from their spikelets (Helbaek, 1952a), they are more likely than bread wheat to be accidentally burnt. For similar reasons, naked barley is less likely to be preserved by carbonization than hulled forms of barley. Large-seeded legumes are unlikely to be carbonized in large amounts as they do not require parching, nor are they likely to be preserved as pottery impressions because of their large size. On the other hand, legumes, and especially the small-seeded types such as vetches, are often found as weeds in cereal crops and could be accidentally preserved if part of the cereal crop was carbonized.

Nut and fruit remains can be preserved through a number of circumstances. Occasionally one finds large quantities of carbonized fruits such as the cache of carbonized apples at Bornholm (Helbaek, 1952b) which were probably carbonized when being dried for storage. Usually, however, only the seeds of fruits or the shells of nuts are preserved. Because many fruit seeds are not destroyed in digestion, they are likely to be preserved in coprolites under suitable conditions of preservation. In such conditions they may be present in large numbers if the individual fruit contains several seeds. On the other hand, carbonized fruit seeds could have been burnt as refuse. Because of this wide variation in preservation, the value of fruit and nuts in the total plant diet is difficult to estimate.

EXAMINATION OF PLANT MATERIAL

Plant remains on archaeological sites have usually been examined from a phylogenetic rather than an economic viewpoint. As a result, the history of the main crop plants is now relatively clear for the Postglacial period. However, less attention has been given to studying the importance of these crops to the economy on a given site.

The statistical treatment of plant remains is also relatively undeveloped. Measurements are usually confined to a statement of the minimum, maximum, and average size of the seed or spikelet part. As this information is often insufficient to allow any statistical tests to be made, its use is of limited value. It is therefore at present impossible to estimate the significance of any size difference between one sample and another.

However, threshing, winnowing, sifting, and other harvesting techniques will tend to remove some grains and seeds from a cereal crop and thus produce a biased sample. Measurements could therefore be misleading unless the circumstances in which the sample occurs are taken into account. If samples of grain from a single archaeological horizon differ according to the contexts in which they are found, it could indicate that the differences have been caused by different activities.

FIELD RESULTS

Soundings 2 m square were excavated at the three sites specifically for the purpose of recovering plant remains; samples were also taken of selected deposits from other trenches. The results obtained from each of the sites are discussed separately.

CHEVDAR

The site of Chevdar lies on the right bank of the River Topolnitsa, 3 km east of the present village and 100 km east of Sofia. Across the river to the south, the slopes of the Sredna Gora rise steeply to a height of 1500 m and are covered in dense forest of oak, beech, and modern pine plantations. The site itself is directly opposite a side valley which gives easy access to the higher mountain slopes. These support alpine pasture now used for summer grazing by sheep and goat which descend to the valleys in the winter. A rough semi-circle of arable land extends from the site, and beyond this are low limestone hills which are today used for rough grazing. The area most suitable for arable cultivation within one hour's walking distance of the site covers about two square kilometres. Although surrounded by hills, the site lies in sunlight throughout the summer from dawn to dusk. This factor could have been of some importance in determining the location of the site; it would have been especially beneficial for the ripening of crops in the summer and for the melting of snow in the spring.

The tell, some 2.5 m in height, has four levels. The first

three contain Karanovo I material and the fourth, Karanovo II. Only the lowest of these levels was investigated in 1970. According to the excavator, Professor G. I. Georgiev, the first settlement was destroyed by fire and thus affords a fortunate 'snap-shot' of one of the earliest villages in Bulgaria.

The preliminary results of 1970 are shown in Table 1. The samples were taken from three different contexts, burnt clay, ovens, and floors. The burnt clay came from ovens and also from daub incorporated in the walls of the houses which were burnt when the settlement was destroyed. The plant remains in the ovens probably represent grain that was either carbonized when it was being parched before storage, or when it was being cooked after it had been stored. The plant remains in the floor deposits were not found in any obvious concentrations and are clearly different from the oven samples. Although the material in the floor deposits may represent 'spill' from grain carbonized in the ovens or from other sources, other possibilities should be considered before arriving at a conclusion. It is possible that the two types of sample are the products of different activities.

The samples from the floor deposits contain a higher percentage of weed seeds than those from the ovens (Table 1). It is therefore probable that weed seeds had been removed from the crop before it was carbonized in the ovens. The grain may have been partly cleaned by winnowing, but another common way of removing weed seeds from grain is to sift the crop through a sieve. This process also tends to remove the smaller grains of cereals from the crop. As the grains of einkorn are thinner and smaller than those of emmer, a higher proportion of einkorn grains would be expected to fall through a sieve. As an experiment, modern samples of emmer and barley, obtained in Bulgaria and containing both einkorn and weed seeds, were sieved through a mesh of 3.35 mm. The results are given in Table 2, and expressed as a scatter diagram in Figure 1. It is evident that most of the einkorn grains (and weed seeds) passed through the mesh. As the grains not retained by the mesh fall through it end-ways, the approximate size of the mesh can be calculated from Figure 1. The breadth and thickness of the grains of emmer are almost the same; thus the mesh size can be calculated as the square root of the transverse area of the largest grain to fall through the sieve. The transverse area of the largest grains which fell through the sieve is about 10 mm² giving a mesh size of 3.15 mm². This is less than the observed size of the sieve mesh as some grains retained by the sieve could have fallen through it had they not lain on the mesh length-ways or been obstructed by other grains. Thus when einkorn was sieved by itself, all the grains passed through the mesh, yet a few were retained when it was sieved with emmer.

The size of grains in oven and floor deposits at Chevdar is shown in Table 3 and as a scatter diagram in Figure 2. The grain on the floor is significantly smaller than that in the ovens; furthermore, the floor samples contain relatively more einkorn and weeds and less bread wheat than the samples from the ovens. It would therefore seem reasonable

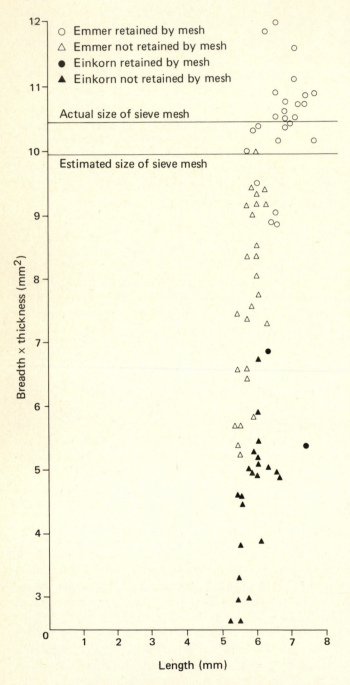

Fig. 1. Effect of sieving a modern sample of emmer with einkorn and weed seeds through a 3.35 mm mesh. Weed seeds: 10 retained by mesh, 28 not retained by mesh.

Table 1.   Chevdar: contents of samples from floors, ovens, and burnt clay

| | Percentage of total sample | | | | | | | | Total no. of seeds in sample |
	Einkorn	Emmer	Bread wheat	Barley	(Cereals)	Legumes	Fruit	Others	
Floors	4.4	30.9	–	13.2	(48.5)	38.5	0.8	12.5	136
(C context)	5.9	29.9	2.6	34.2	(72.5)	12.8	0.9	13.7	117
	1.3	33.9	0.4	40.6	(76.3)	11.6	–	12.1	224
	0.9	18.8	–	25.2	(44.9)	15.6	29.4	10.1	218
Ovens	1.2	94.3	3.1	0.4	(99.0)	0.4	–	0.8	1000
(B context)	2.1	90.7	2.9	2.6	(98.3)	–	–	1.7	1000
	1.4	84.6	1.8	6.6	(94.4)	0.7	1.4	3.5	147
	0.7	7.2	0.8	88.6	(97.3)	0.2	0.6	1.9	1109
Burnt clay (E context)		rare		very common					

Table 2.   Results from sieving modern grain through a mesh 3.35 mm square

| | Length mm | | Breadth mm | | Thickness mm | | Volume mm^3 | Number |
	$\bar{x}$	s^2	$\bar{x}$	s^2	$\bar{x}$	s^2	$\bar{x}$	
(a) Grain retained by mesh								
T. dicoccum	6.82	0.51	3.39	0.19	3.06	0.20	71.01	25
T. dicoccum in sample of barley	6.28	0.42	3.34	0.16	3.05	0.14	66.97	11
H. hexastichum	9.32	0.77	3.59	0.24	2.74	0.23	91.80	25
T. monococcum in sample of T. dicoccum	6.88	–	2.12	–	2.89	–	41.75	2
(b) Grain that passed through mesh								
T. dicoccum	5.88	0.25	2.76	0.30	2.76	0.26	45.50	25
T. dicoccum in sample of barley	5.68	0.40	2.93	0.29	2.59	0.25	43.61	12
H. hexastichum	9.22	0.25	3.02	0.33	2.34	0.27	65.73	25
T. monococcum in sample of T. dicoccum	5.40	0.51	1.60	0.33	2.57	0.23	26.55	23

Table 3.   Chevdar: size of grain from floor and oven deposits

| | Length mm | | Breadth mm | | Thickness mm | | Volume mm^3 | Number |
	$\bar{x}$	s^2	$\bar{x}$	s^2	$\bar{x}$	s^2	$\bar{x}$	
(a) Floors (C context)								
T. dicoccum	5.21	0.49	2.59	0.31	2.32	0.19	31.05	60
T. monococcum	5.02	–	1.90	–	2.42	–	23.09	13
H. hexastichum	4.79	0.50	2.71	0.49	1.91	0.27	24.51	25
(b) Ovens (B context)								
T. dicoccum	5.85	0.53	2.88	0.35	2.79	0.31	47.04	66
T. monococcum	5.65	–	2.18	–	2.75	–	34.40	9
H. hexastichum	6.13	0.26	3.07	0.35	2.30	0.38	43.24	18

that the differences between the floor and oven samples at Chevdar could be interpreted as the result of a sieving process. This would have removed most of the weed seeds, einkorn grains, and the smaller grains of emmer from the crop before it was carbonized in the ovens. If so, the size of the mesh can be calculated as being about 2.5 mm². However, it is well known that carbonization may cause a change in grain size, and any estimate of prehistoric sieve mesh size can only be approximate.

The differences between the plant samples from the ovens and floors are unlikely to have resulted from either inadequate techniques of recovery, or carbonization. The

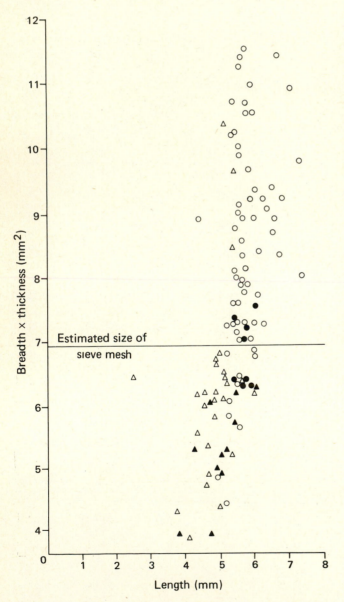

Fig. 2. Chevdar: size of grain in oven and floor samples. (For key see Figure 1.)

samples came from homogeneous and strictly contemporaneous deposits, and great care was taken to isolate each deposit from those around it. As all the plant material was recovered by froth flotation, the difference cannot be due to using different methods of recovery. Furthermore, carbonization could not have differentially altered the composition of the samples from ovens and floors. Only well-preserved specimens were used for the measurements.

The commonest grain at Chevdar is emmer, *T. dicoccum*. There is no evidence at present to suggest that either einkorn or bread wheat was cultivated as a separate crop. However, as bread wheat does not require parching to free the kernels from the husks, it is possible that it is underrepresented in the samples. Yet one would expect that if bread wheat had been cultivated as a separate crop, it would have been preserved in greater numbers when the settlement was destroyed by fire. Barley, of the six-row naked form, appears to be less important than emmer in the oven deposits, although it is as common as emmer in two of the floor samples, and commoner than emmer in the other floor samples as well as the burnt clay. However, as the barley grains in the floor samples are significantly smaller than those in the ovens, much of the barley in the floor deposits could be a result of sieving an emmer crop. The dominance of barley in the samples of burnt clay need not indicate the actual value of barley to the economy, for it is present only as part of the tempering material.

It is difficult to estimate the value of legumes to the economy at Chevdar. As they are less likely to be preserved than cereals, it is possible that they are under-represented in the samples. Legumes would have been a valuable addition to the economy both because of their high protein content and their value to the soil as providers of nitrogen. However, there is no evidence as yet that they were cultivated as a separate crop.

Fruit, especially blackberry, grape, and Cornelian cherry, would appear to have been of minor importance, although when in season could have been a useful additional food.

One can therefore conclude that cereals, particularly emmer, formed the mainstay of the plant husbandry at Chevdar, and that legumes and fruit were less important. The differences between the samples from different types of deposit can be explained as the result of various activities, such as cleaning the grain by sieving it or tempering clay with barley chaff before firing.

KAZANLUK

The site of Kazanluk lies near the centre of the modern town of the same name, 200 km east of Sofia and in the middle of the renowned and extremely fertile Valley of the

Table 4.   Kazanluk: contents of samples from floors and middens

	Einkorn	Emmer	Bread wheat	Barley	(Cereals)	Legumes	Fruit	Others	Total no. of seeds in sample
					Percentage of total sample				
Floors	8.9	55.1	1.2	14.4	(79.4)	10.1	—	9.6	167
(C context)	11.3	60.4	3.3	4.2	(79.2)	7.3	2.3	11.3	576
Middens	3.3	25.0	6.5	14.1	(48.9)	32.6	—	18.5	92
(D context)	—	26.0	1.0	6.3	(33.3)	43.8	2.1	20.8	96
	3.6	40.1	1.0	18.5	(63.2)	25.0	2.4	9.5	168
	3.9	23.5	3.9	5.9	(37.2)	50.9	2.0	9.9	102

Roses. The valley here is 20 km wide between the steep and forested slopes of the Stara Planina to the north and the Sredna Gora to the south. Thus the location of the site is very different from that of Chevdar: in every direction for at least 10 km there extends first-class arable land, with little variation in soil or relief. As the site lies on a series of springs which were tapped by wells during the first settlement, the chief local factor of importance would seem to be the depth of water below the surface. Today there is irrigation near the site and beyond this dry agriculture. However, the effect of the local market makes field observations of less value than at Chevdar. Because the opportunities for intensive cereal agriculture are so much greater than at Chevdar, it is not surprising that the site was occupied for a much longer period, from Karanovo I to the Early Bronze Age. In 1970 work was concentrated upon the lowest level, level 17. The preliminary results are shown in Table 4.

The plant samples at Kazanluk were recovered from two contexts, floors and middens. As at Chevdar, the plant material from the floor deposits was not found in any obvious concentrations. The midden deposits, composed mainly of charcoal, contained relatively few seeds or grains and it is probable that most of this material is no more than refuse. As Table 4 shows, the composition of the samples from the two types of deposits is very different. The floor samples contain more cereals but fewer legumes than the midden samples. These however contain more bread wheat but less einkorn than the samples from the floors.

The plant samples from the floor deposits (Table 4) are similar to those at Chevdar (Table 1). It is therefore reasonable to suppose that they were the result of similar activities. This suggestion is strengthened by the fact that the grain size (Tables 3 and 5) from the floor samples of the two sites does not differ significantly. However, as Table 5 shows, the grain in the midden deposits is significantly larger than that in the floor deposits. One could therefore suggest that it represents grain which was discarded after it had been cleaned of weed seeds. Because the grains of einkorn are smaller than those of emmer, they would tend to be removed from the main crop of emmer in the cleaning process as was demonstrated in the modern experiment described above; therefore, less einkorn would be preserved in the cleaned grain of the midden deposits. On the other hand, grains of bread wheat are plumper than those of einkorn or emmer and so are more likely to be retained by

Table 5.   Kazanluk: size of grains from floor and midden deposits

	Length mm		Breadth mm		Thickness mm		Volume mm^3	Number
	$\bar{x}$	s^2	$\bar{x}$	s^2	$\bar{x}$	s^2	$\bar{x}$	
(a) Floors (C context)								
T. dicoccum	4.99	0.50	2.40	0.06	2.41	0.38	28.87	65
T. monococcum	4.87	0.36	1.61	0.48	2.15	0.68	16.86	64
H. hexastichum	5.27	—	2.87	—	2.13	—	31.71	10
(b) Middens (D context)								
T. dicoccum	6.01	0.56	3.08	0.40	2.77	0.33	45.07	34
T. monococcum	5.61	—	2.09	—	2.75	—	32.23	2
H. hexastichum	6.08	0.54	3.28	0.32	2.29	0.29	45.66	20

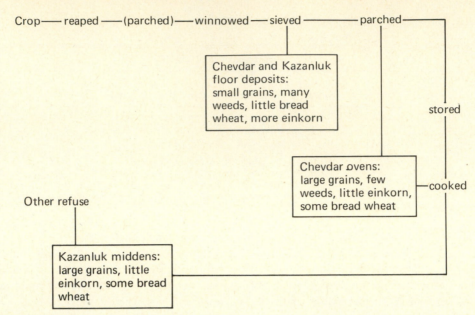

Fig. 3. Cereal preparation activities represented in the plant samples at Chevdar and Kazanluk.

a sieve mesh. This would account for the higher frequency of bread wheat and the lower amount of einkorn in the midden deposits than in the samples from the floors. As Tables 3 and 5 show, the size of grain in the midden deposits at Kazanluk is not significantly different from that in the oven deposits at Chevdar. This also suggests that the grain in the middens was discarded at some stage after the crop had been cleaned. The activities which appear to be represented at Chevdar and Kazanluk are shown in diagrammatic form in Figure 3. If one uses the same method as was employed on the modern grain and on that from Chevdar, the size of mesh used at Kazanluk to produce the observed samples would have been about 2.7 mm² (Fig. 4).

In addition to the grain, the midden deposits yielded remains of many other species, which may or may not have derived from the same sources as the grain. This heterogeneity, characteristic of midden deposits, makes economic interpretations of the remains difficult and hazardous. The above discussion of the Kazanluk midden deposits is offered simply as one possible interpretation of the data.

The commonest crop at Kazanluk is emmer. There is no evidence to suggest that either einkorn or bread wheat was grown as a separate crop. Barley, of the six-row naked form, appears to be less important than at Chevdar and there is no evidence that it was cultivated as a separate crop. On the other hand, it is possible that it is under-represented, as wheat appears to be the chief crop that was being processed. Legumes are common, especially in the midden deposits, but from the evidence available seem to have been less important than cereal cultivation. Fruit appears to have been of minor importance only.

EZERO

The site of Ezero (Dipsiska Mogila) is already well known as one of the most important Eneolithic and Early Bronze Age sites in southern Europe (Georgiev & Merpert, 1966). It lies 3 km south-east of Nova Zagora beside a small lake in lush water meadows which have recently been drained. Apart from this small area of pasture, the surrounding and extremely fertile soil in the area is today wholly under cultivation. In 1970, a sounding 2 m x 2 m and 4 m deep was excavated, in which 140 deposits were isolated. The preliminary results are shown in Table 6. The deposits in the sounding fall into two clearly defined groups: those of the Eneolithic and levels XI and XII of the Early Bronze Age, which contained few structural features, and those above, in the upper parts of the Early Bronze Age levels, which were composed almost entirely of the debris of floors, ovens, and hearths.

In the Eneolithic deposits, plant remains were rare but consistent between samples. Therefore, the remains from twenty-six similar deposits have been combined in the calculations. As no structures were encountered, it is likely that the sounding at this depth lay outside the main area of occupation. Since the circumstances under which the plant remains were burnt are unknown, little can be said about the relative importance of the crops at this time.

The lower levels, levels XI and XII, of the Early Bronze Age consisted of deposits that were very similar to those of the Eneolithic. Few plant remains were found, the sample from level XII being especially small and unsuitable for statistical treatment, but, broadly speaking, the relative frequencies of plants were similar to those of the Eneolithic. This is in sharp contrast to the plant remains in level X that came from an oven in and around which was found a mass of six-row naked barley. If the oven sample is compared with the remains from the earlier levels, it could be interpreted as indicative of a change in the subsistence pattern from a wheat to a barley based economy. However, it would seem as likely to reflect the change in the deposits from which the samples were taken, as a change in the economy.

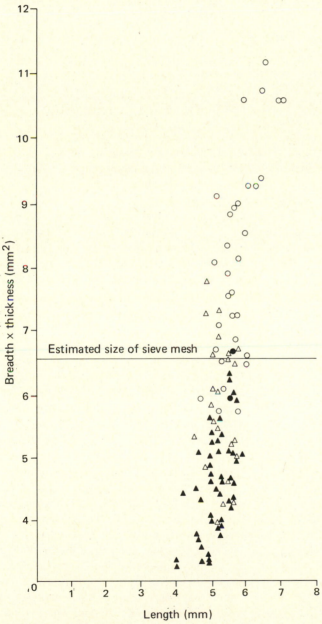

Fig. 4. Kazanluk: size of grain in floor and midden samples. (For key see Figure 1.)

In level IX, a poorly preserved oven was found associated with a floor and a well-defined series of ash deposits, each of which could be isolated. The lowest of these, directly over the floor, consisted entirely of emmer, with only traces of einkorn and bread wheat, and probably represents part of a crop that was being prepared for storage or being cooked. The sample of plant remains from the second ash deposit was more heterogeneous, but the sample from the ash layer above it consisted largely of legumes. The other plants in this sample could be a result of contamination when the deposit was formed, or could be indicative of the quality of the crop itself. The sample above this deposit was smaller and more heterogeneous than the one below it.

The results from Ezero can be compared with those from the two Neolithic sites already discussed. Emmer and six-row naked barley appear to have been the chief cereals at both Chevdar and Kazanluk, and of the two, emmer was probably the more important. However, at Ezero it cannot be concluded whether barley or wheat was the more important crop in the Early Bronze Age, until a wider range of deposits is investigated. At present, neither einkorn nor bread wheat appears to have been important. The greatest difference between the Karanovo I samples from Chevdar and those from the Early Bronze Age at Ezero is seen in the large sample of legumes in level IX at Ezero, although it is possible that these were also cultivated as a separate crop at Chevdar.

DISCUSSION

The results obtained from the field work in 1970 indicate that the composition of plant samples varies considerably between different archaeological contexts. Conclusions on the plant husbandry of a prehistoric site could therefore be misleading unless this factor is considered. To show that this is of general application to other archaeological sites, the implications of these results will be discussed with reference to two important early farming sites, Beidha and Ali Kosh. These have been chosen for a number of reasons: first, they are both the earliest village farming sites yet excavated in their respective areas that have evidence of plant husbandry; secondly, Ali Kosh, like Ezero, has a long sequence of occupation through which the types of deposit are likely to change; and thirdly, the types of deposit found on these sites are broadly similar to those encountered on the three tells just discussed.

At Beidha, it was observed that 'practically all information is derived from imprints in clay from walls and roof of one particular house destroyed in a violent fire during the early existence of the village'. From this, it was concluded that 'the most important cereal grown at Beidha was

Table 6.   Ezero: contents of samples from Eneolithic and Early Bronze Age deposits
(Sample of less than 100 shown in square brackets)

	Einkorn	Emmer	Bread wheat	Barley	(Cereals)	Legumes	Fruit	Others	Total no. of seeds in sample
Eneolithic									
F deposits (26)	10.3	26.5	0.4	13.4	(50.6)	16.9	–	32.5	256
Early Bronze Age									
F deposits									
level XII	[27.0]	[36.2]	–	[5.6]	[(68.8)]	[13.3]	–	[17.9]	[39]
level XI	3.9	45.8	4.9	29.6	(84.2)	12.4	–	3.4	205
B deposits									
level X	–	–	–	100.0	(100.0)	–	–	–	2000
level IX	0.5	98.7	0.2	0.4	(99.8)	0.2	–	–	755
	20.8	31.1	3.5	22.8	(78.2)	19.4	0.6	1.8	151
	5.3	9.3	0.8	2.8	(18.2)	77.5	–	4.3	251
	13.0	31.5	2.5	15.0	(62.0)	13.0	–	18.0	200

the hulled, two-row barley' (Helbaek, 1966). A strikingly similar conclusion would have appeared tempting at Chevdar had the burnt clay alone been examined (Table 1). The evidence from Chevdar suggests that such a conclusion drawn on the basis of one context only could be misleading, especially if the plant remains in it are not a result of some aspect of food production.

At Ali Kosh, a vast quantity of carbonized plant material was recovered by flotation (Hole *et al.*, 1969), and so the site has contributed much evidence crucial to our understanding of the development of plant husbandry in the Near East. From the earliest horizon, the Bus Mordeh phase, 'the plant material was spillings from meals dropped into the fire or ash fringe. . . . Swept up with ash and dirt, the plant remains were thrown into some place where they were often trodden upon and therefore excessively fragmented'. Thus the plant remains were derived from at least two sources, parts of meals and refuse; in the classification of contexts used on the Bulgarian samples, they would be regarded as a midden sample. In this deposit, 'the ash contained literally thousands of carbonised seeds. The vast majority were the systematically collected seeds of local wild legumes like *Astragalus* and *Trigonella*, but also included were coarsely-ground groats of grain and a few whole kernels of emmer wheat and two-row hulled barley' (Hole *et al.*, 1969). From this, it was concluded that 'we see two contemporaneous elements of early agriculture: on the one hand, a heavy dependence upon collection of seeds of wild endemic plants; on the other, cultivation of both wild and domesticated forms of wheat and barley'. At Kazanluk, there were fewer cereal remains in the midden deposits than in the floor samples, while legumes and weed seeds were more common. It was suggested that the plants in these

midden contexts at Kazanluk were derived from several types of activities, and as the material was discarded as refuse the overall contents of the sample could not be taken to represent the actual percentages of the crops that were cultivated.

In the succeeding Ali Kosh phase, there 'was a patch of green clay floor. . . . Included in the floor was a hearth. The ash in this hearth contained many carbonised grains of emmer wheat and two-row hulled barley; some wild legumes were a smaller percentage of the total than they had been in the Bus Mordeh samples'. Thus the sample is this time drawn from a hearth inside a house rather than a midden outside a house. The conclusion drawn is that 'cultivation of winter-grown cereals . . . increased. During the phase, there seems to have been a real tapering-off in the collection of small-seeded wild legumes'. The evidence from Ezero offers a comparison (Table 6) where the difference between a sample drawn from an oven (B context) and a derived (E) context below it is clearly seen. The apparent increase in the importance of cereals, similar to that seen at Ali Kosh, is striking.

In the succeeding Mohammed Jaffar phase, 'a principal change of economy seems to have taken place. Cultivated plants and their attendant weeds fall off, indicating that the plant-producing activity during the period becomes secondary to other occupations, pastoralism and hunting . . . collection of the wild plants of the steppe increased on a huge scale'. The samples from which these conclusions are drawn came from a 'thick ash layer . . . composed of lens after lens of white and black ash. . . . What it suggested most was a dump area just outside a house where hearth contents had been thrown week after week for a considerable length of time' (Hole *et al.*, 1969). This midden deposit is thus quite unlike the hearth deposit that contained the plant remains from the Ali Kosh phase but is similar to that of the Bus Mordeh phase. It is therefore not surprising that 'the carbonised seeds from the ash sample had a somewhat different character from those of the Ali Kosh phase'. In fact, the percentage of cultivated crops in this deposit (3.5 percent) is strikingly similar to that of 3.4 percent in the Bus Mordeh phase, drawn from a similar type of deposit.

These results are analogous to those from Ezero. The deposits from the Eneolithic and levels XI and XII of the Early Bronze Age were similar to each other, but very different from the deposits above in levels IX and X. The two types of deposit yielded different types of plant samples. If one were to consider plant samples drawn from similar types of deposit at Ali Kosh, then there would seem to be little evidence of change in the plant husbandry of the Ali Kosh sequence. A hearth inside a house can be expected to contain a greater proportion of cultivated plants than a midden outside a house. At Kazanluk it is probable that the plant material from the middens represented only the least valued parts of the diet.

The results from Chevdar and Kazanluk show that the size of grain varies according to the archaeological context and the activities by which it becomes incorporated into the soil. Conclusions drawn from the size of grain on, for example, local environmental conditions or crop improvement should therefore take account of this factor. At Ali Kosh, for example, the grains of emmer in the Bus Mordeh phase are described as small compared with those from the subsequent Ali Kosh phase. In this instance, the grains were

recovered from two different contexts that would seem to have been the result of different kinds of activities. If conclusions are therefore to be drawn upon such problems as long-term changes in grain size because of improved agronomic techniques, it seems desirable that only plant remains from similar contexts be compared with each other.

CONCLUSIONS

The results from the field work carried out in Bulgaria in 1970 make it clear that different archaeological contexts contain different and characteristic plant remains. Before conclusions about the crop husbandry practised on a site can be drawn, it is necessary to investigate a variety of contexts within each phase of occupation. Failure to do so could lead to misleading conclusions, particularly when the remains from a deeply stratified site are used as evidence for changes in plant husbandry. In this instance, it is valid only to compare samples in similar contexts from different periods. It is of course preferable if a wide range of deposits are examined from each period. New techniques of recovering plant material now make this feasible. Furthermore, the value of the study of the differences between samples from different contexts and the activities that contributed to their composition has now been demonstrated, and this information can be used in the future to attack more complex problems. Thus, a more detailed and complete picture of the plant husbandry practised by the inhabitants of a prehistoric site is within our reach.

5. THE EXPLOITATION PATTERNS OF A MODERN REINDEER ECONOMY IN WEST GREENLAND

D. A. STURDY

It has long been clear that, before what is believed to be the earliest introduction of domestication, man began to pay especial attention to particular animal species, a process of specialization in obtaining food which is clear from the heavy predominance of one species in many faunas recovered from Palaeolithic sites. With the realization that the domestication of plants and animals is unlikely to be a stage of human economic development which can be observed at a fixed time horizon over a wide area, interest has also focused on those man-animal relationships which cannot be classified as either 'hunting' or 'domestication'. In theory, such intermediate relationships may occur where the optimum relationship between man and the animal he exploits, that is, the relationship which results in the greatest long-term benefit to both species, is not close enough to warrant labelling as 'domestication'. This will particularly be the case where the optimum relationship involves the two species living at some distance from each other for some time, when the original sense of the word domestication is clearly lost. The reindeer is an excellent example both of an animal which was heavily exploited by Palaeolithic man, at some times apparently to the virtual exclusion of all other animals, but which even today is hardly a domestic animal in the sense in which sheep and cows, for example, are domestic in many economies. The exploitation of this species therefore falls into the two gaps in modern concepts of the prehistory of man-animal relationships; the gap between the Palaeolithic hunter and the Neolithic farmer, long entrenched in archaeological thought, and the gap between 'wild' and 'domestic' animals, classes which may exist but which certainly do not describe all animals exploited by man.

This paper considers the present-day exploitation pattern of reindeer in one area, in an attempt to provide some guidelines to research in this field. The intention of the investigations described was to give an example of the methods and principles by which the economic potential of an area, and the natural features occurring in it, may be assessed to deduce the economy practised on the basis of the location of the human habitation sites and, following this, to deduce the relationships which arise in the economy between man and the animals. To this end, a form of site catchment analysis has been pursued, based on the relation between the areas which would be used by the animals, the topographic features which might influence their behaviour, and the sites of the human groups who exploit the animals. The case selected was the reindeer station of Itivnera in west Greenland.

It is a commonplace that the use of ethnographic parallels to interpret archaeological data is at best a hazardous enterprise. This is because ethnographers do not make use of a long time scale. Their data are presented as assessments of the present situation, and there are good reasons why, for the purposes of their discipline, this should be so. But the archaeologist is not necessarily concerned with studies which are paradigms across a developing situation. The principal value of archaeological work may well lie in its opportunities to apply the effects of a long time scale in arriving at an empirical observation of the success or otherwise, in Darwinian terms, of the phenomena which are studied. A study of reindeer economies in Siberia and Norway today is hampered by the developing nature of those economies. Many of the techniques practised in the economy are traditional ones, suited to fairly isolated communities; others are of recent date and are related to a cash economy. It is hard to disentangle the two, which are woven together in the present economic structure; but it is hard also not to suspect that some of the techniques now being practised are out of phase with others and hence that some techniques will be superseded by others already in use, so that the economy is now in a state of flux. Under these conditions, many observations cannot have more than short-term value. The west Greenland reindeer economy is a new one, being about twenty years old; the Norwegian Lapps who run the station have adapted the economy to the exigencies of the situation, and hence the economy may not be the mixture of old and new found in most Old World reindeer economies. It is true that many recent attempts to run reindeer stations in the New World have been apparently successful and have then collapsed (Hadwen & Palmer, 1935; Scheffer, 1951; Leopold & Darling, 1953). But while it is too early to say whether the Greenland station will be long-lived, many of the more obvious lessons of the failure of the Alaskan industry have been applied, particularly in herding techniques and pasture management.

West Greenland was selected for the purposes of this investigation for a number of other reasons, which would enable the data collected to be useful in an elucidation of European Ice Age reindeer economies and perhaps other prehistoric exploitation of deer. No precise ecological parallels to the north European Ice Age tundra-steppe environment exist in the world today. Among other factors, all modern tundra regions suffer from the long dark arctic winter, which has two major effects: first, the temperature differential between summer and winter is probably more exaggerated in the present arctic than in Ice Age tundra regions; and second, the vegetation is affected by the shorter periods when photosynthesis can occur. The abundant heliophyte vegetation of Late Glacial Denmark, discussed by Degerbøl and Krog (1959) is an excellent illustration of this point. It was therefore desirable to select as southerly a region as was compatible with true tundra and a flourishing population of reindeer, to minimize the effect of the dark arctic winter. Further, west Greenland enjoys a peculiar climate, sometimes described as 'temperate maritime arctic', under which is developed a plant community which corresponds better than any other with the plant communities suggested by pollen and macroscopic analyses of Würmian deposits in Europe (Trapnell, 1933; Lang, 1952). In general ecological outline, west Greenland represents a very telescoped version of Ice Age central Europe, when Europe was bounded to the south by Alpine glaciation, as west Greenland is bounded to the east by the great ice-cap; to the west, the Greenland coastal strip is limited by the sea, corresponding to the early stages of the Baltic in Late Glacial Europe when northern Europe was becoming free from ice cover. Many Würmian reindeer sites occur in hilly or mountainous districts, and while literature of reindeer economies in plains country is extensive, there is little material on the effects of broken country on reindeer economies. The west Greenland region is very hilly.

GENERAL TOPOGRAPHY OF THE ITIVNERA DEER RANGES

Some further information is offered here to supplement the map which accompanies this paper. The area lying to the east of the dotted line marked W–W on the map (Fig. 1) is the winter grazing range of the reindeer. The ground is, on the whole, rather lower and flatter than in other parts of the ranges. Sheltered valleys, in the Tungmeradlip tasserssua and the Austmannendal, are useful when the weather is very severe. The vegetation is largely composed of lichen-mats, mostly of the lichen groups (Cladonia spp.) called reindeer-moss, which are of particular importance to the

reindeer in winter when sedge, grass, and brush vegetation is much sparser and at its lowest nutritive value (Lynge, 1921; Egorov, 1965). Between the winter range and Itivnera lies the massif of Aputitoq, inaccessible except in a few places, steep, rocky, and hostile. To the north of the massif, the lower areas towards Kapisigdlit are used in summer by a few hardy sheep, which are stabled in the village in the winter. This region is occasionally visited by the deer in winter. South of the massif lies the Aputitoq Pass, with two small lakes, at a height of about 500 m. This pass is of great importance, and will be discussed later. South of it, the peninsula between Aputitoq and Oriartorfik opens out, where the deer graze in autumn and spring. Although some of the hills on this peninsula rise to 1300 m, the grazing is good, with many lichen-mats, and there are sheltered corries which the reindeer appear to prefer as grazing areas in this region. Within the peninsula, movement is not greatly restricted by landforms, but the western and eastern sides of the peninsula, where the land runs into the fjords, are very steep.

At the western foot of Aputitoq lies the Itivneq, an isthmus between the Itivdleq fjord and a branch of the Godthåbfjord; this isthmus lies below 200 m. West of the isthmus, the ground rises up to Quagssugarssuaq and the summer grazing grounds. This region is mountainous, but there is a belt of gently sloping land abutting the western shore of the Itivdleq; there are also sheltered and relatively flat corries similar to those in the Aputitoq-Oriartorfik peninsula. There is much more shrub and grass vegetation, notably *Salix glauca* the arctic willow, *Betula nana* the dwarf birch, and *Empetrum nigrum* the crowberry. The deer will browse on the willow and occasionally on the birch, but the crowberry was seldom browsed; hence an abundance of crowberry with little other plant cover tends to point to overgrazing on this range. The most heavily browsed shrub seemed to be *Ledum groenlandicum*, Labrador tea. In this, observations on the Greenland summer grazing are in accord with Kelsall's (1960) work on the barren-ground caribou. Some lichen-mats also occur. This region is again part of a peninsula which extends west to Godthåb, but about 30 km down the peninsula from the Itivneq, the terrain becomes extremely hostile, with steep rock faces and cliffs, and much ice in shaded gullies. For this reason the deer do not appear to travel more than 30 km into the peninsula. Only about half of the area of this peninsula used by the reindeer is shown on the map, since more is not relevant to the discussions in this paper.

In 1928 an expedition from Oxford went to the Godthåbfjord and took as its main working area a region about 50 km from the Itivnera ranges. Since the two areas are naturally very similar, Trapnell's account of the general

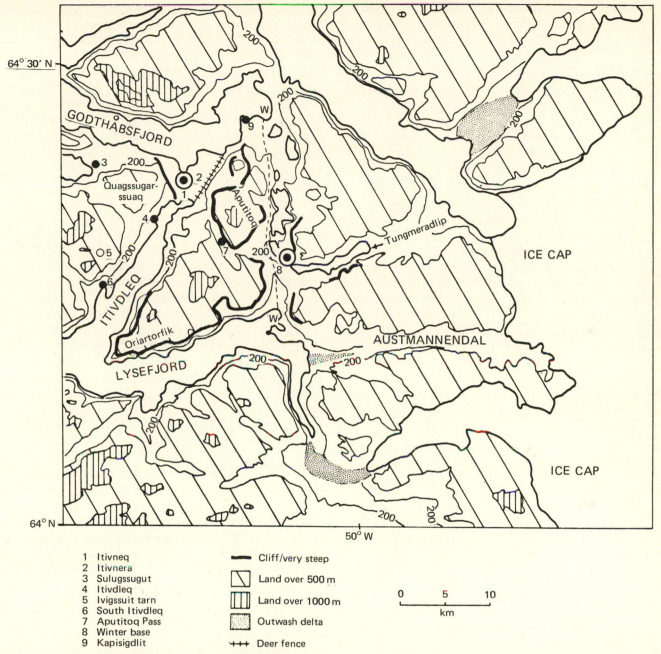

1 Itivneq
2 Itivnera
3 Sulugssugut
4 Itivdleq
5 Ivigssuit tarn
6 South Itivdleq
7 Aputitoq Pass
8 Winter base
9 Kapisigdlit

Cliff/very steep
Land over 500 m
Land over 1000 m
Outwash delta
Deer fence

0   5   10
km

Fig. 1.   Map of Itivnera reindeer station and grazing areas.

ecology (1933) serves as a very good introduction to the Itivnera deer ranges. Members of this expedition also visited a more mountainous district closer to the ice-cap; their observations are of importance, for the Itivnera ranges lie rather closer to the ice-cap than the Oxford expedition's main working area. Trapnell observed that the proximity of the ice-cap leads to a greater predominance of lichen-mat vegetation, and this, in part, explains why the Itivnera winter range is closer to the ice-cap than the other ranges.

NATURAL BARRIERS

Natural barriers will be of importance to the discussions which follow, and therefore what does and does not constitute a natural barrier to reindeer should be stated. Reindeer can swim very well, for each hair is a sealed hollow tube, which gives the animals great buoyancy in the water. They will, however, not swim any distance unless they have to, and they are particularly unwilling to swim more than a minor river when they have calves with them. Thus, the reindeer could almost certainly swim the Itivdleq at its narrowest point, more or less opposite the Itivdleq site, without much difficulty; but they would not do so without considerable incentive. Most of the fjords surrounding the Itivnera ranges are too wide to be swum. From Newhouse's account (1954) of Norwegian reindeer swimming out to islands off the coast of Norway, it appears that 3 km is about the maximum distance that a reindeer herd can cross, and this distance is likely to prove too much for the endurance of yearling animals. Landforms which will impede reindeer movements are cliffs and steep screes. Reindeer are very sure-footed and will climb, apparently effortlessly, slopes which men have difficulty negotiating, but they are not rock-climbers and have not the agility of the ibex. Some slopes in the Greenland ranges are covered with scree with many large boulders, and a mat of mossy vegetation grows over this scree. This mat obscures the interstices between the boulders. The deer will avoid these slopes, since if an animal's hoof penetrates the mat the deer stands a very good chance of a broken leg. Such slopes on the Itivnera ranges often appeared easily traversed from a distance, but if there were no deer tracks across a slope, the attempt to cross it could lead to some difficult moments. These slopes characteristically occur below bluffs or cliffs on the Itivnera ranges, and with the cliffs constitute a formidable barrier to movement in some places.

THE SITES AND THEIR LOCATIONS

The basic terms used in this section are employed with the same meaning as those defined in Vita-Finzi & Higgs (1970) and elsewhere in this volume. The term 'extended territory', however, arose as a result of this work in Greenland; it is therefore worth defining the distinction between the 'site exploitation' and 'extended' territories. The former is the area which is habitually used by the inhabitants of the site for the extraction of their subsistence; the latter is the area that supports resources used by the inhabitants, but that lies outside the exploitation territory and is seldom if ever visited by man. As such the resources in a site extended territory must be mobile. The limits of a site extended territory may be defined naturally, by rivers, cliffs, etc., or defined socially.

Itivnera

Itivnera is the central site for the reindeer station. Among the buildings which have been erected by the Royal Greenland Trading Company are quarters for the herdsmen when they are at the base, and a slaughterhouse and other facilities for butchering the deer. Near the base there are several

miles of fencing, designed to make the control of the animals and the selection of particular animals for slaughter easier during the killing season. This is the only time at which these fences are used. The location of the site, as the central base, is of particular importance. It lies on a neck of land, the Itivneq, which divides two fjords which join beyond the peninsula of the summer grazing grounds to the west. On the west this isthmus is bounded by a line of low cliffs, offering only one or two practical ways over but with fairly easy bypasses at each end of the cliffs where they meet the fjords. To the east the cliffs and screes of the western side of Aputitoq form a good natural boundary, but it is less well-defined than the cliffs to the west. A deer-fence has therefore been constructed running down the eastern edge of the isthmus from fjord to fjord; but this merely straightens out a natural line. In this way the Itivneq forms a small area with only very limited access and exit points, in size about 5 km by rather less than 3 km. Within such an area a large number of reindeer can be pastured only for very short periods, such as the killing season, when it is desirable to have the animals concentrated and near at hand. To this end, the pasture in the area is closely controlled, and some areas are left untouched each year to provide a reserve of pasture. The site also lies between the summer lands and the spring-autumn grounds in the Aputitoq-Oriartorfik peninsula. The winter lands are accessible by a four hour march over the Aputitoq Pass. This pass is the only exit to the east which leads to any grazing of importance, as is obvious from the map.

Itivnera therefore serves multiple functions. It is used for the autumn killing, for which purpose its location is ideal. The natural features around the site determine this killing area by providing a region which lies between summer and autumn grazing grounds, is of limited area, with very few access or exit points, and is therefore a natural corral, but can support all the reindeer for a short period. The site is the base to which supplies are sent and from which the carcases of the deer are shipped out, for its harbour is adequate. It is the home base occupied by the Lapps in summer, at which time the site has as its extended territory the summer grazing grounds; this is also true to a lesser extent of the spring-autumn lands, as will be shown. Its central location, in this particular case, allows it to act as the co-ordinating centre for all seasonal activities, although in most other reindeer economies the distances between summer and winter grazing ranges is much too great to allow one site to be active in both seasons. Because the men at the Itivnera station do not live exclusively on reindeer, but to a large extent on imported foodstuffs, Itivnera does not have an exploitation territory. Clearly, in the Ice Age situation it would have to have had one; this difference will be discussed in detail later.

Aputitoq Pass

The Lapps have built a hut in the middle of Aputitoq Pass. It lies two hours' march from Itivnera and two from the winter base. From the hut access into the Aputitoq-Oriartorfik peninsula is easy. The site, which lies at 500 m, serves two functions. First, it is a night stop or bad weather refuge for herdsmen travelling between the winter base and Itivnera. Second, the hut is used as a night stop for herdsmen when they are driving deer from the winter to the spring grazing, from the spring to the summer grazing, and so on. As such it can be classed among the archaeological site categories defined in Vita-Finzi & Higgs (1970) as both a migration or transit site and a temporary camp. The distinction between these two categories lies in that, while a transit camp is used solely as a place to stop during journeys, the temporary camp serves, but only for a very short period, the same function as a home base, and is used for the same reasons. When used as a temporary camp, the Aputitoq Pass site serves the spring-autumn grazing grounds of the Aputitoq-Oriartorfik peninsula.

Winter base

It will be readily apparent from the map that the winter base is a minor version of Itivnera, in that many of the features which make Itivnera an excellent base for the reindeer station are also present at this site. It is located on the most practicable route in and out of the winter grazing grounds; and as Itivnera is located on the edge of the summer lands, so the winter base is on the edge of the winter lands, on a less effective but definite isthmus. The site is well located for driving deer out of the winter lands preparatory to sending them up into the spring range. Driving the winter range is most easily done by concentrating the deer from a wide area into the trough of the Tungmeradlip, which debouches to the west into a steep little valley which runs out near the winter base. Here there is a rather narrow neck of land leading up to the Aputitoq Pass; this neck of land is limited to the south-west by a very steep slope, and to the north-west by the cliffs and screes of Aputitoq, so that it is roughly triangular in shape, with the base of the triangle running along the base of the depression in which the winter base lies. This depression forms the western boundary of the winter lands and provides a good winter access route to supplies at Kapisigdlit. To the south, the depression continues to the silty and marshy flats, most unattractive to the reindeer, at the mouth of the Austmannendal, whose rich grazing, by contrast, and sheltered position is frequently exploited by the deer in winter. Hence this southern part of the depression is also useful as a driving route, since steep slopes make movement directly into the Aputitoq-Oriartorfik peninsula very difficult

except by way of the Aputitoq Pass. Immediately behind the site, and continuing north up the east side of the depression, is a low line of bluffs similar to those which bound the Itivneq on the west. Again, the massif of Aputitoq leaves only a small area between these bluffs and the mountain, around the winter base. Hence there is formed a very useful natural corral for concentrating and counting animals before sending them into the spring grazing and after clearing the same range at the end of autumn. The corral is not so efficient as its counterpart at Itivnera, but it is certainly the second-best natural corral in the whole range; this factor and the location on a neck of land between two ranges with good access north to Kapisigdlit, form the cardinal points of the location. The extended territory of this site is the winter grazing range and also the spring-autumn range.

Itivdleq site

Two hours' march from Itivnera the Lapps have constructed a small hut on the western shore of the Itivdleq, near a small stream. It is worth observing that the water supply is better and more constant elsewhere in the vicinity, while this stream dries up after two dry days in summer. Hence water supply is not a determining factor in the location. The hills that rise above and to the west are separated by a great corrie, south-west of Quagssugarssuaq on the map, capable of supporting a fair number of deer. From this corrie to Itivnera, the best route passes near the site. Access uphill and to the south is easy enough; one and a half hours' walk leads to another important corrie, and two hours' to a very good grazing region round the Ivigssuit tarn. These grazing areas and corries showed every sign of heavy use by the reindeer, and the more palatable foods in the areas nearer Itivnera were rather overgrazed. The site, in short, serves as a temporary camp for the Lapps during round-ups in the summer lands, and lies below and is well situated in relation to several likely collecting areas. When clearing this area of deer, the animals are bunched and then driven down to the fjord edge, and thence along the shore to the Itivneq. This site, lying at the base of the bunching areas, was designed for use during this operation, and is not used at any other time.

South Itivdleq and Sulugssugut sites

At neither of these sites are there any buildings, but they are both returned to regularly, leaving the usual debris. Both serve precisely the same function as the Itivdleq site, and both lie under great corries. Sulugssugut is two hours' walk from Itivnera, and the two Itivdleq sites are also two hours' walk apart.

HERD MOVEMENTS

To understand the importance of the site locations to the reindeer economy, a brief summary of the herd movements and the techniques by which the deer are moved is useful. The winter grounds are not naturally enclosed, and the deer could go feral by moving into the country to the south. In the winter, therefore, the men take shifts of staying with the deer, sleeping in the snow in reindeer-skin sleeping bags after the fashion common in Norway. Contact with the herds is seldom lost for long, and considerable control of the use of the grazing can be exercised if required. The Lapps in Greenland prefer to rely on the natural expertise of the deer in finding their own food. In April the winter lands are swept for deer, and any outlying animals not in the main closely-knit herds, which usually number from fifty to 200 animals, are collected. The entire population is concentrated in batches of from 200 to 500 near the winter base, and then are sent up the slopes of the Aputitoq Pass and thence into the spring grazing in the Aputitoq-Oriartorfik peninsula. When all the reindeer have been sent into the spring lands, some men stay at the winter base to prevent any animals returning to the winter lands, should they show any inclination to do so, which is rare. The other men go to Itivnera. Hence at this season the spring range is the extended territory of both Itivnera and the winter base. The deer are left alone in the spring range, for it is clear from the map that, with men at Itivnera and the winter base, no deer can leave the Aputitoq-Oriartorfik peninsula without passing within a very few kilometres of the men.

The spring grazing is swept in June, and the animals are then sent into the summer lands across the Itivneq. At this time the Aputitoq Pass site is used for the occasional night. The deer have a natural instinct towards seasonal migration inherited from their Norwegian ancestors, and are not hard to move. When all the reindeer are in the summer lands, the men all return to Itivnera, where the summer is spent in preparing and mending the fences for the autumn slaughter, and in other repairs and the manufacture of equipment. Again the deer are left alone to graze as they will, for Itivnera blocks the exit from the summer lands. The summer is much the easiest time of the year for the men. In late September, usually, the deer are driven in from the summer lands and in this operation the temporary sites in the region are used. The animals are concentrated in the Itivneq, and separated into the animals for slaughter and otherwise by means of the fencing, in small groups at a time. Emphasis in slaughtering is placed generally on the young males, but the sickly or weak of any age or sex will be killed, together with some of the older animals. When there has been a particularly good calving crop, because of fine weather at the right time, more does are killed, and

when the calving crop is poor, or bad weather at some season has reduced numbers, the emphasis on killing barren does, older animals and the young males is strong. Hence the actual killing proportions in the autumn slaughter are highly dependent on yearly variations in climatic conditions and the state of the range, and not on any fixed pattern; and these variations are wide in Greenland. Therefore, were the Itivnera station to be excavated in a few thousand years, the only major trend to emerge from the bones about killing proportions might be a tendency to select young males. The lasso is used for the singling out of animals for slaughter. When the slaughtering is over, the herd movements described are reversed.

In the earlier years of the Itivnera station, the carrying capacity of the range was rather over-estimated. Vibe (1967) who mentions the station in his work on the Greenland fauna, suggested a figure of 3500 deer. However, the pressure which is apparent on the summer grazing near Itivnera, and twenty years' experience, suggests that the optimum figure for the range is about 1800. The area of the winter range is approximately 700 km^2, and hence for the five months that the deer use the winter range about forty hectares per animal are required, corresponding to an annual figure of ninety hectares per deer per year for this sort of grazing. The winter range, however, contains a large number of small lakes, and this figure is therefore too generous for grazing less plentifully endowed with water, where a figure of seventy-five to eighty hectares for lichen-mat range may be more accurate. The spring-autumn grounds are used for three months of the year in total, and have an approximate area of 155 km^2. This corresponds to thirty-six hectares per deer per year; but it should be observed that higher deer densities are possible on range used only for short periods at a time, such as this range, since one of the factors controlling deer densities is the build-up of parasitic infestation, which will be smaller the less prolonged the use of the range. No figures of any accuracy could be obtained for the summer lands, for the author was unable to define exactly the extent of territory used by the reindeer. However, it seems reasonable to suppose that approximately forty hectares per deer per year for grazing other than lichen-rich winter grazing is an acceptable figure, and for the winter grazing about double this amount, or eighty hectares. These figures are in good accord with range carrying capacities and deer densities quoted by Steen (1968) for Norway, Banfield (1954) for the barren grounds of Canada, and Andreev & Savkina (1960) for Siberia.

Some interest attaches to the actual methods of moving the reindeer from one grazing area to another, since this is connected with the problem of the man-animal relationship. The Lapps emphasized that in Greenland the deer are driven, and not herded. What was implied was that herding involves travelling with the animals or in close contact with them; the herdsman may lead his animals or walk behind them, but close contact is the criterion. The Greenland reindeer are moved by allowing the deer to see or smell a man in a given position, so that they will move away from the scent or sight in a desired direction. The author was able to make some detailed observations on rounding-up reindeer and moving them from one area to another by this means. Such a method of moving the animals appears to be a corollary of the principle of leaving the deer alone as much as is compatible with retaining control, which is the keystone of the man-animal relationship. This is true of some other economies, such as sheep on some hill farms of England, but is especially true of the Greenland economy; for since natural features can be used to control the animals and keep them within the extended territories of the bases for more than half the year, the animals are even more 'wild' than most Scandinavian or Siberian herded reindeer.

CONCLUSIONS AND IMPLICATIONS FOR ARCHAEOLOGY

It is clear from the analysis of the site locations and grazing areas presented that, in this case, the relief and nature of the ground play a decisive role in establishing whether the men stay with the reindeer or not. In naturally defined grazing areas, with limited access and exit points, it is adequate to wait at these points and thus block the 'necks' of the grazing areas. The deer appear to benefit from this arrangement, for the station chief emphasized that the more the deer are left alone, the fatter they will be. In winter, when all the exits from the range cannot be blocked by the available labour, closer contact with the animals must be maintained. The sites are located for their corralling features, or for their position on nodes of important communication or migration routes; some are used only as stops during round-ups associated with a change of grazing range. The fact that the sites are all distributed so that the nearest site is two hours' walk away is of great interest in view of the importance of this range suggested by Vita-Finzi & Higgs (1970). Although none of the sites has a true exploitation territory, it is clear that the two hours' walk remains an important economic distance. In the Itivnera ranges forays from the bases are usually over a distance greater than 10 km or two hours' walk, and hence rest-places are established at this range so that the work can be carried out conveniently. In the winter grounds, of course, where the men move much more inside the grazing range, small clusters of debris are more frequent and distributed more widely; such small sites correspond, in Stone Age terms, to finds of a few flints.

Emphasis has been laid on the position of the two home bases on the edge of the extended territories to which they refer and which they help to define by blocking obvious exit points, and on the fact that no site in the Itivnera range can be considered to have a true site exploitation territory. The reason for this latter fact lies in the nature of the food eaten. Much of the food consumed on the station consists of tinned and preserved foods brought to Itivnera by boat or from the settlement at Kapisigdlit. Hence the Lapps are not concerned with everyday subsistence activities on the whole, although they dry a good deal of reindeer meat at the autumn killing period and store it at Itivnera. Extensive use of this practice may be related to the fact already mentioned, and peculiar among reindeer economies, that the same base can be used in both summer and winter. In an archaeological context, where the existence of agriculture in the same area cannot be demonstrated, it is clear that the two home bases at least would have been used more directly for everyday subsistence extracted from the area lying around them, and hence would have had site exploitation territories. However, the Itivnera station, with its outside sources of food, thereby offers a very clear demonstration of the principle of the extended territory uncluttered by other considerations. Archaeologically, a naturally delimited extended territory can be recognized as an extension of the region exploited by the human group without a concomitant increase of input into the economy, just as Itivnera is partly located to define the extended territory which is very seldom visited, but which supports the equivalent of the major resource, in this case the reindeer. It seems likely that the naturally delimited extended territory may be closely connected with the exploitation of animals neither by 'domestication' as it is understood by the keeping of sheep, for example, nor by hunting, that is, killing animals after approaching by stealth. In such intermediate man-animal relationships, where control of the animals is desirable, but minimal contact with them except for killing is also desirable, the use of natural features to assist in herd control is immediately expedient; and allied to this is the desirability of using sites to block off exits from naturally defined grazing ranges, and thus having sites located peripherally to the areas which support the animals.

In this example the extended territories are naturally delimited, but in more heavily populated regions, or areas where such natural barriers do not occur, natural boundaries are likely to be replaced by territorial boundaries. The large herbivores are well-known to be highly territorial animals, as many studies have shown (e.g. Darling, 1956; Spinage, 1969). Hence when the extended territory is not naturally delimited, either the human group must adapt to the territories of the animals exploited or change the territories of the animals; that is, develop a closer relationship with the animals. Which is done will depend on the compatibility of the behaviour of man and the particular animal he is exploiting. Basic subsistence extraction from any home base must normally take place within its exploitation territory, but some mobile resources may be located outside this exploitation territory but still within the territory of the human group living at the base. Hence the precise location of the home base must be a balance between the requirements of the two sorts of territory wherever the extended territory is an advantage. For example, many agricultural communities include a more mobile section of the economy concerned with livestock. The base of the agricultural community is largely determined by the requirements of agriculture, and by the availability of fuel, water, etc. Where limited or long-range transhumance is practised by the livestock section, the agricultural workers will seldom if ever visit the herds' grazing areas, although these areas are an integrated and vital part of the whole economy. Hence the grazing ranges of the herds form the extended territory of the agricultural site, and its location will be influenced to some extent by the requirements of the extended territory, which may, for example, be best exploited by using the base as a 'bottleneck'. In other situations, a more simple exploitation territory may be the best or more successful method of exploiting resources.

Current research is exploring the relation between extended and exploitation territories much further; but it is to be hoped that this study of extended territories occurring without exploitation territories, because of the cash economy in which they occur, may enable the principles to emerge more clearly, and thence to be applied to the more usual and more complex situation. The means by which prehistoric men exploited extended territories, and the ways in which these territories were defined, may have a considerable bearing on the problem of how men can exploit animals whose behaviour is sufficiently at variance with human behaviour to make the close relationships loosely called 'domestic' impossible, but whose exploitation is not best achieved by hunting.

ACKNOWLEDGEMENTS

I am indebted to Dr Chr. Vibe, of the Zoological Institute, Copenhagen, Col. J. Helk, of the Arktisk Institut, Copenhagen, and especially Mr G. Rowley of the Dept of Indian Affairs and Northern Development, Ottawa, for their valuable assistance in preparations for the field work; and to Mr M. J. Luxmoore, my companion in the field. Funds for the field work were provided by the Worts Travelling Scholars Fund and Trinity College, Cambridge.

6. SOILS AND SITE LOCATION IN PREHISTORIC PALESTINE

D. WEBLEY

The purpose of this paper is to record some preliminary assessments of the relationships between site locations and their economic potentials by considering evidence from Palestinian sites in general and the site of Tell Gezer in particular. Except in the case of some of the earliest Neolithic sites, the explanations which have usually been advanced for the growth and position of tell sites are based primarily upon socio-political considerations, such as military defence, and take little or no account of food potential. While socio-political factors undoubtedly influence the location of some sites, even military strategy must cope with the logistics of food and water supply. Thus it is suggested that in most cases economic considerations of resource availability and population size will be the primary factors controlling site location. This suggestion is tested through the economic assessment of prehistoric sites using the method of site catchment analysis (Vita-Finzi & Higgs, 1970). Site catchment analysis establishes the potential for exploitation in a broad sense; it does not attempt to arrive at estimates of site utilization or of the precise economies practised at a particular moment in time. While it is impossible in retrospect to reconstruct prehistoric farm economies in detail, the technique used in this article provides a basis for more detailed site comparisons.

In this study the technique of catchment analysis has not been used to record all ecological parameters, but to concentrate upon those which would have most influenced the human use of an area. If one attempts to classify a site territory. in terms of its economic potential for subsistence agriculture, it could be divided into arable potential, pasture potential, forest potential, and wasteland. A factor common to all these classes is the pedological information which can help to measure their potential fertility. Therefore, the hypothesis is put forward that the distribution of sites will be related to the distribution of soil types, and emphasis has been placed on the controlling role that soils may play in the exploitation of an area.

There are at least five aspects of soils which should be distinguished in site analysis. These are moisture availability, meteorological conditions pertaining to its structure, physical support of plants and animals, plant and animal food potential, strata stability and topographical deficiencies and constraints. In the case of arable exploi-

tation the ease of tillage with primitive tools must be added. This is especially relevant in the case of clay soils that can be cultivated with hoes and mattocks under certain climatic conditions.

SOILS AND SITES

Soil and agricultural studies have been made of well known archaeological sites in Palestine based on the published soil map (Ravikovitch, 1968) to arrive at land use assessments. Consideration was given to the soil's existence and condition at the time of the occupation (Higgs & Vita-Finzi, I. 3). In order to bring together the various factors of land capability, a classification has been designed based upon that of Vita-Finzi & Higgs (1970). Each soil type was assessed for its ability to support pasture and arable crops (Table 1). The general classes may be subdivided into regional classes to include local divergences. Class 1 has been subdivided on the basis of plant food replenishment (1a) and reduction of natural soil fertility through use (1b). Class 2 is divided on the basis of inbuilt deficiencies for plant growth, and the number of categories will vary with local conditions. Here, three have been used: 2a are soils in which the drainage is impeded; 2b are areas where there is excess salt causing salt marshes or deserts; and 2c is where the matrix contains few plant nutrients to sustain growth, as on sand dunes.

A recent distribution map (Anati, 1963) of the country shows Palaeolithic sites limited to the northern sector and succeeding Natufian sites spreading to the south. The Pre-pottery Neolithic extends farther, and by Chalcolithic times distributions were continuous from Egypt to the Lebanon. The Yarmukian pottery Neolithic sites are restricted to the edge of large rivers, and the beginning of tell formation in Early Bronze Age times occurred in the same areas. By the Middle Bronze Age, tells had begun to grow in the northern Negev on wadi banks, and the Early Iron Age settlements continued to grow near rivers until a new diversification was established. Table 2 shows the soil series and their agricultural potential within the catchments of the 222 archaeological sites examined, the last column denotes the number of sites within the vicinity of each soil. Technical descriptions of the soil series may be found in the soil map. Cations expressed as milliequivalents per 100 grams of soil

Table 1.   Prehistoric land capability classification – Israel

Arable	Pasture

Class 1
    Gradient under 15%; soil over 20 cm; well-drained;
      1a – plant foods replenished; 1b – plant foods not
      replaced
	Class 1
	    Good grazing for: sheep, goats, cattle, pigs

Class 2
    Gradient as 1; arable limited; inbuilt deficiencies;
      2a – impeded drainage; 2b – salt excess; 2c –
      impoverished
	Class 2
	    Limited grazing for: some animals – cattle, pigs, goats, camels

Class 3
    Gradient over 20%; no arable possible; erosion possible
	Class 1/2
	    Good grazing (1); soil; Limited (2); rock; rainfall
	      rainfall 600 mm; sheep 300 mm; goat and gazelle
	      and goat

indicate its natural fertility by measuring the plant foods present, but since this figure is also a function of clay content, it has to be balanced in the classifications with drainage and ease of ploughing. The number of sites in each series gives an indication of the favoured soils, but their overall acreages must also be taken into account.

Two different soils per site is the most common situation, one being freely and one poorly drained. Although the presence of hydromorphic soils denotes free water, the two soils have other implications. As regards hunting, game would be attracted and pasture would be favoured in dry seasons by the wet soil. For the arable farmer the slope soils at the junction of slope and swamp would benefit from the constant water source, from which the soil would be fed continually by capillarity, making cereal growth possible where rainfall was minimal. Table 2 shows that soils (A), (B), and (J) provide the most productive natural situations

for arable agriculture. The addition of (C), (D), and (G) widens the scope for natural grazing, while seasonal pastures associated with (I), (M), (O), and (P) provide the basis for transhumance, control of water supplies, or both.

An outstanding distributional feature is that highly successful sites with long and important histories, such as Hazor, have a maximum diversity of habitats and soil types serving them. Within the catchment of that city there are six different soil types, ranging from Limestone Rendsinas which are suitable for pastoral activities, well drained Brown Earths suitable for arable crops within advanced technological societies, to soil mixtures providing well-watered and well-drained deposits re-fertilized by hill wash. To these must be added the swamp and lake margins of Lake Hula which may have provided fowl, fish, and grazing for cattle and pigs. The successful sites were well placed to exploit a number of resources and if one enterprise failed,

Table 2.   Distribution of archaeological sites with soil types and their agricultural potential

	Soil type	Drainage	Cations meq/100	Agricultural class		No. of sites
				Arable	Pasture	
Terra rossa	A	Good	35	1b	1	22
Mediterranean brown earth	B	Good	55	1b	1	15
Rendsina mountain	C	Good	18	2	2	29
Brown basaltic	D	Poor	50	2	2	6
Hamra	E	Good	10	2	1	21
Brown alluvial vertisols	G	Poor	68	2a	2	28
Alluvial	H	Poor	43	2	2	37
Brown steppe	I	Poor	40	2	(1)	15
Colluvial-alluvial	J	Good	27	1a	1a	9
Rendsina valley	K	Poor	25	2b	2	10
Sand dunes	M	Excess	–	2c	(1)	4
Brown skeletal desert	O	Good	11	2c	(1)	10
Stony desert land	P	Excess	9	2c	(1)	7
Loess raw	S	Good	13	(2)	(2)	7
Desert alluvial	X	Good	–	2b	(2)	2

Brackets denote seasonal use.

the others could compensate. One is not denying political and strategic reasons for their location, but emphasizing that their power could be supported economically. That they were able to grow continually from small beginnings is due fundamentally to their varied surroundings.

Although sites are classified as being adjacent to particular soil types, the greater majority are placed *on* freely drained soils. Early settlements are never sited on wet ground. It is only in the Early Iron Age that tells are founded on vertisols and heavy alluvia.

Palaeolithic and Natufian sites occupy situations of maximum soil diversity. El Wad and Nahal Oren have five soil types and habitats within their catchment areas. Bare limestone with islands of Rendsina support grassy fields; the alluvium before the caves merges into the valley vertisols which supported damp oakwoods, and swamps. On the edge of the territory the sea might have provided an additional food source. The situations suggest areas where economies relying upon several animal species could be successful. The Pre-pottery Neolithic sites occupy similar situations.

Neolithic Yarmukian pottery sites show a change of emphasis to the hill-derived alluvium. In areas surrounded by soil with a high salt content unsuitable for plant growth, the main sites (Jericho and Sha'ar Golen) occupy salt-free deposits rich in plant food. These Rendsina mixtures are found in the Betshan, Hula, and Jordan valleys overlying Lisan Marls and must have been accumulating at the time of the prehistoric occupation. They need not imply cereal agriculture (Prausnitz, 1959), but may equally indicate the presence of pastures well-watered by the hill-wash and flushed with plant food, providing areas where animals would naturally congregate. Sites in the Jezreel valley have been used as examples of slope soil exploitation and cereal husbandry. From Yokneam to Meggido they lie adjacent to soils with medium to high salt content (Ravikovitch, 1968), which is a serious limiting factor to cereal growth; these settlements appear to be related more to animal distribution. The limestone soils in their vicinity, whether Rendsina or Terra Rossa, are as suitable for animals as for cereals. Sheep or goats, if allowed to graze freely, move to them in preference to all other soils (Hughes, 1958). Slopes have been shown to provide the better conditions for open forest growth (Reiners & Reiners, 1970) and, by inference, grazing for gazelle and deer, as well as goats. Even within the series, variations occur, and it is only by detailed inspections of individual sites that their potential can be assessed. In the Terra Rossa suite, parts would be unsuitable for cereals with primitive implements due to their high clay content; these would support naturally dry oak forest but could, in suitable climatic regimes, be used with 'slash and

burn' techniques. The shallow profiles on which cereals could be grown would have stunted scrub with roots spreading laterally; here one would find the 'grassy fields' of wild cereals. Exploitation would proceed from the lighter versions towards the deeper and any 'slash and burn' would begin where soil and tree growth was thinner, moving gradually into the deeper profiles as time and need dictated.

From the soil, depth, mechanical analysis, degree of podsolization, and gleying, it would appear that north Israel during the Neolithic had hills clothed with different densities of forest, scrub, and rock outcrops. Towards the valleys, the slopes were covered with thicker well-drained soil where its accumulation was possible, supporting well-grown, broad-leaved trees, and hence browsing animals. Where hill and valley meet and slopes shelve into the wet clays, dense undergrowth dominated. At valley mouths, or where topography led to severe downwash, deltas of colluvial-alluvial material would probably have supported lush vegetation of grass and trees. It is here that agriculturalists would probably settle and animals gather. The valley floor had dense forest, swamp, and salt marsh.

Chalcolithic debris is found from Upper Galilee to Sinai, and for the present study the sites are considered to represent one people. The relationship of the Chalcolithic to the Early Bronze Age is open to debate. The amount of Chalcolithic material found at the base of tells is small compared to that of the Early Bronze Age, and when both are present, it is difficult to isolate time intervals between them. However, no Early Bronze Age pottery was found at Ghussul (Hennessy, 1969). The distributions of many of the Chalcolithic sites cannot be correlated with soil types and suggest Bedouin transhumance groups working within the framework of Early Bronze Age 'city states'. The sitings show a dualism: part of the sites are in water/wadi situations, and the rest in uniform impoverished environments with little water and poor soil where only seasonal occupation is possible. Indeed, even the tell at Ghussul showed what might be interpreted as an indication of seasonal exploitation, the plaster floors being separated only by thin lenses of debris with but three distinct periods in the whole mound. The environs support the evidence from the excavation: the extreme aridity and the salt-laden Lisan Marls suggest a mobile economy, just as today the area is only populated with transient Bedouin herdsmen.

The Proto-Urban and Early Bronze Age situations are closely tied to river valleys, and tell formation established the norm for future land use. In most cases the pattern is similar: all are sited on freely drained land with at least two soil types nearby and, in some cases, three or more. One of the series is usually a heavy wet deposit. A typical site occupies a valley flank on colluvial-alluvial or Terra Rossa materials, with alluvium and vertisols on the valley floor; towards the mountains are light limestone soils. There are few examples of early foundations on single soils; even Ai', on Terra Rossa, lies within the catchment of Bethel, a complementary site with three soil types. The two sites appear never to have been occupied at the same time (Kenyon, 1965).

Throughout the Early Bronze Age the valley siting persists with some exceptions (Tell Hesi on one soil). In the Middle Bronze Age, there is a movement away from the valleys; although some new foundations occur there (Tell Gemma), many are now situated on more uniform soils, such as Tell Ajjul (Middle Bronze Age 1) on the Hamra series and Tell Fara (Middle Bronze Age 2) on Loess. All are still found on dry ground. The Late Bronze Age sites are still more closely related to uniform surroundings (Tell Askelon), although occasionally one finds river sites (Tell Abu Hawan). By the Early Iron Age tells are found on all soils and even on wet, impeded ground.

Evidence has been presented for a pattern of site location based on the exploitation of preferred soils and for movement from them as population pressure increased. The spread from Carmel and Galilee in the Natufian resulted, by Pre-pottery Neolithic times, in the peopling of large areas of soils and environments that were inferior to those of the earlier settlements. The diffusion continued until by the beginning of the Bronze Age the country was covered with a thin spread of settlement. The expansion was occasioned by the search for food and soils needed to grow it.

The appearance of Yarmukian Neolithic sites on river deltas and slope soils in the north indicates a newly developed preference for valley slope soils, water, and plant food replenishment. The Early Bronze Age expansion was similar with less emphasis on plant food replenishment; the colluvial-alluvial mixtures were in short supply and population pressure must have been great enough to cause a move to less fertile districts. The spread of exploitation was confined to limestone Rendsina and slope soils where animals would congregate for water and the flush of pasture after rain, and from where they would move to the hills as pasture receded. This suggests that, in addition to cereals, transhumant animal husbandry played an important part in the economy of these sites. It may have been at this time that large water harvesting came into use, and it would have been a natural outcome of the spread away from the deltas. The beginnings of Middle Bronze Age tell formation in the north Negev illustrates expansion to even less favourable sites; for example, the material from Ramat Matred (Aharoni et al., 1960) suggests that it was only through water collection and transhumance that life there was possible.

Development on uniform soils in the Early Iron Age

occurred in all areas (Tell Ful and Tell Nasbeth) and further advances in irrigation technique saw the Israelite colonization of the Negev (Aharoni et al., 1961). But it is difficult to accept that cereals were the main product, water control may equally allow the extension of pastoral activities through the dry seasons. The sites could be permanent seasonal transhumance centres between the south and north Negev. Indeed, the small size of some of the tells, such as Tell Hesi, would certainly support this case.

AN INDIVIDUAL SITE STUDY – TELL GEZER

Tell Gezer, with a long and important history from the Final Neolithic/Chalcolithic to the Early Iron Age, is situated on the summit of the lower of two hills. Its natural boundaries are provided by the high ground to the east, and to the west by a coastal plain interspersed with low limestone ridges running parallel to the coast. Surrounding the site on all sides, the original land surface is evident as a stone strewn rough pasture standing above the plain. It is occupied by Bedouin whose tents stand on the edges of stony fields delineated by broken natural rock. The Xeroserom is light textured and very stony and has been derived from breakdown products of Nari crusts. About ½ km from the tell the soil is thicker and darker. The deposits near the tell appear to have been continually cultivated; they are very friable with all structure lost, in contrast to those farther to the west where well-formed soil prisms are evident; the latter provides the main arable matrix for the kibbutzim and it varies in thickness with topography, the limestone ridges making it shallower and the valley alluvia deepening it. At the time of the visit (August), irrigated crops of millet, cotton, and vegetables were growing, the water being brought by pipe from outside the catchment area. To the north and south the situation is similar. To the east, the Rendsina persists over the hills with evidence of walls and terracing. A plantation of olives on the derived calcareous material gives way to a Brown Earth farther from the site. About one hour from the site a lake bed is present.

For site catchment analysis, six two-hour walks were made along chosen compass points and notes were kept of topography, soil, and agriculture; visits and interviews with producers within the radius of the site completed the present land utilization picture.

In the catchment the following soils were recognized: (1) Rock dominant; (2) Mountain rendsina; (3) Mediterranean brown earth; and (4) Alluvium.

1. *Rock dominant* areas around the tell are where 50-70 percent of the surface is limestone rock with the depressions filled with a soil that supports grasses which can be grazed.

   (Class: arable 3, pasture 2.)

2. *The rendsina* is low in organic matter and varies in depth from 5 cm at the tell to 50 cm farther away. (Class: arable 3, pasture 1/2.)

3. *The Mediterranean brown earth* is high in organic matter and provides good pasture and some tree growth in its deeper phase. Within the catchment the profile varies and is mixed with a heavier alluvium. (Class: arable 2, pasture 1.)

4. *The alluvium* mixed with (3) at the valley bottom is clayey and drainage is impeded. (Class: arable 2, pasture 2.)

Present-day exploitation

Within the area walked two distinct agricultural regimes were apparent. Bedouin herdsman, and Moshav and Kibbutzim settlements. The total Israeli and Bedouin population now served by the area is seven to eight hundred people.

The Bedouin economy is based on transhumant stock raising, ranging from Beersheba to the present site. The leader, an eighty-year-old man who had seen the group grow from four tents in his youth to the present twenty-five, pointed out that it was imperative to move from the southern base at Beersheba to look for animal grazing; Gezer was better than the Beersheba base, as the pasture lasted three to four months. For most of the year pastoralism had to be supplemented by food purchase. The movement pattern as long as he could remember was three years at Gezer to one at Beersheba; he thought there was a similar crop cycle, cereals failing one year in three at the southern site. The community numbered 200 in twenty-five tents, with one family per tent. They owned a flock of forty sheep and 360 goats of which 10 percent were males; 300 kids were produced each season. In addition they possessed five cows and forty chickens, plus fifteen camels for transport. About 400 animals were sold each year, and it was necessary to buy stock replacements (100) once every four years after the move from the south. Grazing was supplemented with imported fodder, one-quarter of which was paid for by animal sales. Since the community was not self-sufficient, some of the men did other work for part of the year. One of them, isolated from the rest, grew barley on the Rendsina fields around his tent and obtained an average of 4.4 quintals per hectare, a yield which was only obtained in a very good season at Beersheba. Their overall distribution (Fig. 1) shows the tents sited on the light limestone soils with all arable being concentrated there, although grazing also took place on the heavier soil. It was made clear that ploughing of the Brown Earth was impossible without tractors, while on the lighter soils before 1939, donkeys and camels had been used to prepare the

ground for the main cereal crop (barley). It is of interest that the cereal named in the Gezer Calendar is also barley. The analysis showed that the exploitation was marginal in the extreme, and it was only by trade outside the territory that the tribe existed, and the critical population density (Allan, 1965) was between four and twenty-five tents.

The Israeli Moshav and Kibbutz settlements are difficult to assess in relation to the environment, since their origin (1949) was not related to agricultural considerations, but to politico-military ones (Fig. 2). Each site representative said that the initial population was not related to land potential, and as a consequence, settlements designed for 350 families in 1949 had decreased to fifty by 1970, and even these were supported by enterprises not directly involved with the immediate area. Indeed, transport had been provided to exploit land 30 km away. Although each of these three settlements had dairy herds and some irrigated cultivation with emphasis on 'foreign' crops, much of the animal food was imported to the site from outside. The importance of 'exotic' crops to maintain the present population was mentioned, and it was stated that, while wheat produced I£10 per dunum, flowers grown on the same area produced I£2000, per year. In most cases, all produce was sold, since guaranteed prices made it cheaper to buy in than consume one's own produce. Each site had dairy herds composed of up to 250 milch cows with a smaller number of calves fattened indoors and slaughtered as veal. For these enterprises, large quantities of water were needed, which was piped in from outside the area and strictly rationed (each family received 17 000 m^3 per year). Other sources of income were deep litter chickens (four families derived all their income from these at one Moshav), eggs, and flowers. One hundred and fifty families lived on the three settlements giving a total population of five to six hundred people.

For early man the area can only be assessed by obtaining information on the staple crops. At each centre it was agreed that the major limiting factor for cereal growth was the low annual rainfall (350 mm). The rain began at the end of November and continued into April. If none fell after the middle of March, poor yields were to be expected. The soil exploited was the Mediterranean Brown Earth and yields with irrigation were six times those on the lighter Rendsina. The soil could only be worked with tractors, because the clays needed careful and constant working to obtain the best tilth before sowing; failure to do this reduced yields considerably. In the case of the Moshavs, if tractors were not available, the land could only be exploited by grazing animals. Without introduced water, cattle breeding does not appear to be possible and must be discounted as a source of protein in early times. This suggests that the Mediterranean Brown Earth could have

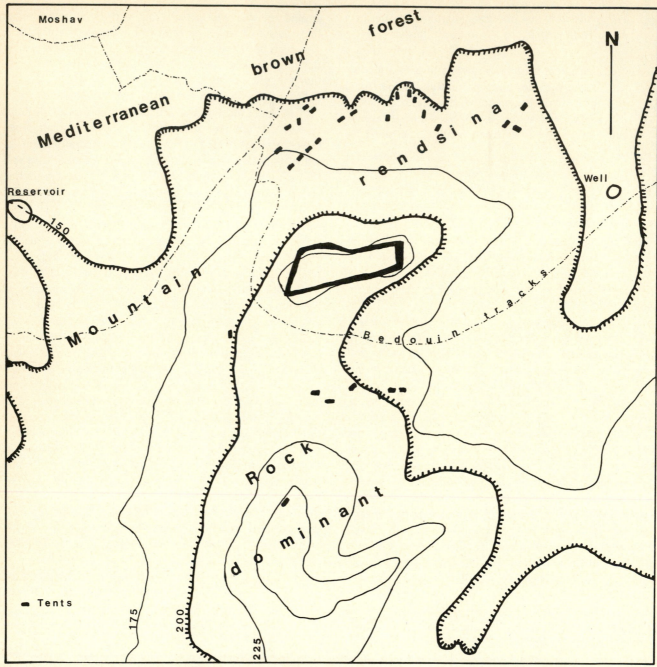

Fig. 1. Tell Gezer land use, 1970. Distribution of Bedouin tents and soil types.

been used most successfully in prehistoric times as grazing for sheep and goats. Water for human and animal consumption was supplied from two sources, the well, still used by the Bedouin, and the large cistern found in the tell.

Prehistoric exploitation

The vegetation undisturbed by crop cultivation would have consisted of areas of rough grass between the bare rock

with thicker vegetation towards the valley bottoms merging into oak forest at wadi edges and in places where the soil was deeper. From the known site history, it is clear that the agriculture must be considered in the light of man's technical competence to deal with the two contrasting soils, the light Rendsina and the Brown Earth. Unlike the Late Bronze Age settlers, the first occupants would not have had implements to cultivate the extremely heavy soil, and their cereals would have been restricted to the Rock Dominant

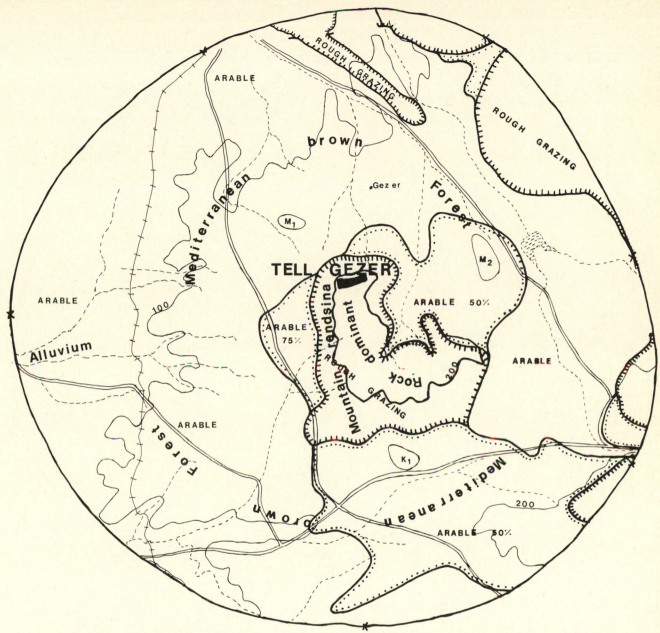

Fig. 2. Tell Gezer land use, 1970. Distribution of settlements, soil types, and land use within site territory. K_1 = kibbutz, M_1, M_2 = moshavs, X = 2 hour boundary.

and Rendsina like the Bedouin of today (Fig. 3). The Rendsina is a structureless deposit due to centuries of continual cultivation, and when originally cropped would yield about 4.4 quintals per hectare, a figure based on its inherent fertility (analysed by Professor S. Ravikovitch of the Hebrew University) and confirmed by the local Bedouin. The Mediterranean Brown Earth filling the valley, grades from light stony near the tell to a deep clay in the valley. It is only the lighter, shallower phase that could have

been ploughed by Late Bronze Age settlers (Fig. 4). Its main area would support good grazing and, when mixed with river derived alluvium, tree growth. The cereal yield for Late Bronze Age times on the ploughable part has been assessed (Ravikovitch) at 7.5 quintals per hectare. Both yields are long-term means taking into account crop losses due to insects, weather, and topographical limitations.

Tables 3 and 4 represent the areas, yields, and man equivalents of the soils in Chalcolithic and Late Bronze Age

175

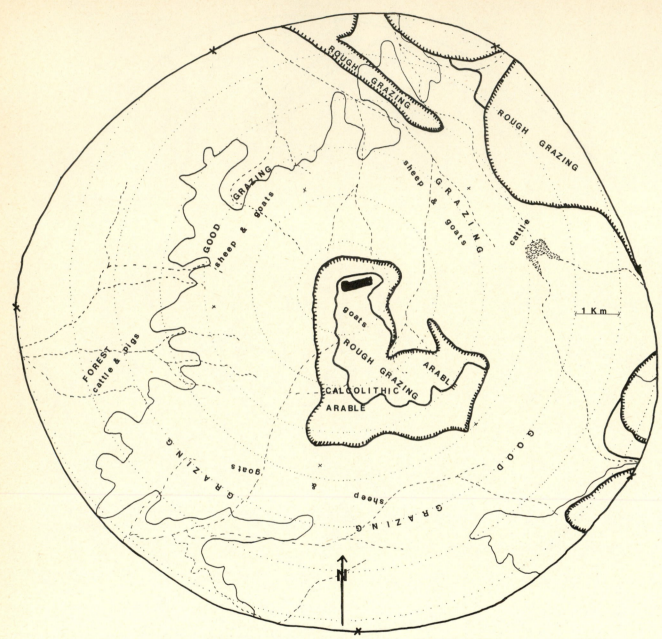

Fig. 3.   Tell Gezer land use, Final Neolithic/Chalcolithic. x = 1 hour boundary, X = 2 hour boundary.

times. The yields have been assessed in two ways: by the total area of each soil, and by allowing for agricultural constraints to production. It is inconceivable that these soils could be cropped every year without leading to exhaustion and abandonment, and since there is no sign of this, allowance must be made for breaks in production. Rotations for the Rendsina are based on examination of the site and the number of fields today in the rock hollows. These were naturally circular but were made sub-square by marginal quarrying to increase their size (probably causing their abandonment, since the soil would be thinner and would dry out more quickly). The survey indicates that 10 percent of the Rendsina would be cropped in any one year. Although a rotation of 1/2 has been suggested (Turkowski, 1969) for the Late Bronze Age cultivation of the Brown Earth, this would not take into account aspects of long-term utilization. In the Tables a rotation of 1/5 for any year has been used to take into account crop rotation, seasonal movements, crop failures through drought, locusts, diseases, etc. The human equivalents are based on the

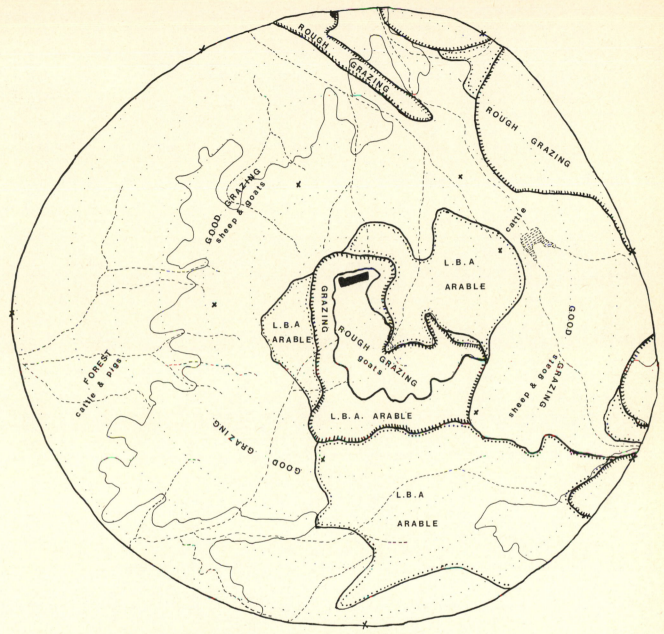

Fig. 4.   Tell Gezer land use, Late Bronze Age/Early Iron Age.

calories needed to provide 70 percent of human requirements per day (2000 calories) and is equivalent to 4.4 quintals of cereals per annum.

Goat production, presented in Table 5, is based on the present-day Bedouin figures and relates to the number of animals present in any one season. More could be supported for shorter periods at maximum spring growth, but not sustained for any length of time. The human equivalents in this case have been calculated as the meat of forty kids or twenty adult goats per annum.

A Biblical reference to city planning (Numbers 35, v) gives a figure of 2000 square cubits (approximately 2 km^2) of land per city; this area is delineated by the boundary stones recorded at Gezer. This figure is in general agreement with Chisholm's (1968) for arable exploitation, although in the case of a Levite settlement (Numbers 35, iii; Joshua 21, xxiii) it is regarded as the common pastoral land of the city. If a circle with a radius of 5 km is used as the limit of cereal production for a city with hamlets (Joshua 16, x) — i.e. the maximum distance of markets from the source of

Table 3.   Area of soil types within 2 hr of Tell Gezer (hectares)

Km	Rock dominant	Rendsina	Shallow brown earth	Deep brown earth	Total brown earth
1	102 (33)	137 (43)	34 (11)	41 (13)	75 (24)
2	245 (19)	219 (17)	380 (30)	412 (33)	792 (69)
3	334 (12)	461 (16)	668 (24)	1366 (48)	2034 (72)
4	361 (7)	664 (13)	905 (18)	3097 (62)	4002 (80)
5	361 (4)	715 (9)	1331 (17)	5451 (69)	6782 (86)
6	361 (3)	961 (8)	1844 (16)	8135 (72)	9979 (88)
7	361 (2)	1478 (10)	2596 (17)	10 941 (71)	13 557 (88)

Note. Figures in brackets % of acreage within area.

Table 4(*a*). Barley yield in quintals per km

Km	Maximum production rendsina	Shallow brown earth	10% rotation rendsina	1/5 rotation shallow brown earth
1	599	256	60	51
2	960	2862	96	572
3	2025	5026	203	1005
4	2914	6812	291	1362
5	3140	10 021	314	2004
6	4221	13 880	422	2776
7	6491	19 547	649	3909

Table 4(*b*). Expressed as human units

1	337	144	34	29
2	540	1610	54	322
3	1139	2827	114	565
4	1639	3831	164	766
5	1766	5637	177	1127
6	2374	7807	237	1561
7	3651	10 994	365	2199

Table 5.   Goat potential within 2 hr Tell Gezer (1 goat per 4 hectares)

Km	Rock dominant	90% rendsina	Shallow brown earth 4/5	Deep brown earth	Total goats	Minus 10% males	Total kids 3/4	Human equivalents
First settlement								
1	13	30	9	10	62	56	42	1
2	30	49	94	109	282	254	190	5
3	41	102	165	337	645	581	438	11
4	45	147	224	765	1181	1063	797	20
5	45	159	330	1346	1880	1692	1269	32
6	45	214	460	2009	2728	2455	1841	46
7	45	329	641	2702	3717	3345	2509	62
Late Bronze Age settlement								
1	13	30	7	10	60	54	40	1
2	30	49	75	109	263	237	180	4
3	41	102	132	337	612	551	413	10
4	45	147	179	765	1176	1058	793	19
5	45	159	263	1346	1813	1632	1224	31
6	45	214	346	2009	2314	2083	1562	39
7	45	329	513	2702	3589	3230	2442	61

Table 6. Population estimates of Middle Eastern tells based on urban areas

Site	Hectares	Population based on density of 125/hectare	Population based on density of 500/hectare
Ai' (Early Iron Age)	1.5	152	739
Arad (Early Bronze Age)	11.2	1220	5625
Tell Ajjul	12.1	1520	6075
Tell Beit Mirsim	3.2	380	1520
Tell Gezer	8.9	1125	4455
Hazor 1	11.2	1220	5625
Hazor (Middle Bronze Age II)	60.7	7591	30 375
Tell Hesi	1.0	127	506
Jericho (Neolithic)	3.2	405	1600
Lackish	7.3	912	3650
Meggido	5.3	652	2632
Tell Nesbeth	3.2	405	1600
Tannarch	4.4	556	2227
Ur	67.8	8350	33 412
Average Old Testament City	2.4	341	1215

production (Clark, 1967) — and the two-hour walk as the grazing range, the population of the Final Neolithic/ Chalcolithic settlement would have been 239 taking into account the agricultural constraints postulated above; if these constraints are not accepted, the maximum population possible would have been 1836. No account has been taken of hunting, but it is unlikely that this would increase the number of people supported; it would provide calories above the basic minimum. The present Bedouin economy illustrates the importance of transhumance, and it might be expected that the earlier settlers would also have gone outside the territory to procure food for their goats. The wanderings and copper mining of the Chalcolithic peoples may be related to this need for outside provisions. Trade, in whatever form, is essential to food supplies in seasonal marginal territories.

The population of Late Bronze Age Gezer is assessed at 1365 with crop rotations, and at 7414 without them. Again hunting would make little difference even though the invention of the wheeled chariot might extend the hunting range. These estimates might be compared with others derived by different means (Table 6) for the population of urban cities (Clark, 1967). Although there is evidence for phenomenally high population densities in Far Eastern cities, for medieval and Greek sites the range lies between eighty and 500 people per hectare with an average of 125 (Russell, 1958). The table gives estimates for various Middle Eastern sites based on 125 and 500 people per hectare.

The lower population figure (1125) for Gezer is in reasonable agreement with the agricultural assessment and the present-day population. If one uses the higher, it could be accepted as the difference between food potential and the degree of urbanization. Whatever population is used, 1000-4000, the site can be placed into the 'Kreisstadt' category of Christaller (1966) and suggests that its immediate influence extended over 35-45 km and, by comparison with German medieval sites (Loesch, 1954), had up to sixteen sites dependent on it.

The exploitation of the earlier periods thus appears to have been similar to that of the present day, the Chalcolithic occupation being equated with the Bedouin and the city states of the Bronze and Early Iron Age with the formalized Kibbutz and Moshav settlements, even to the extent that, like the present foundations, the earlier Gezer was a border settlement (Joshua 16, iii). The water supply for the earlier period has its parallel in the Bedouins' well, the piped water from outside the area has replaced the Late Bronze Age cistern of the Tell thus making the present day occupation possible. There seems no reason to doubt that the area has been fully exploited within the limitations of current technological levels. Its long history is mirrored in the four soil habitats, and to these must be added the lake (not now existing, but a prominent feature on pre-1948 maps). It is of interest that economic expanses of water lie at the periphery of many of the major sites (e.g. Hazor and Bethshan).

The two preceding studies outline an exercise in catchment analysis and reach tentative conclusions on the site of Gezer and the agricultural background of early Palestine. The general study shows a relationship between sites and the fertility of soils around them, and indicates possible associations between historic periods and land use; without the soil map, it is doubtful if these could be shown until many detailed individual site analyses had been completed. Indeed, the consideration of separate cases might pose problems of interpretation different from those of Gezer, and many would be needed to arrive at the picture suggested by the general study. Eventually the food production at Gezer might be more exactly equated with the surroundings by an examination of the organic and inorganic remains retrieved from the site itself. The extension of the technique to other sites will allow demographic and food potential comparisons.

7. EXCAVATIONS AT CAN HASAN III 1969–1970

D. H. FRENCH

with contributions by G. C. Hillman, S. Payne and R. J. Payne

The mound of Can Hasan III is located about 1.5 km north of the village of Can Hasan, which lies about 13 km north-east of Karaman, approximately 320 km south of Ankara (Fig. 1). Excavations took place in May and October to December 1969, and in June 1970. Two aspects which made investigation of this site immediately attractive were the discovery, on the surface, of obsidian tools showing analogy with C-14 dated material from Suberde, and the absence of recognizable 'early' pottery; both of these aspects indicated that the site was 'early', that is, certainly aceramic, probably pre-Çatal and perhaps contemporary with Suberde. The fact that there was little deposition overlying these early levels and that excavation facilities already existed at Can Hasan I added to the interest and suitability of the site. Finally, it was thought that the excavation of the site might contribute to the general theme of the British Academy Major Research Project on the Early History of Agriculture.

A principal factor governing the whole excavation was financial, as initially the available resources were £1250. The aims of the operation, therefore, were to excavate efficiently and effectively within the limits of the available money (that is, 'maximum recovery from minimum-necessary excavation'), and, in particular, to recover materials (e.g. animal bone, plant remains) relevant to the theme of the project.

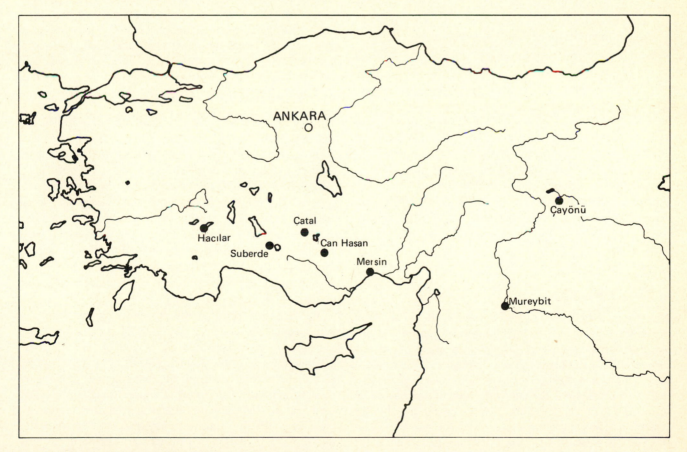

Fig. 1.   Position of Can Hasan III in relation to other early sites.

With these general aims in mind, the work, nevertheless, proceeded empirically. Objectives were formulated and methods revised as the excavation progressed. From the outset, there was an awareness of the meagre size of the samples being recovered but it was decided to concentrate on their qualitative nature. Expressed simply, the intention was to excavate until it seemed there was enough material of the desired kind. Thus, although the size of the samples was only visually estimated, the decision (which was implemented after the excavation had begun) to develop the techniques and methods then current at Can Hasan in order to ensure as a fundamental principle a more mechanical, repeatable standard of recovery was largely taken on theoretical grounds. The consequence of this basic decision led to the water-sieving experiments, an account of which is given by French (1971).

THE MOUND (Fig. 2)

The site, as it now exists above the level of the plain, measures *c.* 100 m × 100 m; the trenches, cut along an E-W transect, gave no indication of original extent. Though planned to provide immediate evidence of spatial variation and functional distribution, these trenches have given only limited information for a lateral cross-section.

STRATIGRAPHY

The deep sounding (Fig. 3) indicated at least seven major deposits, i.e. structural complexes; the lowest two of these were tested by an earth-corer. The maximum depth of deposit is *c.* 6.75 m of which the existing height of the mound (above the surrounding plain) constitutes 2.25 m; the remainder, 4.50 m, is now buried. The last 2.50 m of deposit is below the water level. As observed during excavation, the sequence of deposition is unbroken; it consists largely of groups of floor-lines divided by deposits of clay and wall debris.

STRUCTURES (Fig. 4)

The trenches 49 K and L gave warning of the presence of structures immediately below the plough-soil, and it was therefore decided to undertake a programme of surface-stripping. With flat-bladed shovels, plough soil was removed to a depth of *c.* 0.30 m below the surface; on the flat surface thus exposed the surviving tops of walls were revealed and then planned. This operation was initiated in the autumn of 1969 but completed only in the spring of 1970. Despite the presence of a large Ottoman period pit in the centre of the mound, the surface stripping revealed, after

some difficulty, the surviving lines of walls of a complex of structures which are probably to be considered as houses. An area of 600 m² (20 m × 30 m) was cleared. This figure may represent only 6 percent of the present *hüyük* (*c.* 100 m × 100 m). The trench 49L represents no more than 0.16 percent of the same total area; from this trench 28 m³ of earth was excavated, a minute proportion of the total. There is no indication yet of functional distribution or of specialized locations (i.e. work or activity areas).

Both the stratification (Fig. 3) and the plan recovered by surface stripping (Fig. 4) indicate that within the basic orientation of the site (as revealed), structures were perhaps developed both horizontally (i.e. by insertion into a 'court-yard' area) and vertically (i.e. by superposition of one structure over another).

Walls were built without stone foundations or trenching. Wood reinforcement is not evidenced. Mud-brick was found, but walls were mostly constructed in a 'slab' pisé technique. Wall and floor surfaces were coated with mud plaster and sometimes painted in red, some floor surfaces being made of extremely hard, compacted clay to which small pebbles had been added. Two ovens were found, which had been constructed of fine clay, straw-tempered; one (square 48K) had been built into a wall and was full of earth in which the largest sample (*c.* 500 g) of carbonized plant remains found on the site was accidentally recovered.

D.H.F.

PLANT REMAINS

The plant remains from Can Hasan III are being studied as a source of information on past human activities (seasonal or otherwise) which were directed towards the obtaining of food by exploitation of plant resources. At the same time, information is being sought on past vegetation cover (particularly any tree cover) in the Can Hasan area in all cases where the macroscopic plant remains uncovered can yield relevant data. Vegetation cover is in turn being treated as an indicator of the general potential of the area accessible to the Can Hasan villagers both in broad terms (e.g. grazing potential) and in terms of immediate resources represented by individual plants.

We shall first consider the possibility of answering certain specific questions via the study of macroscopic plant remains. Were domesticated plants present or not? There are two aspects to this problem. First, it is highly improbable that the total spectrum of plant resources utilized by the inhabitants of Can Hasan at a given time will be represented in the plant remains retrievable from the corresponding level of the site; thus we could never state emphatically that domesticated types of plants were absent at the time of occupation. If we accept this limitation as inevitable,

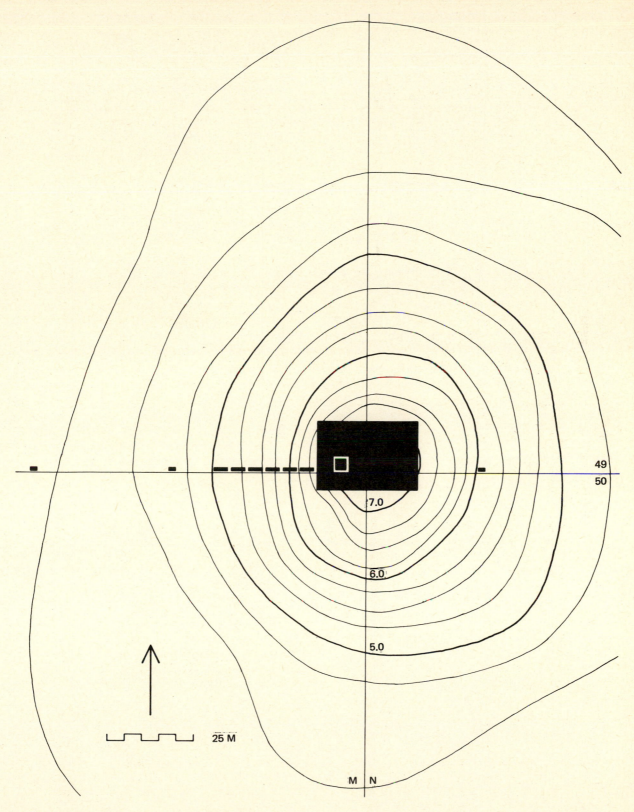

Fig. 2.   Plan of site.

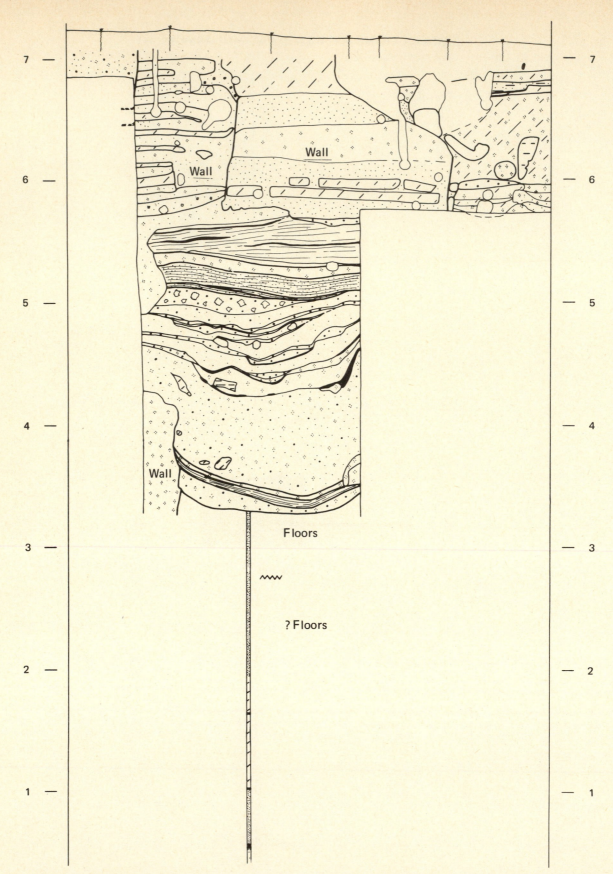

Fig. 3.   South face of Trench 49 L.

184

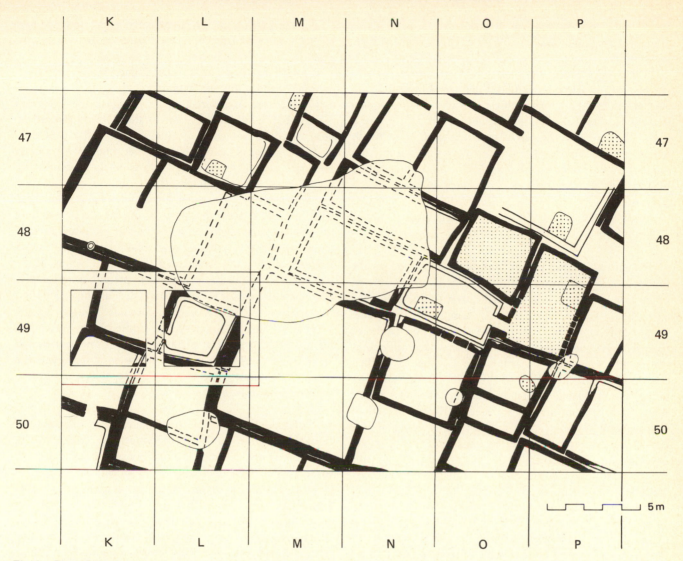

Fig. 4. Plan of structures.

then, secondly, the problem is reduced to one of recognizing in the plant remains present those morphological differences separating wild, segetal, and cultivated types. We are frequently forced to base these distinctions on grade characters for which (in all but the most uniform material) large samples must be measured if the standard errors are not going to bridge the means. (The quantity required will vary with the plant type concerned, the part of the plant preserved and recovered, and its state of preservation.) Even in the cereals where one can often make use of major-gene based (non-grade) characters, large samples are again necessary if one is to be able to distinguish between the products of an occasional outcross (between the crop plant population and nearby stands of wild or segetal relatives) and a 'transitional' crop, with all its traditionally adherent implications of 'incipient domestication'.

Whether or not these plants (identified as either wild or domesticated) were actually cultivated by the settlement at this time is another problem and can often only be solved by consulting other forms of data together with those represented by the plant remains. Grain from domesticated crops may have been imported from elsewhere. On the other hand, wild forms of some crop species would certainly not have developed 'domestic' characters immediately on being taken into cultivation and therefore by themselves do not offer irrefutable proof that they were gathered from wild stands.

Interpretation of identifications in terms of the contribution of a given plant product to the village economy demands a quantitative approach both in the study of plant remains and in parallel studies of the one model available in these extrapolations, that is, the agricultural systems and the techniques and uses of plant products (for food, dyes, drugs, weaving, and building) observable now in the villages of Anatolia.

In deriving information of past vegetation cover, macroscopic remains can indicate that a plant was present in the area but little more (consideration of traded plant products is excluded here). Such a fact could in rare cases prove a useful clue to the existence of environmental factors with which the distribution of that plant species is known (from modern studies) to be unwaveringly associated. Information of this sort can be deduced from mere presence of the relevant remains, but as low concentration in site deposits and very small seed sizes are often involved, large quantities of earth must be processed down to fine size limits.

The extraction techniques used were developed on the principle stressed above that, as well as being capable of processing large quantities of earth down to fine limits, the extraction system must also be based on repeatable, mechanical standards. It is otherwise impossible to define the nature of one's samples in a manner which will permit statistically acceptable procedures to be applied in their analysis. It has been suggested that a mean retrieval of 95 percent of all organic material of minimum diameter greater than 1 mm^2, is possible by the Can Hasan method of water-sieving. Although this appears highly probable, the hypothesis has yet to be tested experimentally. Samples have, however, been taken for this purpose and for assessing the damage inflicted on different types of remains by water-sieving.

Damage to carbonized plant remains caused by water-sieving appears to have been slight. All the material was damp on being excavated. With similar material excavated at Aşvan, 1970, mere contact with water was rarely found to inflict detectable damage. However, surface tension effects can apparently prove highly destructive when extremely dry carbon is brought into contact with water (Hopf, pers. comm.). Slight cracking of some carbonized structures was noted during drying, even when the time available for drying was extended over one week. Since damp carbon is extremely fragile and stores very badly, the carbon excavated here would have had to have been dried in any case. Retrieval of intact cereal glumes and also cereal rachis segments complete with tufts of intact, carbonized, unicellular bristles demonstrates that it is possible for even highly fragile carbonized remains to survive water-sieving.

Non-carbonized plant material (generally seeds or fruits with heavily silicified cell walls) mostly came from the sunken residues. This indicates the necessity of using a system of water-sieving in which this denser fraction is automatically retained.

For the purpose of this preliminary report, four samples of plant remains (out of a total of *c.* 350) were briefly examined in order to be able to give some idea of:

(*a*) the range of plant remains retained by the extraction methods used on this excavation;

(*b*) the sort of information (relevant to the questions asked) that a full examination of the 350 samples might ultimately be expected to provide.

The first sample came from an oven built into a wall on the south side of trench 48K. Approximately 20 percent by weight of the total sample was examined for this preliminary analysis. The remaining samples came from three adjacent levels near the bottom of the deep sounding (trench 49L) just above the present water table, and each of them represents a near-total of plant remains extracted from the digging unit concerned. The identifications of the plant remains in all four samples are presented in Table 1.

Substantiation for identification (such as dimensions and drawings of the structure concerned) is omitted for the purpose of this preliminary list. Some of the very small seeds of wild or segetal plants are as yet unidentified and are not considered here. A full account of these and the remaining samples will follow in another publication, together with drawings and dimensions.

In the fraction of the batch of material so far examined from the closed oven in the uppermost level (48K, 860.2), the remains are dominated by carbonized straw fragments together with charred chaff (rachis segments and occasional glumes, beautifully preserved) and what appears to be the remains of burnt dung. There is very little wood charcoal. Mixed in this are large numbers of intact grains of cereals which conform morphologically to grain of existing domesticated types and which are dominated by the free-threshing wheats. The latter appear to have been the source of the charred chaff. Seeds of probably cultivated legumes and many other plants are also present (see Table 1). The oven thus appears to have been heated by fuels similar to those used in Anatolian villages today: straw, dried dung, and some woody twigs. The three samples from trench 49L again include domesticated-type wheats, though quite different species are involved here.

The possibility of seasonal site occupation can only be superficially evaluated here. On the basis of present-day practices in Central Anatolia, the cereals and legumes would have been harvested in early July and threshed, winnowed, and perhaps sieved during the following weeks through into September. A further period of occupation would have been required for sowing (and perhaps harrowing) these crops, though the time of year involved must remain unknown, as the modern equivalents of the cereal crops represented here include both winter and spring sown

Table 1.   Provisional list of plant types found in preliminary examination of remains from four digging units at Can Hasan III

Plant type	Plant structures represented	No. of structures retrieved and digging-unit context			
		48K 860.2	49L 110.24	49L 110.23	49L 110.21
CEREALS					
Triticum boeoticum spp. *aegilopoides* (1-grained wild einkorn)	grain		2 (+1 ?)		
T. boeoticum spp. *thaoudar* (2-grained wild einkorn)	grain		1 (+2 ?)		
T. monococcum (cultivated einkorn)	grain				
1-grained				1	8
2-grained			4 (+3 ?)		
Einkorn (wild or cultivated)	spikelet forks		8	7	
T. dicoccum (emmer wheat)	grain	cf. 20+	2 (+3 ?)		(?1)
	spikelet forks	present			
T. cf. *aestivium*					
lax-eared (bread wheat)	grain	30+			
	rachis fragments	present			
compact-eared (club wheat)	grain	65+			
	rachis fragments	present			
Secale cereale cf. spp. *segetale* (weed rye)	grain	6	1		
Hordeum distichum (2-rowed hulled barley	grain	40+			
	rachis fragments present				
Hordeum nudum (naked barley, ? 2-rowed)	grain	3 (+5 ?)			
LARGE SEEDED LEGUMES					
Lens cf. *culinaris* (lentil)	seed	8+	4	3	
Vicia ervilia (bitter vetch)	seed	15+	5		17
V. cf. *sativa* (common vetch)	seed		5	40	
OTHER EDIBLES					
Juglans regia (walnut)	endocarp	1 fragment			
Celtis cf. *tournefortii* (hackberry)	endocarp	1	c. 360	c. 520	97
Vitis sylvestris (wild grape)	seed	1			
Prunus sp.	seed + endocarp	1			
Crataegus (a mutipyrenate sp.)	pyrene				1
OTHERS					
Polygonum sp.	fruit			1	1
Chenopodium cf. *album*	seed		1		
Chenopodium sp.	seed	15+			
Atriplex cf. *lasiantha*	fruit + bracteoles	4			
cf. *Silene* sp.	seed	1	(? 1)		
Dianthus sp.	seed	1			
cf. *Ranunculus*	achene		1		
Small-seeded legumes, primarily *Medicago* and/or *Trifolium* spp.	seed	10+	1	4	
cf. *Rosa*	achene	1			
cf. *Lithospermum arvense*	achene		1000's	1000's	1000's
Labiateae	achene	1			
Galium tricorne	fruit	1			
Scirpus cf. *lacustris* (a rush, cf. bulrush)		15+	25	26	1
Carex sp. (a sedge)	fruit including perigynium			1	
Gramineae (small-seeded grasses)	caryopsis + lemma and palea in some cases	43+ (at least 6 spp.)	35 (4 spp.)	32 (4 spp.)	4

Notes

Present = used for rachis remains where no attempt has been made to count the number of rachis internodes of each type.

+ = more to come (whole sample not yet examined).

(+2 ?) = two additional grains of dubious identity.

forms. Tilling could easily have been limited to a single, annual operation timed immediately prior to a spring sowing or else immediately after the harvesting and threshing of mid- or late summer (when it could be followed by, and combined with, an autumn sowing). Of the remaining plants, those which are unlikely to have been weeds of the cereals, and thereby brought in with the grain, appear to have been gathered in late summer or early autumn, e.g. the fruits of *Atriplex lasiantha*, a plant which was presumably gathered as fuel, are generally formed fairly late in the year. Straw and woody weeds cut for fuel are, however, storable, as are walnuts and raisins (see Table 1). It is therefore not possible to state the time of year at which the last fire was lit in this oven, though late summer may be a reasonable guess. To conclude, *minimum* site occupation at this time must have included mid- to late summer together with a further term for sowing which could have involved either an extension of late summer occupation or else a separate period in early spring. However, if the diet of the inhabitants of Can Hasan III was grain-based, movement to separate winter quarters with a six-month grain supply for a small family group would have been inconceivable without the use of pack animals or wheeled transport.　　G.C.H.

ANIMAL BONE

The results of a rapid examination of selected samples of animal bones are shown in Table 2. This list will undoubtedly be increased and changed by further work, but it probably provides a reasonably reliable indication of the relative abundance of the bones of the commoner animals.

A point of considerable interest is the difference between the sample from this site, and that from the Chalcolithic levels at Can Hasan I. Though the lists of species present are very similar, at Can Hasan I the sample is heavily dominated by sheep/goat bones, while at Can Hasan III no species dominates numerically, and *Bos* seems to be the most important animal in terms of meat supply. This difference is particularly significant as the two sites are less than 1000 m apart.

The bone sample from Çatal Hüyük, whose location is broadly similar, is more like that from Can Hasan III, but *Bos* predominates far more strongly, providing 70-80 percent of the identified specimens, and 90 percent of the meat supply (Perkins, 1969). Sieving was not used at Çatal Hüyük, and it is possible that *Bos* is over-represented as a result. If so, Çatal Hüyük might more closely resemble Can Hasan III.

The Chalcolithic levels (3-2A) at Can Hasan I probably represent a mixed farming economy, with primary dependence on the cultivation of cereals and legumes, and the herding of sheep and goats, and some cows — essentially the pattern with which one is familiar in this area today, but with the addition of the horse as a draught animal.

The difference between Can Hasan I and Can Hasan III can be interpreted in several ways. For instance:

(1) Can Hasan III may represent a different economic pattern, also allowing sedentism, which was subsequently replaced by the pattern seen at Can Hasan I. The most obvious possibility along these lines is that one or more of the domesticates that formed an integral part of the Can Hasan I economy was not a domesticate at Can Hasan III.

(2) If the same domesticates were available,

(a) there may have been a local environmental

Table 2.　Provisional list of animal species found in preliminary examination of remains from Can Hasan III

Species	Abundance
LARGER MAMMALS	
Large bovid (probably *Bos*)	common
Sheep/goat (*Ovis/Capra*)	fairly common (*Ovis* certainly present, *Capra* probably present)
Red deer (*Cervus elaphus*)	present (mainly antler fragments)
Equid (probably *Equus hemionus*, the onager)	fairly common
Roe deer (*Capreolus capreolus*)	present
Pig (*Sus scrofa*)	fairly common
OTHER SPECIES	
Hare (*Lepus*)	common
Canids (*Canis, Vulpes*)	fairly common (at least two species present, the more frequent of fox/jackal size, the scarcer of large dog/small wolf size)
Tortoise (*Testudo*)	fairly common
Snakes (Ophidia)	common
Birds (Aves)	present (bones not common, eggshell from fairly large eggs abundant)
Smaller mammals (Rodentia, Insectivora)	abundant in topsoil, otherwise rare
Fish (Pisces)	rare
Amphibia	rare

change, such as a lowering of the water-table accompanying a gradual shrinkage of the Pleistocene lakes in the Karaman basin; this might be expected to favour sheep at the expense of cattle;

(b) an increase in population density might have caused changes in agricultural practice; a possible area for expansion would have been to make a greater use of the hills and mountains to the south and east for sheep grazing; some of the cattle grazing might have been taken up by an extension of cultivation.

When detailed analysis of the faunal and other samples from Can Hasan I and Can Hasan III has been completed, we should be able to arrive at a closer understanding of their economies, and the reasons for the differences between them.

S.P.

WORKED BONE

A large number of bone implements were found, of which a high proportion are well-finished tools rather than just used scraps. The bulk of the collection is made up of tool-types common to most sites — a variety of points made on long bones, particularly on sheep/goat distal metapodia, blunt-ended tools such as scoops also made on long bones, and spatulae made on ribs. A few types are of more particular interest: first, a series of pins (Plate I) made on sheep/goat metapodia, which, although they have parallels at other sites, are considerably longer and finer than usual; secondly, a rather uniform group of pierced spatulae (Plate II); and thirdly, a number of small tubular beads, usually 1-2 cm long. A group of fifteen of these beads (Plate III) were found in the same series of floors which produced most of the pierced spatulae.

R.J.P.

Plate I.   Bone pin made on sheep/goat metapodial: CAN III/261.

Plate II.   Pierced bone spatula: CAN III/33.

Plate III.   Bone beads: CAN III/45.

CHIPPED STONE

Most of the chipped stone is obsidian, which occurs in abundance. Tool types include finely retouched points like those at Mersin (Garstang, 1953), end-scrapers, flake-scrapers, awls, *lames écaillées*, heavy backed blades, and small backed bladelets, some with obliquely truncated tips. Two other features of the obsidian industry are immediately obvious; the presence of large amounts of waste, mainly in the form of small chips, and the absence of the large numbers of parallel-sided blades so common on larger sites.

Flint is less abundant, and is mainly used for sickle-blades, some of which are denticulate. In contrast with the obsidian, there is little flint waste.   S.P.

SUMMARY

The results of the excavation have an intrinsic value, but perhaps of greater importance is the conclusion that it is possible to conceive and carry out a limited and controlled operation which achieves the aims proposed before beginning, and further that such an operation need not take up a disproportionate amount of the time and financial resources available for excavation.

The archaeological results are themselves, to a large extent, the product of the mechanical standards adopted for the excavation. Although certain conclusions could perhaps be drawn, especially with reference to the animal bone collections from Çatal where a preponderance of cattle bone is suggested, it is clear that there will be difficulties in assessing the results of other sites in the light of the Can Hasan III operation. Before attempting to discern patterns in subsistence economies, it may be that a number of sites will have to be re-excavated in order to provide a clearer basis for comparison.   D.H.F.

FINANCES

The total costs were approximately £3000, a sum which includes *c.* £250 expended on the development and production of the water-sieving equipment. Funds were procured from the Crowther-Beynon Fund of The Museum of Archaeology and Ethnology, Cambridge University, and, through the generosity of Major Russell, a grant was received from the Russell Trust. Financial support was also provided by the British Institute of Archaeology at Ankara.

8. CAN HASAN III, THE ANATOLIAN ACERAMIC, AND THE GREEK NEOLITHIC

SEBASTIAN PAYNE

The recently excavated Anatolian aceramic site of Can Hasan III (French *et al.*, III. 7) is one of a group of similar aceramic sites (Aceramic Hacılar, Suberde, Aşıklı Hüyük) which have been investigated during the past twelve years. It seems reasonable to regard these sites as a group not only because of broad resemblances in artefacts and architecture, but also because they form a group geographically (Fig. 1), and can plausibly be seen as ancestral to the ceramic Neolithic in the same area at sites such as Çatal Hüyük and Erbaba. The available ^{14}C dates (Fig. 2) place these acer-

amic sites in the seventh millennium, while most of the dates from the ceramic Neolithic at Çatal Hüyük fall in the first half of the sixth millennium (using the 5568 half-life).

In the context of current investigation of the origins and development of agriculture, the interpretation of these sites, the earliest known settlement mounds in Central and Western Anatolia, is of great interest. Are they, as some authors would suggest, the villages of hunter/gatherers or 'incipient' cultivators and domesticators, or, as others would suggest, are they fully fledged farming villages,

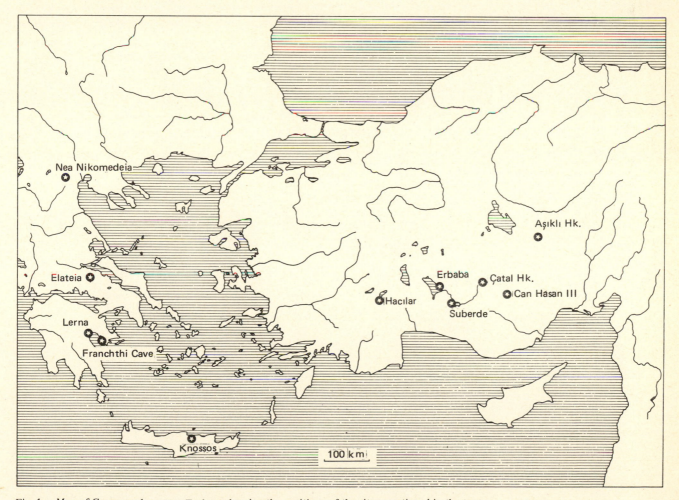

Fig. 1. Map of Greece and western Turkey, showing the positions of the sites mentioned in the text.

191

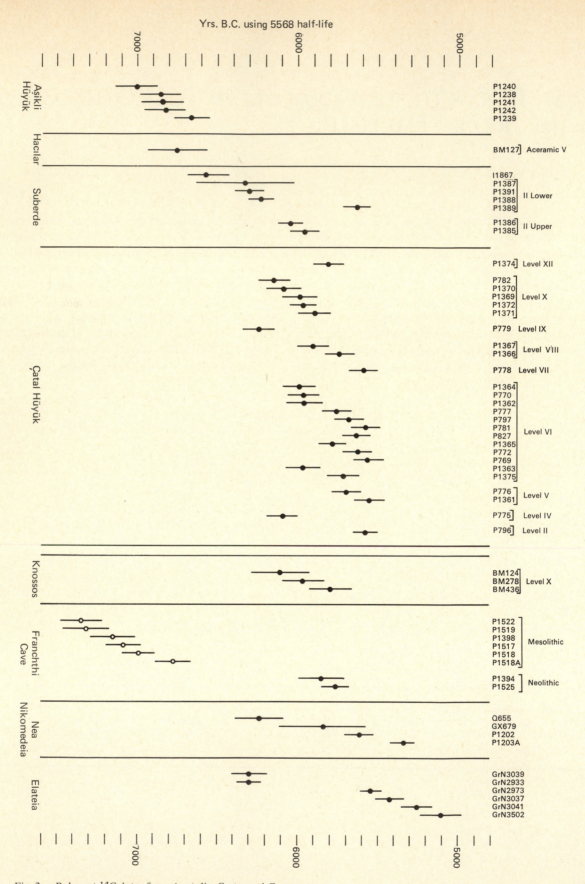

Fig. 2.   Relevant ^{14}C dates from Anatolia, Crete, and Greece.

192

dependent on crop cultivation and domestic animals? Traditionally, this question is approached by examining the plant and animal remains.

THE PLANT REMAINS

Information is only available about two of the sites. From Aceramic Hacılar (Helbaek, 1970) a single ash sample included:

(? Wild) Einkorn	*Triticum boeoticum*
Emmer	*T. dicoccum*
Hulled two-row barley	*Hordeum* cf. *spontaneum*
Naked six-row barley	*Hordeum vulgare* var. *nudum*
Lentil	*Lens esculenta*

Preliminary examination of a few of the available samples of seeds from Can Hasan III has revealed the presence of:

Wild einkorn	*Triticum boeoticum*
Cultivated einkorn	*T. monococcum*
Emmer	*T. dicoccum*
Bread wheat (both lax-eared and compact-eared)	*T.* cf. *aestivum*
Hulled two-row barley	*Hordeum distichum*
Naked ? two-row barley	
Lentil	*Lens* cf. *culinaris*

as well as a wide range of other species.

Thus at both sites there is good evidence for the cultivation of wheat, barley and lentils, and the possibility that other plants were also cultivated cannot be excluded. One cannot, however, from the plant remains themselves, assess whether agriculture played an important part in the economy of these sites or not.

THE ANIMAL REMAINS

The only sample that has been studied in detail is that from Suberde (Perkins & Daly, 1968). This indicated that the main source of meat was sheep, and that goat, *Bos*, pig and red deer were also important. Other species occurring in smaller quantities included dog. Perkins and Daly argue that, apart from the dog, all the animals were wild and that this was a hunters' village, but they give no positive evidence for this view. Indeed, their comment that none of the sheep was over three years old is of considerable interest, conflicting on the one hand with their picture of 'cooperative drives, slaughtering whole flocks at a time', and agreeing well on the other hand with data from sites where it is reasonably assumed that sheep and goats were domestic — such as Neolithic and Bronze Age Lerna (Gejvall, 1969), or Neolithic Knossos (Jarman & Jarman, 1968); it would not

be unreasonable to suggest that this could be interpreted as providing evidence that the sheep at Suberde were not wild.

A good sample of animal bones is also available from Can Hasan III, and is being studied at present. Preliminary inspection indicates that the main meat source was *Bos*, and that sheep/goat, pig and an equid (probably onager) were also important; other species present in smaller quantities include red and roe deer, and at least two species of canid.

From the other two sites less information is available. Nineteen identifiable bones were recovered from aceramic Hacılar, eleven of sheep/goat, and the remainder of *Bos*, dog, fallow deer and hare. A sample from Aşıklı Hüyük, collected by Dr I. A. Todd from a section cut by the river, included sheep, goat, *Bos*, pig, equid and hare.

Thus the available evidence about animal domestication at these sites is very scanty; at the one site about which we have much information, sheep — arguably domesticated — appear to have provided much of the meat supply, but we do not know how important meat was in the diet. About the other species (apart from dog), and at the remaining sites, there is as yet too little evidence to allow us to assess the man-animal relationships involved: there is no evidence, for instance, at Suberde, that the other species were domesticated — but equally there is no evidence that they were wild.

Examination of the plant and animal remains only partly answers the question posed at the beginning of this paper. If the criteria used are valid, there is some evidence for cultivation and animal domestication at these sites — but little evidence about how important these activities were.

THE LOCATION AND NATURE OF THE SITES

Examination of the positions of these sites adds a little more to the picture. Aşıklı Hüyük lies at a local widening in the narrow fertile intermontane valley of the Melendiz Çay, which is at present cutting into the site. Hacılar and Suberde are in wider intermontane lake basins — Hacılar on fertile alluvium close to a spring and also near one of the rivers running into Lake Burdur, and Suberde on a small knoll where Lake Suğla meets the southern end of the Seydişehir alluvial plain, near a spring and a river running into the lake. The position of Can Hasan III is more difficult to assess: it lies in the Karaman plain on the alluvial fan of the Selereki river near Pleistocene lake marls which are subject to winter flooding (de Meester, 1970). As the fan has been growing actively during the Holocene — three or four metres of deposit have built up round the site since its occupation – the local environment of the site has probably changed substantially, but it seems reasonable to suppose that it lay on the fan, fairly near its edge, and probably close to the river: the *Scirpus* seeds found in the deposits indicate that water was not far away at the time. If, as seems not improbable, a similar site lies beneath Çatal Hüyük (Mellaart, 1964, p. 73, but see also Mellaart, 1970a) its location is similar to that of Can Hasan III – in the Konya plain, on the alluvial fan of the Çarşamba river – again an actively growing fan building out over Pleistocene lake marls.

The nature of the sites suggests more or less sedentary occupation of long duration – the architecture is substantial, and the deposits are deep. It seems unlikely that this would have been possible if subsistence was primarily based on hunting and gathering, for which these sites are not particularly well placed: it is worth noting that fish and bird bones were scarce at Suberde (Perkins & Daly, 1968) despite its lakeside position, and they were scarce also at Can Hasan III. Agriculturally, however, the positions of these sites make better sense: each probably had available an area of fertile well-watered loamy alluvium, and a reliable water supply – this is particularly noteworthy in an area where such locations are scarce. Therefore it seems reasonable to infer that the availability of these soil and water conditions was a determining factor in the location of these sites – and that their occupants were substantially dependent on the exploitation of these soils.

As for the question of animal domestication, the site of Knossos (Evans, 1964, 1968) casts an interesting, if perhaps unexpected, light on these sites. In the earliest occupation at Knossos, dated to *c.* 6000 B.C. (Fig. 2), cow, sheep, goat, pig and dog are present, as also are emmer, einkorn, bread wheat, naked and hulled barley and lentils. Evans comments:

> There is nothing to suggest that the Knossos culture represents a local development in Crete, since there is at present no satisfactory evidence for any earlier human inhabitants there, nor is there anything to suggest that the species of wild animals and grasses

necessary for the independent development of such a food-producing economy were present.

(Evans, 1968, p. 272)

This implies that by 6000 B.C. cow, sheep, goat, pig and dog were already sufficiently domestic to be transported by sea, and thus were probably fully domestic within the sense in which this term is normally understood. Where did they come from? The evidence from mainland Greece suggests that the Neolithic was intrusive there at about the same time as in Crete (Fig. 2) – whether it is actual groups of people or simply the technology and domesticates that are intrusive is irrelevant to the present argument. Franchthi Cave (Jacobsen, 1969), with a sequence from the end of the Pleistocene to the Late Neolithic, provides important evidence for this view. As Evans himself comments, the obvious place to look for the origins of the Knossos Neolithic is in western Turkey. Unfortunately, no sites of this period have yet been excavated on the west coast of Turkey. On the Anatolian plateau, however, these aceramic sites provide a plausible if distant origin for the Knossos Neolithic and the Neolithic in Greece: the dates fit, and all the necessary plants and animals are present. This strongly suggests that not only the sheep and dogs, but also the goats, cattle and pigs present in the Anatolian aceramic were already domesticated or in the process of being domesticated. Also the occurrence of bread wheat at Knossos no longer seems so surprisingly early against the background of Can Hasan III.

Thus the available evidence suggests that already in the seventh millennium, the pattern of settled village life which was later to spread over so wide an area, dependent on cereal and legume cultivation and domestic sheep, goats, cattle and pigs, was already established in Central and Western Anatolia, and that these Anatolian aceramic sites were, in the fullest sense, farming villages.

ACKNOWLEDGEMENT

I am grateful to Dr Todd for the opportunity to examine the sample of animal bones from Aşıklı Hüyük.

LYNNE GOLDSTEIN

CONCLUSION: THE BIOLOGY OF DOMESTICATION

J. B. HUTCHINSON

The domestication of animals and plants, and the enormous changes in morphology and physiology that have resulted, constitute an evolutionary phenomenon of the greatest interest to biologists. The whole process is of such recent origin that much of the genetic stock of the earlier phases of domestication, and indeed many of the wild types from which domestic races sprang, are still living and available for study. The understanding of genetic processes gained in the past half century has made possible experimental analysis of the evolution of domestic races, and this has led to new and more informed interest among biologists in the beginning of domestication, and in the times and places where it occurred.

In crop studies, the foundations were laid by de Candolle,[1] who assembled the knowledge of the relationships of cultivars with their wild counterparts that was then available, and brought order for the first time into what had been a diffuse and vague field of enquiry. There the matter rested until Vavilov,[2] stimulated by his contact with Bateson and the early Mendelians at the John Innes Institute, set out his theory of the distribution of variability in crop plants, and his deduction from it of their centres of origin. It is from Vavilov's work that modern studies of crop plant evolution are derived.

It soon became clear that the centres of origin of crop plants which Vavilov identified were closely related to centres of development of civilization itself. Thus evolutionary biologists discovered an interest in common with archaeologists in the origins, in time and place, of the cultures dependent upon agriculture which were the forerunners of modern civilization.

The sources of information which the biologist can tap are the genotype of a cultivar, its geographical, morphological, and genetic relationships with other cultivars and with wild species, and the genetic consequences of the evolutionary process by which the cultivar became differentiated from its wild ancestor. From archaeology the biologist gains information on the time scale of the process he is studying, and material from excavations against which he can check his genetic deductions. Thus the two disciplines are complementary, and arising out of this complementation there is the prospect of a further check of deductions by genetic experiment.

Biological and archaeological studies are in agreement in the identification of two major centres of domestication of crop plants, in the Middle East and in Mexico. The domestication of major groups of crop plants in these two centres is well established. It is argued elsewhere in this volume that the tendency to regard these centres as unique centres of domestication, either in time or in place, is unjustified. In a sense, the botanical evidence is clearly in support of the view that the origin of agriculture is a much more widely spread phenomenon. Vavilov first postulated six centres of origin of cultivated plants. Later he increased the number to eleven or twelve. More recent work has tended to discount the importance of centres, and to show that 'the origin is no origin at all but a gradual transformation extending over wide areas and long periods . . .'.[3] Study of the crop composition of early agricultural systems has proceeded far enough now to show that domestication has gone on in all of the regions in which agriculture is long established.

Crop botanists have generally assumed that this wide ranging domestication went on by a process of culture spread. Doggett,[4] for instance, wrote of domestication of *Sorghum*: 'We may suggest that the Cushites grew emmer wheat, and being accustomed to cereals, developed some of the local plants, including *Eleusine* millet, teff, flax and sorghum, for use in areas less well suited to wheat.' Similarly, in considering the history of the crop plants of India, a natural and convenient frame of reference is provided by the hypothesis that agriculture was introduced into India from the centre of origin of temperate agriculture in the Middle East. The crop plants of the Middle East — in particular wheat, barley, peas and lentils — were brought by the first farmer invaders. Then, as Doggett suggested in Africa, as the farmers approached the climatic limits of their crops they domesticated local plants to replace them and to provide the means of spread into further regions. Thus rice, the *Brassica* oilseeds, and the *Phaseolus, Cajanus* and *Dolichos* pulses were added to the list of crops.

Belief in the importance of culture diffusion as a factor in the development of farming systems is strengthened by the appearance in India at an early date of African cereals. There are three of these, sorghum, bulrush millet (*Pennisetum*) and finger millet (*Eleusine*), and their African origin is established on the botanical criteria of the African distribution of their wild relatives. Likewise there is a group of crop plants long growing in India whose relatives are to be found in south-east Asia, and these also must have been introduced into India at an early date. Sugar cane and bananas belong to this group. Finally, the fifth group of Indian crop plants is that originating in the American continent, maize, potatoes, the American *Phaseolus* beans, and tobacco. Of their introduction there is considerable, though incomplete, historical evidence.

The pattern is largely consistent with a hypothesis that Old World agriculture originated in the Middle East and spread to India by two routes, one through Iran and Baluchistan, and one through Africa, to be followed by local domestication of a range of indigenous plants of which rice was the most important. However, the argument that such a theory should not be accepted without critical examination makes it necessary to look carefully at facts not easily explained on the theory of Middle Eastern origin. First, the south-east Asian crop plants have no connection with the Middle East, and there is no obvious way in which they could be accounted for by diffusion from a single culture centre. Secondly, though the botanical and archaeological evidence are in agreement that rice must have been domesticated in India, there seems also to be good evidence that it was domesticated in south-east Asia and China. Indeed, Darlington & Janaki Ammal's 'gradual transformation extending over wide areas and long periods' fits the domestication of rice admirably.

Evidently diffusion from a single centre is not sufficient to account for the establishment of agriculture in India. Not only so, but the dating so far established does not give an adequate picture of the relations between India and the Middle East and Africa. Knowledge of agricultural civilizations in India begins with the Harappan. But the Harappans already had important constituents of Middle Eastern, African, and indigenous Indian groups of crop plants by 2000 B.C.[5] Moreover, on the evidence of the fragment examined by Gulati and Turner,[6] they were skilled in the art of spinning and weaving the indigenous cotton, which is not an easy textile raw material. It seems unlikely that Harappan agriculture could have arisen, equipped with a repertoire of crop plants and a skilled textile craft, without a long antecedent gestation period. And for this, Neolithic farming in the Baluchistan valleys seems inadequate. Until we know more of the human cultures that preceded the Harappan, we cannot assess the importance of culture spread and indigenous innovation, in the establishment of agriculture in India.

The study of the beginnings of domestication of livestock is even more difficult than the corresponding crop studies. The degree of differentiation of domestic animals from their wild relatives is less than of crop plants from their progenitors, and the important characters of the domesticate, such as udder size in milk animals, and fleshing in meat producers, leave no trace in the archaeological record. One may hope that information may be forthcoming on wool comparable with that on cotton elicited by Gulati and Turner and Chowdhury and Buth.[7] Nevertheless, there is nothing among domestic animals comparable to the tough rachis in the Old World cereals as an index of progress in domestication, and no sequence of morphological change such as that by which the history of the domestication of maize has been worked out.

The exploitation of animals by man can be traced over a much longer period than the exploitation of plants. The suggestion that man/animal relationships approaching those of domestication may go back into the Palaeolithic is therefore of particular significance.

Most of the hunting and herding communities were in the Old World. The predominance of Old World communities has continued throughout the period of animal domestication. One of the unsolved problems of the development of agriculture is the very small contribution of the New World to animal domestication. No New World animal has been used for milk production, and none for draught. The Andean cameloids have been used in a small way as beasts of burden and for the production of textile fibres, and these, the guinea pig and the turkey have been used for meat. This is all, and the impact on human culture of animal domestication in the New World is trivial.

In the Old World, on the other hand, animal domestication has gone on in the Middle East, in Europe, and in the Indo-Pakistan sub-continent. The distinction between the western and the Indian domestications is particularly interesting. Allchin[8] has summarized the available information, and has pointed out that in cattle the Indian domestication was based on the local humped zebu type, though there was knowledge of the European humpless type through contact with Mesopotamia. He suggests that most if not all the Indian domestications were local, and on the basis of the rather inadequate dating so far available, it appears that communities dependent on cattle for meat, and even for draught or load bearing, were as early in peninsular India as in the Indus valley in the north-west. Thus the Indian information also supports the view that animal domestication may have gone on over a much longer time scale than is commonly supposed.

Perhaps the most important contribution of biology to the study of agricultural prehistory is the experimental study of the genetic systems through which the evolution of crop plants and domestic animals came about. The first project in this field was Fisher's study[9] of the evolution of dominance in a group of 'fancy' characters in poultry. Fisher postulated that the dominance of these characters was the result of selection by man in the early stages of domestication, in circumstances where crossing occurred between the domestic flocks and wild jungle fowl from which they had been derived. He went on to show by experimental cross-breeding that the genetic situation was in fact as he had proposed.

The importance of this study in relation to agricultural prehistory is that it was the first demonstration of a long persisting genetic consequence of the conditions under which domestication took place. Higgs and Jarman have drawn attention to the frequency with which intercrossing between domesticated and wild animals still occurs, and it is satisfactory to be able to endorse their view with experimental evidence of the consequences of intercrossing during the taming of such an advanced domesticate as the fowl.

Recently, experimental evidence of a more general nature has been presented, which illuminates the genetic system operating during domestication without isolation from the wild parental species. Thoday,[10] working with *Drosophila*, has shown that selection in opposite directions in an interbreeding population will result in the establishment of two morphologically and genetically distinct groups, even though gene exchange continues between them. Doggett has shown how this concept clarifies the genetic situation in *Sorghum*, where in Africa the cultivated forms are accompanied by weedy relatives which resemble the cultivars with which they are associated, but differ from them in those characters such as shattering panicle, hard seed coat and semi-perennial habit, that contribute to success as a weed of cultivation and a colonist of abandoned land. Reappraisal of the status of the cottons of field margins and abandoned lands, and of the weedy rices, indicates that this genetic situation, described by Thoday as disruptive selection, is one of great importance in crop plant evolution. It appears that there is no need to postulate isolation in order to account for the emergence of distinct races adapted to the circumstances of cultivation. Such races may arise under selection while interbreeding with the wild parent persists.

The biology of domestication is a continuing process. On the one hand, the genetic consequences of early domestication are still to be detected in cultivated races and also in their wild and weedy relatives. On the other, the process can be studied in the current development of new domestications. In plants, *Hevea* rubber and the grasses or legumes on which the pastoral industry of Australia depends, are examples. Among animal species are the musk-ox discussed by Wilkinson (III. 1) and some of the African antelopes that are being exploited in ecological situations unsuitable for traditional livestock husbandry. In the study of this continuing process, which has given rise to the agriculture by which human communities are supported, the archaeologist and the biologist are engaged in a fruitful partnership.

[1] A. de Candolle, *Origine des Plantes Cultivés* (1882).

[2] N. I. Vavilov, *Botanical Geographic principles of Selection*, Lenin Acad. of Agric. Sci. of the Inst. of Pl. Br. in the U.S.S.R. (1935).

[3] C. D. Darlington and E. K. Janaki Ammal, *Chromosome Atlas of Cultivated Plants* (Allen & Unwin, 1945).

[4] H. Doggett in J. B. Hutchinson (ed.), *Essays in Crop Plant Evolution* (Cambridge, 1965).

[5] Vishnu-Mittre, in *Trans. Base Res. Inst., 31* (1968), 87.

[6] A. M. Gulati and A. J. Turner, in *Ind. Cent. Cotton Cttee, Tech. Lab. Bull., 17* (1928).

[7] *Ibid.*; K. A. Chowdhury and G. M. Buth, in *Nature, 227* (1970), 85.

[8] F. R. Allchin, in P. J. Ucko and G. W. Dimbleby (ed.), *The Domestication and Exploitation of Plants and Animals* (Duckworth, 1969).

[9] R. A. Fisher, in *Phil. Trans. Roy. Soc. B., 225* (1935), 195.

[10] J. M. Thoday, in *Genetics Today, 3* (Pergamon Press, 1964), 533.

BIBLIOGRAPHY

Åberg, E. (1963) Discussion: origin and phylogeny. *Barley Genetics I. Proc. 1st int. Barley Genet. Symp.* 32.

Acanfora, M. O. (1962-3) Gli scavi di Valle Ottara presso Cittaducale. *Bull. Paletn. ital.* **14**, 73-154.

Aharoni, Y., Evenari, M., Shannon, L. & Tadmor, N. H. (1960) The ancient desert agriculture of the Negev. *Israel Explor. J.* **10**, 23-36 and 97-111.

(1961) Ancient agriculture in the Negev. *Science, N.Y.* **133**, 979-96.

Alessio, M., Bella, F., Cortesi, C. & Turi, B. (1969) University of Rome Carbon-14 dates VII. *Radiocarbon* **11**, 482-98.

Alessio, M., Bella, F., Improta, S., Belluomini, G., Cortesi, C. & Turi, B. (1970) University of Rome Carbon-14 dates VIII. *Radiocarbon* **12**, 599-616.

Allan, W. (1965) *The African Husbandman.* Edinburgh: Oliver and Boyd.

Allen, D. & Mech, D. (1963) Wolves versus moose on Isle Royale. *Natn. geogr. Mag.* **123**, 200-19.

Althin, C.-A. (1954) Man and environment. A view of Mesolithic material in Southern Scandinavia. *Meddn Lunds Univ. hist. Mus.* 269-93.

Altuna, J. (1963) Fauna de mamíferos del yacimiento prehistórico de Aitzbitarte IV. *Munibe* **15** (3-4), 105-24.

(1967) Fauna de mamíferos de la caverna de Marizulo. In Excavaciones en Marizulo, by M. Laborde, J. M. de Barandiarán, T. Atauri & J. Altuna. *Munibe* **19**, 261-98.

Anati, E. (1963) *Palestine before the Hebrews.* London: Jonathan Cape.

Anderson, J. (1895) Notice of a cave recently discovered at Oban. *Proc. Soc. Antiq. Scotl.* **29**, 211-30.

Andreev, V. N. & Savkina, Z. P. (1960) Reindeer pastures and meadows of the Far North of the U.S.S.R. *Proc. 8th int. Grassld Congr.* 166-8.

Anfossi, L. (1958-61) Terza campagna di scavi sistematici all'Arma dello Stefanin (Val Pennavaira-Albenga). *Quarternaria* **5**, 348.

(1967) Vaso di tipo campaniforme nell'Arma di Nasino (Val Pennavaira-Albenga). *Atti XII Riun. scient. Ist. ital. Preist. Protost.* 237-49.

Aranzadi, T. de & Barandiarán, J. M. de (1935) Exploraciones en la Caverna de Santimamiñe (Basondo: Cortézubi). Exploraciones en la Caverna de Lumentxa (Lequeitio). *Yacim. Azilienses y Paleolítecos* 3.

Asdell, S. A. (1964) *Patterns of Mammalian Reproduction,* 2nd ed. London: Constable.

Baker, H. G. (1965) Characteristics and modes of origin of weeds. In *The Genetics of Colonizing Species*, ed. H. G. Baker & G. L. Stebbins. New York and London: Academic Press.

Baker, R. R. (1970) Bird predation as a selective pressure on the immature stages of the cabbage butterflies, *Pieris rapae* and *P. brassicae. Proc. zool. Soc. Lond.* **162**, 43-59.

Banfield, A. W. F. (1954) Preliminary investigation of the barren-ground caribou, parts 1 and 2. *Wildl. Mgmt Bull., Ottawa* ser. 1, **10A** and **10B**.

Barandiarán, J. M. de & Sonneville-Bordes, D. de (1964) Magdalénian Final et Azilien d'Urtiaga (Guipúzcoa): Étude statistique. In *Miscelanea en Homenaje al Abate Henri Breuil,* ed. E. Ripoll Perelló, vol. 1, pp. 163-71. Barcelona: Instituto de Prehistória y Arqueología.

Barocelli, P. (1953) L'ultimo decennio di studi preistorici in Italia. *Bull. Paletn. ital.* **8** (6), 3-36.

Bárta, J. (1957) Pleistozäne Sanddünen bei Sered' und ihre paläolithische und mesolithische Besiedlung. *Slov. Archeol.* **5** (1), 45-50.

ar-Yosef, O. & Tchernov, E. (1966) Archaeological finds and the fossil faunas of the Natufian and microlithic industries at Hayonim Cave (Western Galilee, Israel). *Israel J. Zool.* **15**, 104-40.

Basse de Ménorval, E. (1966) Ancienne circonscription de Paris (région nord). *Gallia Préhist.* **9**, 437-46.

Bate, D. M. A. (1940) Fossil antelopes of Palestine in Natufian (mesolithic) times, with descriptions of new species. *Geological Magazine* **77**, 418-43.

Bell, G. D. H. (1965) The comparative phylogeny of the temperate cereals. In *Essays on Crop Plant Evolution,* ed. Sir J. Hutchinson, pp. 70-102. Cambridge: Cambridge University Press.

Belyaev, D. K. (1969) Domestication of animals. *Sci. J.* **5**, 47-52.

Benac, A. (1962) Studien zur Stein und Kupferzeit im nordwestlichen Balkan. *Ber. Römisch-Germanischen Komm. 1961* **42**, 1-170.

Bernabó Brea, L. (1950) Yacimientos paleolíticos del sudeste de Sicilia. *Ampurias* **12**, 115-44.

Berry, R. J. (1964) The evolution of an island population of the house mouse. *Evolution, Lawrence, Kansas* **18**, 468-83.

(1969a) Non-metrical skull variation in two Scottish colonies of the Grey seal. *Proc. zool. Soc. Lond.* **157**, 11-18.

(1969b) The genetical implications of domestication in animals. In *The Domestication and Exploitation of Plants and Animals*, ed. P. J. Ucko & G. W. Dimbleby, pp. 207-17. London: Duckworth.

Bertram, C. K. R. & Bertram, G. C. L. (1968) The Sirenia as aquatic meat-producing herbivores. *Symp. zool. Soc. Lond.* **21**, 385-91.

Bigalke, R. C. & Neitz, W. O. (1954) Indigenous ungulates as a possible source of new domesticated animals. *J. S. Afr. vet. med. Ass.* **25**, 45-54.

Binford, L. R. (1968) Post-Pleistocene adaptations. In *New Perspectives in Archaeology*, ed. S. R. Binford & L. R. Binford, pp. 313-41. Chicago: Aldine.

Binford, L. R. & Binford, S. R. (1966) A preliminary analysis of functional variability in the Mousterian of Levallois facies. *Am. Anthrop. (Spec. publs)* **68** (2: 2), 238-95.

Bishop, A. H. (1914) An Oronsay shell-mound – a Scottish pre-Neolithic site. *Proc. Soc. Antiq. Scotl.* **48**, 52-108.

Black, J. D. (1968) *The Management and Conservation of Biological Resources*. Philadelphia: F. A. Davis Company.

Blair, W. F. (1957) Changes in vertebrate populations under conditions of drought. *Cold Spring Harb. Symp. quant. Biol.* **22**, 273-5.

Boessneck, J. (1962) Die Tierreste aus der Argissa-Magula vom präkeramischen Neolithikum bis zur mittleren Bronzezeit. In Die deutschen Ausgrabungen auf der Argissa-Magula in Thessalien, I, by V. Milojčić, J. Boessneck & M. Hopf, pp. 27-99. *Beitr. urgesch. frühgesch. Archäol. Mittelmeer-Kulturraumes* **2**.

(1963) In Seeburg, Burgäschisse-Süd; Die Tierreste, by J. Boessneck, J.-P. Jéquier & H. R. Stampfli. *Acta Bernensia* **2**, Teil 3.

Boessneck, J., Jéquier, J.-P. & Stampfli, H. R. (1963) Seeberg, Burgäschisee-Süd; Die Tierreste. *Acta Bernensia* **2**, Teil 3.

Bökönyi, S. (1969a) Archaeological problems and methods of recognising animal domestication. In *The Domestication and Exploitation of Plants and Animals*, ed. P. J. Ucko & G. W. Dimbleby, pp. 219-29. London: Duckworth.

(1969b) A Lepenski-vir-i öskori telep gerinces faunája. *Különlenyomat az Archaeologiai Ertesitö* **96** (2), 157-60.

(1970) Animal remains from Lepenski vir. *Science, N.Y.* **167**, 1702-4.

Bolomey, A. (1970) Cîteva observaţii asupra faunei de Mamifere din straturile Romanello-Aziliene de la Cuina-Turcului. In Epipaleoliticul de la Cuina-Turcului-Dubova, by A. Păunescu. *Studii Cerc. Istorie Veche* **21**, 3-47.

Bordes, F. & Fitte, P. (1964) Microlithes du Magdalénien Supérieur de la Gare de Couze. In *Miscelánea en homenaje al Abate Henri Breuil*, ed. E. Ripoll Perelló, vol. 1, pp. 259-67. Barcelona: Instituto de Prehistoria y Arqueología.

Borgoras, W. C. (1904) The Chuckchee. I. Material Culture. Publs of the Jesup North Pacific Expedition. *Mem. Am. Mus. nat. Hist.* **7**.

Borzatti von Löwenstern, E. (1964) La fauna pleistocenica della Grotta delle Mura (Monopoli-Bari). *Atti IX Riun. scient. Ist. ital. Preist. Protost.* 143-50.

(1965) La Grotta-Riparo de Uluzzo C. *Riv. Sci. preist.* **20** (1), 1-31.

(1969) Industrie romanelliane e neolitiche nella grotta delle Prazziche (Novaglie-Lecce). *Riv. Sci. preist.* **24**, 91-143.

Bosold, K. (1966) *Geschlechts- und Gattungsunterschiede an Metapodien und Phalangen Mitteleuropäischer Wildwiederkauer*. Munich: Institut für Palaeoanatomie, Domestikationsforschung und Geschichte der Tiermedizin der Universität München.

Bouchud, J. (1956) Faune de l'Abri Pagès. In L'Abri Pagès à Rocamadour et la question de l'Azilien dans le Lot, by A. Niederlender, R. Lacam & D. de Sonneville-Bordes, pp. 444-6. *Anthropologie, Paris* **60**.

Boule, M. & Villeneuve, L. de (1927) La grotte de l'Observatoire à Monaco. *Archs Inst. Paléont. hum.* **1**.

Bovio Marconi, J. (1953) Incisioni rupestri all'Addaura (Palermo). *Bull. Paletn. ital.* **8** (5), 5-22.

(1954-5) Nuovi graffiti preistorici nelle grotte del M. Pellegrino (Palermo). *Bull. Paletn. ital.* **9** (64), 57-72.

Braidwood, R. J. & Howe, B. (1960) Prehistoric investigations in Iraqi Kurdistan. *Studies in Ancient Oriental Civilization* **31**.

Braidwood, R. J. & Willey, G. R. (1962) Conclusions and afterthoughts. In *Courses towards Urban Life*, ed. R. J. Braidwood & G. R. Willey, pp. 330-59. Viking Fund Publications in Anthropology **32**. Edinburgh: Edinburgh University Press.

Broholm, H. C. (1926-34) Nouvelles trouvailles du plus ancien âge de la pierre. Les trouvailles de Holmegaard et de Svaerdberg. *Mém. Antiq. du Nord*, 1-128.

(1928) Langøfundet. En Boplads fra den aeldre Stenalder paa Fyn. *Aarb. f. nord. Oldk. og Hist.* 3 Raekke, **18**, 129-90.

Bulmer, R. (1968) The strategies of hunting in New Guinea. *Oceania* **38**, 302-18.

Bunge, W. (1966) Theoretical geography. *Lund Stud. Geogr. Ser. C.* **1**, 73-87.

BIBLIOGRAPHY

Burt, W. H. (1943) Territoriality and home range concepts as applied to mammals. *J. Mammal.* **24**, 346-52.

Burton, A. C. & Edholm, O. G. (1945) *Man in a Cold Environment.* London: Arnold.

Butzer, K. (1964) *Environment and Archaeology.* London: Methuen.

Callen, E. O. (1967) The first New World cereal. *Am. Antiq.* **32**, 535-8.

Çambel, H. & Braidwood, R. J. (1970) An early farming village in Turkey. *Scient. Am.* **222** (3), 50-6.

Cardini, L. (1947) Gli strati paleolitico e mesolitico di Arene Candide. *Riv. Stud. Liguri* **29**.

Carr-Saunders, A. M. (1922) *The Population Problem: A Study in Human Evolution.* Oxford: Clarendon Press.

Carruthers, D. (1949) *Beyond the Caspian. A Naturalist in Central Asia.* London and Edinburgh: Oliver and Boyd.

Cayeux, L. (1960) Note sur un ancien habitat néolithique occidental à la limite des anciens marais du Havre. *Bull. Soc. préhist. fr.* **57**, 553-6.

Chagnon, N. A., LeQuesne, P. & Cook, J. M. (1971) Yanomamö hallucinogens: anthropological, botanical, and chemical findings. *Curr. Anthrop.* **12**, 72-4.

Chaplin, R. E. (1969) The use of non-morphological criteria in the study of animal domestication from bones found on archaeological sites. In *The Domestication and Exploitation of Plants and Animals*, ed. P. J. Ucko & G. W. Dimbleby, pp. 231-45. London: Duckworth.

Chard, C. S. (1963) The Nganasan: wild reindeer hunters of the Taimyr Peninsula. *Arct. Anthrop.* **1**, 105-21.

Cheynier, A. (1965) *Comment vivait l'homme des cavernes à l'âge du renne.* Paris: Les Éditions du Scorpion.

Chisholm, M. (1968) *Rural Settlement and Land Use*, 2nd ed. London: Hutchinson.

Christaller, W. (1966) *Central Places in Southern Germany*, English edition. Englewood Cliffs, N.J.: Prentice-Hall.

Churchill, D. M. & Wymer, J. J. (1965) The kitchen midden site at Westward Ho! , Devon, England: ecology, age, and relation to changes in land and sea level. *Proc. prehist. Soc.* **31**, 74-84.

Clark, C. (1967) *Population Growth and Land Use.* London: Macmillan.

Clark, J. G. D. (1947) Sheep and swine in the husbandry of prehistoric Europe. *Antiquity* **21**, 122-36.

  (1952) *Prehistoric Europe: The Economic Basis.* London: Methuen.

  (1954) *Excavations at Star Carr.* Cambridge: Cambridge University Press.

  (1962) A survey of the Mesolithic Phase in the Pre-history of Europe and South-west Asia. *Atti del VI Congr. Int. delle Scienze Preistoriche e Protostoriche, Rome.* **1**, 97-111.

  (1967) *The Stone Age Hunters*, 112-23. London: Thames and Hudson.

  (1970a) *World Prehistory: a New Outline.* Cambridge: Cambridge University Press.

  (1970b) *Aspects of Prehistory.* Berkeley: University of California Press.

  (1971) *Star Carr.* Addison-Wesley Modular Program in Anthropology. Reading, Massachusetts.

Clark, J. G. D. & Piggott, S. (1965) *Prehistoric Societies.* New York: Knopf.

  (1970) *Prehistoric Societies,* 142-6. London: Penguin.

Clason, A. T. (1967) *Animal and Man in Holland's Past*, 2 vols. Groningen: J. B. Wolters.

Clot, A. B. (1840) Aperçu Général sur l'Egypte, Paris.

Clutton-Brock, J. (1963) The origins of the dog. In *Science in Archaeology*, ed. D. Brothwell & E. S. Higgs, 1st ed., pp. 269-74. London: Thames and Hudson.

  (1969) Carnivore remains from the excavations of the Jericho Tell. In *The Domestication and Exploitation of Plants and Animals*, ed. P. J. Ucko & G. W. Dimbleby, pp. 337-45. London: Duckworth.

  (1971) The primary food animals of the Jericho Tell from the Proto-Neolithic to the Byzantine period. *Levant* **3**, 41-55.

Colombo, B. (1957) On the sex ratio in man. *Cold Spring Harb. Symp. quant. Biol.* **22**, 193-202.

Combier, J. (1959) Informations Archéologiques. Circon-scriptions des antiquités préhistoriques–Grenoble. *Gallia Préhist.* **2**, 193-214.

  (1967) Le Paléolithique de l'Ardèche. *Publs Inst. Préhist. Univ. Bordeaux* **4**.

Conde de la Vega del Sella (1930) Las cuevas de la Riera y Balmori (Asturias). *Com. Investnes paleont. prehist.* **38**, 1-116.

Coon, C. S. (1951) *Cave Explorations in Iran, 1949.* Phila-delphia: University Museum, University of Pennsyl-vania.

  (1957) *Seven Caves.* London: Jonathan Cape.

Coulonges, L. (1928) Le gisement préhistorique du Mar-tinet à Sauveterre-la-Lémance (Lot-et-Garonne). *Anthropologie, Paris* **38**, 495-503.

  (1935) Les gisements préhistoriques de Sauveterre-la-Lémance (Lot-et-Garonne). *Archs Inst. Paléont. hum.* **14**.

  (1963) Magdalénien et Périgordien Post-Glaciaires: Grotte de la Berie del Rey (Lot-et-Garonne). *Gallia Préhist.* **6**, 1-29.

Cowan, I. McT. & McCrory, W. (1970) Variation in the mountain goat, *Oreamnos americanus. J. Mammal.* **51**, 60-73.

Cranstone, B. A. L. (1969) Animal husbandry: the evidence from ethnography. In *The Domestication and Exploitation of Plants and Animals*, ed. P. J. Ucko & G. W. Dimbleby, pp. 247-63. London: Duckworth.

Crawford, I. A. (In press) Report on The Udal, North Uist. *Antiquity*.

Crisler, L. (1956) Some observations on wolves hunting caribou. *J. Mammal.* **37**, 337-46.

Daniel, M. J. (1963) Early fertility of red deer hinds in New Zealand. *Nature, Lond.* **200**, 380.

Darling, F. F. (1956) *A Herd of Red Deer.* London: Oxford University Press.

Dart, R. A. (1967) Mousterian osteodontokeratic objects from Geula Cave (Haifa, Israel). In The Geula Caves — Mount Carmel, by E. Wreschner, M. Avnimelech, E. Schmid, G. Haas & R. A. Dart, pp. 69-140. *Quaternaria* 9.

Dasmann, R. F. & Mossman, A. S. (1961) Commercial use of game mammals on a Rhodesian ranch. (Mimeographed circular.)

Davidson, P. E. (1967) A study of the oystercatcher (*Haematopus ostralegus* L.) in relation to the fishery for cockles (*Cardium edule* L.) in the Burry Inlet, South Wales. *Fishery Invest., Lond.* ser. 2, **25**, 1-28.

Degerbøl, M. (1933) Danmarks Pattedyr i Fortiden i Sammenligning med recente Former. *Meddr. dansk. Naturh. Foren.* **96**, 357-641.

(1942) In Dyrholmen, en Stenalderboplads paa Djursland, by T. Mathiassen, M. Degerbøl & J. Troels-Smith. *K. danske Vidensk. Selsk. Ark. -Kunsthist. Skr.* **1** (1), 1-212.

(1943) Om Dyrelivet i Aamosen i Stenalderen. In Stenalderbopladser i Aamosen, by T. Mathiassen, pp. 165-206. *Nord. Fortidsminder* 3 (3).

(1961) On a find of a Preboreal domestic dog (*Canis familiaris* L.) from Star Carr, Yorkshire, with remarks on other Mesolithic dogs. *Proc. prehist. Soc.* **27**, 35-55.

(1962) Ur und Hausrind. *Z. Tierzucht. ZuchtBiol.* **76**, 243-51.

(1963) Prehistoric cattle in Denmark and adjacent areas. In *Man and Cattle*, ed. A. E. Mourant & F. E. Zeuner, pp. 68-79. *Occ. Pap. R. anthrop. Inst.* **18**.

Degerbøl, M. & Fredskild, B. (1970) The Urus (*Bos primigenius* Bojanus) and Neolithic domesticated cattle (*Bos taurus domesticus* Linné) in Denmark. *Biol. Skr.* **17**, 1-234.

Degerbøl, M. & Iversen, J. (1945) The *Bison* in Denmark. *Danm. geol. Unders. Raekke 2*, **73**, 1-62.

Degerbøl, M. & Krog, H. (1959) The reindeer in Denmark. *Biol. Skr.* **10** (4).

de Meester, T. (1970) *Soils of the Great Konya Basin, Turkey.* Centre for Agricultural Publishing and Documentation, Wageningen.

Dever, W. G. (1968) Gezer — a Palestinian mound re-excavated. *Raggi* **8** (3).

Dewar, J. M. (1915) The relation of the oystercatcher to its natural environment. *Zoologist* **19**, 281-91, 340-6, 376-83, 426-31, 458-65.

Diem, K., ed. (1962) *Documenta Geigy, Scientific Tables*, 6th ed. Macclesfield, Cheshire: Geigy (UK) Ltd. Pharmaceuticals Division.

Dimbleby, G. W. (1967) *Plants and Archaeology.* London: John Baker.

Dimitrieva, E. L. (1960) Fauna Krimskikh stoyanok Zamil Koba II i Tash Aïr I. In Peshtchernaya Stoyank Tash Aïr, kak osnova periodizatsii poslepaleoliticheskikh kultur Krima, by D. A. Krainov, pp. 166-88. *Mater. Issled. Archeol. SSSR* **91**.

Doggett, H. (1970) *Sorghum.* London & Harlow: Longman.

Dorst, J. (1970) The Charles Darwin Foundation for the Galapagos Islands. *Nat. & Resour.* **6**, 11-14.

Drew, I, M., Perkins, D. & Daly, P. (1971) Prehistoric domestication of animals: effects on bone structure. *Science, N.Y.* **171**, 280-2.

Drinnan, R. E. (1958) The winter feeding of the oyster-catcher (*Haematopus ostralegus*) on the edible mussel (*Mytilus edulis*) in the Conway Estuary, North Wales. *Fishery Invest., Lond.* ser. 2, **22**, 1-15.

Ducos, P. (1957) Étude de la faune du gisement Néolithique de Roucadour (Lot). *Bull. Mus. Anthrop. préhist. Monaco* **4**, 165-88.

(1958) Le gisement de Chateauneuf-lez-Martigues (B.-du-R.). Les mammifères et les problèmes de domestication. *Bull. Mus. Anthrop. préhist. Monaco* **5**, 119-33.

(1968) L'origine des animaux domestiques en Palestine. *Publs Inst. Préhist. Univ. Bordeaux* **6**.

(1969) Methodology and results of the study of the earliest domesticated animals in the Near East (Palestine). In *The Domestication and Exploitation of Plants and Animals*, ed. P. J. Ucko & G. W. Dimbleby, pp. 265-75. London: Duckworth.

Dumitrescu, V. (1965) Principalele rezultata ale primelor două campanii de Săpături din Aşezarea Neolitică Tîrzie de la Căscioarele. *Studii Cerc. Istorie Veche* **16**, 215-37.

Dyson, R. H., Jr. (1953) Archaeology and the domestication of animals in the Old World. *Amer. Anthrop.* **55**, 661-73.

Dzieciołowski, R. (1970) Relations between the age and size of red deer in Poland. *Acta theriol.* **15**, 253-68.

Eaton, R. L. (1969) Cooperative hunting by cheetahs and

BIBLIOGRAPHY

jackals and a theory of domestication of the dog. *Mammalia* **33**, 87-92.

Edwards, W. D. (1967) The Late-Pleistocene extinction and diminution in size of many mammalian species. In *Pleistocene Extinctions*, ed. P. S. Martin & H. E. Wright, Jr., pp. 141-54. New Haven and London: Yale University Press.

Egorov, O. V. (1965) *Wild ungulates of Yakutia.* Jerusalem: Israeli Program for Scientific Translations, 1967.

Ehrlich, P. R. & Raven, P. H. (1969) Differentiation of populations. *Science, N.Y.* **165**, 1228-31.

Elder, W. H. (1965) Primaeval deer hunting pressures revealed by remains from American Indian middens. *J. Wildl. Mgmt* **29**, 366-70.

Ellison, L. (1960) Influence of grazing on plant succession of rangelands. *Bot. Rev.* **26**, 1-78.

Escalon de Fonton, M. (1956) Préhistoire de la Basse-Provence. *Préhistoire* **12**, 1-164.

(1966) Du paléolithique supérieure au mésolithique dans le Midi Méditérranéen. *Bull. Soc. préhist. fr.* **63**, 66-180.

Estes, R. D. & Goddard, J. (1967) Prey selection and hunting behaviour of the African wild dog. *J. Wildl. Mgmt* **31**, 52-70.

Evans, J. D. (1964) Excavations in the Neolithic settlement of Knossos, 1957-60. Part I. *A. Brit. Sch. Archaeol., Athens* **59**, 132-240.

(1968) Knossos Neolithic, Part II. *A. Brit. Sch. Archaeol., Athens* **63**, 239-76.

Evans, L. T. & Dunstone, R. L. (1970) Some physiological aspects of evolution in wheat. *Aust. J. biol. Sci.* **23**, 725-41.

Ewbank, J., Phillipson, D. W., Whitehouse, R. D. & Higgs, E. S. (1964) Sheep in the Iron Age: a method of study. *Proc. prehist. Soc.* **30**, 423-6.

Ewer, R. F. (1968) *Ethology of Mammals.* London: Logos Press Limited.

Fitte, P. & Sonneville-Bordes, D. de (1962) Le Magdalénien VI de la Gare de Couze. *Anthropologie, Paris* **66**, 217-54.

Flannery, K. V. (1969) Origins and ecological effects of early domestication in Iran and the Near East. In *The Domestication and Exploitation of Plants and Animals*, ed. P. J. Ucko & G. W. Dimbleby, pp. 73-100. London: Duckworth.

Fletcher Valls, D. (1956) Problèmes et progrès du Paléolithique et du Mésolithique de la Région de Valencia (Espagne). *Quartär* 7/8, 66-90.

Foster, J. B. (1964) Evolution of mammals on islands. *Nature, Lond.* **202**, 234-5.

Frank, P. W., Boll, C. D. & Kelly, R. W. (1957) Vital statis-

tics of laboratory cultures of *Daphnia pulex* DeGeer as related to density. *Physiol. Zool.* **30**, 287-305.

Fraser, F. C. & King, J. E. (1954) Faunal remains. In *Excavations at Star Carr*, by J. G. D. Clark, pp. 70-95. Cambridge: Cambridge University Press.

French, D. H. (1971) An experiment in water-sieving. *Anatolian Studies* **21**, 59-64.

Frenzel, F. (1960) Die Vegetations- und Landschaftszonen Nord-Eurasiens während der letzten Eiszeit und während der postglazialen Warmezeit. *Abh. math. naturwiss. Kl.*, Wiesbaden **6**.

Fuller, W. A. (1962) The biology and management of the bison of Wood Buffalo National Park. *Wildl. Mgmt Bull., Ottawa* **1**, 1-52.

Gagnière, S. (1959) Circonscription d'Aix-en-Provence. *Gallia Préhist.* **2**, 214-52.

(1966) Circonscription de Provence-Côte d'Azur-Corse. *Gallia Préhist.* **9**, 585-622.

Gaillard, C. (1934) Contribution à l'étude de la faune préhistorique de l'Egypte. *Archs Mus. Hist. nat. Lyon.* **14** (3), 1-125.

Gaillard, C., Pissot, J. & Côte, C. (1927) L'abri préhistorique de la Genière a Serrières-sur-Ain. *Anthropologie, Paris* **37**, 1-36.

(1928) L'abri sous roche préhistorique de Sault et l'Abri Trosset, à Serrières-sur-Ain. *Anthropologie, Paris* **38**, 449-77.

Galbreath, E. C. (1938) Post-glacial fossil vertebrates from East-Central Illinois. *Geol. Ser., Fld Mus. Nat. Hist.* **6** (20), 303-13.

Garrod, D. A. E. (1926) *The Upper Palaeolithic Age in Britain.* Oxford: Clarendon Press.

(1942) Excavations at the cave of Shuqbah, Palestine, 1928. *Proc. prehist. Soc.* **8**, 1-20.

(1955) Palaeolithic spear-throwers. *Proc. prehist. Soc.* **21**, 21-35.

Garrod, D. A. E. & Bate, D. M. A. (1937) *The Stone Age of Mount Carmel*, vol. 1. Oxford: Clarendon Press.

Garstang, J. (1953) *Prehistoric Mersin.* Oxford: Clarendon Press.

Gauthier, P. & Paccard, M. (1962) L'Abri Edward (Commune de Méthamis-Vaucluse). *Cah. ligur. Préhist. Archéol.* **11**, 10-20.

Gejvall, N.-G. (1969) *Lerna, a Pre-Classical Site in the Argoilid. Vol. I: The Fauna.* Princeton: American School of Classical Studies at Athens.

Georgiev, G. I. & Merpert, N. I. (1966) The Ezero mound in South-east Bulgaria. *Antiquity* **40**, 33-7.

Gervais, P. (1855) *Les trois Règnes de la Nature: Histoire naturelle des Mammifères.* Paris: Curmod.

Gill, N. T. & Vear, K. C. (1966) *Agricultural Botany.* London: Duckworth.

Godwin, H. (1965) The beginnings of agriculture in North West Europe. In *Essays on Crop Plant Evolution*, ed. Sir J. Hutchinson, pp. 1-22. Cambridge: Cambridge University Press.

González Echegaray, J. (1964) Excavationes en la Terrezeda 'el Khiam', Jordania. *Biblthca praehist. Hispana* **5**.

Gorman, C. (1971) The Hoabinhian and after: subsistence patterns in Southeast Asia during the late Pleistocene and early Recent periods. *Wld Archaeol.* **2**, 300-20.

Graindor, M.-J. (1965) Circonscription de Caen. *Gallia Préhist.* **8**, 21-31.

Graziosi, P. (1928) La Grotta di Talamone. *Atti prima Riun. Archo Antrop. Etnol.* **58**, 122-52.

(1962) *Levanzo. Pitture e incisioni.* Firenze: Sansoni.

Grigson, C. (1969) The uses and limitations of differences in absolute size in the distinction between the bones of aurochs (*Bos primigenius*) and domestic cattle (*Bos taurus*). In *The Domestication and Exploitation of Plants and Animals*, ed. P. J. Ucko & G. W. Dimbleby, pp. 277-94. London: Duckworth.

Groves, C. P., Ziccardi, F. & Toschi, A. (1966) Sull'asino selvatico africano. *Ric. Zool. appl. Caccia* **5**, 1-30.

Gubser, N. J. (1965) *The Nunamiut Eskimos – Hunters of Caribou.* New Haven and London: Yale University Press.

Guthrie, R. D. (1968) Paleoecology of a Late Pleistocene small mammal community from interior Alaska. *Arctic* **21**, 223-44.

Hadwen, S. & Palmer, L. (1935) Reindeer in Alaska. *U.S. Dept. Agric. Bull.* **1089**.

Hagedoorn, A. L. (1945) *Animal Breeding.* London: Crosby Lockwood and Son.

Hancock, D. A. (1959) The biology and control of the American whelk tingle, *Urosalpinx cinerea* Say., on English oyster beds. *Fishery Invest., Lond.* ser. 2, **22**, 1-66.

Hancock, D. A. & Urquhart, A. E. (1965) The determination of natural mortality and its causes in an exploited population of cockles (*Cardium edule* L.). *Fishery Invest., Lond.* ser. 2, **24**, 1-40.

Harlan, J. R. (1967) A wild wheat harvest in Turkey. *Archaeology* **20**, 197-201.

Harlan, J. R. & Zohary, D. (1966) Distribution of wild wheats and barley. *Science, N.Y.* **153**, 1074-80.

Harris, D. R. (1967) New light on plant domestication and the origins of agriculture: a review. *Geogrl Rev.* **57**, 90-107.

Hartley, W. (1964) The distribution of grasses. In *Grasses and Grasslands*, ed. C. Barnard, pp. 29-46. London & Melbourne: Macmillan.

Haskin, H. H. (1950) The selection of food by the common oyster drill, *Urosalpinx cinerea* Say. *Proc. natn. Shellfish Assoc.* 62-8.

Hawkes, J. G. (1969) The ecological background of plant domestication. In *The Domestication and Exploitation of Plants and Animals*, ed. P. J. Ucko & G. W. Dimbleby, pp. 17-30. London: Duckworth.

Heiser, C. B. (1965) Sunflowers, weeds, and cultivated plants. In *The Genetics of Colonizing Species*, ed. H. G. Baker & G. L. Stebbins, pp. 391-401. New York and London: Academic Press.

Helbaek, H. (1952a) Early crops in Southern England. *Proc. prehist. Soc.* **17**, 194-233.

(1952b) Preserved apples and *Panicum* in the prehistoric site of Nørre Sandegaard, Bornholm. *Acta archaeol.* **23**, 107-15.

(1959) Domestication of food plants in the Old World. *Science, N.Y.* **130**, 365-72.

(1960a) Comment on *Chenopodium* as a food plant in prehistory. *Ber. geobot. ForschInst. Rübel* **31**, 16.

(1960b) The paleoethnobotany of the Near East and Europe. In Prehistoric investigations in Iraqi Kurdistan, by R. J. Braidwood & B. Howe, pp. 99-118. *Studies in Ancient Oriental Civilization* **31**.

(1964) First impressions of the Çatal Hüyük plant husbandry. *Anatol. Stud.* **14**, 122.

(1966) Pre-pottery Neolithic farming at Beidha. In Five seasons at the Pre-pottery Neolithic village of Beidha in Jordan, by D. Kirkbride, pp. 61-7. *Palest. Explor. Q.* **98**.

(1969) Plant collecting, dry-farming, and irrigation agriculture in prehistoric Deh Luran. In Prehistory and human ecology of the Deh Luran Plain, by F. Hole, K. V. Flannery & J. A. Neely, pp. 383-426. *Mem. Mus. Anthrop. Univ. Mich.* **1**.

(1970) The plant husbandry of Hacilar. In *Excavations at Hacilar*, by J. Mellaart, pp. 189-244. Edinburgh: Edinburgh University Press.

Hennessy, J. B. (1969) Preliminary report on the first season of excavations at Teleilat Ghussul. *Levant* **1**, 1-24.

Herre, W. (1961) Ist *Sus (Porcula) salvanius* Hodgson 1847 eine Stammart von Hausschweinen? *Z. Tierzücht. ZüchtBiol.* **76**, 265-81.

(1963) The science and history of domestic animals. In *Science and Archaeology*, ed. D. Brothwell & E. S. Higgs, pp. 235-49. London: Thames and Hudson.

(1968) Zoologische Betrachtungen zu Aussagen über den Domestikations Beginn. *Palaeohistoria* **14**, 283-5.

Herre, W. & Requate, H. (1958) Die Tierreste der paläolithischen Siedlungen Poggenwisch Hasewisch, Borneck und Hopfenbach bei Ahrensburg. In *Die jungpaläolithischen Zeltanlagen von Ahrensburg*, by A. Rust, pp. 23-7. Neumünster: Karl Wachholtz.

Herre, W. & Roehrs, M. (1971) Domestikation und Stammesgeschichte. In *Die Evolution der Organismen*, ed. W. Herre, B. Rensch, M. Roehrs & F. Schwanitz, vol. 2, pp. 29-174. Stuttgart: Gustav Fischer Verlag.

Hescheler, K. & Kuhn, E. (1949) Die Tierwelt. In *Urgeschichte der Schweiz*, by O. Tschumi, vol. 1, pp. 121-368. Frauenfeld: Huber.

Hester, J. J. (1968) Comments on Davies, Hugot, and Seddon, Origins of African agriculture symposium. *Curr. Anthrop.* **9**, 497-8.

Heusser, C. J. (1961) Some comparisons between climatic changes in northwestern North America and Patagonia. *Ann. N.Y. Acad. Sci.* **95**, 642-57.

Hickling, C. F. (1965) Herbivorous fish in a water economy. *J. appl. Ecol.* **2**, 413.

Higgs, E. S. (1962a) Fauna. In Excavations at the Early Neolithic site at Nea Nikomedeia, Greek Macedonia (1961 season), by R. J. Rodden. *Proc. prehist. Soc.* **28**, 267-88.

(1962b) A metrical analysis of some prehistoric domesticated animal bones from Cyrenaican Libya. *Man* **62**, 119-22.

(1967a) Environment and chronology — the evidence from mammalian fauna; & Domestic animals. In *The Haua Fteah (Cyrenaica)*, by C. B. M. McBurney, pp. 16-44, 313-19. Cambridge: Cambridge University Press.

(1967b) Faunal fluctuations and climate in Libya. In *Background to Evolution in Africa*, ed. W. W. Bishop & J. D. Clark, pp. 149-63. Chicago and London: University of Chicago Press.

Higgs, E. S. & Jarman, M. R. (1969) The origins of agriculture: a reconsideration. *Antiquity* **43**, 31-41.

Higgs, E. S. & Vita-Finzi, C. (1966) The climate, environment and industries of Stone Age Greece, part II. *Proc. prehist. Soc.* **32**, 1-29.

Higgs, E. S., Vita-Finzi, C., Harris, D. R. & Fagg, A. E. (1967) The climate, environment and industries of Stone Age Greece, part III. *Proc. prehist. Soc.* **33**, 1-29.

Higham, C. F. W. (1967) Stock rearing as a cultural factor in prehistoric Europe. *Proc. prehist. Soc.* **33**, 84-106.

(1968) Faunal sampling and economic prehistory. *Z. Säugetierk.* **33**, 297-305.

(1969) The metrical attributes of a sample of bovine limb bones. *Proc. zool. Soc. Lond.* **157**, 63-74.

Ho, Ping-Ti. (1969) The loess and the origin of Chinese agriculture. *Am. hist. Rev.* **75** (1), 1-36.

Hoare, W. H. B. (1930) *Conserving Canada's Muskoxen.* Ottawa: F. C. Acland.

Hobler, P. M. & Hester, J. J. (1969) Prehistory and environment in the Libyan desert. *S. Afr. archaeol. Bull.* **23**, 120-30.

Hole, F. & Flannery, K. V. (1967) The prehistory of southwestern Iran: a preliminary report. *Proc. prehist. Soc.* **33**, 147-206.

Hole, F., Flannery, K. V. & Neely, J. A. (1969) Prehistory and human ecology of the Deh Luran plain. *Mem. Mus. Anthrop. Univ. Mich.* **1**.

Hooijer, D. A. (1961) The fossil vertebrates of Ksar 'Akil, a palaeolithic rock shelter in the Lebanon. *Zool. Verhandel* **49**, 1-67.

Howard, H. E. (1920) *Territory in Bird Life.* London: John Murray.

Hughes, R. E. (1958) Sheep population and environment in Snowdonia. *J. Ecol.* **46**, 169-90.

Hutchison, M. (1970) Artificial rearing of some East African antelopes. *Proc. zool. Soc. Lond.* **161**, 437-42.

Jacobsen, T. W. (1969) Excavations at Porto Cheli and vicinity, preliminary report, II: the Franchthi Cave, 1967-68. *Hesperia* **38**, 343-81.

Jarman, M. R. (1969) The prehistory of Upper Pleistocene and Recent cattle. Part 1: East Mediterranean, with reference to North-West Europe. *Proc. prehist. Soc.* **35**, 236-66.

(1971) Culture and economy in the north Italian Neolithic. *Wld Archaeol.* **2**, 255-65.

Jarman, M. R. & Jarman, H. N. (1968) The fauna and economy of Early Neolithic Knossos. In Knossos Neolithic, Part II, by J. D. Evans, pp. 241-64. *A. Brit. Sch. Archaeol., Athens* **63**.

Jarman, M. R., Vita-Finzi, C. & Higgs, E. S. (In press) Site catchment analysis in archaeology. In *Settlement Patterns and Urbanisation*, ed. P. J. Ucko, G. W. Dimbleby and R. Tringham.

Jażdżewski, K. (1965) *Poland.* London: Thames and Hudson.

Jennings, J. D. (1957) Danger Cave. Memoir 14, Society of American Archeology. *Am. Antiq.* **23** (2: 2).

Jéquier, J.-P. (1963) In Seeberg, Burgäschisee-Süd; Die Tierreste, by J. Boessneck, J.-P. Jéquier & H. R. Stampfli. *Acta Bernensia* **2**, Teil 3.

Jewell, P. A. (1962) Changes in size and type of cattle from prehistoric to mediaeval times in Britain. *Z. Tierzücht. ZüchtBiol.* **77**, 159-67.

(1963) Cattle from British archaeological sites. In *Man and Cattle*, ed. A. E. Mourant & F. E. Zeuner, pp. 80-101. *Occ. Pap. R. anthrop. Inst.* **18**.

(1966a) The concept of home range in mammals. In *Play, Exploration and Territory in Mammals*, ed. P. A. Jewell & C. Loizos, pp. 85-109. *Symp. zool. Soc. Lond.* **18**.

(1966b) Breeding season and recruitment in some British mammals confined on small islands. In *Comparative*

Biology of Reproduction in Mammals, ed. I. W. Rowlands, pp. 89-116. *Symp. zool. Soc. Lond.* **15**.

Johansen, K. F. (1914-19) Une station du plus ancien âge de la pierre dans la tourbière de Svaerdborg. *Mém. Antiq. du Nord*, 241-359.

Johnson, L. A. S. (1970) Rainbow's end: the quest for an optimal taxonomy. *Syst. Zool.* **19**, 203-39.

Jørgensen, S. (1956) Kongemosen-Endnu en Aamose-Boplads fra aeldre Stenalder. *Kuml*, 23-40.

Julander, O., Robinette, W. L. & Jones, D. A. (1961) Relation of summer range condition to mule deer productivity. *J. Wildl. Mgmt* **25**, 54-60.

Kelsall, J. P. (1960) Co-operative studies of the barren-ground caribou. *Wildl. Mgmt Bull., Ottawa*, ser. 1, **15**.

Kenyon, K. M. (1957) Excavations at Jericho. *Palest. Explor. Q.* **89**, 101-7.

(1965) *Archaeology in the Holy Land*, 2nd ed. London: Methuen.

(1969) The origins of the Neolithic. *Advmt Sci., Lond.* **26**, 144-60.

Kettlewell, H. B. D. (1961) The phenomenon of industrial melanism in Lepidoptera. *A. Rev. Ent.* **6**, 245-62.

King, J. E. (1962) Report on animal bones. In Excavations at the Maglemosian sites at Thatcham, Berkshire, by J. Wymer, pp. 355-61. *Proc. prehist. Soc.* **28**.

Kirkbride, D. (1966) Five seasons at the Pre-pottery Neolithic village of Beidha in Jordan. *Palest. Explor. Q.* **98**, 8-72.

Klein, D. R. (1970) Tundra ranges north of the boreal forest. *J. Range Mgmt* **23**, 8-14.

Klein, D. R. & Olson, S. T. (1960) Natural mortality patterns of deer in Southeast Alaska. *J. Wildl. Mgmt* **24**, 80-8.

Klein, R. G. (1969) *Man and Culture in the Late Pleistocene.* San Francisco: Chandler.

Knorre, E. P. (1961) Results and perspectives of moose domestication. *Pap. Pechora-Ilych State Reservation* **9**, 5-177. (Translation in files of Canadian Wildlife Service, Ottawa.)

Kuckuck, H. (1970) Primitive wheats. In *Genetic Resources in Plants – Their Exploration and Conservation*, ed. O. H. Frankel & E. Bennett, pp. 249-66. Oxford and Edinburgh: Blackwell Scientific Publications.

Kurtén, B. (1959) Rates of evolution in fossil mammals. *Cold Spring Harb. Symp. quant. Biol.* **24**, 205-15.

(1965) The Carnivora of the Palestine caves. *Acta zool. fenn.* **107**, 1-74.

(1967) Some quantitative approaches to dental micro-evolution. *J. dent. Res.* **46**, 817-28.

(1968) *Pleistocene Mammals of Europe.* London: Weidenfeld and Nicolson.

Lacam, R., Niederlender, A. & Vallois, H.-V. (1944) Le gisement mésolithique du Couzoul de Gramat. *Archs Inst. Paléont. hum.* **21**.

Landauer, W. & Chang, T. K. (1949) The Ancon or Otter sheep. History and genetics. *J. Hered.* **40**, 105-12.

Lang, H. (1952) Zur späteiszeitlichen Vegetations- und Florengeschichte Südwestdeutschlands. *Flora* **139**, 243-94.

Laplace-Jauretche, G. (1953) Les couches à escargots des cavernes pyrénéennes et le problème de l'Arisien de Piette. *Bull. Soc. préhist. fr.* **50**, 199-211.

Lawrence, B. (1967) Early domestic dogs. *Z. Säugetierk.* **32** (1), 44-59.

Lee, R. B. (1968) What hunters do for a living, or how to make out on scarce resources. In *Man the Hunter*, ed. R. B. Lee & I. DeVore, pp. 30-48. Chicago: Aldine.

(1969) ! Kung Bushman subsistence: an input-output analysis. In *Environment and Cultural Behaviour*, ed. A. P. Vayda, pp. 47-79. Garden City, New York: Natural History Press.

Leeds, A. (1965) Reindeer herding and Chukchi social institutions. In *Man, Culture, and Animals*, ed. A. Leeds & A. P. Vayda, pp. 87-128. Washington, D.C.: American Association Advancement Science.

Legnani, F. & Stradi, F. (1963) Gli scavi nella caverna dei Ciclami nel Carso triestino. *Atti VII Riun. scient. Ist. ital. Preist. Protost.* 31-8.

Leopold, A. S. & Darling, F. F. (1953) *Wildlife in Alaska.* New York: Ronald Press.

Leroi-Gourhan, A. (1961) Les fouilles d'Arcy-sur-Cure (Yonne). *Gallia Préhist.* **4**, 3-16.

(1965) *Préhistoire de l'Art Occidental.* Paris: L. Mazenod.

Lilienfield, F. A. (1951) H. Kihara: Genome-analysis in *Triticum* and *Aegilops*. X. Concluding review. *Cytologia* **16**, 101-23.

Lindemann, W. (1956) Transplantation of game in Europe and Asia. *J. Wildl. Mgmt* **20**, 68-70.

Loesch, A. (1954) *The Economics of Location*, English edition. New Haven: Yale University Press.

Loeser, C. J. (1968) The rationalization of the global distribution of domesticated animals. *J. dev. Areas* **3**, 67-76.

Long, C. A. (1969) An analysis of patterns of variation in some representative mammalia. Part 2: studies on the nature and correlation of measures of variation. In *Contributions in Mammalogy*, ed. J. Knox Jones, Jr., pp. 289-302. Lawrence: University of Kansas Press.

Lumley, H. de (1969) Une cabane acheuléenne dans la Grotte du Lazaret (Nice). *Mem. Soc. préhist. fr.* **7**.

Lundelius, E. L., Jr. (1967) Late-Pleistocene and Holocene faunal history of central Texas. In *Pleistocene Extinctions*, ed. P. S. Martin & H. E. Wright, Jr., pp.

287-319. New Haven and London: Yale University Press.

Lynge, B. (1921) Studies on the lichen flora of Norway. *Skr. VidenskSelsk. Christiania* Mat.-naturv. Kl. 1 7.

McBurney, C. B. M. (1967) *The Haua Fteah (Cyrenaica) and the Stone Age of the South-east Mediterranean.* Cambridge: Cambridge University Press.

McMeekan, C. P. (1940, 1941) Growth and development in the pig with special reference to carcass quality and characters. *J. agric. Sci., Camb.* **30**, 276-344, 387-436, 511-69, **31**, 1-49.

McMeekan, C. P. & Hammond, J. (1940) The relation of environmental conditions to breeding and selection for commercial types in pigs. *Emp. J. exp. Agric.* 8, 6-10.

MacPherson, A. H. (1965) The origin of diversity in mammals of the Canadian arctic tundra. *Syst. Zool.* **14**, 153-73.

Madariaga, B. (1963) Análisis paleontológico de la fauna terrestre y marina de la Cueva de la Chora. In Cueva de la Chora (Santander), by J. González Echegaray, M. A. García Guinea & A. Begines Ramírez, pp. 51-76. *Excavaciones Arqueológicas en España* **26**.

Malavolti, F. (1951-2) Richerche di preistoria emiliana: scavi nella stazione neo-eneolitica del Pescale (Modena). *Bull. Paletn. ital.* 8 (4), 13-38.

Mangelsdorf, P. C. (1965) The evolution of maize. In *Essays on Crop Plant Evolution*, ed. Sir J. Hutchinson, pp. 23-49. Cambridge: Cambridge University Press.

Mangelsdorf, P. C., MacNeish, R. S. & Galinat, W. C. (1964) Domestication of corn. *Science, N.Y.* **143**, 538-45.

Mason, I. L. (1963) In *Man and Cattle*, ed. A. E. Mourant & F. E. Zeuner, pp. 18-19. *Occ. Pap. R. anthrop. Inst.* **18**.

Mayr, E. (1963) *Animal Species and Evolution.* Cambridge, Mass.: Belknap Press.

Mellaart, J. (1964) Excavations at Çatal Hüyük, 1963. *Anatol. Stud.* **14**, 39-120.

(1970*a*) *Excavations at Hacilar.* Edinburgh: Edinburgh University Press.

(1970*b*) *Anatolian Neolithic settlement patterns.* London research seminar on Archaeology and related subjects, meeting on 'Settlement Patterns and Urbanisation', Dec. 1970.

Méroc, L. (1967) Circonscription de Midi-Pyrénées. *Gallia Préhist.* **10**, 389-411.

Millotte, J.-P. (1967) Circonscription de Franche-Comté. *Gallia Préhist.* **10**, 365-87.

Movius, H. L. (1942) *The Irish Stone Age.* Cambridge: Cambridge University Press.

(1953) The Mousterian cave of Teshik Tash, South-eastern Uzbekistan, Central Asia. *Bull. Am. Sch. prehist. Res.* **17**, 11-71.

(1966) The hearths of the Upper Perigordian and Aurignacian horizons at the Abri Pataud, les Eyzies (Dordogne), and their possible significance. In *Recent Studies in Paleoanthropology*, ed. J. D. Clark & F. C. Howell, pp. 296-325. *Am. Anthrop. (Spec. Publs)* **68** (2).

Müller, H.-H. (1959) Die Tierreste von Alt-Hannover. *Hannov. Gesch.* **12**, 181-259.

Murie, A. (1944) The wolves of Mt McKinley. *Fauna natn. Pks. U.S.* **5**.

Murray, J. (1970) *The First European Agriculture.* Edinburgh: Edinburgh University Press.

Musil, R. (1970) Domestication of the dog already in the Magdalenian? *Anthropologie* 8 (1), 87-8.

Neel, J. V. (1970) Lessons from a 'primitive' people. *Science, N.Y.* **170**, 815-22.

Neuville, R. (1951) Le paléolithique et le mésolithique du Désert de Judée. *Archs Inst. Paléont. hum.* **24**.

Newhouse, J. (1954) *Reindeer are wild too.* London: John Murray.

Nicolăescu-Plopşor, C. S. & Păunescu, A. (1961) Azilianul de la Baile Herculane în lumina noilor cercetări. *Studii Cerc. Istorie Veche* **12**, 203-13.

Niethammer, G. (1963) *Die Einbürgerung von Säugetieren und Vögeln in Europa.* Hamburg and Berlin: Paul Parey.

Obermaier, H. (1924) *Fossil Man in Spain.* New Haven: Yale University Press.

Paccard, M. (1952) Le gisement sauveterrien et néolithique de la grotte d'Unang, Vaucluse. *Bull. Soc. préhist. fr.* **49**, 226-9.

(1956) Du Magdalénien en Vaucluse: l'Abri Soubeyras à Ménerbes. *Cah. ligur. Préhist. Archéol.* **5**, 3-33.

Palma di Cesnola, A. (1962) Contributi alla conoscenza delle industrie epigravettiane nell'Italia centro-meridionale. *Riv. Sci. preist.* **17** (1), 1-75.

Palma di Cesnola, A. & Borzatti von Löwenstern, E. (1963) Gli scavi dell'Istituto Italiano di Preistoria e Protostoria nel Salento durante l'ultimo triennia. *Atti VIII Riun. scient. Ist. ital. Preist. Protost.* 27-43.

Păunescu, A. (1964) Cu privire la perioda de Sfîrşit a Epipaleoliticului în Nord-Vestul şi Nord-Estul Romîniei şi unele persistente de lui în neoliticul vechi. *Studii Cerc. Istorie Veche* **15**, 321-36.

Payne, S. (1968) The origins of domestic sheep and goats: a reconsideration in the light of the fossil evidence. *Proc. prehist. Soc.* **34**, 368-84.

(1969*a*) Animal bones. In Excavations at Porto Cheli and vicinity, preliminary report, II: the Franchthi Cave, 1967-68, by T. W. Jacobsen, pp. 350-4. *Hesperia* **38**.

(1969*b*) A metrical distinction between sheep and goat

metacarpals. In *The Domestication and Exploitation of Plants and Animals*, ed. P. J. Ucko & G. W. Dimbleby, pp. 295-306. London: Duckworth.

Peek, J. M., Lovaas, A. L. & Rouse, R. A. (1967) Population changes within the Gallatin elk herd, 1932-65. *J. Wildl. Mgmt* **31**, 304-16.

Péquart, M. & Péquart, S. J. (1954) *Hoëdic. Deuxième station nécropole du Mésolithique côtier Armoricain.* Anvers: De Sikkel.

Péquart, M., Péquart, S. J., Boule, M. & Vallois, H. V. (1937) Téviec. Station-nécropole Mésolithique du Morbihan. *Archs. Inst. Paléont. hum.* **18**.

Percival, J. (1921) *The Wheat Plant.* London: Duckworth.

Pericot García, L. (1942) *La Cueva del Parpalló (Gandia).* Madrid: Instituto Diego Velazquez.

(1945) La cueva de la Cocina (Dos Aguas). *Archos Prehist. Levant.* **2**, 39-72.

Perkins, D. (1964) Prehistoric fauna from Shanidar, Iraq. *Science, N.Y.* **144**, 1565-6.

(1966) The fauna from Madamagh and Beidha, a preliminary report. In Five seasons at the Pre-pottery Neolithic village of Beidha in Jordan, by D. Kirkbride, pp. 66-7. *Palest. Explor. Q.* **98**.

(1969) Fauna of Çatal Hüyük: evidence for early cattle domestication in Anatolia. *Science, N.Y.* **164**, 177-9.

Perkins, D. & Daly, P. (1968) A hunters' village in Neolithic Turkey. *Scient. Am.* **219**, 97-106.

Perrot, J. (1960) Le gisement Natoufien de Mallaha (Eynan), Israël. *Anthropologie, Paris* **70**, 437-83.

Peters, E. (1934) Das Mesolithikum der oberen Donau. *Germania* **18**, 81-9.

Peterson, R. L. (1957) Changes in the mammalian fauna of Ontario. In *Changes in the Fauna of Ontario*, ed. F. A. Urquhart, pp. 43-58. Toronto: University of Toronto Press.

Picton, H. D. (1961) Differential Hunter Harvest of elk in two Montana herds. *J. Wildl. Mgmt* **25**, 415-21.

Pidoplichko, I. G. (1969) *Pozdnepaleoliticheskie Zhilishtcha iz Kostei Mamonta na Ukraine. (Late Paleolithic Dwellings of Mammoth Bones in the Ukraine.)* Kiev: Akademii Nauk Ukrainskoi SSR Institut Zoologii.

Piette, E. (1906a) Études d'ethnographie préhistorique: 10-1. Le chevêtre. *Anthropologie, Paris* **17**, 27-53.

(1906b) Fibules Pleistocènes. *Rev. Préhist.* **1**, 3-15.

Pinchot, G. B. (1970) Marine farming. *Scient. Am.* **223**, 14-21.

Posselt, J. (1963) The domestication of the eland. *Rhod. J. agric. Res.* **1**, 81-7.

Poulain-Josien, T. (1964) In Gisements tardenoisiens de l'Aisne, by J. Hinout, pp. 93-4. *Gallia Préhist.* **7**.

Prausnitz, M. W. (1959) The first agricultural settlements in Galilee. *Israel Explor. J.* **9**, 166-74.

Radmilli, A. M. (1953) Gli scavi della Grotta Polesini (Ponte Lucano, Tivoli). *Bull. Paletn. ital.* **8** (5), 23-31.

(1963) Il Mesolitico nel Carso triestino. *Atti VII Riun. scient. Ist. ital. Preist. Protost.* 39-43.

Radmilli, A. M. & Cremonesi, G. (1963) Note di preistoria abruzzese. *Atti VII Riun. scient. Ist. ital. Preist. Protost.* 127-53.

Raikes, R. (1967) *Water, Weather and Prehistory.* London: John Baker.

Ravikovitch, S. (1968) *Soil Map of Israel.* Jerusalem: Hebrew University Faculty of Agric. Rehovot.

Reed, C. A. (1960) A review of the archaeological evidence on animal domestication in the prehistoric Near East. In Prehistoric investigations in Iraqi Kurdistan, by R. J. Braidwood & B. Howe, pp. 119-45. *Studies in Ancient Oriental Civilization* **31**.

(1961) Osteological evidence for prehistoric domestication in southwestern Asia. *Z. Tierzücht. ZüchtBiol.* **76**, 31-8.

(1965) Imperial Sassanian hunting of pig and fallow-deer, and problems of survival of these animals today in Iran. *Postilla* **92**, 1-23.

(1969) The pattern of animal domestication in the prehistoric Near East. In *The Domestication and Exploitation of Plants and Animals*, ed. P. J. Ucko & G. W. Dimbleby, pp. 361-80. London: Duckworth.

Reiners, W. A. & Reiners, N. W. (1970) Energy and nutrient dynamics of forest floras in Minnesota forests. *J. Ecol.* **58**, 497-519.

Renfrew, J. M. (1969) The archaeological evidence for the domestication of plants: methods and problems. In *The Domestication and Exploitation of Plants and Animals*, ed. P. J. Ucko & G. W. Dimbleby, pp. 149-72. London: Duckworth.

Requate, H. (1958) Die Knochenreste von Pinnberg-Ahrensberg. In *Die Funde vom Pinnberg*, by A. Rust, pp. 26-7. Neumünster: Karl Wachholtz.

Reverdin, L. (1930) La station préhistorique du Col des Roches près du Locle (Neuchâtel). *Jber. schweiz. Ges. Urgesch.* **22**, 141-58.

Richter, C. P. (1954) The effects of domestication and selection on the behaviour of the Norway rat. *J. natn. Cancer Inst.* **15**, 727-38.

Riley, R. (1965) Cytogenetics and the evolution of wheat. In *Essays on Crop Plant Evolution*, ed. Sir J. Hutchinson, pp. 103-22. Cambridge: Cambridge University Press.

Riley, R., Unrau, J. & Chapman, V. (1958) Evidence on the origin of the B genome of wheat. *J. Hered.* **49**, 91-8.

Roe, F. G. (1951) *The North American Buffalo.* Toronto: University of Toronto Press.

Roehrs, M. (1961) Biologische Anschauungen über Begriff

und Wesen der Domestikation. *Z. Tierzücht. Zücht-Biol.* **76**, 7-23.

Rolls, E. C. (1969) *They all ran wild.* Sydney: Angus and Robertson.

Rudebeck, G. (1950) The choice of prey and mode of hunting of predatory birds with special reference to their selective effect. *Oikos* **2**, 65-88.

    (1951) The choice of prey and mode of hunting of predatory birds with special reference to their selective effect. *Oikos* **3**, 200-31.

Ruiter, L. de (1958) Natural selection in *Cepaea nemoralis. Archs. Neerl. Zool.* **12**, 571-3.

Russell, J. C. (1958) Late ancient and mediaeval populations. *Trans. Am. phil. Soc.* **48** (3), 1-152.

Rust, A. (1943) *Die Alt- und Mittelsteinzeitlichen Funde von Stellmoor.* Neumünster in Holstein: Archäologisches Institut des Deutschen Reiches.

Ryder, M. L. (1969) Changes in the fleece of sheep following domestication (with a note on the coat of cattle). In *The Domestication and Exploitation of Plants and Animals*, ed. P. J. Ucko & G. W. Dimbleby, pp. 495-521. London: Duckworth.

Sahlins, M. D. (1968) In *Man the Hunter*, ed. R. B. Lee & I. DeVore, pp. 85-9. Chicago: Aldine.

Salisbury, Sir E. (1961) *Weeds and Aliens.* London: Collins.

Salmon, S. C. & Hanson, A. A. (1964) *The Principles and Practice of Agricultural Research.* London: Leonard Hill.

Sarasin, F. (1918) In Die steinzeitlichen Stationen des Birstales zwischen Basel und Delsberg, by H. G. Stehlin. *Neue Denkschr. schweiz. naturf. Ges.* **54** (2), 79-291.

Sarasin, F. & Stehlin, H. G. (1924) Die Magdalénien-Station bei Ettingen (Baselland). *Denkschr. schweiz. naturf. Ges.* **59** (1), 1-26.

Sarauw, G. F. L. (1911) Maglemose. Ein steinzeitlicher Wohnplatz im Moor bei Mullerup auf Seeland, verglichen mit verwandten Fundten. *Prähist. Z.* **3**, 52-104.

Sarkar, P. & Stebbins, G. L. (1956) Morphological evidence concerning the origin of the B genome in wheat. *Am. J. Bot.* **43**, 297-304.

Schaller, G. B. (1967) *The Deer and the Tiger.* Chicago and London: University of Chicago Press.

    (1968) Hunting behaviour of the cheetah in the Serengeti National Park, Tanzania. *East. Afr. Wildl. J.* **6**, 95-100.

Scheffer, V. B. (1951) The rise and fall of a reindeer herd. *Sci. Monthly* **73**, 356-61.

Schmid, E. (1963) Die Tierknochen. In Birsmatten-Basisgrotte, by H.-G. Bandi, pp. 93-100. *Acta Bernensia* **1**.

Schwanitz, F. (1966) *The Origin of Cultivated Plants*, English edition. Cambridge: Harvard University Press.

Scott, J. P. (1958) *Animal Behaviour.* Chicago: University of Chicago Press.

Scotter, G. W. (1965) Reindeer ranching in Fennoscandia. *J. Range Mgmt* **18**, 301-5.

Semenov, S. A. (1964) *Prehistoric Technology*, English edition. London: Cory, Adams and Mackay.

Shikama, T. & Okafujı, G. (1958) Quaternary cave and fissure deposits and their fossils in Akiyosi District, Yamaguti Prefecture. *Sci. Rep. Yokohama natn. Univ. Sect. II. Biological and geological sciences* **7**, 43-103.

Shirokogoroff, S. M. (1935) *Psychomental Complex of the Tungus.* London: Kegan, Paul, Trench, Trubner.

Silver, I. A. (1969) The ageing of domestic animals. In *Science in Archaeology*, ed. D. Brothwell & E. S. Higgs, 2nd ed., pp. 283-302. London: Thames and Hudson.

Simpson, G. G., Roe, A. & Lewontin, R. C. (1960) *Quantitative Zoology*, revised ed. London and Burlingame: Harcourt Brace and Co.

Skinner, M. F. & Kaisen, O. C. (1947) The fossil *Bison* of Alaska and a preliminary revision of the genus. *Bull. Am. Mus. nat. Hist.* **89**, 123-256.

Slicher van Bath, B. H. (1963) *The Agrarian History of Western Europe A.D. 500-1850.* London: Edward Arnold.

Slobodkin, L. B. (1962) *Growth and Regulation of Animal Populations.* New York: Holt.

Smalley, I. J. (1968) The loess deposits and Neolithic Culture of northern China. *Man* **3** (2), 224-41.

Smith, H. S. (1969) Animal domestication and animal cult in dynastic Egypt. In *The Domestication and Exploitation of Plants and Animals*, ed. P. J. Ucko & G. W. Dimbleby, pp. 307-14. London: Duckworth.

Snyder, L. L. (1957) Changes in the avifauna of Ontario. In *Changes in the Fauna of Ontario*, ed. F. A. Urquhart, pp. 26-42. Toronto: University of Toronto Press.

Sonneville-Bordes, D. de (1960) *Le Paléolithique supérieur en Périgord.* Bordeaux: Delmas.

Spencer, D. L. & Lensink, C. J. (1970) The muskox of Nunivak Island, Alaska. *J. Wildl. Mgmt* **34**, 1-15.

Spinage, C. A. (1969) Territoriality and social organisation of the Uganda defassa waterbuck, *Kobus defassa ugandae. J. Zool.* **159**, 329-61.

Spurway, H. (1955) The causes of domestication: an attempt to integrate some ideas of Konrad Lorenz with evolutionary theory. *J. Genet.* **53**, 325-62.

Stamp, L. D. (1958) The measurement of land resources. *Geogrl. Rev.* **48**, 1-15.

Steen, E. (1968) Some aspects of the nutrition of semi-domestic reindeer. *Symp. zool. Soc. London* **21**, 117-28.

Stefansson, V. (1943) *The Friendly Arctic*. New York: Macmillan.

(1946) *Not by Bread Alone*. New York: Macmillan.

Steffensen, J. (1958) Stature as a criterion of the nutritional level of Viking Age Icelanders. *Árbók hins Íslenzka Fornleifafélags, Third Viking Congress*, 39-51.

Stewart, D. R. M. (1963) Development of wildlife as an economic asset. *Bull. epizoot. Dis. Afr.* **11**, 167-71.

Strickon, A. (1965) The Euro-American ranching complex. In *Man, Culture, and Animals*, ed. A. Leeds and A. P. Vayda, pp. 229-58. Washington, D.C.: American Association Advancement Science.

Struever, S. (1968) Flotation techniques for the recovery of small-scale archaeological remains. *Am. Antiq.* **33**, 353-62.

Sumner, F. B. (1909) Some effects of external conditions upon the white mouse. *J. exp. Zool.* **7**, 97-155.

Taber, R. D. (1961) Wildlife administration and harvest in Poland. *J. Wildl. Mgmt* **25**, 353-63.

Takahashi, R. (1955) The origin and evolution of cultivated barley. *Adv. Genet.* **7**, 227-66.

(1963) Further studies in the phylogenetic differentiation of cultivated barley. *Barley Genetics I. Proc. 1st int. Barley Genet. Symp.* 19-31.

Talbot, L. M., Payne, W. J. A., Ledger, H. P., Verdcourt, L. D. & Talbot, M. H. (1965) The meat production potential of wild animals in Africa. *Tech. Commun. Commonw. Bur. Anim. Breed. Genet.* **16**.

Tåning, A. V. (1952) Experimental study of meristic characters in fishes. *Biol. Rev.* **27**, 169-93.

Taschini, M. (1964) Il livello mesolitico del Riparo Blanc al Monte Circeo. *Bull. Paletn. ital.* **15** (73), 65-88.

Taylor, J. (1968) *Salmonella* in wild animals. *Symp. zool. Soc. Lond.* **24**, 51-73.

Taylor, W. E. J., Jr. (1966) An archaeological perspective on Eskimo economy. *Antiquity* **40**, 114-20.

Teal, J. J., Jr. (1958) Golden fleece of the arctic. *Atlantic* **201**, 76-81.

(1970) Domesticating the wild and woolly musk ox. *Natn. geogr. Mag.* **126**.

Telfer, E. S. (1967) Comparison of moose and deer winter range in Nova Scotia. *J. Wildl. Mgmt* **31**, 418-25.

Tener, J. S. (1965) *Muskoxen in Canada*. Ottawa: Queen's Printer.

Thomas, S. E. (1954) Appendix I. Sjöholmen, Site 179. In The chronology of the Stone Age settlement of Scania, Sweden. I. The Mesolithic settlement, by C.-A. Althin, pp. 169-87. *Acta archaeol. Lund.* ser. 4, **1**.

Thomsen, T. & Jessen, A. (1902-7) Une trouvaille de l'ancien âge de la pierre. La trouvaille de Braband. *Mém. Antiq. du Nord*, 162-232.

Thomson, D. F. (1939) The seasonal factor in human culture. *Proc. prehist. Soc.* **10**, 209-21.

Tozzi, C. (1966) Il giacimento mesolitico de Capo d'Acqua (l'Aquila). *Bull. Paletn. ital.* **17** (75), 13-25.

Trapnell, C. G. (1933) Vegetational types in the Godthaab fjord. *J. Ecol.* **21**, 294-334.

Treus, V. & Kravchenko, D. (1968) Methods of rearing and economic utilization of eland in the Askaniya-Nova Zoological Park. *Symp. zool. Soc. Lond.* **21**, 395-411.

Tringham, R. (1969) Animal domestication in the Neolithic cultures of the south-west part of Europaean U.S.S.R. In *The Domestication and Exploitation of Plants and Animals*, ed. P. J. Ucko & G. W. Dimbleby, pp. 381-92. London: Duckworth.

Troels-Smith, J. (1953) Ertebøllekultur-Bondekultur. *Aarb. f. nord. Oldk. og Hist.* **43**, 5-62.

Turkin, N. V. & Satunin, K. A. (1902) *Zveri Rossii*. Quoted in Results and perspectives of moose domestication, by E. P. Knorre. *Pap. Pechora-Ilych State Reservation* **9**, 5-177. (Translation in files of Canadian Wildlife Service, Ottawa.)

Turkowski, L. (1969) Peasant agriculture in the Judean Hills. *Palest. Explor. Q.* **101**, 21-33.

Turville-Petre, F. (1932) Excavations in the Mugharet el Kebarah. *J. R. anthrop. Inst.* **62**, 271-6.

Valoch, K., Pelíšek, J., Musil, R., Kovanda, J. & Opravil, E. (1969) Die Erforschung der Kůlna-Höhle bei Sloup im Mährischen Karst (Tschechoslowakei). *Quartär* **20**, 1-45.

van Zeist, W. (1969) Reflections on prehistoric environment in the Near East. In *The Domestication and Exploitation of Plants and Animals*, ed. P. J. Ucko & G. W. Dimbleby, pp. 35-46. London: Duckworth.

van Zeist, W. & Bottema, S. (1966) Palaeobotanical investigations at Ramad. *Ann. Arch. Arabs Syriennes* **16**, 179-80.

van Zeist, W. & Casparie, W. A. (1968) Wild einkorn and barley from Tell Mureybit in Northern Syria. *Acta bot. neerl.* **17**, 44-55.

Vaufrey, R. (1928) Le paléolithique italien. *Archs Inst. Paléont. hum.* **3**.

(1951) Étude paléontologique I. Mammifères. In Le paléolithique et le mésolithique du Désert de Judée by R. Neuville, pp. 198-217. *Archs Inst. Paléont. hum.* **24**.

Vibe, Chr. (1967) Arctic animals in relation to climatic fluctuations. *Meddr Grønland* **170** (5).

Vilain, R. (1966) Le gisement de Sous-Balme à Culoz (Ain)

et ses industries microlithiques. *Docums Lab. Géol. Fac. Sci. Lyon* **13**.

Vita-Finzi, C. (1966) The Hasa Formation. *Man* **1**, 386-90.

(1969*a*) Fluvial geology. In *Science in Archaeology*, ed. D. Brothwell & E. S. Higgs, 2nd ed., pp. 135-50, London: Thames and Hudson.

(1969*b*) *The Mediterranean Valleys*. Cambridge: Cambridge University Press.

Vita-Finzi, C. & Higgs, E. S. (1970) Prehistoric economy in the Mount Carmel area of Palestine: site catchment analysis. *Proc. prehist. Soc.* **36**, 1-37.

Waechter, J. d'A. & Seton-Williams, V. M. (1938) The excavations at the Wadi Dhobai 1937-38. *J. Palest. orient. Soc.* **18**.

Weber, W. (1950) Genetical studies on the skeleton of the mouse. 3. Skeletal variation in wild populations. *J. Genet.* **50**, 174-8.

Wendorf, F. (1968) Late Palaeolithic sites in Egyptian Nubia. In *The Prehistory of Nubia*, ed. F. Wendorf, vol. 2, pp. 791-953. Dallas: Fort Burgwin Research Center & Southern Methodist University Press.

Westerby, E. (1927) *Stenalderbopladser ved Klampenborg*. Copenhagen: C. Λ. Reitzel.

Whitehead, G. K. (1964) *The Deer of Great Britain and Ireland*. London: Routledge and Kegan Paul.

Wiener, G. & Purser, A. F. (1957) The influence of four levels of feeding on the position and eruption of incisor teeth in sheep. *J. agric. Sci., Camb.* **49**, 51-5.

Wilkinson, P. F. (1971*a*) Oomingmak: a model for man-animal relationships in prehistory. *Curr. Anthrop.* (in press).

(1971*b*) The domestication of the musk ox. *Polar Rec.* (in press).

(1971*c*) The first verified occurrence of twinning in musk oxen. *J. Mammal.* **52**, 358.

(1971*d*) Neolithic postscript. *Antiquity* (in press).

(1972) Predation and prehistory in North America. In *Models in Archaeology*, ed. D. L. Clarke (in preparation). London: Methuen.

Windels, F. (1948) *The Lascaux Cave Paintings*. London: Faber and Faber.

Winge, H. (1900) In *Affaldsdynger fra Stenalderen i Danmark*, by A. P. Madsen, S. Müller, C. Neergaard, C. G. J. Petersen, E. Rostrup, K. J. V. Steenstrup & H. Winge. Copenhagen: C. A. Reitzel.

Woodburn, J. (1968) An introduction to Hadza ecology. In *Man the Hunter*, ed. R. B. Lee & I. DeVore, pp. 49-55. Chicago: Aldine.

Wright, B. S. (1960) Predation on big game in East Africa. *J. Wildl. Mgmt* **24**, 1-15.

Wynne-Edwards, V. C. (1962) *Animal Dispersion in Relation to Social Behaviour*. Edinburgh and London: Oliver and Boyd.

Wyss, R. (1957) Eine mesolithische Station bei Liesbergmühle (Kt. Bern). *Z. schweiz. Archäol. Kunstgesch.* **17** (1), 1-13.

Yazan, Y. & Knorre, Y. (1964) Domesticating elk in a Russian national park. *Oryx* **7**, 301-4.

Youngson, R. W. (1970) Rearing red deer calves in captivity. *J. Wildl. Mgmt* **34**, 467-70.

Zei, M. (1953) Esplorazione di grotte nei pressi di Sezze — Romano. *Bull. Paletn. ital.* **8** (5), 102-7.

Zervos, C. (1959) *L'Art de l'Epoque du Renne en France*. Paris: Cahiers d'Art.

Zeuner, F. E. (1963*a*) *A History of Domesticated Animals*. London: Hutchinson.

(1963*b*) The history of domestication of cattle. In *Man and Cattle*, ed. A. E. Mourant & F. E. Zeuner, pp. 9-19. *Occ. Pap. R. anthrop. Inst.* **18**.

Zimmerman, E. C. (1963) Nature of land biota. In *Man's Place in the Island Ecosystem*, ed. F. R. Fosberg, pp. 57-64. Honolulu: Bishop Museum Press.

Zimmermann, W. (1961) Zur Domestikation der Chinchillas. *Z. Tierzücht. ZüchtBiol.* **76**, 343-8.

Zohary, D. (1960) Studies on the origin of cultivated barley. *Bull. res. Coun. Israel* **9D**, 21-42.

(1965) Colonizer species in the wheat group. In *The Genetics of Colonizing Species*, ed. H. G. Baker & G. L. Stebbins, pp. 403-23. New York and London: Academic Press.

(1969) The progenitors of wheat and barley in relation to domestication and agricultural dispersion in the Old World. In *The Domestication and Exploitation of Plants and Animals*, ed. P. J. Ucko & G. W. Dimbleby, pp. 47-66. London: Duckworth.

(1970) Centers of diversity and centers of origin. In *Genetic Resources in Plants — Their Exploration and Conservation*, ed. O. H. Frankel & E. Bennett, pp. 33-42. Oxford and Edinburgh: Blackwell Scientific Publications.

NAME INDEX

Åberg, E., 21
Acanfora, M. O., 131
Aharoni, Y. et al., 172
Alessio, M. et al., 129
Alexander, J., 63, 64
Allan, W., 173
Allchin, F. R., 196
Allen, D., 94
Allibone, T. E., x
Altuna, J., 131
Anati, E., 169
Andreev, V. N., 166
Asdell, S. A., 74, 79

Baker, H. G., 22-3
Baker, R. R., 94
Banfield, A. W. F., 166
Barfield, L., 25
Barocelli, P., 131
Bar-Yosef, O., 120
Basse de Ménorval, E., 131
Bate, D. M. A., 119, 120
Bell, G. D. H., 16, 23
Belyaev, D. K., 88, 90, 108, 109
Berry, R. J., 87, 114
Bertram, C. K. R. & G. C. L., 110
Bigalke, R. C., 109
Binford, L. R., 11, 97
Binford, S. R., 97
Boessneck, J., 3, 71, 85, 95, 129
Bökönyi, S., 5, 7, 77, 83, 92, 111, 114, 121, 129, 135, 136
Bordes, F., 54
Borgoras, W. C., 101
Borzatti von Löwenstern, E., 130, 131
Bottema, S., 4, 21
Boule, M., 71
Braidwood, R. J., viii, 3, 8, 11, 22, 30
Bulmer, R., 6, 94, 110
Bunge, W., 32
Burt, W. H., 30
Burton, A. C., 98
Buth, G. M., 196
Butzer, K., 21

Callen, E. O., 10
Çambel, H., 3, 22
Candolle, A. de, 195
Carr-Saunders, A. M., 12, 29, 30
Carruthers, D., 6
Casparie, W. A., 17, 19
Chagnon, N. A. et al., 114
Chang, T. K., 74
Chaplin, R. E., 121
Chapman, V., 24
Chard, C. S., 117
Charles, J. A., ix, 25, 39-48
Childe, V. G., 11
Chisholm, M., 31, 33, 177
Christaller, W., 179
Chowdhury, K. A., 196
Clark, J. G. D., vii-x, 9, 10, 27, 131, 136, 179
Clason, A. T., 92, 131, 134, 135
Clot, A. B., 123

Clutton-Brock, J., 6, 120, 123
Colombo, B., 93
Coon, C. S., 49, 76, 121, 122
Cowan, I. McT., 87, 89
Cranstone, B. A. L., 114
Crawford, I. A., 41
Crisler, L., 94

Daly, P., 61, 84, 193, 194
Daniel, M. J., 133
Darling, F. F., 132, 134, 161, 167
Darlington, C. A., 196
Dart, R. A., 8
Davidson, P. E., 94
Degerbøl, M., 4, 85, 86, 90, 91, 162
de Meester, T., 193
Dennell, R. W., 26, 39, 48, 149-59
Dever, W. G., 124
Dewar, J. M., 94
Dimbleby, G. W., x, 11
Dimitrieva, E. L., 130
Doggett, H., 6, 195, 197
Dorst, J., 110
Drew, I. M., 84
Drinnan, R. E., 94
Ducos, P., 7, 75, 83, 92, 120, 121, 123, 124, 130, 131
Dumitrescu, V., 131
Dunstone, R. L., 17
Dyson, R. H. Jr., 91
Dzieciołowski, R., 134

Eaton, R. L., 8
Edholm, O. G., 98
Edwards, W. D., 86
Egorov, O. V., 162
Ehrlich, P. R., 6, 7, 87, 88
Elder, W. H., 95
Ellison, L., 22
Estes, R. D., 94
Evans, J. D., 4, 21, 194
Evans, L. T., 17
Ewbank, J. et al., 78
Ewer, R. F., 87

Faegri, K., 81
Fisher, R. A., 196
Fitte, P., 54
Flannery, K. V., 3, 19, 26, 30, 85, 92, 115, 121, 122, 150
Fletcher Valls, D., 131
Foster, J. B., 6, 88, 89
Frank, P. W. et al., 87
Fredskild, B., 85
French, D. H., 53, 63, 64, 181-90, 191
Frenzel, F., 115
Fuller, W. A., 94

Gaillard, C., 122
Galbreath, E. C., 4
Galinat, W. C., 7, 15
Garrod, D. A. E., 9, 119, 120
Garstang, J., 190
Gejvall, N.-G., 69, 193
Georgiev, G. I., 152, 156

Gervais, P., 109
Gill, N. T., 20, 23
Goddard, J., 94
Godwin, H., vii, x, 39
Gonzalez Echegaray, J., 120
Gorman, C., 9, 11
Grigson, C., 71, 85, 87
Grimes, W. F., x
Groves, C. P. *et al.*, 6
Gubser, N. J., 95
Gulati, A. M., 196
Guthrie, R. D., 91

Hadwen, S., 161
Hagedoorn, A. L., 86
Hancock, D. A., 94
Hanson, A. A., 20
Harlan, J. R., 16, 18, 22
Harris, D. R., 10
Hartley, W., 117
Haskin, H. H., 94
Hawkes, C. F. C., vii
Hawkes, J. G., 22
Heiser, C. B., 22
Helbaek, H., 4, 7, 11, 15, 16, 17, 18, 19, 25, 39, 150, 151, 158, 193
Hennessy, J. B., 171
Herre, W., 6, 83, 85, 87, 88, 90
Hester, J. J., 8, 25
Heusser, C. J., 86
Hickling, C. F., 110
Higgs, E. S., vii, viii, 3-13, 15, 26, 27-36, 39, 77, 84, 88, 95, 96, 97, 100, 111, 114, 118, 119, 124, 129, 131, 133, 164, 165, 167, 169, 197
Higham, C. F. W., 65, 92, 136
Hillman, G. C., 182-8
Ho, Ping-Ti, 9, 11
Hoare, W. H. B., 95
Hobler, P. M., 8
Hole, F., 3, 30, 85, 92, 122, 150, 158
Hooijer, D. A., 119
Hopf, M., 186
Howard, H. E., 29
Howe, B., 3, 8, 11, 30
Hughes, R. E., 171
Hutchinson, J. B., vii, x, 195-7

Iverson, J., 81, 91

Jacobsen, T. W., 63, 64, 194
Janaki Ammal, E. K., 196
Jarman, H. N., ix, 3, 5, 6, 13, 15-26, 39-48, 129, 193
Jarman, M. R., 3-13, 15, 39, 77, 78, 83-96, 111, 114, 123, 125-47, 193, 197
Jennings, J. D., 30
Jéquier, J.-P., 71, 85, 129, 132, 133
Jewell, P. A., 30, 85, 93
Johnson, L. A. S., 111
Jope, E. M., vii, x
Julander, O. *et al.*, 93

Kaisen, O. C., 90
Kelsall, J. P., 162
Kenyon, K. M., 120, 123, 124, 172
Kettlewell, H. B. D., 90
Kirkbride, D., 122
Klein, D. R., 93, 94, 117
Klein, R. G., 101
Knorre, E. P., 6, 13, 85, 108, 114, 115
Kollau, W., 71, 75, 78
Kravchenko, D., 108

Krog, H., 162
Kuckuck, H., 23
Kurtén, B., 78, 86, 90

Landauer, W., 74
Lang, H., 162
Lawrence, B., 4
Leakey, M. D., 101
Lee, R. B., 30, 116, 118
Leeds, A., 6, 108, 117
Legge, A. J., ix, 7, 25, 39-48, 97-103, 115, 119-24
Lensink, C. J., 93
Leopold, A. S., 161
Leroi-Gourhan, A., 84, 101
Lilienfield, F. A., 21, 24
Loesch, A., 179
Loeser, C. J., 109, 115, 117
Long, C. A., 91
Lumley, H. de, 101
Lundelius, E. L. Jr, 91
Lynge, B., 162

McBurney, C. B. M., 49, 66
McCrory, W., 87, 89
MacNeish, R. S., viii, 7, 15
MacPherson, A. H., 88, 91
Malavolti, F., 131
Mangelsdorf, P. C., 5, 7, 10, 15
Marriott, J., 64
Mason, I. L., 85
Mayr, E., 86
Mech, D., 94
Mellaart, J., 194
Merpert, N. I., 156
Morgan, L. H., 27
Movius, H. L., 101
Müller, H.-H., 132
Murie, A., 94
Murray, J., 135, 140
Musil, R., 4

Neel, J. V., 87
Neely, J. A., 3, 122, 150
Neuville, R., 120
Newhouse, J., 164
Niethammer, G., 116
Nietz, W. O., 109
Nilsson, S., 27
Nobis, G., 30

Okafuji, G., 4
Olson, S. T., 93, 94

Paccard, M., 131
Palmer, L., 161
Payne, R. J., 189
Payne, S., ix, 3, 44, 47, 49-81, 87, 90, 91, 125, 129, 136, 188-9, 190, 191-4
Peek, J. M. *et al.*, 93
Percival, J., 17-18, 19, 20
Pericot García, L., 131
Perkins, D., 3, 4, 7, 61, 84, 92, 121, 124, 188, 193, 194
Perrot, J., 120
Peterson, R. L., 91
Peyrony, D., 54
Phillips, C. W., x
Picton, H. D., 132-3
Pidoplichko, I. G., 4
Piette, E., 84
Piggott, S., vii

Pinchot, G. B., 110
Posselt, J., 108
Prausnitz, M. W., 171
Purser, A. F., 76

Raikes, R., 34
Raven, P. H., 6, 7, 87, 88
Ravikovitch, S., 169, 171, 175
Reed, C. A., 3, 4, 11, 85, 91, 112, 123, 132
Reiners, W. A., & N. W., 171
Renfrew, A. C., 63, 64
Renfrew, J. M., 4, 21, 24, 26
Reverdin, L., 131
Richter, C. P., 90, 108
Riley, R., 16, 18, 19, 23, 24
Roberts, J. A. F., 87
Roe, F. G., 95
Roehrs, M., 6, 87, 88, 90
Rolls, E. C., 109
Rudebeck, G., 94
Ruiter, L. de, 90
Russell, J. C., 179
Rust, A., 71, 75
Ryder, M. L., 90

Sahlins, M. D., 118
Salisbury, E., 22, 23, 150
Salmon, S. C., 20
Sarkar, P., 19, 24
Satunin, K. A., 115
Savkina, Z. P., 166
Schaller, G. B., 94
Scheffer, V. B., 161
Schmid, E., 129
Schwanitz, F., 16, 17, 20
Scotter, G. W., 109
Semenov, S. A., 9
Seton-Williams, V. M., 123
Seward, A., vii
Shikama, T., 4
Shirokogoroff, S. M., 6, 95
Silver, I. A., 76, 121
Simpson, G. G. et al., 89
Skinner, M. F., 90
Slicher van Bath, B. H., 140
Slobodkin, L. B., 12, 140
Smalley, I. J., 11
Smith, H. S., 115
Snyder, L. L., 91
Sonneville-Bordes, D. de, 54
Spencer, D. L., 93
Spinage, C. A., 167
Spurway, H., 114
Stamp, L. D., 36
Stampfli, H. R., 71, 85, 129
Stebbins, G. L., 19, 24
Steen, E., 166
Stefansson, V., 95, 101
Steffensen, J., 78
Streuver, S., 39
Strickon, A., 109

Sturdy, D. A., ix, 30, 161-8
Sumner, F. B., 90

Taber, R. D., 138
Takahashi, R., 24
Talbot, L. M. et al., 108, 116
Tåning, A. V., 90
Taylor, J., 110
Taylor, W. E. J. Jr, 115
Tchernov, E., 120
Teal, J. J. Jr, ix, 107
Telfer, E. S., 91
Tener, J. S., 88, 93
Thoday, J. M., 197
Thomson, D. F., 29
Todd, I. A., 193, 194
Trapnell, C. G., 162, 163
Treus, V., 108
Tringham, R., 6, 54
Turkin, N. V., 115
Turkowski, L., 176
Turner, A. J., 196
Turville-Petre, F., 119
Tyler, C., 79

Unrau, J., 24
Urquhart, A. E., 94

van Zeist, W., 4, 17, 19, 21, 22
Vaufrey, R., 120, 130
Vavilov, N. I., 195
Vear, K. C., 20, 23
Vibe, Chr., 166
Vilain, R., 131
Villeneuve, L. de, 71
Virri, T. J., 31
Vita-Finzi, C., viii, 8, 9, 26, 27-36, 118, 124, 131, 133, 164, 165, 167, 169
von Thünen, J. H., 30, 33

Waechter, J. d'A., 123
Weber, W., 87
Webley, D., 31, 169-80
Wendorf, F., 9, 25
West, R. G., vii
Wheeler, M., viii
Whitehead, G. K., 91, 132
Wiener, G., 76
Wilkinson, P. F., ix, 4, 6, 78, 83-96, 107-18, 123, 133, 197
Willey, G. R., 11
Windels, F., 84
Woodburn, J., 9, 95, 116
Wright, B. S., 94
Wynne-Edwards, V. C., 12, 28, 87, 131

Yazan, Y., 108
Youngson, R. W., 85

Zervos, C., 84
Zeuner, F. E., 5, 6, 8, 11, 12, 84, 85, 91, 109, 114, 115
Zimmermann, W., 109
Zohary, D., 16, 17, 21, 22, 23, 24, 25

GENERAL INDEX

Abri Pataud, 101
Abri Sous-Balme, 131
Aegilops
    modern distribution of, 21
    morphological changes in, 19, 23-4
Africa
    early agriculture in, 3, 195, 197
    modern exploitation strategies in, 95, 116-17
African buffalo, selective breeding of, 109
Ai', 172
Ain Mallaha, 8, 102, 103, 120
Aitzbitàrte, 131
Ali Kosh, 24, 39, 121, 123, 150
    domesticated animals at, 3, 4, 92
    domesticated cereals at, 16, 21, 157-9
allometry, 87
America
    early agriculture in, 3
    early domestication in, 4, 10, 195, 196
animal bones, 65-81
    analysis and interpretation of, 68-81, 89-90, 125, 188-9, 193
    calculation of number of individuals, 60-1, 68-9
    difficulty of identifying species, 77, 125-6
    improved recovery of, 59-61, 65
    as indicators of season of occupation, 78-9
    reasons for presence on site, 68
    relative importance of different species, 68-71
    representation of different age classes, 76-7
    standards for treatment and publication of, 123
animal husbandry,
    defined, 8
    new areas of, 107-10
    New World contribution to origins of, 196
    origins of, 3-13, 85-6, 132
    productivity of different species, 137-8
    transhumant, 172, 173
antler, seasonal availability of, 78, 79
Apple Creek, 39
Argissa-Magula, 3, 4, 129
Asia
    early agriculture in, 3
    early domestication in, 4, 11
Aşıklı Hüyük, 191, 193
Asprochaliko, 34, 97, 131
    cave climate of, 98-100, 103
Aşvan, 53, 186

Ban Kao, 9
Barley (England), 78
barley
    early domestication of, 4, 7, 15-26, 194
    introduction into Europe, 13
    modern distribution of wild form, 16, 21-3, 25
    origins of, 24-5
    preservation of, 151
bâtons de commandement as part of bridle, 84
Bedouin economy, 173, 175, 177, 179
Beidha, 24, 34, 123, 157
    barley at, 4, 7, 16, 17, 18, 158
    gazelle at, 122
    goat at, 4, 121, 123, 124
Belt Cave, 76, 122
Bergman's rule, 78, 86

Bethel, 172
birds, 78, 79, 194
    extension of range, 79
    selective predation by, 94
Birsmatten, 129, 130
bison, 126
    morphological changes in, 90-1
    selective predation on, 94, 95
bone tools, 76, 189
Bornholm, 151
Bos primigenius, 71, 89
Burgäschisee-Süd, *see* Seeberg . . .

Cambridge, Lion Yard, 54, 63
Can Hasan, 54, 59, 63, 71, 77, 191-4
    animal remains at, 188-9, 193, 194
    excavations at, 181-190
    houses at, 182
    plant remains at, 182-8, 194
caribou, 108, 114
    selective predation on, 94, 117
    sexual segregation among, 95
carnivores, morphological changes in, 88, 90
cassowary, domestication of, 110, 112
Çatal Hüyük, 4, 7, 181, 188, 190, 191, 194
cattle
    Chillingham, 88
    docility of modern, 85
    early domestication of, 4, 85, 194, 196
    introduction into Europe, 13, 125
    in Mesolithic and Neolithic sites, 126, 128, 135, 136, 193, 194
    size changes resulting from climatic change, 86
cave climates, 97-103
    measurement of, 97-100
Çayönü, 3, 4
cereals
    annual requirement of family group, 19
    changes of grain shape and size as indicators of domestication, 17, 20
    development of tough rachis, 4, 5, 6, 17-18, 19-20, 23, 196
    modern distribution of, 20-4
    see also individual plants
Chateauneuf-lez-Martigues, 130
Chevdar, 48, 151-4, 155, 156, 157, 158, 159
chinchilla, domestication of, 109-10
Chukchi skin house, 101
climatic change, 17, 21-2, 34, 86, 91, 119
Col des Roches, 131
Cova Negra, 131
crop plant evolution, 15, 195; *see also under* individual plants
crop rotation, 18, 138

deer, 93, 125-47
    selective predation on, 94, 95, 130-1
    see also red deer, roe deer, wapiti
Deh Luran Plain, 122
demographic characteristics
    as indicators of domestication, *see* domestication
    of human populations, 93
distance as limiting factor in exploitation, 30-2, 33
distribution of past animal populations, 91-2
Divostin, 129
docility of small breeds, supposed, 85

dog
 early domestication of, 4, 5, 6, 193, 194
 introduction into Europe, 13
 neglected by Eskimos, 85
 selective predation by, 94
domestication
 artistic and artefactual evidence for, 84, 115, 123
 biology of, 195-7
 criteria used to identify, 3-13, 83-96, 114; analysis of slaughter
  pattern, 121, 122-3; demographic characteristics of population, 3, 7, 71, 74, 75, 76-7, 92-5, 121, 193; morphological
  changes, 7, 16-17, 20, 89-91, 95-6, 121; size differences, 6,
  74-5, 77-8, 84-7, 89
 definitions of, 8, 15-16, 83, 96, 111-12
 developmental stages in, 114-15
 experimental, 107-18
 geographical evidence on early, 91-2, 115-16
 various models of origins and spread of, viii, 11-13, 15-16, 85,
  92, 125, 135
 see also individual animals and plants

economic prehistory, aims of, 13, 96, 112, 118
economies, prehistoric, 111-12
 conscious selective hunting, 133
 development of, 135-9
 herding, 133
 labour-intensive, 138-9
 mobile, 28-9, 30
 mobile-sedentary, 29, 188
 red deer-pig based, 126, 129, 130, 135, 136, 137
 sedentary, 29, 30, 124, 194
 sheep-goat-pig-cattle based, 129, 130, 135, 136, 139
einkorn
 early domestication of, 4, 19, 24, 194
 modern distribution of wild form, 19
 preservation of, 151
 size changes in, 17
eland, domestication of, 83, 85, 108, 112, 114, 116
elephant, domestication of, 8, 84
elk
 domestication of, 6, 13, 112, 114, 115
 in European Mesolithic sites, 128
 experimental domestication of, 108, 114
 selective predation on, 95
 size and docility, 85
El Khiam, 120, 123
emmer
 early domestication of, 4, 17, 24, 194
 modern distribution of wild form, 21, 22
 preservation of, 151
 weed seeds in, 149
epigenetic variation, 87-8, 89, 90
epiphyseal fusion, 75, 76, 92, 121
Erbaba, 191
Eskimo snow houses, 101
Espelugues, 84
excavation techniques
 inadequacy of traditional, 46, 49, 52, 61, 63, 65
 on microlithic sites, 54
 see also plant remains
exploitation territory, 133, 167, 168
Ezero, 48, 156-7, 158, 159

fire, used in caves, 101
fish
 bones of, 78, 194
 grass carp, 110, 112
 milkfish, 110, 112
 morphological changes in, 90
 mullet, 110

Fondo Tomollero, 136
fox, selective breeding of, 109, 112, 115
Franchthi Cave, 54, 63, 194
froth flotation, 25, 39-48
 collector mixture, 41
 design of equipment, 41-4
 effectiveness as against water separation, 41
 method of use, 44-7
 principles of, 40-1
 rate of operation, 45
 sampling techniques used with, 47-8
 and soil washing, 46-7

Galapagos tortoise, protection of, 110
game-cropping, 110, 112
gazelle
 domestication of, 8, 115, 120-4
 in Natufian sites, 119-24
 selective predation on, 94
gene flow, 87
genetic drift, 5, 78
genome analysis, 23-4
Ghussul, 171
globe thermometer, 98
goat
 early domestication of, 4, 75, 92, 123-4, 194
 in early Neolithic sites, 129, 193, 194
 introduction into Europe, 13, 125
 reproduction, 79, 177
gregariousness as pre-adaptation for domestication, 114-15
Grotta delle Prazziche, 130, 131
Grotta Mangiapane, 129, 130
Grotta Ulluzzo, 131
Grotte de l'Observatoire, 71
Grotte de Pech-Merle, 84
Grotte du Lazaret, 101
Grotte du Renne, 101
Grotte d'Unang, 131

Hacılar, 4, 24, 191, 193
Haua Fteah, 77
Hayonim, 120
Hazor, 170
Hekelingen, 135
horse
 bones at modern Can Hasan, 71, 77
 early domestication of, 84
 in European Mesolithic sites, 126, 128-9
 interbreeding with wild population, 6

India
 early agriculture in, 195-6
 early animal domestication in, 196
Indian buffalo, domestication of, 109
industrial melanism, 90
interbreeding between wild and domestic populations, 6-7, 114, 197
isolation of populations, 5-7, 87-8, 96
Isolino, 131
Isturitz, 84

Jarmo, 4, 16, 21, 24
Jericho, 4, 16, 24, 29, 124
 gazelle at, 120, 123
 soil types at, 171

kangaroo, selective breeding of, 109
Kastritsa, 29, 97, 128, 129, 131
 cave climate of, 98-100, 103
Kazanluk, 48, 154-6, 157, 158, 159
Kebarah Cave, 102-3, 119

kill-off, pattern of, 77, 78, 133-4, 193
Knossos, ix, 3, 4, 21, 48, 129, 135-6, 193, 194
Kostienki, 101
Ksar 'Akil, 119

La Ferrassie, 30
La Gare de Couze, 54
Langeveld, 135
Lascaux, 84
Laugerie-Basse, 84
Laugerie-Haute, 30
Le Basse di Valcalaona, 33
legumes
    early domestication of, 194
    preservation of, 151, 154
Lepenski vir, 129, 136
Lerna, 69, 193
Le Solutré, 84

maize, early domestication of, 5, 7, 10, 15
Marizulo, 131
Mas d'Azil, 84
Megiddo, 29, 171
    land use around, 32
Mersin, 190
millet, early domestication of, 10
mink, domestication of, 108, 112
Mohenjo-daro, 34
Molino Casarotto, 48, 130, 133, 136-7, 139
    red deer at, 129, 131, 134, 136
mollusca
    morphological changes in, 90
    oyster farming, 110, 113
Monte Tondo, 134, 136
moose, selective predation on, 94, 112
morphological changes resulting from human action
    animal, 7, 83, 88-91, 95-6, 196
    plant, 16-17, 19-20, 23-5, 196
mortality curve, 92-3
mouflon, 87, 91
Mugharet el Wad, 119, 121, 171
Munhatta, 75, 123
Mureybit, 8, 17, 19, 20, 24
musk-ox, 88, 117
    domestication of, 107-8, 110, 112, 113, 114, 197
    rate of calving, 93
    selective predation on, 94
    size and docility, 85, 107

Nahal Oren (Wadi Fellah)
    animal remains at, 120-1, 123
    gazelle at, 120-1, 122-4
    modern exploitation pattern of area, 32
    soil types at, 171
    use of froth flotation at, 45-7, 120
Natufian sites, 9, 102, 119-24, 171
Nea Nikomedeia, ix, 3, 4, 71, 75, 129
Neolithic Revolution, viii
Neolithic transition in Europe, 129
    changing patterns of animal exploitation in, 129-30
neoteny, 87
Non Nok Tha, 9
Norway rat, domestication of, 108, 110

Olduvai Gorge, artificial shelter at, 101
ostrich, domestication of, 109

Pan-p'o, 9
Parpalló, 30, 131

pig
    early domestication of, 4, 6, 85, 194
    introduction into Europe, 13
    in Mesolithic and early Neolithic sites, 125, 126, 129, 130, 135, 136, 193, 194
    patterns of exploitation of, 138
    selective predation on, 95
plant husbandry
    defined, 8, 26
    origins of, 3-13
plant remains
    archaeological context of, 149, 150-1, 158-9
    collection of: at Can Hasan, 186-8; by dense media separation, 39; by froth flotation, 25, 39-48, 149; improved by new excavation techniques, 46, 47; by water separation, 39; by visual inspection, 39
    interpretation of, 149-59, 182, 185-6, 193
    preservation of, 149-51, 186
Pescale, 131
pollen analysis, limitations for identification of domestication, 39
Pompei, 34
Porto Cheli, 129
pottery
    grain impressions on, 150
    improved recovery of, 54-9
predation
    random, 94, 96
    selective, 7, 94-5
    see also individual animals

Ramat Matred, 172
Raymonden-Chancelade, 84
red deer
    domestication of, 85, 132
    economies based on, 130-1, 135, 136, 137
    in Mesolithic and Neolithic sites, 125, 126-8, 129-30, 193
    morphological changes in, 91
    patterns of exploitation of, 131-5, 138, 139-40
    reproductive pattern, 133-4, 138
    selective predation on, 95, 129, 131
reindeer, 6, 13, 79, 108, 117
    domestication of, 109, 114, 161, 167
    grazing requirement, 166
    herd movements, 166-7
    patterns of exploitation of, 161-8
    swimming ability of, 164
restricted breeding, 5, 74, 87
rhinoceros, selective predation on, 95
rice
    cultivation of, 9, 11
    domestication of, 196
Rivoli, 134, 136-7
roe deer, 125, 126, 128, 130, 193
Romanelli, 128
Roucadour, 131

St Michel d'Arudy, 84
saiga antelope, selective breeding of, 109, 114
sampling techniques, 47-8, 63, 80
    biased samples, 53, 61, 65, 68, 76, 149
    random sampling, 65-6
Săpături, 131
secondary products of animals, 71
Seeberg Burgäschisee-Süd, 75, 95
    domesticated cattle at, 71, 85
    red deer at, 129-30, 131, 132, 133, 134
selection
    human, 5, 7, 20, 96, 133
    natural, 114

selection pressure, 17-18
selective breeding, 8, 12, 77, 87, 88, 90, 111
    of elk, 108
    of musk-ox, 107
    of other animals, 108-10, 112, 114
    technological requirements for, 114
    see also individual animals
settlement area, Biblical references to, 177
settlement patterns, 8-9
Sha'ar Golen, 171
Shanidar Cave, 3, 7, 121, 123
sheep
    advantages of small size, 86
    early domestication of, 3-4, 5, 92, 123-4
    in early Neolithic sites, 130, 135, 136, 193, 194
    interbreeding between wild and domesticated, 87
    introduction into Europe, 13, 125
    otter sheep, 74
    St Kilda sheep, 93
    structure of fleeces and fibres, 90
    see also mouflon
Sheikh Ali, 29
Shuqbah, 102, 119-20
Sidari, 125
sieving
    coarse, 44, 47
    dry, 49, 53, 54, 63, 152-3
    water, 46, 47, 52-63, 65, 182, 186
Sitagroi, 53, 54, 59, 61, 63, 66, 76
site catchment analysis, 26, 27-36, 118, 161, 169
    field methods, 32-3, 36, 172
site location, 169-80
    and economic potential, 169, 193-4
size changes in animals
    and Bergman's rule, 78, 86
    as indicator of domestication, 4, 5, 6, 74-5, 77-8, 84-7, 90, 108
    and isolation, 87-8
    problems of interpretation, 77-8
    in wild populations, 6, 78, 86, 88, 90-1
'slash and burn' cultivation, 171
soil type and site location, 169-80
sorghum, 6, 195, 197
spelt
    cultivation of, 19, 20, 24
    preservation of, 151
Spirit Cave, 11
Star Carr, viii, 4, 125, 128, 131, 133
Stellmoor, 71, 74
stone tools
    at Can Hasan, 190
    improved recovery of, 54
Suberde, 8, 181, 191, 193, 194

Tabun, 102
Taibe, 123

Tamaulipas, 11
tapir, selective breeding of, 109, 114
Tash Aïr, 130
Taubach, 95
Tehuacán Valley, 10, 11
Tell Abu Hawan, 172
Tell Ajjul, 172
Tell Askelon, 172
Tell es-Sawwan, 4
Tell Fara, 172
Tell Ful, 172
Tell Gemma, 172
Tell Gezer, 45, 48, 124, 169
    patterns of exploitation at, 173-80
    soil types at, 172-7, 178, 179
Tell Hesi, 172
Tell Nasbeth, 172
Tell Ramad, 4, 21
territoriality in humans, 29-30, 36
tooth eruption, 75, 76, 78, 92
    effect of nutrition on, 76
Torri, 134, 136
Toukh, 122

Udal, The, 41

Valle Ottara, 131
variation in animal populations, 88-90
Vatte di Zambana, 129
Videlles, 131
Vlaardingen, 131, 132, 134-5, 139
Vogelenzang, 135

Wadi Dhobai, 123
Wadi el Mughara, 35, 36
wapiti, 115, 132
weed seeds, information provided by, 149-50
wheat
    early domestication of, 4, 15-26, 194
    introduction into Europe, 13
    modern distribution of wild form, 16, 21-3
    origins of, 24
    preservation of, 151, 154
    weeds in, 150
wolf, 4, 6, 93
    selective predation by, 94

Yokneam, 171

Zamil Koba, 130
Zawi Chemi Shanidar, 3, 7, 92
zebra, selective breeding of, 109, 112, 116